AF758249

LIBERAL DEMOCRACIES AND THE TORTURE OF THEIR CITIZENS

This book analyses and compares how the USA's liberal allies responded to the use of torture against their citizens after 9/11. Did they resist, tolerate or support the Bush Administration's policies concerning the mistreatment of detainees when their own citizens were implicated and what were the reasons for their actions? Australia, the UK and Canada are liberal democracies sharing similar political cultures, values and alliances with America; yet they behaved differently when their citizens, caught up in the War on Terror, were tortured.

How states responded to citizens' human rights claims and predicaments was shaped, in part, by demands for accountability placed on the executive government by domestic actors. This book argues that civil society actors, in particular, were influenced by nuanced differences in their national political and legal contexts that enabled or constrained human rights activism. It maps the conditions under which individuals and groups were more or less likely to become engaged when fellow citizens were tortured, focusing on national rights culture, the domestic legal and political human rights framework, and extant political opportunities.

Liberal Democracies and the Torture of Their Citizens

Cynthia Banham

•HART•
PUBLISHING
OXFORD AND PORTLAND, OREGON
2017

Hart Publishing
An imprint of Bloomsbury Publishing Plc

Hart Publishing Ltd
Kemp House
Chawley Park
Cumnor Hill
Oxford OX2 9PH
UK

Bloomsbury Publishing Plc
50 Bedford Square
London
WC1B 3DP
UK

www.hartpub.co.uk
www.bloomsbury.com

Published in North America (US and Canada) by
Hart Publishing
c/o International Specialized Book Services
920 NE 58th Avenue, Suite 300
Portland, OR 97213-3786
USA

www.isbs.com

HART PUBLISHING, the Hart/Stag logo, BLOOMSBURY and the Diana logo are trademarks of Bloomsbury Publishing Plc

First published 2017

© Cynthia Banham 2017

Cynthia Banham has asserted her right under the Copyright, Designs and Patents Act 1988 to be identified as Author of this work.

All rights reserved. No part of this publication may be reproduced or transmitted in any form or by any means, electronic or mechanical, including photocopying, recording, or any information storage or retrieval system, without prior permission in writing from the publishers.

While every care has been taken to ensure the accuracy of this work, no responsibility for loss or damage occasioned to any person acting or refraining from action as a result of any statement in it can be accepted by the authors, editors or publishers.

All UK Government legislation and other public sector information used in the work is Crown Copyright ©. All House of Lords and House of Commons information used in the work is Parliamentary Copyright ©. This information is reused under the terms of the Open Government Licence v3.0 (http://www.nationalarchives.gov.uk/doc/open-government-licence/version/3) except where otherwise stated.

All Eur-lex material used in the work is © European Union, http://eur-lex.europa.eu/, 1998–2016.

British Library Cataloguing-in-Publication Data
A catalogue record for this book is available from the British Library.

ISBN: HB: 978-1-50990-684-0
ePDF: 978-1-50990-682-6
ePub: 978-1-50990-683-3

Library of Congress Cataloging-in-Publication Data

Names: Banham, Cynthia, author.

Title: Liberal democracies and the torture of their citizens / Cynthia Banham.

Description: Oxford [UK] ; Portland, Oregon : Hart Publishing, 2017. | Includes bibliographical references and index.

Identifiers: LCCN 2016045781 (print) | LCCN 2016046046 (ebook) | ISBN 9781509906840 (hardback : alk. paper) | ISBN 9781509906833 (Epub)

Subjects: LCSH: Torture (International law) | Terrorism (International law) | September 11 Terrorist Attacks, 2001. | Terrorism—Prevention—Law and legislation. | Torture—United States.

Classification: LCC KZ7170 .B33 2017 (print) | LCC KZ7170 (ebook) | DDC 364.6/7—dc23

LC record available at https://lccn.loc.gov/2016045781

Typeset by Compuscript Ltd, Shannon
Printed and bound in Great Britain by TJ International Ltd, Padstow, Cornwall

To find out more about our authors and books visit www.hartpublishing.co.uk. Here you will find extracts, author information, details of forthcoming events and the option to sign up for our newsletters.

This book is for Leo

CONTENTS

ACKNOWLEDGEMENTS

I would like to acknowledge the many colleagues and friends from the Australian National University, the University of Queensland and beyond, who provided the inspiration, encouragement and intellectual engagement that contributed to this book.

First, to Hilary Charlesworth, who supervised the 2015 doctoral thesis on which this book was based and then provided me with the opportunity of a post-doctoral year at the School of Regulation and Global Governance (RegNet) at the ANU to develop it. It was a privilege to work with you, and I thank you for your guidance, support and belief.

To Christian Reus-Smit, who first inspired me to undertake a PhD by inviting me to accept a visiting fellowship when he was head of the Department of International Relations at the ANU. Thank you for your kindness, generosity and assistance, particularly with forming the early ideas underpinning this book.

There were many others from whose insights and comments this book benefited, including my panel member, Jacinta O'Hagan, as well as Heather Rae, Andrew Phillips, Pete Van Ness and Robert Goodin.

RegNet is a wonderfully enriching and enjoyable research community in which to work. I would like to pay tribute to the many kind and generous people I crossed paths with there and at the ANU more broadly. They include, amongst others: Emily Tannock, Miranda Forsyth, Natasha Tusikov, Blayne Haggart, Emma Larking, Benjamin Authers, Romina Paskotic and Daniel Marston. To my other Canberra friends, thank you for your companionship throughout the process, especially Kirsty McNeil and Rebecca Irwin.

In addition, I thank my doctoral thesis examiners, as well as the reviewer engaged by Hart Publishing, whose feedback I found immensely helpful in refining my arguments for the book. I would like to express my gratitude to the individuals—lawyers, journalists, and civil society activists, from Australia, the UK and Canada—who agreed to be interviewed for this work. Thanks to Carolyn Brewer for copy-editing and also to Hart Publishing.

Lastly, to my family. My love and gratitude go to my parents, John and Lori, and siblings, Juliette, Anthony and Sebastian. To my amazing husband Michael and our dear son Leo: thank you for your unending support, patience and devotion. I love you both so much.

Cynthia Banham
Canberra
July 2016

TABLE OF CASES

Australia

Canada

Council of Europe

United Kingdom

United States of America

TABLE OF LEGISLATION

Australia

Canada

United Kingdom

United States of America

TABLE OF TREATIES

1

Introduction

Overview

Torture is prohibited by international law. This includes under the United Nations Convention Against Torture and Other Cruel, Inhuman or Degrading Treatment or Punishment (CAT), which 158 states have accepted. The use of torture is inconsistent with fundamental values underpinning liberal democracies. Liberalism is a political tradition distinguished by the supreme value it places on the liberty of the individual, while torture disregards the sanctity of human dignity, autonomy and freedom.

Despite this, torture continues to be used by many states today—141 at last count, according to Amnesty International—including liberal democracies.[1] This was underscored by the public release in December 2014 of the United States Senate Select Committee on Intelligence's *Committee Study of the Central Intelligence Agency's Detention and Interrogation Program*.[2] The Committee's report presented detailed documentary evidence that detainees in the United States' (US) 'war on terror' were subjected to torture and other cruel, inhuman or degrading treatment. As the Committee chairman, Dianne Feinstein, stated in her 'Foreword' to the report, 'it is my personal conclusion that, under any common meaning of the term, CIA detainees were tortured'.[3] The modern prevalence of state torture, including that sanctioned by liberal democracies after 11 September 2001, highlights the gap that exists between law and practice when it comes to human rights.

The war on terror was launched by the US in response to the devastating terrorist attacks of 11 September that killed nearly 3,000 people in New York City, Washington, DC and rural Pennsylvania.[4] Much has been written about how

[1] Amnesty International, 'Torture in 2014: 30 years of broken promises', Stop ~~Torture~~ Media Briefing, 13 May 2014.

[2] United States Senate Select Committee on Intelligence, *Committee Study of the Central Intelligence Agency's Detention and Interrogation Program*, 2014.

[3] Dianne Feinstein, 'Foreword' in United States Senate Select Committee on Intelligence, *Committee Study of the Central Intelligence Agency's Detention and Interrogation Program*, 2014, 4, fas.org/irp/congress/2014_rpt/ssci-rdi.pdf.

[4] Jonathan Hafetz, *Habeas Corpus After 9/11: Confronting America's New Global Detention System* (New York, NY: New York University Press, 2011) 11.

torture came to form part of the US Bush Administration's detainee interrogation policy in that broadly conceived war.[5] This book is primarily concerned with a subject to which less attention has been directed: how the liberal allies of the US responded to the torture of their own citizens detained in the war on terror. These allies included the United Kingdom (UK), Canada and Australia. All three provided political and military support for the US invasion of Afghanistan in October 2001. They also had citizens (and, in the case of the UK, residents too) detained in the war on terror, who alleged mistreatment and/or torture. Surprisingly, despite sharing similar legal and political systems and common values, including a respect for human rights, these liberal democracies behaved differently when confronted with their citizens' claims of torture.

Australia, for example, was indifferent for many years to allegations of the torture of two citizens detained at Guantánamo Bay, the US Naval Base in Cuba where the Bush Administration held hundreds of individuals captured in the war on terror.[6] When one of the citizens, Mamdouh Habib, gave a public account of his torture in Pakistan and Egypt after returning home in 2005, the Australian Government suggested that he should not be believed, and that anyone who did take his claims seriously was prejudiced in favour of Al-Qaeda and was anti-American.[7] Canada, on the other hand, established a public judicial inquiry in 2004 into allegations that one of its citizens, Maher Arar, had been tortured in Syria, where he was sent by US officials for interrogation.[8] The Canadian inquiry resulted in the first officially documented description of the US practice of extraordinary rendition—the same ordeal to which Habib was subjected.[9] The UK was different again from Australia and Canada in its response to the detention of its citizens at Guantánamo Bay. Amid international concerns that detainees were being tortured, the UK began repatriating its nine citizens in early 2004; all were returned home by January 2005.[10] In addition, the UK refused to allow its citizens to be

[5] For example David Cole, 'The taint of torture: The roles of law and policy in our descent to the dark side', *Houston Law Review* 49(1) (2012), 53–69; Alfred McCoy, *A Question of Torture: CIA Interrogation, from the Cold War to the War on Terror* (New York, NY: Holt Paperbacks, 2006); Joseph Margulies, *Guantánamo and the Abuse of Presidential Power* (New York, NY: Simon & Schuster Paperbacks, 2006); Jonathan Hafetz, *Habeas Corpus After 9/11: Confronting America's New Global Detention System* (New York, NY: New York University Press, 2011); Philippe Sands, *Torture Team: Rumsfeld's Memo and the Betrayal of American Values* (New York, NY: Palgrave Macmillan, 2008); Jamie Mayerfeld, 'Playing by our own rules: How US marginalization of International Human Rights Law led to torture', *Harvard Human Rights Journal* 20 (2007), 89–140.

[6] Donald Rumsfeld, 'DoD news briefing—Secretary Rumsfeld and Gen. Myers', US Department of Defense, 27 December 2001.

[7] 2UE, 'Interview—2UE IV with John Laws—Habib', 14 February 2005 (Alexander Downer).

[8] Commission of Inquiry into the Actions of Canadian Officials in Relation to Maher Arar, *Report of the events relating to Maher Arar: Analysis and recommendations*, 2006, http://epe.lac-bac.gc.ca/100/206/301/pco-bcp/commissions/maher_arar/07-09-13/www.ararcommission.ca/eng/index.htm.

[9] Reg Whitaker, 'Arar: The affair, the inquiry, the aftermath', *IRPP Policy Matters* 9(1) (2008), 9.

[10] Neil A Lewis, 'Red Cross finds detainee abuse in Guantánamo', *New York Times*, 30 November 2004, 1.

tried by the US military commission process, which permitted the use of evidence obtained by coercion.[11] The UK noted this was because the commissions failed to offer 'sufficient guarantees of a fair trial in accordance with international standards'.[12] Despite this, Australia and Canada allowed their citizens to be tried under the Guantánamo Bay military commissions.

In this book, I examine why these three liberal allies responded differently to their citizens' claims of torture in the war on terror. In other words, why did states sometimes live up to their international human rights commitments regarding the ban on torture and sometimes not? The question is complex, because so many different factors came to bear on the issue of detainee treatment in what was a time of heightened national security tension and heated political debate in the aftermath of the 9/11 terrorist attacks. My intention is not to rank liberal democracies in terms of their human rights records based on how they responded to the torture of citizens. Rather, I examine the factors that promoted the toleration of torture by liberal democracies, and those that restrained such impulses.

The argument presented in this book for why liberal democracies behaved differently when their citizens were tortured overseas is made on the foundation of detailed empirical analysis of what occurred inside the three countries during the first 10 years of the war on terror. Essentially, my contention is that liberal democracies, in responding to breaches of the international norm and laws prohibiting torture, were influenced by nuanced but important differences in their domestic political and legal contexts that enabled or constrained civil society activism on human rights.

Contemporary liberal international scholarship argues that domestic civil society is a crucial player in efforts to promote international human rights.[13] Whether domestic actors are able to positively influence states, however, depends on the existence of appropriate agents with adequate political will and capability, factors heavily influenced by the domestic context and which vary across states.[14] The liberal international model is often applied to examining human rights outcomes across different regime types, where freedoms and restrictions on political mobilisation can vary dramatically according to whether the political system is authoritarian or democratic.[15] This study is, however, concerned with outcomes across different liberal democracies. Citizenries in liberal democracies also operate

[11] Johan Steyn, 'Guantánamo Bay: The legal black hole', *International and Comparative Law Quarterly* 53(1) (2004), 1–15.

[12] Lord Goldsmith, 'Lord Goldsmith's speech in full', 25 June 2004, http://news.bbc.co.uk/2/hi/uk_news/politics/3839153.stm.

[13] James Ron and David Crow, 'Who trusts local human rights organizations? Evidence from three World regions', *Human Rights Quarterly* 37 (2015), 188–89.

[14] Eric Neumayer, 'Do international human rights treaties improve respect for human rights?', *Journal of Conflict Resolution* 49(6) (2005), 950.

[15] Beth A Simmons, *Mobilizing for Human Rights: International Law in Domestic Politics* (New York, NY: Cambridge University Press, 2009) 16.

in legal and political environments that can differ in significant ways that affect human rights activism.

Three domestic factors are isolated and examined as a part of a framework of enabling and constraining factors that can influence rights activism. In brief, the first is the country's political culture, and the way its history and prior experiences of human rights infractions condition the polity's particular awareness of rights. Second is the country's national institutional human rights framework, which includes constitutional and legislative rights protections and provides important levers for mobilisation around rights issues. The third is political opportunity, a more transient factor that offers incentives for or discouragement of activism in the form of a more open or closed political environment for mobilisation. These three political and legal structures are interrelated. Political culture can influence a polity's institutions, while institutions in turn can be established (or dismantled) deliberately in an attempt to forge a new rights culture. Opportunities can rely on activists framing claims according to dominant community understandings, or on accessing or constructing unifying mobilising structures.[16] This enabling and constraining framework is discussed at length in Chapter 3. The different configurations of these factors across the three polities had important consequences for how executive governments in the UK, Australia and Canada responded to allegations that citizens and residents detained in the war on terror were tortured.

Civil societies are not, of course, homogeneous. It is not suggested that preferences of members of civil society are necessarily progressive or predetermined in favour of human rights. Furthermore, civil society agendas can change over time; they can be influenced by events and by the passage of time following traumatic events like terrorism. This study does not conceive of civil society as a monolithic entity, nor assign to it an inherently normative purpose. Rather, it assumes two basic points. First, most people value their own human rights: they generally care when they perceive their rights, and those of fellow citizens (as opposed to more distant foreigners), as threatened in serious ways. Secondly, in every liberal democracy different groups exist whose mandates include, specifically or broadly, defending human rights. This study is concerned with mapping the conditions under which such individuals and groups are more or less likely to become engaged when citizens' rights not to be tortured are violated. I explain what I mean by civil society and outline some critiques of its role in shaping rights agendas in Chapter 3.

The questions I pose in this book relate to the issue of political accountability, and whether states were ultimately held accountable by their domestic constituencies for their treaty obligations and human rights commitments regarding torture. Accountability involves the assurance that public officials are answerable for their behaviour, can be compelled to inform and justify their decisions, and may be

[16] Sidney Tarrow, *Power in Movement: Social Movements and Contentious Politics* (New York, NY: Cambridge University Press, 1998) 71–72.

subject to sanctions for those decisions.[17] Whether states faced robust demands from citizens for accountability on international human rights breaches when a gap emerged between law and practice regarding torture, depended on particular configurations of various political and legal factors that encouraged or hindered that process and that differed across countries. Accountability of states that used torture in the war on terror—or that permitted it to be used, including against their own citizens—has been varied and inadequate. President Barack Obama, for example, refused to pursue prosecutions of US officials who ordered or carried out torture.[18] Given this, the topic of torture and liberal democracies is a timely and important one.

The remainder of this chapter sets out the cases and methodology, and outlines the plan of the book.

The Cases

The selection of Australia, the UK and Canada as case studies is based on their similarities as countries that nonetheless had different responses to the torture issue in the war on terror. The three polities share a British heritage, are all members of the Commonwealth with common law legal systems and possess strong records of ratifying international human rights treaties. They have different domestic human rights frameworks, however. Australia has a federal constitution but no national bill of rights. The UK has no written constitution but is networked into an effective regional human rights system through its membership of the Council of Europe, a consequence of which is that in 1998 it enacted the Human Rights Act (which gave effect to rights under the European Convention on Human Rights as domestic statutory rights).[19] Canada has a federal constitution and a constitutional bill of rights, namely the Canadian Charter of Rights and Freedoms.

It is also important to acknowledge foreign policy differences between Australia, the UK and Canada that may have impacted on their responses to the war on terror. While they are all US allies, their relationships with the superpower are influenced by different geostrategic factors. Canada, for example, shares a border with the US, a much more powerful neighbour, posing particular cultural, economic and foreign policy challenges.[20] Australia is the most geographically

[17] Enrique Peruzzotti, 'The societalization of horizontal accountability: Rights advocacy and the Defensor del Pueblo de la Nacion in Argentina' in *Human Rights, State Compliance, and Social Change: Assessing National Human Rights Institutions*, ed Ryan Goodman and Thomas Pegram (New York, NY: Cambridge University Press, 2012) 246.

[18] Mark Mazzetti and Scott Shane, 'Interrogation memos details harsh tactics by the CIA', *New York Times*, 16 April 2009, 1.

[19] Rayner Thwaites, *The Liberty of Non-Citizens* (Oxford: Hart Publishing, 2014) 137.

[20] Allan Kornberg and Harold D Clarke, *Citizens and Community: Political Support in a Representative Democracy* (Cambridge: Cambridge University Press, 1992) 18.

isolated of the allies and historically has carried a deep sense of insecurity that has shaped its heavy reliance on America's friendship.[21] For the UK, retaining a close US alliance is sometimes seen as a way for the former imperial power to exercise influence over global affairs beyond its current position.[22] Differences in the three states' alliances, discussed further in Chapters 5–7, meant the UK and Australia supported the US invasion of Iraq in 2003, while Canada did not.[23] Domestically, executive governments were under a range of pressures unique to their polity. For example, the UK had more citizens (and residents) detained in the war on terror than did Australia or Canada. The specific involvement of the states in their citizens' detention also varied. This involvement ranged from turning a blind eye to mistreatment and torture, to greater levels of complicity, such as knowingly supplying information that led to their own citizens' capture or assisted in their interrogations. In addition, the UK was involved in ongoing inquiries into allegations that its military personnel used torture against non-citizens in Iraq.[24]

I mention these differentiating factors to highlight the complexities and multiple political layers involved in understanding the states' responses to the issue of torture in the war on terror. I do not claim to provide here a complete explanation for why liberal democracies responded as they did to torture—only greater understanding of some of the important influences that had a bearing on their behaviours. My particular interest is in better understanding the responses of states to the torture of citizens and residents by examining the role civil society activism played in shaping that response.

Within each of the three case studies I focus on two people or groups of people, based primarily on how representative they were of each state's (sometimes internally inconsistent) approaches to the torture issue. In Australia, I focus on David Hicks and Habib, Australia's only citizens held at Guantánamo Bay. In the UK, I compare two groups of people rather than two particular individuals—the nine UK citizens and six residents detained at Guantánamo. In Canada I examine the case of Arar, a dual Canadian-Syrian citizen who, like Habib, was subjected to extraordinary rendition to Syria (though Arar was never detained at Guantánamo Bay), and Omar Khadr, Canada's only citizen at Guantánamo who was captured at age 15 in Afghanistan. Extraordinary rendition was the US practice, used increasingly after 11 September 2001, of transferring individuals, who had no access to a legal proceeding in which to challenge that transfer, for interrogations to a country

[21] Anthony Burke, *In Fear of Security: Australia's Invasion Anxiety* (Sydney: Pluto Press, 2001).

[22] Tim Dunne, '"When the shooting starts": Atlanticism in British security strategy', *International Affairs* 80(5) (2004), 898.

[23] Kim Richard Nossal, 'Defense policy and the atmospherics of Canada–US relations: The case of Harper conservatives', *American Review of Canadian Studies* 37(1) (2007), 24.

[24] International Criminal Court, 'Prosecutor of the International Criminal Court, Fatou Bensouda, reopens the preliminary examination of the situation in Iraq', statement, 13 May 2014, https://www.icc-cpi.int//Pages/item.aspx?name=otp-statement-iraq-13-05-2014.

where they were at risk of torture.[25] Since my interest lies in the different ways in which liberal democracies responded to the torture of their citizens overseas, I treat arguments that could technically be regarded as being about detention (though still implicating torture) as issues about torture. For example, torture was at the heart of the practice of extraordinary rendition. Torture was also central to concerns about the treatment of detainees at Guantánamo Bay, including those held by the International Committee of the Red Cross (ICRC).[26]

My decision to focus on the torture of citizens, rather than foreigners, is based on claims made by liberal states about the particular obligations they owe nationals as members of a defined political community. I employ such liberal claims as a test of liberal credentials: in the case of torture of their own members, did liberal states look after their own? The liberal distinction between citizens and non-citizens is founded on ideas about citizenship as membership of a political community. Citizenship defines bounded populations with a specific set of rights and duties, excluding 'others' on the grounds of nationality.[27] Post-World War II ideas about the universality of human rights sometimes conflict, however, with liberal states' attempts to discriminate between citizens and non-citizens in certain rights matters.[28] Some scholars argue that older notions of nation-based citizenship are being destabilised and a new, more cosmopolitan concept of citizenship is developing.[29] This blurring of the line between citizens and non-citizens is interesting for the way the UK treated its residents who were tortured, and I discuss it in Chapter 6.

I study the decade after 11 September 2001 in depth, but include relevant developments until the end of 2015. This time frame enables a study of changes of government in all three case study countries, and covers the return of all Australian, UK and Canadian citizens and residents from Guantánamo Bay. This period also encompasses the change in US administrations from President George W Bush, whose administration instigated the post-9/11 torture policies, to President Obama, who banned torture.[30] This is significant because, after Obama's election, it presumably became easier for the allies to be critical of the Bush Administration's torture policies and practices.

This book adopts a comparative case study approach. It is based on inductive research, where I seek to identify patterns from the evidence and select theoretical tools based on my early findings. It uses qualitative analysis, derived from media

[25] Margaret L Satterthwaite, 'Rendered meaningless: Extraordinary rendition and the Rule of Law', *The George Washington Law Review* 75 (2007), 1336.

[26] Lewis, 'Red Cross finds detainee abuse in Guantánamo', 1.

[27] Yasemin Nuhoglu Soysal, *Limits of Citizenship: Migrants and Postnational Membership in Europe* (Chicago, IL: University of Chicago Press, 1994) 2.

[28] David Cole and Jules Lobel, *Less Safe, Less Free: Why America is Losing the War on Terror* (New York, NY: The New Press, 2007) 39.

[29] Soysal, *Limits of Citizenship*, 1, 119; Saskia Sassen, *Territory Authority Rights: From Medieval to Global Assemblages* (Princeton, NJ: Princeton University Press, 2008 [2006]) 307.

[30] Executive Order No 13,491, 74 Fed Reg No 16, 22 January 2009.

reports and other relevant publicly available texts, as well as a small number of semi-structured interviews, to draw out similarities and differences between cases. My approach is 'contextual'.[31] To understand liberal democracies' legal and policy approaches to human rights and torture after 9/11, I argue that it is necessary to provide a detailed, nuanced, contextual examination that takes account of historical, political, legal and organisational factors that can affect how states respond.

For each case study country, I selected two mainstream newspapers, nominally representing opposite sides of the political spectrum (progressive and conservative) and reflecting different ownerships. Newspapers displaying different political views were chosen in order to ensure that as wide a spectrum of dominant views on the torture issue in a polity was captured as possible. I identified all individual newspaper articles from each publication that dealt directly with torture in the war on terror, Guantánamo Bay and the torture of the particular country's individual citizens and residents who were detained by the US or subjected to extraordinary rendition.

Based on an initial analysis of these newspaper articles, I constructed a narrative of what occurred in each state with respect to the unfolding of its responses to the torture issue, in terms of the executive, judicial and legislative arms of government and civil society. From this narrative, I identified important public texts (primary and secondary sources) for closer study. These included government press releases, reports and transcripts of media interviews; records of judicial proceedings; records of parliamentary proceedings, including speeches and committee reports; non-governmental organisation (NGO) press releases and reports; and additional media articles, including transcripts of television programs and opinion articles. I also identified the main actors in the torture debate within each case, including political elites, and members of civil society. I assessed a group or an individual to be influential or important if they were frequently mentioned in newspaper reports as playing an important role or speaking out on the torture issue, or if they made a significant interjection into public debate. I then identified a small number of actors from the political and civil society spheres to interview, on the basis that they might help to clarify or confirm an issue or a hunch that arose from the narrative.[32]

Plan of the Book

The book proceeds as follows. Chapter 2 addresses contradictions between liberal theory and torture policy. Chapter 3 discusses prevailing liberal international

[31] Kent Roach, *The 9/11 Effect: Comparative Counter-Terrorism* (New York, NY: Cambridge University Press, 2011) 5.

[32] Many interviewees requested their names not be used, and accordingly I have chosen not to name any interviewees unless they expressly indicated a preference otherwise.

relations and international law theories for understanding state behaviour on international human rights. It shows how these compliance theories can provide a useful foundation for explaining differences between liberal democracies, by focusing on features of the domestic political and legal context that can affect mobilisation on human rights. It outlines in detail a framework of enabling and constraining factors for activism that helps explain why it is easier for domestic actors to mobilise under certain conditions and harder under others.

Chapter 4 examines the key developments in the US after 11 September 2001 that led to torture becoming a tool in the war on terror. I outline briefly what occurred in the different political spheres in the US (the executive, legislature, judiciary and civil society). I do not make the US an object of study beyond setting out in detail what occurred in that country with respect to torture, as the necessary background against which the behaviour of the three allies is to be analysed.

Chapters 5, 6 and 7 are the core case study chapters, where I provide detailed narratives of how Australia, the UK and Canada responded to the torture of citizens. I set out the actions of the executive, parliament, the courts and civil society. I then analyse the behaviour of domestic non-state actors through the framework of enabling and constraining factors influencing rights activism.

In Chapter 8, I bring together my findings and conduct more detailed comparative analysis of the cases. I draw conclusions about the potential for civil society to play a vital role in achieving state accountability on contentious international human rights matters, and how the effectiveness of civil society activism can be influenced in significant ways by the domestic political and legal context.

2

Torture and Liberal Democracies

Introduction

This chapter addresses the contradictions between liberal theory and torture policy. I briefly outline the nature of the modern prohibition on torture and discuss the fundamental attributes of liberal thought, showing why torture flouts its most essential values. I then describe how, historically, liberals have justified torture, and note how some of these arguments were evident in the contemporary discourse around the treatment of detainees after 11 September 2001.

The Prohibition on Torture

Torture is banned without exception by international law and is—rhetorically at least—unacceptable to most, especially liberal, states. No other practice, except slavery, is as universally and unanimously condemned in law and human convention.[1] The prohibition on torture constitutes a basic human rights norm, where a norm is defined as 'collective expectations for the proper behaviour of actors with a given identity'.[2] Western legal systems have declared the prohibition against torture to have the status of *jus cogens* or a peremptory norm of international law from which no derogation is permitted.[3] Torture's prohibition helps express what it means to be modern and progressive—it is emblematic of the larger commitment by liberal states to non-brutality in the legal system.[4]

[1] Henry Shue, 'Torture', *Philosophy and Public Affairs* 7(2) (1978), 124.

[2] Peter Katzenstein, 'Introduction: Alternative perspectives on national security' in *The Culture of National Security: Norms and Identity in World Politics*, ed Peter Katzenstein (New York, NY: Columbia University Press, 1996) 5.

[3] See, eg, in *R v Bow Street Metropolitan Stipendiary Magistrate, ex p Pinochet Ugarte (No 3)* [1999] 2 All ER 897 (HL).

[4] John T Parry, *Understanding Torture: Law, Violence, and Political Identity* (Ann Arbor, MI: University of Michigan Press, 2010) 81; Jeremy Waldron, 'Torture and positive law: Jurisprudence for the White House', *Columbia Law Review* 105(6) (2005), 1681.

Yet torture was, historically, rejected for quite pragmatic reasons. Torture was outlawed by Western states in the middle of the eighteenth century. Its abolition is frequently linked to Enlightenment thinkers such as Voltaire and Cesare Beccaria, whose powerful writing on the subject shocked the conscience of Europe.[5] John Langbein, however, has described as a 'fairy tale' the explanation that abolition happened as a result of moral outrage and persuasive arguments pointing out incurable deficiencies in the jurisprudence of torture.[6] His rigorous historical account establishes that the banning of torture came about not because of politics or the work of publicists, but for juristic reasons and much earlier, due to a revolution in the law of proof and the introduction of free judicial evaluation of the evidence.[7] Torture, states had realised by the seventeenth century, did not work, and far more reliable methods of determining criminal guilt emerged.

Torture today is prohibited by international law under the International Covenant on Civil and Political Rights (ICCPR) (Article 7) and the United Nations Convention Against Torture and Other Cruel, Inhuman or Degrading Treatment or Punishment (CAT). What exactly constitutes torture, however, is difficult to define, in part because drawing a line between it and other forms of abuse involves a normative judgement.[8] The CAT is the most extensive international law document addressing the issue of state torture and abuse. It defines torture in Article 1(1) as:

> Any act by which severe pain or suffering, whether physical or mental, is intentionally inflicted on a person for such purposes as obtaining from him or a third person information or a confession, punishing him for an act he or a third person has committed or is suspected of having committed, or intimidating or coercing him or a third person, or for any reason based on discrimination of any kind, when such pain or suffering is inflicted by or at the instigation of or with the consent or acquiescence of a public official or other person acting in an official capacity.

Torture, then, according to the CAT, involves the intentional infliction of physical or mental pain by or at the behest of the state, in order to extract information, punish, intimidate or coerce. The CAT goes on in Article 2 to stipulate that no exceptional circumstances whatsoever can be invoked to justify torture. By prohibiting exceptions to the ban on torture, some legal scholars argue, international law makes the definition of torture the central legal issue.[9] The CAT shifts the zone

[5] John H Langbein, *Torture and the Law of Proof: Europe and England in the Ancien Regime* (Chicago, IL: University of Chicago Press, 2006) 10.

[6] ibid.

[7] ibid, 4, 11.

[8] Jeremy Waldron, 'Vagueness in law and language: Some philosophical issues', *California Law Review* 82(3) (1994), 526–29; see also Edward Peters, *Torture: Expanded Edition* (Philadelphia, PA: University of Pennsylvania Press, 1999) 152–53.

[9] John T Parry, 'The shape of modern torture: Extraordinary rendition and ghost detainees', *Melbourne Journal of International Law* 6(2) (2005), 520.

of contention for states wanting to use torture from the idea of exceptional circumstances to interpretations of legal definitions. Governments wanting to maintain a formal adherence to the CAT can interpret the definition of torture in a way that permits their proposed coercive conduct. This is facilitated by the fact that the Convention arguably leaves room for states to engage in coercive treatment that falls short of torture.[10]

Developments in the US after 11 September 2001 provided a vivid illustration of how denying exceptions to the prohibition on torture can result in an outcome whereby the definition of torture becomes the central controversy. Bush Administration lawyers based their legal justifications for approving coercive techniques, in part, on a contorted definition of torture, where 'torture' applied only to the most extreme conduct. The lawyers claimed that torture had to be 'equivalent in intensity to the pain accompanying serious physical injury, such as organ failure, impairment of bodily function, or even death', to contravene US international law obligations.[11]

Liberalism

What is signified by the assertion that the taboo on torture 'goes to the heart of what it means to be a liberal democracy'?[12] Jeremy Waldron argues that torture is a 'legal archetype'. That is, it is incompatible with the Western legal system because it is contrary to its very spirit, which is based on 'respect for human dignity even in extremis' and the idea that law, while forceful, is not savage or brutal.[13] To appreciate the basis for these ideas, an exposition of liberalism's central tenets is useful.

Liberal thought has a lengthy history, and contemporary scholars emphasise different attributes when defining liberalism's essential values. Pre-eminent among its values is individual freedom. Liberalism's core ideas can be traced to the formulation of seventeenth-century political philosopher John Locke, 'Freedom of Men under Government, is, to have a standing Rule to live by, common to every one of that Society, and made by the Legislative Power erected in it.'[14] Most accounts of liberalism emphasise tolerance, privacy, commitments to constitutionalism and the rule of law—values all connected to the freedom of the individual.[15] Political

[10] ibid, 526.

[11] Memorandum from Jay S Bybee, Assistant Attorney-General, to Alberto R Gonzalez, Counsel to the President, 1 August 2002, in *The Torture Papers: The Road to Abu Ghraib*, ed Karen J Greenberg and Joshua L Dratel (New York, NY: Cambridge University Press, 2005).

[12] Jutta Brunnée and Stephen J Toope, *Legitimacy and Legality in International Law: An Interactional Account* (New York, NY: Cambridge University Press, 2010) 230.

[13] Waldron, 'Torture and positive law', 1726–727.

[14] John Locke, 'Second treatise', *Two Treatises of Government*, ed Peter Laslett (Cambridge: Cambridge University Press, 1988 [1689]) 282.

[15] Anthony Arblaster, *The Rise and Decline of Western Liberalism* (Oxford: Basil Blackwell, 1984) 55.

philosopher John Gray stresses four fundamental elements of liberalism.[16] It is individualist, in asserting the moral primacy of the individual against any collective; egalitarian, conferring on all people the same moral status; universalist, affirming the moral unity of the human species over historical or cultural associations; and meliorist, believing in the improvability of the world through human effort. Liberalism's universalism, as will be shown, is thought by some critics to embody a potentially dangerous intolerance of difference.[17]

As a political system, liberalism can be understood as an attempt to limit the power of the state for the sake of guaranteeing or protecting individual freedom.[18] The liberal state is one in which the government is limited by stringent rules, and a liberal political order must contain constitutional constraints on the arbitrary exercise of governmental authority.[19] Liberalism is thus sometimes described as 'anti-tyrannical', underpinned by the fundamental belief that the power of the state should be limited in pursuit of the goal of individual freedom.[20] The US, the UK, Australia and Canada are examples of liberal democracy, a form of government in which the liberal tradition coexists and is balanced by a commitment to democracy. Although historically liberalism has been associated with democracy, they are distinct political traditions. While the liberal tradition is constituted by the rule of law and respect for individual rights and liberty, the older democratic tradition is associated with the equality of citizens and popular sovereignty.[21] There is an inbuilt tension in liberal democratic government that, theoretically, operates as a safety net against inequality and abuse of power. This tension exists because democratic principles ensure that the government is responsive to the will of the people, yet sometimes the majority wishes to see individual liberties curtailed.

Torture isolates and humiliates individuals, stripping them of their inherent dignity, and thus violates in the most fundamental way the values the liberal state exists to uphold. Torture instrumentalises pain in the pursuit of inflicting punishment or obtaining information. It imposes physical and psychological agony on an utterly vulnerable individual in order to break and mutilate that person's will.[22] Torture's essential opposition to liberalism is manifest in the relationship that exists between the torturer and the victim, which is one of brutal, total domination. The defencelessness of the victim is what makes torture more morally repugnant

[16] John Gray, *Liberalism* (Milton Keynes: Open University Press, 1986) x.

[17] Joseph Slaughter, 'A question of narration: The voice in international human rights law', *Human Rights Quarterly* 19(2) (1997), 416–17.

[18] Stephen Holmes, *Passions and Constraint: On the Theory of Liberal Democracy* (Chicago, IL: University of Chicago Press, 1995) 18.

[19] Gray, *Liberalism*, 73–74.

[20] Holmes, *Passions and Constraint*, 18.

[21] Chantal Mouffe, *The Democratic Paradox* (London: Verso, 2000) 2–3.

[22] Jeremy Waldron, *Torture Terror and Trade-offs: Philosophy for the White House* (Oxford: Oxford University Press, 2010) 5.

to liberals than killing.[23] Torture is inflicted precisely to 'tyrannize and dominate the victim', and is thus, in a political sense, 'a microcosm, raised to the highest level of intensity, of the tyrannical political relationships that liberalism hates the most'.[24] When conducted by the state, the practice of torture is unbounded government power.

Justifying Modern Torture

The modern, near-universal, legal and moral condemnation of torture is, however, not the whole story. Torture thrives in the contemporary world—a situation attributed to, amongst other factors, the growth of the security state in the twentieth century, the emergence of anticolonial insurgencies and the rise of terrorism.[25] Moreover, it has been used over decades in diverse conflicts by liberal democracies at home and abroad. Torture was used by the French state in colonial Algeria in the late 1950s and early 1960s, with far-reaching implications for Algeria's eventual realisation of its independence.[26] As I discuss in Chapter 6, torture was also used by the British state against suspected Irish Republican paramilitaries in the civil conflict in Northern Ireland in the 1970s, and before that by British occupying forces in Kenya and Cyprus in the 1950s and in Aden in the 1960s.[27] The United States Central Intelligence Agency's (CIA) early forays into torture have been tied to Cold War politics.[28] Alfred McCoy argues that the genealogy of CIA torture techniques used in the war on terror can be traced 'from their origins in the 1950s to their present-day perfection'.[29] The CIA used torture in Vietnam in the 1960s, and exported it to Latin America over the next two decades.[30]

Darius Rejali notes there is a long, unbroken, though largely forgotten history of torture in democracies at home and abroad using modern 'clean techniques' of physical torture.[31] Many current-day torture techniques are clean as opposed to scarring because, while physical in nature, they leave few marks. They are also often done in 'predictable combinations'. The French, for example, used torture

[23] Henry Shue, 'Torture' in *Torture: A Collection*, ed Sanford Levinson (New York, NY: Oxford University Press, 2004) 51.

[24] David Luban, 'Liberalism, torture, and the ticking bomb', *Virginia Law Review* 91(6) (2005), 1430.

[25] Waldron, 'Torture and positive law', 1684.

[26] Pierre Vidal-Naquet, *Torture: Cancer of Democracy—France and Algeria 1954–62* (Harmondsworth: Penguin Books, 1963) 15; Slaughter, 'A question of narration', 421.

[27] Ian Cobain, *A Secret History of Torture* (Berkeley, CA: Counterpoint, 2012).

[28] Alfred McCoy, *A Question of Torture: CIA Interrogation, from the Cold War to the War on Terror* (New York, NY: Holt Paperbacks, 2006) 7.

[29] ibid, 5.

[30] ibid, 12.

[31] Darius Rejali, *Torture and Democracy* (Princeton, NJ: Princeton University Press, 2007) 4.

by electricity along with water torture in Algeria.[32] According to Rejali, most of these clean torture methods were pioneered by liberal democracies, including the British, French and American governments, many in the last hundred years.[33] Thus, while pre-Enlightenment torture was frequently carried out as a public spectacle, the distinguishing feature of modern torture is that it is hidden. Torture today is a secret practice that survives under conditions of deniability, a political practice that must be known but not seen.[34] Modern torturers favour pain that intimidates the prisoner alone.[35] Contemporary torture's purpose is not just about inflicting severe pain to extract information or to punish, but to dominate and ascribe responsibility to the victim for the pain incurred.[36] How does this style of torture fit with liberalism? A fundamental point is that liberalism is a contested concept, and its central contestation—what liberty means—is connected to the way in which some liberals justify torture.

Many of the internal philosophical contestations that plague liberal thinking relate to fundamental disagreements over how liberty, or freedom, should be defined. Is it freedom from something, or freedom to do something? The former notion envisages a more minimalist conception of the state's function in guaranteeing individual freedom. It suggests freedom from coercion or interference, and is often labelled negative liberty.[37] The latter conception implies a much more active role for the state, in setting up the conditions for individuals to achieve their potential. This is often described as positive liberty.[38] Whether liberty is defined in negative or positive terms has major implications for how we think about the state's role in ensuring personal freedom and, more specifically, where the limits on state power should lie. Political philosophers quarrel about the validity of conceptualising liberty in positive/negative terms, with some arguing the difference is illusory.[39] My interest lies in a different dispute concerning the dangers of viewing liberty in a positive sense.

The central argument made against conceiving of individual liberty in a positive way is that such an understanding implies there exists a single political ideal, and that the state has a legitimate role in promoting and projecting the values associated with such a model life. Negative liberty, on the other hand, recognises that 'human goals are many, not all of them commensurable, and in perpetual

[32] ibid, 5.

[33] ibid.

[34] Paul W Kahn, *Sacred Violence: Torture, Terror, and Sovereignty* (Ann Arbor, MI: University of Michigan Press, 2008) 3.

[35] Rejali, *Torture and Democracy*, 35.

[36] John T Parry, 'Escalation and necessity: Defining torture at home and abroad' in *Torture: A Collection*, ed Levinson, 154.

[37] Isaiah Berlin, 'Two concepts of liberty' in *Liberty: Isaiah Berlin*, ed Henry Hardy (Oxford: Oxford University Press, 2002) 169.

[38] ibid, 177–78.

[39] Shue makes this argument. The positive/negative conception, he argues, is founded on a moral distinction between action and omission of action that is 'morally bankrupt', because the prioritising

rivalry with one another'.[40] John Gray illuminates this dichotomy through his discussion of liberalism's 'two faces', which he conceives of in terms of the dual competing notions of liberal toleration. One side of the debate views toleration as the pursuit of an ideal form of life, where liberal institutions are seen as 'applications of universal principles'; the other understands liberal toleration to mean the search for terms of peace among different ways of life.[41] Isaiah Berlin's exposition of positive liberty suggests how some extreme understandings might lend themselves to liberal justifications of more tyrannical practices. Berlin construed positive liberty as deriving from the wish of individuals to be their own masters, and argues that this carries a danger of authoritarianism when applied not only to one's inner life, but also to one's relations with other members of society.[42] This is because self-mastery implies that, if I am rational, what is right for me must be right for others who are rational like me—in other words there 'must exist one and only one true solution to any problem'.[43] Recalcitrant human beings must be moulded 'to my pattern'.[44] Taken to the level of government, for Berlin such a way of thinking—that the ends of all rational beings must fit into a single, universal, harmonious pattern—suggests authoritarian structures.[45]

Not only liberal scholars caution against understandings of liberalism that would ultimately lead to authoritarianism. Political theorist Carl Schmitt, a critic of liberal constitutionalism, also saw peril in liberalism's universalist ideals. Liberal ideology embodies the possibility of justifying one's actions on the basis of a claim to universal moral principles and, as such, Schmitt thought there was no natural limit to what one might do to make the world safe for liberalism.[46] Liberalism, he wrote, perceives the adversary—those who do not ascribe to liberal beliefs—not just as an enemy but as 'an outlaw of humanity'.[47] Indeed, liberalism has a lengthy imperialist history of treating the 'Other' differently. Many prominent nineteenth-century liberal thinkers, for example, supported a non-egalitarian political system that excluded individuals who were regarded as lacking the capacity to exercise rights and freedoms enjoyed by white men.[48]

Warnings about the potential dangers of understanding liberty in a positive sense become compelling in the context of torture. Torture relies upon a

of negative liberties over positive favours the privileged. See Henry Shue, *Basic Rights: Subsistence, Affluence, and US Foreign Policy* (Princeton, NJ: Princeton University Press, 1996) 51.

[40] Berlin, 'Two concepts of liberty', 216.

[41] John Gray, *Two Faces of Liberalism* (New York, NY: The New Press, 2000) 2.

[42] Berlin, 'Two concepts of liberty', 178, 191.

[43] ibid, 191.

[44] ibid, 192.

[45] ibid, 200.

[46] Tracy B Strong, 'Foreword' in Carl Schmitt, *The Concept of the Political*, trans George Schwab et al (Chicago, IL: University of Chicago Press, 1996 [1932]) xxii–xxiii.

[47] Carl Schmitt, *The Concept of the Political*, trans George Schwab et al (Chicago, IL: University of Chicago Press, 1996 [1932]) 79.

[48] Jennifer Pitts, *A Turn to Empire: The Rise of Imperial Liberalism in Britain and France* (Princeton, NJ: Princeton University Press, 2005); Uday Mehta Singh, *Liberalism and Empire: A Study in Nineteenth-Century British Liberal Thought* (Chicago, IL: University of Chicago Press, 1999).

distinction being made between 'us' (innocent citizens) and 'them' (the enemy), between what we may do or countenance doing to each other as fellow members of a liberal political community, and what we may do or countenance doing to outsiders.[49] Such a differentiation between two categories of human beings—our civilised selves and the barbaric terrorists—was a common rhetorical device used by liberal democracies in the war on terror. This binary was evident in the days after 11 September 2001, when US President George W Bush declared, 'Every nation, in every region, now has a decision to make. Either you are with us, or you are with the terrorists.'[50] The implied understanding was that '"terrorists" do not have the right to full human rights protection'.[51] There was a noticeable racial dimension to the post-9/11 distinction of the terrorist 'Other'. It is argued that 9/11 facilitated the consolidation of a new category that grouped together persons who appeared 'Middle Eastern, Arab, or Muslim' and whose members were identified as terrorists and 'disidentified as citizens'.[52] These stereotypes, to which I return in Chapters 5–7, recall the imperialist logic of liberal political thought.[53]

Modern liberals employ another important device to justify torture. This one centres on the idea of 'the exception', defined by Schmitt as a situation that cannot be codified in the existing legal order, best characterised as 'a case of extreme peril, a danger to the existence of the state'.[54] Whether an extreme emergency exists, and how to eliminate it, is determined by the sovereign, who 'stands outside the normally valid legal system', though he belongs to it, 'for it is he who must decide whether the constitution needs to be suspended in its entirety'.[55] Contemporary scholars have linked Schmitt's writings with liberal justifications of torture after 11 September 2001, arguing that modern liberal legal orders are defined by ideas of the exception and commitments to violence.[56] What David Luban calls the 'liberal ideology of torture' insists that the sole purpose of torture must be intelligence gathering to prevent catastrophe.[57] It is necessary; those who inflict it are motivated not by cruelty but by looming disaster; it is the exception not the rule; and therefore torture has nothing to do with state tyranny. In such circumstances, this reasoning asserts that the use of torture is self-defence and does not even merit the epithet 'torture'.[58]

[49] Waldron, *Torture Terror and Trade-offs*, 5.

[50] George W Bush, 'Address to a Joint Session of Congress and the American people', Washington, DC, 20 September 2001.

[51] Andrea Liese, 'Exceptional necessity: How liberal democracies contest the prohibition of torture and ill-treatment when countering terrorism', *Journal of International Law and International Relations* 5(1) (2009), 42.

[52] Leti Volpp, 'The citizen and the terrorist', *UCLA Law Review* 49(5) (2002), 1576.

[53] Pitts, *A Turn to Empire*, 4.

[54] Carl Schmitt, *Political Theology*, trans George Schwab (Chicago, IL: University of Chicago Press, 2005 [1922]) 6.

[55] ibid, 7.

[56] Parry, *Understanding Torture*, 82.

[57] Luban, 'Liberalism, torture, and the ticking bomb', 1439.

[58] ibid, 1440.

The liberal construct for rationalising torture is embodied in the 'ticking time bomb' hypothetical, a scenario frequently drawn upon after 11 September 2001 by those wishing to justify the use of torture in the war on terror.[59] According to this scenario, torture is warranted in order to extract information from an individual that would enable authorities to locate and defuse a bomb, and thus prevent the deaths of many innocents. Liberal legal scholar Alan Dershowitz went as far as to argue for the use of torture warrants—or judicially regulated state torture in such a situation.[60] He argued this position on the grounds that, since torture would probably be used anyway in preventing imminent terrorism events, it would be better normatively to assure 'accountability and neutrality' on such occasions through the use of warrants. The 'ticking time bomb' scenario disassembles under scrutiny. As Henry Shue has argued, it idealises, adding positive features beyond reality, and abstracts, removing negative ones, and thereby constructs 'a disastrously misleading analogy from which to derive conclusions about reality'.[61] A paradox emerges here, then, between international law, which is resolute in its prohibition on torture, and state practice, which allows for exceptions on the basis of existential threats to national security.

The particular steps by which torture came to be employed by the Bush Administration after the terrorist attacks of 11 September 2001 are outlined in detail in Chapter 4. By way of summary here, it can be noted that the conduct of the Bush Administration with regard to detainees captured in the war on terror had the effect of creating the space for torture to become an intelligence-gathering tool.

The US detainee policies were founded on a series of premises, including that the adversary—Al-Qaeda, the terrorist organisation believed to be responsible for the terrorist attacks, and its supporters—was to be regarded as a new kind of enemy, requiring a different kind of response.[62] One feature of the detainee policies was legal in nature and involved reinterpreting or rejecting international human rights and humanitarian law regarding the detention and interrogation of detainees captured in what was identified as a 'different kind of war', on the basis that they did not apply to this novel situation.[63] The other feature of the US detainee policies was normative. It engaged many of the liberal justifications for using illiberal practices against non-deserving individuals discussed previously, including the 'us' and 'them' distinction and the idea of the exception.

[59] ibid.

[60] Alan Dershowitz, 'Tortured reasoning' in *Torture: A Collection*, ed Levinson, 266–67.

[61] Henry Shue, 'Torture in dreamland: Disposing of the ticking bomb', *Case Western Reserve Journal of International Law* 37 (2&3) (2006), 231.

[62] George W Bush, 'President holds prime time news conference', White House, Washington, DC, 11 October 2001.

[63] ibid.

The Bush Administration's actions permitting the use of aggressive interrogation practices met resistance from some parts of the US Government, including the Federal Bureau of Investigation (FBI) and the US military, though such objections were largely ignored.[64]

Conclusion

The global norm against torture and the international law codifying it were undermined by the war on terror. This was achieved by liberal democracies despite the fundamental conflict between liberal values and the state practice of torture. The US response to the Al-Qaeda threat represented a serious challenge to this key principle of international human rights law that drew in the liberal allies of the US. This book examines how Australia, the UK and Canada responded to this challenge to the norm against torture when the rights of their own citizens and residents were at issue. What factors contributed to liberal democracies sometimes tolerating torture, and what factors limited such tendencies?

[64] Jonathan Hafetz, *Habeas Corpus After 9/11: Confronting America's New Global Detention System* (New York, NY: New York University Press, 2011) 41–42.

3

Enabling and Constraining Activism

Introduction

In this chapter I begin by showing how liberal international relations and international law theories for understanding state behaviour on international human rights can provide a useful foundation for explaining differences between liberal democracies. I focus on features of the domestic political and legal context that can affect mobilisation on rights, and then outline a framework of enabling and constraining factors for rights activism that helps to explain why it is easier for domestic actors to mobilise on human rights issues under certain domestic political and legal conditions, and harder under others.

Explaining State Behaviour on International Human Rights

Why do states uphold international human rights commitments? This question is of particular interest to scholars, because on matters of human rights, unlike other areas of international law, states have little incentive to police other states' non-compliance with norms and treaties that concern their actions towards their own citizens and do not directly threaten or harm other states.[1] Answering this question has given rise to a substantial compliance literature loosely associated with the liberal schools of international relations and international law. Liberalism in this context refers to the theory that state preferences derived from domestic and transnational social pressures—rather than state capabilities—influence state behaviour.[2] Liberal international theory sees individuals and private groups as the

[1] Oona A Hathaway, 'Do human rights treaties make a difference?', *The Yale Law Journal* 111(8) (2002), 1938.

[2] Andrew Moravcsik, 'The new liberalism' in *The Oxford Handbook of International Relations*, ed Christian Reus-Smit and Duncan Snidal (Oxford: Oxford University Press, 2008) 236.

fundamental actors in international politics, and assumes that the domestic and international spheres are inextricably linked.[3] It abandons the realist concept of states as unitary actors, arguing that states are made up of a large number of actors with different interests, which is why domestic politics matters.[4] Liberal international law scholarship thus argues that global rules and principles can have a profound impact on the behaviour of states, based on the important role that internal state-society relations play in determining external state behaviour.[5]

Human Rights as Power Mediators

Before looking at some of the liberal treaty compliance theories more closely, I consider a preliminary question: How are human rights to be conceived?[6] This study adopts a pragmatic approach to human rights, which emphasises their political quality and the way they can be harnessed by non-state actors in contests with the state over incursions on individual freedoms. This view understands human rights as a public normative practice of global scope, whose central concern is to protect individuals against the consequences of certain actions and omissions of their governments.[7] This challenges a more orthodox, or moral, view of human rights that sees them as being held by all individuals by virtue of their humanity.[8]

The notion of human rights as providing an armoury against the potential exercise of excessive or arbitrary power has long been present in the scholarship on rights. John Locke described the natural right to freedom as a 'fence against tyranny'.[9] More recently, Henry Shue posited that the chief purpose of rights is 'to provide some minimal protection against utter helplessness to those too weak to protect themselves'.[10] While not denying the moral basis for rights, I view

[3] Andrew Moravcsik, 'Taking preferences seriously: A liberal theory of international politics', *International Organization* 51(4) (1997), 516; Anne-Marie Slaughter, 'A liberal theory of international law', *American Society of International Law Proceedings* 94 (2000), 241.

[4] Eric Neumayer, 'Do international human rights treaties improve respect for human rights?', *Journal of Conflict Resolution* 49(6) (2005), 930.

[5] Andrew Moravcsik, 'The origins of human rights regimes: Democratic delegation in postwar Europe', *International Organization* 54(2) (2000), 217–52; Xinyuan Dai, 'The conditional nature of democratic compliance', *Journal of Conflict Resolution* 50(5) (2006), 690–713.

[6] For a comprehensive overview of the field of the philosophical foundations of human rights, see Rowan Cruft, S Matthew Liao and Massimo Renzo (eds), *Philosophical Foundations of Human Rights* (Oxford: Oxford University Press, 2015).

[7] Charles R Beitz, *The Idea of Human Rights* (Oxford: Oxford University Press, 2009) 14.

[8] RJ Vincent, *Human Rights and International Relations* (New York, NY: Cambridge University Press 1986) 9; see also John Tasioulas, 'Towards a philosophy of human rights', *Current Legal Problems* 65(1) (2012), 1–30.

[9] John Locke, 'Second treatise' in *Two Treatises of Government*, ed Peter Laslett (Cambridge: Cambridge University Press, 1988) 279.

[10] Henry Shue, *Basic Rights: Subsistence, Affluence, and US Foreign Policy* (Princeton, NJ: Princeton University Press, 1996) 18.

international human rights in terms of how they are used by citizenries in disputes with the state in a way that is fundamentally political in nature. So while behind specific human rights lies an implied notion of the moral individual, of particular interest for this study is how they are used as 'power mediators, normative principles that materially weak actors can invoke to alter the power relationship between themselves and materially preponderant political agents or institutions, usually sovereign states'.[11]

Individual rights empower civil society actors, who can invoke them in order to influence government policies and actions. As such, international human rights can be thought of as functioning as 'public standards of critique to which citizens and residents, domestic rights activists, and social movement actors can refer in order to hold their own governments accountable', especially if these governments have signed on to the relevant human rights treaties.[12] Rights are invoked by domestic actors, who declare their own rights and strategically invoke human rights treaties 'in order to strengthen their critique of arbitrariness and oppression in the polities and social structures in which they live' and to make respect for rights an accepted criteria for the internal legitimacy of their political system. I note that the notion of 'arbitrary' has a broad meaning in international treaty law and jurisprudence that goes beyond simply being against the law. I return to this concept in Chapter 8, but note here that the arbitrary exercise of power includes elements of inappropriateness, injustice, lack of predictability and due process of law, and of the unreasonable.[13]

International human rights principles and laws can thus provide ammunition for activists and non-governmental organisations (NGOs) to assist in organising against and pressuring governments. They can also provide a textual and interpretive template for domestic courts and legislatures, whose judgments or reports can be used by civil society actors as focal points in their activism.[14] This political understanding of rights informs my understanding of the compliance literature that seeks to explain why, and when, states obey international human rights law.

The Role of Domestic Actors in Human Rights Treaty Compliance

Some treaty compliance theories focus on the impact that transnational human rights advocacy networks have on improving the international human rights

[11] Christian Reus-Smit, 'Human rights in a global ecumene', *International Affairs* 87(5) (2011), 1210.

[12] Jean Cohen, *Globalization and Sovereignty: Rethinking Legality, Legitimacy, and Constitutionalism* (New York, NY: Cambridge University Press, 2012) 216.

[13] Human Rights Committee, *Views: Communication No 458/1991*, UN Doc CCPR/C/51/D/458/1991 (21 July 1994) (*Mukong v Cameron*), [9.8].

[14] David Luban, 'Human rights pragmatism and human dignity' in *Philosophical Foundations of Human Rights*, ed Rowan Cruft, S Matthew Liao and Massimo Renzo (Oxford: Oxford University Press, 2015) 264.

performance of states.[15] I am more interested in the growing body of work that focuses on the role of domestic actors in norm and treaty compliance.[16] This literature argues that domestic civil society is a crucial player in international efforts to promote human rights and that, without organised pressure 'from below', governments will rarely translate international human rights laws and commitments into meaningful reform.[17] Human rights change requires civic groups to engage in sustained, committed and sometimes risky collective action.[18] Progress on human rights begins 'with a build-up of domestic pressures' and 'depends on mobilized groups in domestic civil society pressuring for greater democracy, and using the space provided by democratic institutions to vigilantly defend and protect these rights'.[19] Essentially, this literature argues that human rights treaties affect state behaviour because they alter domestic politics through the channel of social mobilisation.[20] Domestic groups can use the international human rights regime to pressure their domestic government into better respect for human rights.[21]

Beth Simmons has demonstrated empirically that international law can affect domestic politics in ways that exert positive influences on how governments behave towards their citizens.[22] Simmons posits that treaties can trigger three domestic mechanisms: affecting elite-initiated agendas, supporting litigation and sparking political mobilisation.[23] In encouraging mobilisation, Simmons highlights the relationship between citizenries and their governments, arguing that international human rights agreements have the potential to influence domestic

[15] Margaret E Keck and Kathryn Sikkink, *Activists Beyond Borders* (Ithaca, NY: Cornell University Press, 1998).

[16] For example, Eric Neumayer, 'Do international human rights treaties improve respect for human rights?', *Journal of Conflict Resolution* 49(6) (2005), 925–53; Beth A Simmons, *Mobilizing for Human Rights: International Law in Domestic Politics* (New York, NY: Cambridge University Press, 2009); Thomas Risse, Stephen C Ropp and Kathryn Sikkink (eds), *The Persistent Power of Human Rights: From Commitment to Compliance* (New York, NY: Cambridge University Press, 2013); Xinyuan Dai, 'The conditional effects of international human rights', *Human Rights Quarterly* 36(3) (2014), 569–89; Linda Camp Keith, Banks P Miller and Jennifer Holmes, 'How draconian are the changes to US asylum law? A monthly time series analysis', *Human Rights Quarterly* 37(1) (2015), 155; James Ron and David Crow, 'Who trusts local human rights organizations? Evidence from three world regions,' *Human Rights Quarterly* 37 (2015), 188–239.

[17] Ron and Crow, 'Who trusts local human rights organizations?', 188–89.

[18] ibid, 189.

[19] Thomas Risse and Kathryn Sikkink, 'Conclusions' in *The Persistent Power of Human Rights: From Commitment to Compliance*, ed Thomas Risse, Stephen C Ropp and Kathryn Sikkink (New York, NY: Cambridge University Press, 2013) 295.

[20] Simmons, *Mobilizing for Human Rights*, 12; Risse and Sikkink, 'Conclusions', 277.

[21] Neumayer, 'Do international human rights treaties improve respect for human rights?', 930.

[22] Simmons, *Mobilizing for Human Rights*, 4. Previous empirical studies of treaty compliance were more doubtful. One suggested it was 'overly optimistic' to expect that being a party to the ICCPR would produce an observable direct impact on state behaviour. Another provided evidence that human rights treaties may sometimes lead to poorer human rights practices within countries that ratify them. See Linda Camp Keith, 'The United Nations International Covenant on Civil and Political Rights: Does it make a difference in human rights behaviour?', *Journal of Peace Research* 36(1) (1999), 95–118; Hathaway, 'Do human rights treaties make a difference?'

[23] Simmons, *Mobilizing for Human Rights*, 14.

politics 'because they suggest new ways for individuals to view their relationship with their government and with each other'.[24] International rights commitments 'serve notice that governments are accountable—domestically and externally—for refraining from the abuses proscribed by their own mutual agreements'.[25] They focus actors' expectations, help define the size of the expectations gap and can alter political demands for compliance, primarily from domestic constituencies.[26] Other scholars similarly argue that the key mechanism of influence for international human rights institutions (norms and treaties) is to utilise and empower domestic constituents. International norms and treaties do this by informing citizens, legitimising human rights initiatives, enabling the strategic use of international norms and suggesting focal points for activists.[27]

These various international liberal accounts of compliance broadly agree that no general theory of human rights change is possible, and that it makes more sense to try to establish the conditions under which states are more likely to feel bound to comply with global rights principles.[28] For human rights norms and law to affect state behaviour, 'there must be conditions for domestic groups, parties, and individuals and for civil society to persuade, convince, and perhaps pressure governments into translating the formal promise of better human rights protection into actual reality'.[29] In the various accounts, two critical qualities stand out, without which domestic mobilisation on international human rights is unlikely to occur or be effective in pressuring the state. They are ability and will—sometimes framed on the part of the state, sometimes on the part of domestic civil society.[30] Different scholars emphasise particular scenarios in which this is most likely to occur. Thomas Risse and Kathryn Sikkink, for example, identify regime type and material and social vulnerability to pressure as being determinants of the willingness of states to comply with norms and treaties, while state capacity and the centralisation of rule implementation affect its ability to bring about positive human rights change.[31] Simmons frames the key criteria for compliance in terms of means and motive. Thus, domestic actors must have both the motive and the means realistically to press their governments to take international human rights treaties seriously.[32] This is more likely to occur, she argues, in moderately democratic and transitional regimes where institutions are most fluid.[33]

[24] ibid, 141.
[25] ibid, 4–5.
[26] ibid, 14.
[27] Dai, 'The conditional effects of international human rights', 577, 579, 581, 582.
[28] Risse and Sikkink, 'Conclusions', 276; Dai, 'The conditional effects of international human rights', 572; Neumayer, 'Do international human rights treaties improve respect for human rights?', 950.
[29] Neumayer, 'Do international human rights treaties improve respect for human rights?', 950.
[30] Risse and Sikkink, 'Conclusions', 286–87.
[31] ibid.
[32] Simmons, *Mobilizing for Human Rights*, 153.
[33] ibid, 16.

Implicit in this reasoning about the conditions for state compliance with international human rights is that they are heavily dependent on the national context and vary from state to state. As such, liberal compliance theories are most often used to theorise differences in international human rights outcomes across different regime types. Hence Risse and Sikkink argue that democratic states tend to be more willing to comply with human rights norms, though this is enhanced where the state is also vulnerable to external pressures on rights, unlike, say, the US, which is too powerful to care.[34] This is similar to Simmons's findings that treaties have most impact in less stable, transitioning democracies. Simmons also postulates, however, that rights mobilisation is relatively low in long-term democracies because of the apathy of citizens who take rights for granted.[35] Another study argues that ratification of human rights treaties becomes more beneficial to human rights the more democratic the country and the stronger a country's civil society.[36]

The tendency in the compliance literature to generalise about the human rights performances of particularly long-term liberal democracies was challenged after 11 September 2001, when the US transgressed international rights standards. One critique suggested that traditional models for human rights change had overlooked the possibility of domestic support for human rights violations in liberal democracies and the existence of competing global norms such as the maintenance of security.[37] They discounted the possibility that a country that had already ratified and implemented international treaties on a core human rights norm could experience a reversal of these commitments.[38] It was pointed out that even established norms experience ongoing internal dynamism, and their content may be revised in the course of attempts to extend or challenge their meanings.[39] Hence the argument put more recently by scholars in the aftermath of 9/11 is that international human rights norms require constant vigilance and reinforcement by a range of state and non-state actors in order to sustain such rights.[40] This argument is at the heart of the interactional account of international human rights developed by Jutta Brunnée and Stephen Toope. They contend that norms, if they are to prevail and maintain compliance pull, must be repeatedly reasserted

[34] Risse and Sikkink, 'Conclusions', 287–88, 294.

[35] Simmons, *Mobilizing for Human Rights*, 152–53.

[36] Neumayer, 'Do international human rights treaties improve respect for human rights?', 950.

[37] Anja Jetschke and Andrea Liese, 'The power of human rights a decade after: From euphoria to contestation?' in *The Persistent Power of Human Rights*, ed Risse et al, 41–42.

[38] Kathryn Sikkink, 'The United States and torture: Does the spiral model work?' in *The Persistent Power of Human Rights*, ed Risse et al, 145; see also Tim Dunne, '"The rules of the game are changing": Fundamental human rights in crisis after 9/11', *International Politics* 44(2–3) (2007), 269–86; Kate Nash, *The Cultural Politics of Human Rights: Comparing the US and UK* (New York, NY: Cambridge University Press, 2009) 47.

[39] Mona Lena Krook and Jacqui True, 'Rethinking the life cycles of international norms: The United Nations and the global promotion of gender equality', *European Journal of International Relations* 18(1) (2010), 117.

[40] Risse and Sikkink, 'Conclusions', 295.

by wide and disparate communities of legal practice, comprising an array of state and non-state actors.[41]

While many liberal international theorists focus on differences between states of diverse regime types, I am concerned with differences in international human rights implementation among countries of similar regime type. Liberal international theory offers a fruitful starting position for analysis in directing us to examine the local conditions for the mobilisation of domestic actors on international human rights in a particular polity. Did conditions in liberal democracies after 9/11 support a willingness and ability on the part of citizens to mobilise in the face of international human rights breaches? We cannot assume that domestic actors, even across liberal democracies with similar political and legal systems, necessarily faced the same conditions for activism, nor possessed the same level of motivation or means to mobilise. The domestic political and legal context is critical for understanding why actors in some liberal democracies might robustly challenge their states on their international human rights behaviour, but not in others. This is because every domestic context is characterised by particular features that can help or hinder human rights activism.

The Civil Society–State Relationship

This volume places domestic actors at the centre of the study of human rights activism and its influence on state behaviour. Domestic actors include the three levels of government—the executive, legislature and judiciary—in addition to civil society. In a human rights context, interested civil society actors interact with the courts and individual members of Parliament in seeking to influence the behaviour of the executive.

I understand civil society to mean the social arena in which citizens freely assemble, interact, and express opinions about matters of general interest and concern, without being subject to coercion. This definition is informed by Jürgen Habermas's exposition of the 'public sphere'—the social domain of discourse where public opinion is formed.[42] Drawing on Habermas, Jean Cohen and Andrew Arato theorise civil society to mean a domain of social interaction that exists apart from the formal economy and the state, key elements of which are the public sphere and voluntary associations, and which is stabilised by fundamental rights including freedom of communication and association and the protection of privacy.[43]

[41] Jutta Brunnée and Stephen J Toope, *Legitimacy and Legality in International Law: An Interactional Account* (New York, NY: Cambridge University Press, 2010) 102.

[42] Jürgen Habermas, 'The public sphere' in *Jürgen Habermas on Society and Politics: A Reader*, ed Steven Seidman (Boston, MA: Beacon Press, 2005) 231.

[43] Jean Cohen and Andrew Arato, *Civil Society and Political Theory* (Cambridge, MA: MIT Press, 1992) ix, 412, 440–41. Cohen and Arato acknowledge arguments as to whether the economy should

Civil society is a capacious category and operates domestically and transnationally. In this study, I focus on five categories of civil society actors that were most involved in the torture issue: the legal profession, domestic and transnational human rights NGOs, religious-based organisations (especially Muslim community groups), the media and family members.[44] The media, under a traditional liberal model, occupy a position as public watchdog, acting as a check on political power.[45] Of course, as with the rest of civil society, the media cannot always be relied upon to perform this accountability role.

Civil society has an important role to play in guarding against abuse of power and overreach by the state. Ernest Gellner describes this as counterbalancing the central agency of order: while not preventing the state from fulfilling its role as keeper of the peace, civil society can nevertheless stop it from dominating the rest of society.[46] Civil society does this by engaging in political accountability. Accountability is about answerability towards others with a legitimate claim to demand an account.[47] By political accountability, I mean that the obligation to be accountable rests with the government, usually the executive, while the entitlement to demand accountability resides with the citizenry, though it is sometimes realised through other bodies. In a liberal democracy accountability is central, because it is a system of government based on popular sovereignty, and because of the underlying condition of vulnerability to power.[48]

I noted in Chapter 2 that a central preoccupation of liberal democracy as a political system is with defining and limiting the exercise of political power in order to minimise the possibility that the coercive power of the state will threaten individual liberties. One way of doing this is through the traditional doctrine of the tripartite separation of powers, where power to govern is distributed between the executive, the parliament and the judiciary, and each group, working within a defined area of responsibility, maintains a check on the other arms of government. A broader way of conceiving of political accountability is necessary in order to understand civil society's role in constraining power. Republican theory conceives of liberty as the desire not to be dominated.[49] Critical to understanding how

be included in the civil society concept; they contend it should not be, because 'the spontaneous forces of the capitalist market economy can represent as great a danger to social solidarity, social justice, and even autonomy as the administrative power of the modern state' (ibid, viii).

[44] For a discussion of why the intimate sphere is often overlooked—because women's issues have traditionally been considered private—see Mary Kaldor, *Global Civil Society: An Answer to War* (Cambridge: Polity, 2003) 48–49.

[45] Pippa Norris, 'Watchdog journalism' in *The Oxford Handbook of Public Accountability*, ed Mark Bovens, Robert E Goodin and Thomas Schillemans (Oxford: Oxford University Press, 2014) 525.

[46] Ernest Gellner, *Conditions of Liberty: Civil Society and its Rivals* (London: Penguin Books, 1996) 5.

[47] Mark Bovens, Thomas Schillemans and Robert E Goodin, 'Public accountability' in *The Oxford Handbook of Public Accountability*, ed Bovens et al, 4, 6.

[48] Mark E Warren, 'Accountability and democracy' in *The Oxford Handbook of Public Accountability*, ed Bovens et al, 39.

[49] Michael Barnett, 'Building a Republican peace: Stabilizing states after war', *International Security* 30(4) (2006), 95; see also Mlada Bukovansky, 'Liberal states, international order, and legitimacy: An appeal for persuasion over prescription', *International Politics* 44(2–3) (2007), 180.

to achieve freedom from domination is the notion of pluralised 'separations of powers'.[50] This idea advocates republics radically pluralising their vision of how to separate powers within the state, so that the state has many branches of separated powers rather than just the traditional legislature, judiciary and executive.[51] Civil society is one branch of a pluralised notion of separated powers, operating alongside the traditional tripartite model. Ideally, in this model, no one centre of power is so dominant as to be able to crush any other separated power, without the other separated powers mobilising to defeat that domination.[52]

Civil society members can operate as 'accountability agents' in that they are self-appointed and self-authorised, and make public claims based sometimes on law, but often on morality, against powerful governmental institutions.[53] Accountability agents 'pay attention to the conduct and performance of powerful governmental and private institutions', and 'make evaluative judgments about whether they are sufficiently respectful of the rights of individuals, or appropriately accountable for the effects of their actions'.[54] Having made these judgments, accountability agents give voice to their claims and rouse others to support them. Accountability agents can monitor the state, contest governmental decisions, denounce the unlawful actions of public officials and expose governmental wrongdoing.[55] They can also activate the operation of agencies such as the judiciary or legislative investigation commissions, which would otherwise not act.[56] Domestic civil society derives its legitimacy to carry out the role of accountability agent from the fact that it is a part of the national polity, yet sits outside the embedded structure of influence in the political system.[57] The role of civil society in standing up for human rights is a kind of constitutional function, in that democratic discourse—an intrinsic feature of civil society—plays a role in generating and maintaining rights.[58] Civil society also makes rights meaningful by bridging the gap between politics and law, through 'building, supporting, and reinforcing a culture of resilience with respect to constitutional and human rights'.[59] In practical terms, civil society carries out

[50] John Braithwaite, Hilary Charlesworth and Aderito Soares, *Networked Governance of Freedom and Tyranny: Peace in Timor-Leste* (Canberra: ANU E Press, 2012) 296.

[51] ibid, xii.

[52] ibid, 128.

[53] Mark H Moore, 'Accountability, legitimacy, and the court of public opinion' in *The Oxford Handbook of Public Accountability*, ed Bovens et al, 633.

[54] ibid.

[55] Enrique Peruzzotti, 'The societalization of horizontal accountability: Rights advocacy and the Defensor del Pueblo de la Nación in Argentina' in *Human Rights, State Compliance, and Social Change: Assessing National Human Rights Institutions*, ed Ryan Goodman and Thomas Pegram (New York, NY: Cambridge University Press, 2012) 249.

[56] ibid, 251.

[57] Larry Diamond, 'What civil society can do to reform, deepen, and improve democracy', paper presented to the workshop on Civil Society, Social Capital, and Civic Engagement in Japan and the United States, 12–13 June 2001, 8.

[58] Cohen and Arato, *Civil Society and Political Theory*, 395.

[59] David Cole, 'Where liberty lies: Civil society and individual rights after 9/11,' *Wayne Law Review* 57(4) (2011), 1256.

this role in generating and giving content to human rights by engaging in contentious politics—that is, collective political struggle involving episodic, public interaction among makers of claims and that involves government.[60]

Civil societies are not monolithic, and individuals and groups will not always serve a checking role in terms of pressuring the state to comply with international human rights law. There are many reasons for this. The relationship between the state and civil society, whether cooperative or fractious, varies across liberal democracies and sometimes according to the political party in power. The nature of the relationship may depend upon the ideological settings of the government. I discuss this further in Chapters 5–7. Briefly, some party ideologies envisage a legitimate role for civil society in the democratic process, while others do not. This can affect how civil society perceives its interests at a given time, including in relation to critiquing official human rights policies. Civil society groups may also be constrained in their role in holding the executive accountable due to a reliance on government funding or access to its people and processes.[61]

Another reason why civil society may not fulfil a checking role on human rights is because of the need to maintain broader public support. The imperative for some NGOs to remain viable can sometimes manifest itself in opportunistic behaviour that leads organisations to engage in issue selection—choosing concerns or cases that are more likely to attract support from the public, donors and the media.[62] The war on terror did not, in general, produce popular human rights victims, though some individuals were more unpopular than others (this was especially evident in the cases of two citizens, Mamdouh Habib in Australia and Omar Khadr in Canada, discussed in Chapters 5 and 7). Related to this point are concerns about the representativeness of civil society and the underlying power structures, values and historical inequities that influence which human rights causes and which victims mainstream or dominant NGOs (particularly transnational ones) are willing to take on. Jai Sen argues, for example, that civil society is a site of power and exclusion, ruled by norms of 'civility', where those considered not to conform (the 'incivil' or, worse because of their purported criminal intent, 'uncivil') are subjugated and either ignored or destroyed.[63] Similarly, others argue that international human rights NGOs are engaged in a political project to

[60] Douglas McAdam, Sidney Tarrow and Charles Tilly, *Dynamics of Contention* (New York: Cambridge University Press, 2001) 5.

[61] Kaldor, *Global Civil Society*, 92; Chiara Cordelli, 'How privatization threatens the private', *Critical Review of International Social and Political Philosophy* 16(1) (2013), 81.

[62] See generally R Charli Carpenter, 'Setting the advocacy agenda: Theorizing issue emergence and nonemergence in transnational advocacy networks', *International Studies Quarterly* 51(1) (2007), 99–120; Alexander Cooley and Ron James, 'The NGO scramble: Organizational insecurity and the political economy of transnational action', *International Security* 27(1) (2002), 5–39; Clifford Bob, *The Marketing of Rebellion: Insurgents, Media, and International Activism* (New York, NY: Cambridge University Press, 2005).

[63] Jai Sen, 'The power of civility: Some critical reflections on global civil society', paper presented at *Global Civil Society: More or Less Democracy?* World Social Forum, Nairobi, Kenya, 22 January 2007, 54.

replicate a vision of society based on the industrial democracies of the north.[64] These critiques of civil society will be returned to in later chapters in relation to the issue of whether certain groups were willing, especially at first, to stand up for the rights of suspected Muslim terrorists who were predominantly from Middle Eastern backgrounds.

Sections of civil society may also sometimes support the executive's downgrading of human rights norms, especially in a time of high national security threat. This occurred in relation to the use of torture in the war on terror. There were instances of journalists, legal academics, legal organisations and think tanks arguing the case for torture across many liberal democracies after 11 September 2001.[65] Such views were expressed against the background of the Bush Administration's arguing or implying that torture was both necessary and effective as a means of obtaining critical intelligence about terrorism.[66] Civil society encompasses a range of individuals and groups with diverse interests and values, not all of them supportive of human rights or of human rights for everybody. Where particular civil society members supported torture, we see echoes of the ideas discussed in Chapter 2 about the dangerous potential of some conceptions of liberalism that encompass universalist beliefs demanding conformity to an ideal form of life.

My interest lies in thinking critically about civil society as a realm of power where basic legal freedoms can be achieved. Whether they are achieved or not depends, at least in part, on non-state actors being willing and able to mobilise on human rights and assume the role of moderating state power.

The Enabling and Constraining Framework

How are we to assess whether a polity's domestic conditions supported activism on human rights? The conditions for mobilisation in a liberal democracy, in terms of whether they encourage or inhibit activism on rights, can be analysed through the lens of the enabling and constraining factors that are particular to the domestic political and legal context. I consider three types of factors: a state's political culture, particularly in relation to rights; its political and legal institutions; and

[64] Makau Mutua, 'Human rights international NGOs: A critical evaluation' in *NGOs and Human Rights: Promise and Performance*, ed Claude E Welch (Philadelphia, PA: University of Pennsylvania Press, 2001) 151.

[65] See, eg, Alan M Dershowitz, *Why Terrorism Works: Understanding the Threat, Responding to the Challenge* (New Haven, CT: Yale University Press, 2002) 145; Mirko Bagaric and Julie Clarke, 'Not enough official torture in the world? The circumstances in which torture is morally justifiable', *University of San Francisco Law Review* 39(3) (2005), 581–616; Michael Ignatieff, *The Lesser Evil: Political Ethics in an Age of Terror* (Edinburgh: Edinburgh University Press, 2005).

[66] See, eg, Dick Cheney, 'The Vice President appears on Meet the Press with Tim Russert', *NBC News*, 16 September 2001.

political opportunities for pressuring governments on rights issues. Some of these domestic legal and political features are more fixed, some are more temporal. In many respects they are interrelated. Political culture, for example, can influence the kind of institutions a state has, and institutions can affect a polity's awareness of rights. Similarly, opportunities can rely on activists framing claims according to dominant cultural understandings that will resonate with the wider public, and on accessing existing institutions. Activists may also, through their activism, influence a polity's awareness of rights and the way its institutions operate (and sometimes, the government's attitude towards those institutions). I treat these three factors separately but note their interdependence.

Political Culture

One feature of the domestic political and legal context that can affect activism on human rights is the country's political culture and, specifically, the way it shapes a polity's ideas about rights. By rights culture, I mean the way historical legacies precondition how members of a modern polity think about themselves as rights-bearing individuals and influence their willingness to act on new cases of rights infractions. I analyse the rights cultures of Australia, the UK and Canada through historical legacies and experiences of rights, and domestic debates around rights.

Culture is an inherently vague concept, the name given to the abstracted customs of a social group and, in many ways, an empirically derived construct.[67] The concept of culture is derived from anthropological literature. Clifford Geertz described political culture as 'an historically transmitted pattern of meanings', according to which members of a polity interpret their experiences and decide upon their actions.[68] It provides the background meanings—the metaphors and historical events—by which specific beliefs and arguments are consciously judged and which actors intentionally use to frame problems.[69] Political culture defines the range of acceptable possible alternatives from which groups or individuals may, other circumstances permitting, choose a course of action.[70] The point of examining political culture in the context of arguments about human rights is premised on a particular understanding about the actions of domestic actors in making rights claims against the state. That is, such actions involve contentious

[67] Neil J Smelser, 'Culture: Coherent or incoherent' in *Theory of Culture*, ed Richard Münch and Neil J Smelser (Berkeley, CA: University of California Press, 1992) 19.

[68] Clifford Geertz, *The Interpretation of Cultures* (New York, NY: Basic Books, 1973) 89.

[69] Neta C Crawford, *Argument and Change in World Politics: Ethics, Decolonization, and Humanitarian Intervention* (Cambridge: Cambridge University Press, 2002) 59.

[70] David Elkins and Richard Simeon, 'A cause in search of its effect, or what does political culture explain?', *Comparative Politics* 11(2) (1979), 131.

politics, and political power rests largely upon expectations, communications and shared sentiments that are shaped by political culture.[71] Similarly, in the sphere of global politics, the process of foreign policy-making and international relations is characterised by political arguments that are based on beliefs that gain their content and are intelligible through and within historically situated cultures of the community in question.[72]

Sally Engle Merry's work dealing with the way culture mediates how international human rights are translated, or 'vernacularized', in the local context is helpful in thinking about how community understandings about rights can vary according to the particular polity.[73] Vernacularisation is the process by which ideas from transnational and international sources travel to small communities and are adapted to local institutions and meanings.[74] Ideas about human rights are embedded in shared cultural assumptions about the nature of the person, the community and the state that are particular to political communities and do not necessarily translate easily from one setting to another.[75] These local understandings encompass questions such as: what are rights, which rights matter, who has them, are they a good thing, are they necessary, whose job is it to uphold them, and what should happen when particular rights are breached?

A nation's rights culture affects civil society's awareness about rights and, importantly, its sense of legitimacy in contesting rights claims against the government. A strong rights culture requires a consciousness about rights at different levels of the polity, and is one in which human rights are embedded in the everyday thinking of policy-makers, legislators, the judiciary and the wider community.[76] Crucially, for rights to have meaning, it is up to individual citizens and groups to demand them.[77] Thus, as Cass Sunstein argues, rights 'will not exist without a rights-bearing culture, that is, a culture in which ordinary people are at least sometimes willing to take serious personal risks by challenging powerful people by insisting that rights are at stake'.[78] Rights consciousness in the context of the citizens' relationship with their government comprises a strong persuasion that

[71] Lucian W Pye, 'Introduction: The elusive concept of culture and the vivid reality of personality', *Political Psychology* 18(2) (1997), 247.

[72] Crawford, *Argument and Change in World Politics*, 13–14.

[73] Sally Engle Merry, *Human Rights and Gender Violence: Translating International Law into Local Justice* (Chicago, IL: University of Chicago Press, 2006); Sally Engle Merry, 'Transnational human rights and local activism: Mapping the middle,' *American Anthropologist* 108(1) (2006), 38–51.

[74] Merry, 'Transnational human rights and local activism', 39.

[75] Merry, *Human Rights and Gender Violence*, 3.

[76] David Kinley and Christine Ernst, 'Exile on Main Street: Australia's legislative agenda for human rights', *European Human Rights Law Review* 1 (2012), 158–70.

[77] Julie A Mertus, 'Human rights and civil society in a new age of American exceptionalism' in *Human Rights in the 'War on Terror'*, ed Richard Ashby Wilson (New York, NY: Cambridge University Press, 2005) 324.

[78] Cass R Sunstein, 'Rights after communism', *East European Constitutional Review* 4(1) (1995), 61.

individuals have rights and 'that when we are wronged there must be remedies, that patterns of illegitimate authority can be challenged'.[79]

Whether civil society is encouraged and supported by its nation's rights culture to take such a stand can depend on the country's history. A country's national historical experiences confer upon its people a shared (though often contested) consciousness through which current human rights issues are interpreted. Political culture is a product of the collective history of a political system.[80] It is general, deeply subjective, and reflects conflict and pluralism.[81] Cultural norms are not necessarily shared equally among all citizens or branches of the state; rather, there will be those that are predominant and considered shared values by a broad cross-section of the population.[82] There often exist competing narratives about a country's national historical experiences, where dominant narratives are contested, including by immigrant minorities and indigenous peoples. As such, the exercise of identifying a rights culture will always be partial and exclusionary.[83]

A state's historical legacies and experiences of rights can help explicate rights culture. These include colonial legacies (whether as coloniser or colonised), and the country's previous encounters with political violence and torture. Louis Hartz's liberal fragment theory is insightful for thinking about rights legacies.[84] Australia and Canada formed as colonial offshoots or 'fragments' of Britain and, in Canada's situation, also of France. Hartz directs us to reflect on these early origins in order to appreciate the nuances in the political cultures of the former settler societies, including their different conceptions of liberalism and rights.[85] His argument is that residues of the political ideas that prevailed at the time Australia and Canada broke away from Europe, and reflecting the particular circumstances in which that separation occurred, can be found in these polities' modern-day political cultures.

Another historical influence I consider is the state's previous experiences of political violence. Historical experiences of terrorism can shape countries' responses to new terrorist threats in ways that affect state and non-state actors. A small number of studies of liberal democracies and terrorism have made such a link.[86] According to some accounts, countries like the US that, prior to 11 September

[79] Hendrik Hartog, 'The constitution of aspiration and "the rights that belong to us all"', *The Journal of American History* 74(3) (1987), 1014.

[80] Lucian Pye, 'Introduction: Political culture and political development' in *Political Culture and Political Development*, ed Lucian Pye and Sidney Verba (Princeton, NJ: Princeton University Press, 1965) 8.

[81] Margaret Radin, *Reinterpreting Property* (Chicago, IL: University of Chicago Press, 1993) 169.

[82] David Schneiderman, 'Property rights and regulatory innovation comparing constitutional cultures', *International Journal of Constitutional Law* 4(2) (2006), 374.

[83] ibid.

[84] Louis Hartz, '*The Founding of New Societies: Studies in the History of the United States, Latin America, South Africa, Canada and Australia* (New York, NY: Harcourt Brace Jovanovich, 1964).

[85] ibid, 3.

[86] For example, see David A Charters (ed), *The Deadly Sin of Terrorism: Its Effect on Democracy and Civil Liberty in Six Countries* (Westport, CT: Greenwood Press, 1994); Philip Gordon and Jeremy Shapiro, *Allies at War America, Europe, and the Crisis over Iraq* (New York, NY: McGraw-Hill, 2004).

2001, had little knowledge of domestic terrorism, had a much lower tolerance for vulnerability than Europe, which had more experience.[87] In Europe, societies have 'internalised the notion that terrorism, given its roots in deep social alienation and its tenacious resistance to purely repressive means, can never be completely eradicated'.[88] Other accounts suggest that decades of terrorism at home can damage a state's liberal ethical commitment to democracy.[89] Australia, the UK and Canada had very different histories with respect to terrorism. I will argue that significant prior experiences of domestic terrorism can render certain sections of the polity more alert to the potentially negative consequences of a state's counter-terrorism responses for incursions of civil liberties.

Political culture influences, and is influenced by, the institutional framework of a state. Rights culture is a dynamic and fluid concept, consisting of ideas and practices that are continually changing because of contradictions among them, or because members adopt new ideas and institutions, including ideas from other cultural systems.[90] Thus domestic rights cultures can be developed in order to improve the human rights policies of states. A polity's dominant understandings about rights can shape its institutions, but states may also establish new institutions (or dismantle or replace existing ones) in order to bring about a change in rights culture. I examine this reciprocal relationship between culture and institutions through domestic debates around issues of rights awareness. An example of these debates includes those relating to the institutionalisation of rights and whether or not rights should be codified. These debates sometimes reference dominant historical narratives and can reveal a state's intent with respect to rights protection. They can be insightful for what they tell us about a polity's traditional understandings of liberty, how members see their relationship with the state, and how liberties should be protected in the future.

I suggest that a stronger rights culture can facilitate human rights activism by giving citizens a greater awareness of human rights and legitimacy in making rights claims against the state.

Political and Legal Institutions

A second, related enabling or constraining factor that can affect human rights activism is a state's political and legal institutions, specifically its national human rights framework. For this I draw on the literature concerning the impact a country's institutional settings can have on policy outcomes in influencing, guiding,

[87] Gordon and Shapiro, *Allies at War America, Europe, and the Crisis over Iraq*, 60.

[88] ibid.

[89] Bruce W Warner, 'Great Britain and the response to international terrorism' in *The Deadly Sin of Terrorism*, ed Charters, 37; Noemi Gal-Or, 'Countering terrorism in Israel,' in *The Deadly Sin of Terrorism*, ed Charters, 162.

[90] Merry, *Human Rights and Gender Violence*, 11.

redirecting, magnifying and inhibiting policy battles.[91] I examine three kinds of domestic institutions in terms of their effects on human rights mobilisation: parliamentary committee systems, bills of rights, and domestic legislation prohibiting torture.

Institutionalist theory seeks to explain variations in the behaviour of similar states subject to the same international conditions and constraints through the particular domestic structures and coalition-building processes of the country involved.[92] Institutions can be defined as relatively stable collections of rules and practices, embedded in structures of resources that make action possible.[93] Institutions wield considerable power:

> They create actors and meeting places and organize the relations and interactions among actors. They guide behaviour and stabilize expectations. Specific institutional settings also provide vocabularies that frame thought and understandings and define what are legitimate arguments and standards of justification and criticism in different situations … Institutions, furthermore, allocate resources and empower and constrain actors differently.[94]

Hence, institutions order democratic political life, defining the setting within which governance and policy-making must take place.[95] The institutionalist argument contends that organisational structures of the state—shaped and reshaped by a confluence of historical forces—exert an influence over policy choice.[96] A state's domestic institutions affect the degree of power that any one set of actors has over policy outcomes, and they influence an actor's definition of his or her own interests. In this way, organisational factors affect both the degree of pressure an actor can bring to bear on policy and the likely direction of that pressure.[97]

I examine three kinds of domestic institutions in terms of the effects they have on human rights mobilisation. The first is the parliament, which can in some liberal democratic systems play a significant role in checking executive policies and conduct on human rights, especially through the parliamentary committee system. As well as participating in these forums, members of parliament can directly ask questions of and lobby ministers. The parliament straddles the executive and citizenry, and can play an important coercive, or at least persuasive, role with respect

[91] G John Ikenberry, 'Conclusion: An institutional approach to American foreign policy', *International Organization* 42(1) (1988), 219–43.

[92] Thomas Risse-Kappen, 'Public opinion, domestic structure, and foreign policy in liberal democracies', *World Politics* 43(4) (1991), 479–80.

[93] James G March and Johan P Olsen, 'The logic of appropriateness' in *The Oxford Handbook of Public Policy*, ed Michael Moran, Martin Rein and Robert Goodin (Oxford: Oxford University Press, 2008) 691.

[94] ibid.

[95] ibid.

[96] Ikenberry, 'Conclusion', 220, 223.

[97] Peter A Hall, *Governing the Economy: The Politics of State Intervention in Britain and France* (Cambridge: Polity Press, 1986) 19.

to shaping policy decisions ultimately taken by the executive.[98] Theoretically, the legislature gives a voice to citizens and civil society groups through these avenues, and provides an opening into the political system and the policy-making processes of the executive government. In practice, however, a parliament's effectiveness can vary across different political systems. As a result of divergent historical developments, the parliaments of Australia, the UK and Canada are constituted slightly differently. This is especially the case with respect to their upper houses, with implications for the institutions' practical power, willingness to stand up to the executive and political legitimacy. In addition, interactions between the parliament and other, external political institutions differ across the three polities. The UK's membership of the Council of Europe, for example, has important implications for the Parliament's oversight functions, as I discuss in Chapter 6.[99]

A bill or charter of rights or human rights act is another example of an institution that can dramatically shape behaviour on human rights. The UK and Canada have bills of rights (or similar human rights frameworks), while Australia does not. Disagreement exists between proponents and critics of bills of rights over whether the judiciary's role in interpreting them is a desirable mechanism in a liberal democracy.[100] However, even detractors acknowledge the powerful effect a bill of rights has in empowering civil society actors.[101] It operates in two ways to improve human rights: by providing judicially enforceable mechanisms to those who believe their rights have been violated; and by deepening respect for human rights more generally within a polity.[102]

Another institution of relevance in influencing activism on international torture is a state's domestic laws criminalising torture (which states are required to enact under the Convention Against Torture and Other Cruel, Inhuman or Degrading Treatment or Punishment, Article 2). After 11 September 2001, laws in Australia, the UK and Canada with respect to torture differed in terms of whether they were piecemeal or more comprehensive. While these domestic laws did not necessarily have a direct bearing on the cases of detainees, they did reflect the states' commitments to the prohibition against torture in a way that, I argue, influenced how activists perceived their chances of success in making claims based on this norm.

While a state's institutions have a powerful effect on policy outcomes, they provide parameters for action, rather than dictating a specific action.[103] I suggest that

[98] Philip Norton, *Parliament in British Politics* (London: Palgrave MacMillan, 2005) 11–12.

[99] ibid, 149–52.

[100] Tom Campbell, 'Human rights-based judicial review: It seems a good idea at the time', *Dissent* (Spring 2008).

[101] FL Morton and Rainer Knopff, *The Charter Revolution and the Court Party* (Toronto: Broadview Press, 2000) 13.

[102] George Williams, 'Constructing a community-based bill of rights' in *Protecting Human Rights: Instruments and Institutions*, ed Tom Campbell, Jeffrey Goldsworthy and Adrienne Stone (Oxford: Oxford University Press, 2003) 247–48.

[103] March and Olsen, 'The logic of appropriateness', 695.

it is easier for citizenries to hold governments to account on human rights where relevant and robust institutional tools exist that facilitate mobilisation.

Political Opportunities

A third, related enabling or constraining factor affecting human rights activism is political opportunity. A more transient factor than rights cultures or institutions, political opportunity also offers incentives for or discouragement of activism in the form of a more open or closed political environment. I examine a number of different kinds of political opportunities relevant to the cases. They included the political party in power (in terms of its particular ideology or attitude towards civil society and/or human rights), the electoral cycle, the unity of the government, and any relevant issues playing out concurrently that resonated with concerns about the torture of detained citizens and residents.

Ideas about political opportunity are drawn from the social movement literature.[104] These ideas focus attention on the opening and closing of political space, and the notion that motivated individuals or groups will respond to the apertures and constraints that the larger political environment offers.[105] Political opportunity structures are dynamic, often fleeting, and sometimes accidental. They can be defined as 'consistent—but not necessarily formal or permanent—dimensions of the political environment that provide incentives for collective action by affecting people's expectations for success or failure'.[106] Changes in political opportunities and constraints create important incentives for initiating new phases of contention.[107] Opportunities reveal allies and expose the weaknesses of enemies; and once they do, they communicate crucial information for movement formation.[108] Sidney Tarrow explains how this occurs:

> The opening of opportunities provides external resources to people who lack internal ones; openings where there were only walls before; alliances that did not previously seem possible; and realignments that appear capable of bringing new groups to power.[109]

According to Tarrow, there are four major ways in which political opportunity structures can be seen to expand.[110] One enlargement of opportunity structure

[104] Sidney Tarrow, *Power in Movement: Social Movements and Contentious Politics* (New York, NY: Cambridge University Press, 1998).

[105] William A Gamson and David S Meyer, 'Framing political opportunity' in *Comparative Perspectives on Social Movements: Political Opportunities, Mobilizing Structures, and Cultural Framings*, ed Doug McAdam, John D McCarthy and Mayer N Zald (New York, NY: Cambridge University Press, 1996) 277; David S Meyer, 'National human rights institutions, opportunities, and activism' in *Human Rights, State Compliance, and Social Change*, ed Goodman and Pegram, 329.

[106] Tarrow, *Power in Movement*, 76–77.

[107] ibid, 7.

[108] ibid, 72.

[109] ibid, 89.

[110] Sidney Tarrow, '"Aiming at a moving target": Social science and the recent rebellions in Eastern Europe', *Political Science and Politics* 24(1) (1991), 14–15.

occurs when levels of access to institutional participation have begun to open up, such as at election time. Another expansion emerges when political alignments are in disarray and new realignments have not yet formed. A third kind of political opportunity structure presents when there are major conflicts within the political elite of which challengers can take advantage. A final avenue of expanded opportunity occurs when challengers are offered the help of influential allies from within, or outside, the system. Political opportunity structure has effects at different, interacting levels, including that of citizens, groups and elites.[111] Increasing political opportunities can widen the space within which citizens perceive that they can legitimately make claims. They can provide new openings for organisers to build movements and attract more support. Expanding political opportunities can also offer new possibilities for elites within the polity to expand their influence and achieve their policy goals.

Political opportunity structures can therefore assist in understanding variations in the strategies, structures and outcomes of similar movements that arise in different places.[112] Actors, routinely engaged in exercises of state accountability on matters such as protecting human rights, watch out for such opportunities ceaselessly.[113] One way to think about this vigilance by civil society is in terms of a 'briefcase' image. That is, sometimes ideas for social change initiatives 'come in a flash of inspiration, and at other times they are carried around in a briefcase for years until the right opportunity presents itself'.[114] In other words, actors interested in political change often must bide their time until the right political opportunity presents. However, political opportunities are limited in terms of the change they can precipitate. External, more stable structural factors, such as the strength or weakness of the state, and the forms of repression used by the state, can inhibit the potential effectiveness of political opportunities.[115] The effective exploitation of opportunities relies on their being perceived as such by political challengers or activists. The use of external opportunities requires activists to employ known repertoires of contention, to frame their messages dynamically and to access or construct unifying mobilising structures.[116] Political opportunities thus have an inevitable cultural component requiring recognition and framing.[117] Hence, a

[111] ibid, 15.

[112] Sidney Tarrow, 'National politics and collective action: Recent theory and research in Western Europe and the United States', *Annual Review of Sociology* 14 (1988), 430.

[113] Margaret E Keck and Kathryn Sikkink, 'Transnational advocacy networks in the movement society' in *The Social Movement Society: Contentious Politics for a New Century*, ed David S Meyer and Sidney Tarrow (Lanham, MD: Rowman and Littlefield Publishers, 1998) 223.

[114] Julie A Mertus, *Bait and Switch: Human Rights and US Foreign Policy*, 2nd edn (New York, NY: Routledge, 2008) 182.

[115] Tarrow, *Power in Movement*, 71.

[116] ibid, 71–72.

[117] Mayer N Zald, 'Culture, ideology, and strategic framing' in *Comparative Perspectives on Social Movements*, ed McAdam et al, 271.

polity's symbolic and institutionalised cultural assumptions, discussed above, feed into the defining of political opportunities.

A number of different kinds of political opportunities (openings and closings of the political system) were common to Australia, the UK and Canada, and presented at different times. They included the political party in power in terms of whether it supported NGOs publicly advocating on government policy. Another related to the discipline or unity of a government, where disunity meant vulnerability to outside pressure because of increased possibilities for civil society lobbying of political elites. A government's unity can be influenced by the election of minority governments, which have to rely for power on agreements with minor parties. A government's vulnerability to pressure from activists can also be affected by other issues playing out in the domestic polity at the same time that resonate with the concern in question. For example, the issue of the 2003 Iraq war played out differently in the three cases, and was deeply unpopular in some states but not in others, with implications for activism on detainee torture. Another type of political opportunity involved the electoral cycle. Elections can make politicians pay attention to what the public wants and reflect public demands in their policies and performance.[118] Elections can thus sometimes offer critical points of pressure, providing important opportunities to influence the executive in the course of ongoing, cumulative, human rights campaigns.

I suggest that a more open polity, in the form of one offering more points of vulnerability of the government, can present greater incentives for mobilisation.

Conclusion

Understanding why liberal democracies responded differently to allegations that their citizens were tortured in the war on terror is a complex puzzle. However, I have argued that it can be conceived of as a problem of why states sometimes comply, and sometimes do not, with international human rights commitments. States, including liberal democracies for whom respecting international human rights forms a key part of their national and global identities, are more likely to comply with norms and treaties when they face pressure from domestic actors to do so. Whether such individuals and groups apply pressure, and whether that pressure is effective, depends on the existence of favourable conditions for human rights activism, equipping them with sufficient will and ability to challenge the state in contests over rights. These conditions vary across liberal democracies according to the domestic political and legal context, particular features of which

[118] Mark N Franklin, Stuart Soroka and Christopher Wlezien, 'Elections' in *The Oxford Handbook of Public Accountability*, ed Bovens et al, 399.

enable or constrain mobilisation on rights. These enabling and constraining factors can influence civil society's ability to mobilise in a practical sense and shape its members' interests in an ideational sense. I contend that a strong human rights culture, and having the right institutional tools and political opportunities, can make it easier for civil society to mobilise on human rights.

The existence of such conditions does not mean that civil society will necessarily engage in activism on a particular international human rights issue. I have noted a number of other factors that also had a bearing on how governments in Australia, the UK and Canada responded to the issue of the treatment of citizens detained in the war on terror, including alliance politics, national security imperatives, and the number of affected citizens and residents. Activism can also be influenced by the self-interest of activists. My argument is that, amongst all these different pressures, civil society activism can have an important bearing on state responses to contentious international human rights issues, and that the existence of certain conditions—a high level of rights awareness across different parts of the polity, and robust levers and political incentives—can make activism easier.

I apply this framework of the enabling and constraining factors affecting human rights activism to a detailed examination of Australia, the UK and Canada. The framework helps realise a central objective of this study: to map the conditions under which civil society is more or less likely to become engaged when fellow citizens are tortured, and thus to provide a deeper understanding of liberal democracies' responses to the torture issue.

4

America's Use of Torture After 9/11

Introduction

The terrorist attacks against the United States (US) on 11 September 2001 triggered a profound shift in human rights discourse and policy. For decades, the US had been a world leader, if a sometimes inconsistent one, on human rights.[1] Yet the US-led counter-terrorism response to the tragic events of that day embody what Martin Scheinin, the first United Nations Special Rapporteur on human rights and counter-terrorism, described as the 'worst-ever backlash' against the promotion and protection of human rights since their emergence after World War II.[2] According to the Bush Administration, the 9/11 attacks 'changed everything'.[3] America, it claimed, faced an unparalleled threat, which necessitated a new approach to fighting terrorism. This 'new paradigm', as President George W Bush described it, was one in which respect for human rights was effectively treated as a luxury that could no longer be indulged.[4]

In this chapter, I chronicle the US deviation from basic human rights values, prompted by the terrorist attacks, and provide the background for the analysis of the three case studies that follow. I explain how torture became an important policy tool in the Bush Administration's counter-terrorism armoury. I chart the events that pressured the Bush Administration to change its policies on detainee treatment, as well as the impact Barack Obama's presidency had in bringing an end to the use of torture by the US. I then outline the different roles of Congress, the judiciary and civil society in supporting or resisting the development of the torture policies. I argue that the shift in US policy on torture after 9/11 had

[1] Martha Finnemore, 'Legitimacy, hypocrisy, and the social structure of unipolarity: Why being a unipole isn't all it's cracked up to be', *World Politics* 61(1) (2009), 84.

[2] Martin Scheinin, 'Resisting panic: Lessons about the role of human rights during the long decade after 9/11' in *The Cambridge Companion to Human Rights Law*, ed Conor Gearty and Costa Douzinas (New York, NY: Cambridge University Press, 2012) 293.

[3] *Meet the Press, NBC News*, 14 September 2003 (Dick Cheney), transcript.

[4] George W Bush, to the Vice President et al, 7 February 2002, memorandum, in *The Torture Papers: The Road to Abu Ghraib*, ed Karen J Greenberg and Joshua L Dratel (New York, NY: Cambridge University Press, 2005), 134–36.

implications for America's close allies, Australia, Canada and the UK. This was for reasons of alliance politics, and because of America's influence on shared principles and ideas.

The Executive

In this section I consider the US executive government's position on the prohibition against torture in three phases: before and after 9/11; and following the backlash against its detainee treatment policies, which intensified after the revelations of prisoner abuse at Abu Ghraib Prison in Iraq.

Before 11 September 2001

Prior to the attacks on 11 September 2001, US public support for the prohibition against torture appeared unequivocal.[5] Certainly the US Constitution, domestic laws and jurisprudence supported this stance, as did America's commitment to relevant international treaties and its public diplomacy. The US public position on torture in this period is best summed up by a 1999 State Department statement to the United Nations Committee Against Torture, emphatically rejecting the use of state torture:

> Torture is prohibited by law throughout the United States. It is categorically denounced as a matter of policy and as a tool of state authority. Every act constituting torture under the Convention [Against Torture and Other Cruel, Inhuman or Degrading Treatment or Punishment] constitutes a criminal offence under the law of the United States. No official of the Government, federal, state or local, civilian or military, is authorized to commit or to instruct anyone else to commit torture. Nor may any official condone or tolerate torture in any form. No exceptional circumstances may be invoked as a justification of torture.[6]

The US Constitution does not prohibit torture as such, but rather, under the Eighth Amendment, bans 'cruel and unusual punishments'. Finding an absolute constitutional ban on torture is difficult.[7] Because of this, US courts have looked to a number of different Amendments, including the Fourth (on unreasonable

[5] Harold Hongju Koh, 'Friedmann Award Essay: A world without torture', *Columbia Journal of Transnational Law* 43(3) (2004), 642.

[6] United States of America, *Consideration of Reports Submitted by States Parties Under Article 19 of the Convention, Initial Reports of States Parties due in 1995, Addendum*, Report to Committee Against Torture, CAT/C/28/Add.5, UN Doc 9 February 2000, [6].

[7] John T Parry, 'The shape of modern torture: Extraordinary rendition and ghost detainees', *Melbourne Journal of International Law* 6(2) (2005), 528.

searches and seizures), Fifth (on self-incrimination) and Fourteenth (on due process).[8] Read together, these provisions have been interpreted as providing a nationwide standard of treatment forbidding torture, beneath which no government entity may fall.[9]

In addition, the US has ratified a number of treaties that expressly prohibit the use of torture. Following World War II, it was instrumental in the conference that gave rise to the 1949 Geneva Convention Relative to the Treatment of Prisoners of War (Third Geneva Convention), which prohibits the torture of prisoners of war.[10] It ratified the four 1949 Geneva Conventions in 1955, and applied them to detainees captured in the Korean and Vietnam Wars, even when its own soldiers were mistreated.[11] The US is a party to two further treaties banning torture (and cruel, inhuman or degrading treatment or punishment): the 1966 International Covenant on Civil and Political Rights (ICCPR) and CAT.[12]

Torture is also illegal under a number of domestic US laws, including the Federal Torture Statute, which prohibits torture undertaken outside of the US. The War Crimes Act makes it an offence for a US national or member of the US armed forces to commit a war crime, defined as a 'grave breach' of the Geneva Conventions, including torture, punishable by (up to) the death penalty. In addition, the US has enacted a number of other statutes to implement its treaty obligations, including the Torture Victim Protection Act of 1991, the Foreign Affairs Reform and Restructuring Act of 1998 and the Alien Tort Statute (ATS). The last of these gives US courts jurisdiction over any civil action by an alien for a tort committed in violation of the law of nations or treaty of the US.[13]

Despite these legal prohibitions, there exists a history of the US sanctioning torture in particular situations, notably during the Cold War. The participation of the Central Intelligence Agency (CIA) in clandestine programs involving torture

[8] Philip Alston and Ryan Goodman, *International Human Rights: The Successor to International Human Rights in Context* (Oxford: Oxford University Press, 2013) 264–65.

[9] United States of America, *Consideration of Reports Submitted by States Parties Under Article 19 of the Convention, Initial Reports of States Parties due in 1995, Addendum*, [49]; see also Jamie Mayerfeld, 'Playing by our own rules: How US marginalization of international human rights law led to torture', *Harvard Human Rights Journal* 20 (2007), 123.

[10] Joseph Margulies, *Guantánamo and the Abuse of Presidential Power* (New York, NY: Simon & Schuster Paperbacks, 2006) 76.

[11] ibid, 77–78.

[12] The US ratified the ICCPR and CAT with the declaration that they were not self-executing and with the reservation that they went no further than pre-existing constitutional rights; see John T Parry, *Understanding Torture: Law, Violence, and Political Identity* (Ann Arbor, MI: The University of Michigan Press, 2010) 60.

[13] The ATS was successfully invoked in the case of *Filártiga v Peña-Irala*, 630 F 2d 876 (2d Cir 1980), brought by two Paraguayan citizens who sued a Paraguayan official (all three were resident in the US) over the torture and killing of their family member in Paraguay. However, the 2013 US Supreme Court decision in *Kiobel v Royal Dutch Petroleum Co*, 133 S Ct 1659 (2013), substantially curtailed future applications of the ATS, with the Court ruling that it generally does not apply beyond America's borders, but rather only when the facts of the case 'touch and concern the territory of the United States … with sufficient force' (at 1669) (majority opinion).

in the second half of the twentieth century has been well documented.[14] The CIA codified research conducted in the 1950s into psychological torture in the secret 'KUBARK Counter-intelligence Interrogation' manual in 1963, and spent the next 30 years propagating these techniques among anti-communist allies across Asia and Latin America.[15] This included during the Vietnam War, under the 'Phoenix program', as well as in Latin America via its Spanish-language counter-insurgency manuals from the late 1960s through to the early 1990s. Until 11 September 2001, there was, however, no public endorsement of torture by US governments.[16]

After 11 September 2001

A shift in US policy with respect to torture occurred after 11 September 2001, with the US President explicitly claiming the authority to ignore domestic and international prohibitions against its use.[17] After 9/11, senior members of the executive government admitted, without remorse, that they had approved the waterboarding of detainees.[18] Courts in the US had previously found that waterboarding—a procedure in which subjects are made to feel like they are being drowned—constituted torture.[19]

The 9/11 attacks were devastating, shocking in their scale, method and location. Nearly 3,000 people were killed when terrorists hijacked four commercial jet airliners, crashing two into the World Trade Center in New York, one into the Pentagon and another into a field in Pennsylvania.[20] The attacks sent the Bush Administration into panic, with officials fearing further assaults.[21] President Bush described the attacks, soon attributed to Al-Qaeda, a global Islamist terrorist group headed by Osama bin Laden, as 'acts of war'.[22]

The legal basis for the US war on terror that ensued was founded on a 'use of force' joint resolution, approved by Congress and signed into law on 18 September

[14] Alfred McCoy, *A Question of Torture: CIA Interrogation, from the Cold War to the War on Terror* (New York, NY: Holt Paperbacks, 2006) 60; Parry, *Understanding Torture*, 141–51.

[15] Alfred McCoy, 'Mind maze: The CIA's pursuit of psychological torture' in *The United States and Torture: Interrogations, Incarceration, and Abuse*, ed Marjorie Cohn (New York, NY: New York University Press, 2011) 26, 30, 33.

[16] Jeremy Waldron, *Torture Terror and Trade-offs: Philosophy for the White House* (Oxford: Oxford University Press, 2010) 187; Margulies, *Guantánamo and the Abuse of Presidential Power*, 82; McCoy, *A Question of Torture*, 211.

[17] Jonathan Hafetz, *Habeas Corpus After 9/11: Confronting America's New Global Detention System* (New York, NY: New York University Press, 2011) 25.

[18] Donald Rumsfeld, *Known and Unknown: A Memoir* (New York, NY: Sentinel, 2011) 583–84.

[19] The Constitution Project, *The Report of the Constitution Project's Task Force on Detainee Treatment* (2013) 355, http://detaineetaskforce.org/pdf/Full-Report.pdf.

[20] Hafetz, *Habeas Corpus After 9/11*, 11.

[21] Jane Mayer, *The Dark Side: The Inside Story of How the War on Terror Turned into a War on American Ideals* (New York, NY: Doubleday, 2008) 4.

[22] George W Bush, 'Remarks by the President in photo opportunity with the National Security Team', White House, Washington, DC, 12 September 2001; 'Address to a Joint Session of Congress and the American people,' Washington, DC, 20 September 2001.

2001.[23] The Bush Administration's framing of the 9/11 attacks, legally and discursively, as acts of war rather than criminal acts, was a deliberate political strategy designed to allow the President more expansive powers.[24] This was reflected in a legal memorandum of the Department of Justice's Office of Legal Counsel (OLC), which claimed that presidential power during wartime was 'at its zenith'.[25]

A second feature of the Bush Administration's discourse responding to 9/11 was the characterisation of the conflict as unprecedented. According to President Bush, this was 'a different kind of war that requires a different type of approach and a different type of mentality'.[26] The framing of the Al-Qaeda threat as novel was used to legitimise the Administration's position that the war on terror necessitated its own unique rules and the long-established laws of war no longer applied.[27] The Attorney General, John Ashcroft, articulated this argument, 'Every day that passes with out-dated statutes and the old rules of engagement is a day that terrorists have a competitive advantage'.[28] Vice President Cheney hinted very early at the lawlessness to come:

> We also have to work, though, sort of the dark side, if you will … A lot of what needs to be done here will have to be done quietly, without any discussion, using sources and methods that are available to our intelligence agencies.[29]

On 7 October 2001, America launched airstrikes against Afghanistan, where the Taliban regime was accused of harbouring Al-Qaeda.[30] Australia, the UK and Canada all committed military forces to the ensuing conflict. An immediate consequence was the detention of large numbers of people suspected of being members either of the Taliban or of Al-Qaeda.[31] Many were held in Afghanistan, while others were taken there after being arrested in other countries.[32] The vast majority of

[23] Senate Joint Resolution Providing for the Authorization for Use of Military Force, SJ RES 23, 107th Congress (2001).

[24] John E Owens, 'Congressional acquiescence to presidentialism in the US "war on terror"' in *The 'War on Terror' and the Growth of Executive Power*, ed John E Owens and Riccardo Pelizzo (New York, NY: Routledge, 2010) 43.

[25] John Yoo, Deputy Assistant Attorney General, to Timothy Flanagan, Deputy Counsel to the President, 25 September 2001, memorandum, in *The Torture Papers: The Road to Abu Ghraib*, ed Greenberg and Dratel, 3–24.

[26] George W Bush, 'President holds prime time news conference', White House, Washington, DC, 11 October 2001.

[27] Richard Jackson, 'Language, policy and the construction of a torture culture in the war on terrorism', *Review of International Studies* 33(3) (2007), 356.

[28] Evidence to House Committee, US Congress, 24 September 2001 (John Ashcroft, Attorney General).

[29] Dick Cheney, 'The Vice President appears on Meet the Press with Tim Russert', *NBC News*, 16 September 2001.

[30] George W Bush, 'Presidential address to the nation', White House, Washington, DC, 7 October 2001.

[31] Philippe Sands, *Lawless World* (New York, NY: Penguin Books, 2005) 155.

[32] Alston and Goodman, *International Human Rights*, 415.

detainees were handed over to US military forces by either Pakistan or the Afghan Northern Alliance, the group fighting the Taliban inside Afghanistan.[33]

The Bush Administration grappled with what to do with the detainees.[34] In November 2001, President Bush issued a military order announcing that detainees would be tried by military commissions outside the usual US military courts-martial system.[35] This decision caused considerable consternation within the US Government, especially among military lawyers, whose concerns were rebuffed by Bush Administration officials.[36] The proposed military commissions lacked the presumption of innocence and the right of appeal to a civilian court, permitted evidence obtained through coercion, and claimed the authority to try offences never before recognised as war crimes.[37] A number of senior military lawyers tried to amend parts of the military commission plan when they first learned of it, but were 'marginalized'.[38]

In late December 2001, Defense Secretary Rumsfeld announced that the detainees would be held at the US Naval Base at Guantánamo Bay, Cuba.[39] This location was selected because, the Bush Administration argued, foreign nationals held there would not have access to US courts.[40] According to an OLC memorandum, detainees at Guantánamo Bay could not bring habeas corpus claims, nor challenge the constitutionality of their detention, the use of military commissions or their denial of rights under international treaties.[41] The first detainees began arriving at Guantánamo Bay on 11 January 2002; in time, some 775 prisoners were held there.[42] Among those detained at Guantánamo Bay were two Australian citizens, one Canadian citizen, nine UK citizens and a number of UK residents.

With the arrival of prisoners at Guantánamo Bay, Rumsfeld announced that the detainees would be regarded as 'unlawful combatants' and denied any rights under the Geneva Conventions.[43] This decision had far-reaching repercussions for how detainees came to be treated, and has been described as the 'Original Sin' that made the adoption of torture at Guantánamo Bay and in secret CIA prisons possible.[44]

[33] Margulies, *Guantánamo and the Abuse of Presidential Power*, 69; the US promised large rewards for the capture of 'al-Qaida and Taliban murderers'.

[34] Rumsfeld, *Known and Unknown: A Memoir*, 565–66.

[35] Executive Order No 57,831, 66 Fed Reg No 2, 16 November 2001.

[36] Hafetz, *Habeas Corpus After 9/11*, 17.

[37] ibid, 17–18.

[38] Mayer, *The Dark Side*, 88.

[39] Donald Rumsfeld, 'DoD news briefing—Secretary Rumsfeld and Gen. Myers', US Department of Defense, 27 December 2001.

[40] Hafetz, *Habeas Corpus After 9/11*, 29.

[41] Patrick Philbin, Deputy Assistant Attorney General, and John Yoo, Deputy Assistant Attorney General, to William J Haynes, General Counsel, Department of Defense, 28 December 2001, memorandum, in *The Torture Papers: The Road to Abu Ghraib*, ed Greenberg and Dratel, 29-37.

[42] Hafetz, *Habeas Corpus After 9/11*, 31.

[43] Donald Rumsfeld, 'DoD news briefing—Secretary Rumsfeld and Gen. Myers', news briefing, US Department of Defense, 11 January 2002.

[44] Mark Danner, *Torture and Truth: America, Abu Ghraib, and the War on Terror* (New York, NY: New York Review Books, 2004) 42.

The Geneva Conventions form part of international humanitarian law, and set out the rules governing the detention, interrogation and release of prisoners by states. While they acknowledge that not all detainees qualify as prisoners of war, Common Article 3 establishes a baseline of treatment for all captives. It states in part:

> In the case of armed conflict not of an international character occurring in the territory of one of the High Contracting Parties, each Party to the conflict shall be bound to apply, as a minimum, the following provisions:
>
> (1) Persons taking no active part in the hostilities, including members of armed forces who have laid down their arms and those placed 'hors de combat' by sickness, wounds, detention, or any other cause, shall in all circumstances be treated humanely …
>
> To this end, the following acts are and shall remain prohibited at any time and in any place whatsoever with respect to the above-mentioned persons:
>
> (a) violence to life and person, in particular murder of all kinds, mutilation, cruel treatment and torture …

The Bush Administration's arguments justifying the decision not to apply the Geneva Conventions to detainees are set out in legal memoranda from early 2002. White House Counsel, Alberto Gonzales, encapsulated the Administration's thinking, writing that the 'war against terrorism' was a 'new kind of war', which placed a 'high premium … on the ability to quickly obtain information from captured terrorists'.[45] This 'new paradigm renders obsolete Geneva's strict limitations on questioning of enemy prisoners and renders quaint some of its provisions', he wrote. This view was based on the reasoning that the Geneva Conventions did not apply to members of Al-Qaeda because a non-state actor could not be a party to international agreements governing war; they did not apply to the Taliban because Afghanistan was a failed state; Common Article 3 did not apply at all because the conflict was international in scope; and, in response to arguments that the Geneva Conventions had the status of customary law, customary law was non-binding on the President.[46]

Not all members of the Bush Administration agreed with the decision relating to the Geneva Conventions.[47] The Secretary of State, Colin Powell, argued that not applying the Geneva Conventions to the conflict in Afghanistan would 'reverse over a century of US policy and practice … and undermine the protections of the law of war' for US troops.[48] Ultimately, President Bush ignored the warnings of Powell and others. The President determined that the Geneva Conventions would

[45] Alberto Gonzales, to the President, 25 January 2002, memorandum, in *The Torture Papers: The Road to Abu Ghraib*, ed Greenberg and Dratel, 118-121.

[46] John Yoo, Deputy Assistant Attorney General, and Robert Delabunty, Special Counsel, to William Haynes II, General Counsel, Department of Defense, 9 January 2002, memorandum, in *The Torture Papers: The Road to Abu Ghraib*, ed Greenberg and Dratel, 38-79.

[47] Danner, *Torture and Truth*, 75.

[48] Colin Powell to Counsel to the President [and] Assistant to the President for National Security Affairs, 26 January 2002, memorandum, in *The Torture Papers: The Road to Abu Ghraib* (ed Greenberg and Dratel) 122-25.

not apply to Al-Qaeda; that although the US would apply the Conventions to the conflict with the Taliban, Taliban detainees were not prisoners of war but 'unlawful combatants'; and lastly, that Common Article 3 applied to neither group. As a matter of policy, President Bush stated, detainees would be treated 'humanely, and, to the extent appropriate and consistent with military necessity, in a manner consistent with the principles of Geneva'.[49]

As the war on terror continued, the Bush Administration grew increasingly frustrated by the scarcity of intelligence it was obtaining on Al-Qaeda.[50] In early to mid-2002, officials began building further practical and legal foundations for the use of more aggressive interrogation techniques.[51] This effort was also driven by the capture of some 'high value' detainees, who were believed to be withholding crucial information.[52] Military and CIA officials consulted psychologists and instructors versed in the US military's Survival, Evasion, Resistance, Escape (SERE) program, in which soldiers were trained to resist torture if captured, in order to source ideas about extreme interrogation methods.[53] Meanwhile, OLC lawyers drafted memoranda about the specific legal limitations on interrogations imposed by domestic and international law with regard to torture. The critical memoranda were issued in the period 2002 to 2005. They related to interrogations to be carried out by the military at Guantánamo Bay and the CIA at its secret prisons.[54]

Three OLC memoranda issued in August 2002 were the most significant in relation to giving a green light to torture. One argued that US interrogation techniques not defined as torture under domestic law would not violate America's obligations under the CAT because of an 'understanding' entered by the US on ratifying the Convention (an argument since disputed by international law scholars).[55] A second addressed the permissible standards of conduct under the federal statute criminalising torture, which implemented US obligations under the CAT.[56] This memorandum concluded that the statute prohibited only 'extreme acts', and that for conduct to constitute physical torture, it must 'be equivalent in intensity to the pain accompanying serious physical injury, such as organ failure, impairment of bodily function, or even death', while mental torture 'must result in significant psychological harm of significant duration'. This definition was taken

[49] Bush to the Vice President et al, memorandum, 7 February 2002.

[50] David Cole, *The Torture Memos: Rationalizing the Unthinkable* (New York, NY: The New Press, 2009) 13.

[51] Constitution Project, *The Report of the Constitution Project's Task Force on Detainee Treatment*, 138.

[52] Cole, *The Torture Memos*, 14.

[53] ibid, 13.

[54] Philippe Sands, *Torture Team: Rumsfeld's Memo and the Betrayal of American Values* (New York, NY: Palgrave Macmillan, 2008) 74.

[55] John Yoo, Deputy Assistant Attorney General, to The Honourable Alberto R Gonzales, Counsel to the President, 1 August 2002, memorandum, in *The Torture Papers: The Road to Abu Ghraib*, ed Greenberg and Dratel, 218-222.

[56] Jay S Bybee, Assistant Attorney General, to Alberto R Gonzalez, Counsel to the President, 1 August 2002, memorandum, in *The Torture Papers: The Road to Abu Ghraib*, ed Greenberg and Dratel, 172–217.

from a Medicare statute that had nothing to do with torture, a much-ridiculed legal manoeuvre described by legal scholars as bizarre.[57] This memorandum also maintained that even if an interrogator's conduct amounted to torture, no criminal penalties would apply if the interrogator acted at the behest of the President, whose Commander-in-Chief powers could not be constrained by Congress. This position was a constitutional distortion that ignored the leading Supreme Court case on executive power (*Youngstown Sheet & Tube Co v Sawyer*).[58] The memorandum also opined that in the current circumstances, necessity or self-defence might justify interrogation methods that violated the criminal prohibition on torture—positions again unsupported by legal authority.[59] The third memorandum explicitly concerned 10 interrogation techniques the CIA wished to use.[60] The methods included waterboarding, repeatedly slamming detainees into walls, extreme sleep deprivation, facial holding and slapping, grasping, confining detainees in boxes for long periods, locking detainees in boxes with insects, wall standing and stress positions. The memorandum determined, disingenuously, that even when all of the methods were used in combination, they would not inflict severe physical pain or suffering or prolonged mental harm, and would thus not violate the Federal Torture Statute.

Together, the underlying purpose of the various memoranda was to ensure legal cover from criminal prosecution for interrogators and to provide a 'golden shield' for state-sanctioned torture.[61] The memoranda made inaccurate assertions about the state of the law on torture that have been widely considered by legal scholars to be arguments about what the authors, or recipients, wanted the law to be, rather than assessments of what the law actually was.[62]

By mid-2002, the Bush Administration knew many detainees at Guantánamo Bay had no connection to Al-Qaeda.[63] Rumsfeld, however, was frustrated at the lack of intelligence coming from detainees, and pressure was building on interrogators.[64] In October 2002, the director of intelligence at Guantánamo Bay, Lieutenant Colonel Jerald Phifer, sought approval for three categories of new 'counter-resistance strategies'.[65] They ranged from yelling and deception

[57] Sands, *Torture Team*, 179; David Luban, 'Liberalism, torture, and the ticking bomb' in *The Torture Debate in America*, ed Karen J Greenberg (New York, NY: Cambridge University Press, 2006) 56.

[58] Luban, 'Liberalism, torture, and the ticking bomb', 67; Kathleen Clark, 'Ethical issues raised by the OLC torture memorandum', *Journal of National Security Law & Policy* 1(1) (2005), 461; *Youngstown Sheet & Tube Co v Sawyer* 343 US 579 (1952).

[59] Luban, 'Liberalism, torture, and the ticking bomb', 64, 66

[60] Jay S Bybee, Assistant Attorney General, to John Rizzo, Acting General Counsel of the Central Intelligence Agency, 1 August 2002, memorandum, in Cole, *The Torture Memos*, 106–27.

[61] Hafetz, *Habeas Corpus After 9/11*, 23; see also Cole, *The Torture Memos*, 20.

[62] Clark, 'Ethical issues raised by the OLC torture memorandum', 458.

[63] Scott Horton, 'Did Bush know Guantánamo prisoners were innocent?', *Harper's Magazine* (New York), 9 April 2010.

[64] Hafetz, *Habeas Corpus After 9/11*, 38.

[65] Jerald Phifer, LTC, to Commander, Joint Task Force 170, 11 October 2002, memorandum, in Danner, *Torture and Truth*, 167–68.

(Category I); to the use of stress positions, isolation, sensory deprivation, loud noise, hooding, 20-hour interrogations, forced nudity, forced grooming and dogs (Category II); to convincing the detainee his family was dead or would be harmed, exposure to cold weather or water, waterboarding and 'non-injurious' contact such as grabbing, poking and pushing (Category III). Until then, the US Army had to comply with the Intelligence Interrogation Field Manual 34-52 when conducting interrogations, which complied with the Geneva Conventions and stipulated that the 'use of force, mental torture, threats, insults, or exposure to unpleasant and inhumane treatment of any kind' was prohibited by law and was not authorised or condoned by the US Government.[66] It fell to a relatively junior military lawyer with no background in international law, Lieutenant Colonel Diane Beaver, to provide the legal advice supporting Phifer's request.[67] Her memo opined that the proposed strategies did not violate federal law, as long as they were necessary to 'achieve a legitimate government objective' and were not used 'maliciously or sadistically for the very purpose of causing harm'.[68] Beaver's reasoning was based on the false premise that 'no international body of law directly applies'.[69] This was because the President had already determined that the Geneva Conventions did not apply to detainees. In December 2002, Rumsfeld approved Category I and II techniques and the 'use of mild, non-injurious physical contact' from Category III.[70] Rumsfeld added a note on giving his approval, 'however, I stand for 8–10 hours a day. Why is standing limited to 4 hours?'

The interrogations taking place at Guantánamo Bay caused considerable disquiet across parts of the Government, especially the military and the Federal Bureau of Investigation (FBI).[71] The FBI withdrew its agents from military interrogations and launched an internal investigation. One FBI officer reported witnessing a detainee 'almost unconscious on the floor', in an unventilated room, with 'a pile of hair next to him. He had apparently been literally pulling his own hair out throughout the night'.[72] Navy General Counsel Alberto Mora was so disturbed by the new interrogation techniques, which he believed could produce 'effects reaching the level of torture', that he took his concerns to Rumsfeld's staff on multiple occasions, eventually putting them in a memorandum to the Defense Secretary's General Counsel, William Haynes, in early January 2003.[73]

[66] Philippe Sands, 'Terrorists and torturers' in *The United States and Torture*, ed Cohn, 266–67; United States Army, *Intelligence Interrogation Field Manual 34-52*, 28 September 1992.

[67] Sands, *Torture Team*, 64–65.

[68] Diane Beaver, 'Legal brief on proposed counter-resistance strategies', 11 October 2002, in Danner, *Torture and Truth*, 170–77.

[69] Sands, *Torture Team*, 66–67.

[70] William J Haynes, General Counsel, to Secretary of Defense, 27 November 2002, memorandum, in Danner, *Torture and Truth*, 181–82.

[71] Sands, *Torture Team*, 45, 112–30.

[72] Hafetz, *Habeas Corpus After 9/11*, 42; Mark Denbeaux and Jonathan Hafetz, *The Guantánamo Lawyers: Inside a Prison Outside the Law* (New York, NY: New York University Press, 2009) 248–49.

[73] Sands, *Torture Team*, 135–40.

In response to these concerns, Rumsfeld rescinded his December 2002 order approving the three categories of interrogation techniques and established a working group to examine detainee interrogations.[74] However, relying on an OLC memorandum that argued the President had complete discretion as Commander-in-Chief over interrogations, the working group approved 35 interrogation techniques, including isolation, forced grooming, sleep deprivation, and facial and stomach slapping, many of which were later approved by Rumsfeld.[75]

In October 2003, in a sign of growing international concern over the Bush Administration's detainee policies, the International Committee of the Red Cross (ICRC), which had been visiting Guantánamo Bay since January 2002, broke with its traditional public silence. It described as intolerable the fact that Guantánamo Bay was being used as 'an investigation center, not a detention center'.[76] Privately the ICRC raised concerns with the US as to whether 'psychological torture' was being carried out there.[77]

In parallel with the development of the harsh interrogation system at Guantánamo Bay, the CIA was establishing its own detention regime, setting up a global network of secret prisons, and acquiring executive authority to engage in practices the US has admitted constituted torture.[78] The CIA's pivotal role in the war on terror, and the foundation for its subsequent detainee program, was settled on 17 September 2001, when President Bush signed a (still-classified) presidential finding, authorising it to kill or capture (and interrogate) suspected terrorists anywhere in the world.[79] The CIA's detention and interrogation regime had two notable features: the use of 'black sites' and the practice of 'extraordinary rendition'.[80] Black sites were covert prisons set up by the CIA in various locations around the world, including Afghanistan, Thailand, Poland, Romania and Lithuania.[81] The ICRC was denied access to these sites and their prisoners, known as 'ghost detainees', and the Government did not admit to their existence until

[74] Donald Rumsfeld, to Commander USSOUTHCOM, 15 January 2003, memorandum, in *The Torture Papers: The Road to Abu Ghraib*, ed Greenberg and Dratel, 239.

[75] Working Group, 'Working Group Report on detainee interrogations in the global war on terrorism: Assessment of legal, historical, policy, and operational considerations', 4 April 2003, in *The Torture Papers: The Road to Abu Ghraib*, ed Greenberg and Dratel, 286-359; Donald Rumsfeld, to Commander, US Southern Command, 16 April 2003, memorandum, in *The Torture Papers: The Road to Abu Ghraib*, ed Greenberg and Dratel, 360-365.

[76] Neil A Lewis, 'Red Cross criticizes indefinite detention in Guantánamo Bay', *New York Times*, 10 October 2003, 1.

[77] Neil A Lewis, 'Red Cross finds detainee abuse in Guantánamo', *New York Times*, 30 November 2004, 1.

[78] Charlie Savage, 'US tells UN panel of steps to revise interrogation policy', *New York Times*, 12 November 2014, 17.

[79] Hafetz, *Habeas Corpus After 9/11*, 53.

[80] Constitution Project, *The Report of the Constitution Project's Task Force on Detainee Treatment*, 163–201.

[81] ibid, 177.

2006.[82] Extraordinary rendition involved the illegal transfers of prisoners to third countries known to torture for interrogation.[83] These countries included Jordan, Egypt, Syria, Morocco, Libya, Iraq and Uzbekistan, though many other countries collaborated in the process (including the UK, which allowed its territory Diego Garcia to be used for rendition flights).[84] The practice directly contravened obligations set out in the CAT, which under Article 3 prohibits states sending individuals to places where they could be tortured.

While my primary concern is with the responses of US allies to the torture of their citizens detained in the war on terror, how the Bush Administration treated US citizens bears mentioning. The differential treatment of American detainees became a point of pressure for advocates of detainees in other countries to use against their governments. British lawyers, for example, argued that UK detainees should be tried in the US domestic courts, as was occurring in the case of US nationals.[85] American citizen, John Walker Lindh, for instance, was captured in Afghanistan and returned to the US, where he entered a plea deal in the federal court in 2002 and was sentenced to a 20-year prison term.[86]

Two further cases involving the detention of US citizens, Yaser Hamdi and Jose Padilla, made their way to the US Supreme Court. Hamdi was captured in Afghanistan and initially transported to Guantánamo Bay in January 2002, but three months later he was transferred to a naval prison in Virginia when his captors realised he was an American citizen.[87] A case challenging Hamdi's detention as an 'enemy combatant', who could be held without access to the US court system, was eventually heard by the US Supreme Court, which ruled against the Government in 2004. Justice Sandra Day O'Connor noted that 'A state of war is not a blank check for the President.'[88] Hamdi was released from detention and returned to his home in Saudi Arabia.[89] Padilla was arrested entering the US at Chicago's O'Hare International Airport in 2002.[90] The Bush Administration declared Padilla

[82] International Committee of the Red Cross, 'ICRC report on the treatment of fourteen "high value detainees" in CIA custody', Report WAS 07/76, 14 February 2007, 3; Hafetz, *Habeas Corpus After 9/11*, 58.

[83] Constitution Project, *The Report of the Constitution Project's Task Force on Detainee Treatment*, 167–68. The use of renditions by the US first began in the 1980s, when terrorist suspects were captured overseas and brought back to America to face prosecution (ibid, 165, 166). After 11 September 2001, the program changed and expanded, its purpose shifting from delivering suspects to trial to imprisoning them solely to extract intelligence. See Hafetz, *Habeas Corpus After 9/11*, 53.

[84] Open Society Justice Initiative, *Globalizing torture: CIA secret detention and extraordinary rendition*, Open Society Foundations, February 2013, 6, www.opensocietyfoundations.org/reports/globalizing-torture-cia-secret-detention-and-extraordinary-rendition.

[85] Julian Borger, 'Camp X-ray Britons begin court challenge', *Guardian*, 20 February 2002, 14.

[86] Neil Lewis, 'American who joined Taliban pleads guilty', *New York Times*, 15 July 2002, 1.

[87] Margulies, *Guantánamo and the Abuse of Presidential Power*, 101.

[88] *Hamdi v Rumsfeld*, 542 US 507, 536 (2004).

[89] Margulies, *Guantánamo and the Abuse of Presidential Power*, 156.

[90] Hafetz, *Habeas Corpus After 9/11*, 47.

an enemy combatant on the basis that he was 'closely associated with al Qaeda', and he was transferred to a naval prison in South Carolina. Padilla's lawyers challenged his detention. The Supreme Court avoided making a decision about whether Padilla's detention was legal, instead finding in 2004 that his case had been filed in the wrong court.[91] His lawyers filed a new habeas corpus application in a different court, and the case again made its way through the appeals courts.[92] Two days before the Bush Administration was due to respond to Padilla's request for the US Supreme Court to review his case a second time, the government announced it was indicting him on terrorism-related charges in the federal court, and he was transferred to civilian custody.[93] Padilla was convicted in 2007 and sentenced to a lengthy prison term.

Abu Ghraib

The development of harsh interrogation techniques for use by the CIA and interrogators at Guantánamo Bay affected prisoners of war captured in Iraq, which was invaded by the US and its allies (including Australia and the UK, though not Canada) in March 2003.[94] Although the Geneva Conventions officially applied to detainees in that conflict, such was the confusion and culture created by policy decisions taken by the Bush Administration with respect to detention and interrogation in other theatres of the war on terror, that the abusive practices soon spread to Iraq.[95]

In April 2004, revelations were aired by the media about abuses of Iraqi prisoners of war at Abu Ghraib Prison, attracting worldwide condemnation and drawing fresh scrutiny of US detainee policies.[96] The CBS program *60 Minutes II* revealed that 17 soldiers in Iraq had been removed from duty after photographs surfaced showing US soldiers abusing and humiliating Iraqi detainees. The *New Yorker's* Seymour Hersh subsequently revealed details of a damning report by the Army investigator into the abuse.[97] Major General Antonio Tabuga had examined the actions of the military police running the US prisons in Iraq and found that 'numerous incidents of sadistic, blatant, and wanton abuses were inflicted on several detainees' between October and December 2003.[98] Tabuga also discovered

[91] *Rumsfeld v Padilla*, 542 US 426 (2004).

[92] Hafetz, *Habeas Corpus After 9/11*, 144.

[93] ibid, 145–46.

[94] Philip Zelikow, 'Codes of conduct for a twilight war', *Houston Law Review* 49(1) (2012), 3.

[95] Hafetz, *Habeas Corpus After 9/11*, 44; Senate Committee on Armed Services, US Congress, *Inquiry Into the Treatment of Detainees in US Custody: Report*, 2008, xxiii; Constitution Project, *The Report of the Constitution Project's Task Force on Detainee Treatment*, 104–05.

[96] 'Abuse of Iraqi POWs by GIs probes', *60 Minutes II*, CBS, 28 April 2004.

[97] Seymour Hersh, 'Torture at Abu Ghraib', *New Yorker*, 10 May 2004, 42–53; Seymour Hersh, 'Chain of command,' *New Yorker*, 17 May 2004, 38–52.

[98] 'The Tabuga Report' in Danner, *Torture and Truth*, 277–328.

that 'ghost detainees' had been brought into Abu Ghraib by the CIA, and were kept hidden from ICRC survey teams.[99]

The global reaction to the Abu Ghraib revelations was scathing. The international media called for Rumsfeld's resignation.[100] Human rights NGOs accused the Bush Administration of war crimes.[101] United Nations human rights experts demanded access to detainees held by the US in Iraq, Afghanistan and Guantánamo Bay.[102] The US military launched further investigations into the Abu Ghraib abuses. Among them, the report of Major General George Fay and Lieutenant General Anthony Jones found that the primary causes of abuse were misconduct by a 'small group of morally corrupt soldiers and civilians' and a failure of leadership.[103] Another report, by former Defense Secretary James Schlesinger, found that the 'augmented techniques' developed for interrogations at Guantánamo Bay 'migrated to Afghanistan and Iraq where they were neither limited nor safeguarded'.[104]

The Bush Administration's response to the furore surrounding the Abu Ghraib abuse revelations was inconsistent and misleading. Publicly, President Bush and his Defense Secretary dissociated themselves from the conduct, blaming it on a few renegade soldiers.[105] President Bush reaffirmed the US commitment to the prohibition on torture, declaring on the UN International Day in Support of Victims of Torture that 'America stands against and will not tolerate torture'.[106] Under pressure, the Bush Administration released a number of its interrogation memoranda, including two of the August 2002 OLC memoranda previously mentioned, some of which had already been leaked to the press.[107] In a June 2004 media briefing, White House Counsel Alberto Gonzales denied any link between the interrogation memoranda and the Abu Ghraib abuses.[108] Following Gonzales' press conference,

[99] ibid, 303.

[100] 'Resign, Rumsfeld', *Economist*, 6 May 2004.

[101] Amnesty International, 'USA: Pattern of brutality and cruelty—war crimes at Abu Ghraib', press release, 7 May 2004.

[102] Lynch, Colum, 'UN investigators appeal to US: Human rights workers seeking access to detention centers', *Washington Post*, 26 June 2004, 17.

[103] 'The Fay-Jones Report', August 2004, in *The Torture Papers: The Road to Abu Ghraib*, ed Greenberg and Dratel, 989.

[104] 'The Schlesinger Report', August 2004, in *The Torture Papers: The Road to Abu Ghraib*, ed Greenberg and Dratel, 915.

[105] George W Bush, 'President Bush welcomes Canadian Prime Minister Martin to White House', White House, Washington, DC, 30 April 2004; Donald Rumsfeld, 'Secretary of Defense Rumsfeld and General Myers Speech at Abu Ghraib Prison', speech delivered at Abu Ghraib Prison, Baghdad, 13 May 2004.

[106] George W Bush, 'President's statement on the UN International Day in support of victims of torture', 26 June 2004.

[107] Jack Goldsmith, *The Terror Presidency: Law and Judgment Inside the Bush Administration* (New York, NY: WW Norton & Company, 2009) 157.

[108] Alberto Gonzales, 'Press briefing by White House Counsel Judge Alberto Gonzales, DoD General Counsel William Haynes, DoD Deputy General Counsel Daniel Dell'Orto and Army Deputy Chief of Staff for Intelligence General Keith Alexander', White House, Washington, DC, 22 June 2004.

the Bush Administration rescinded the controversial August 2002 memorandum redefining torture and publicly issued a replacement.[109] This December 2004 memorandum repudiated torture, saying it was 'abhorrent to both American law and values and to international norms'.[110] However, the new memorandum declined to address the issue of the President's power to authorise torture, saying it was unnecessary to do so, since he had given an 'unequivocal directive' that the US did not torture.[111] Moreover, buried in a footnote in the memorandum was the remark that, having reviewed the OLC's prior opinions addressing the treatment of detainees, 'we … do not believe that any of their conclusions would be different under the standard set forth in this memorandum'.[112]

In addition, in May 2005 the US Justice Department prepared a series of new memoranda making it clear that the President's assurances on the US commitment to the prohibition against torture did not affect the CIA's detainee interrogation programs.[113] One memorandum determined that specific techniques intended for use by the CIA on Al-Qaeda detainees did not, on their own, constitute torture.[114] This was based on the fact that American soldiers subjected to SERE techniques had not exhibited signs of severe physical pain or suffering, or prolonged mental harm. A second memorandum concluded that when all of the techniques were applied to a single suspect in combination, they still did not rise to the level of torture.[115] A third memorandum concluded, implausibly, that none of the CIA techniques constituted cruel, inhuman or degrading treatment, and so did not breach US obligations under the CAT.[116] Some Bush Administration officials, including the Secretary of State Condoleezza Rice, and the President himself, were uneasy with aspects of the CIA detention policies.[117] Efforts by State Department lawyers to contest the OLC's opinions, particularly concerning the meaning of the cruel, inhuman and degrading treatment standard as it applied to CIA interrogations, were disregarded.[118] Together, the memoranda drafted in the wake of the Abu Ghraib scandal assured the CIA that efforts underway in Congress to unambiguously prohibit all cruel, inhuman and degrading treatment would not

[109] Goldsmith, *The Terror Presidency*, 159.

[110] Levin, Daniel, Acting Assistant Attorney General, to James B Comey, Deputy Attorney General, 30 December 2004, memorandum, in Cole, *The Torture Memos*, 128.

[111] ibid, 130.

[112] ibid, 130, fn 8.

[113] Cole, *The Torture Memos*, 11.

[114] Steven Bradbury, Principal Deputy Assistant Attorney General, to John Rizzo, Senior Deputy General Counsel, Central Intelligence Agency, 10 May 2005, memorandum, in Cole, *The Torture Memos*, 152.

[115] ibid, 199.

[116] Steven Bradbury, Principal Deputy Assistant Attorney General, to John A Rizzo, Senior Deputy General Counsel, Central Intelligence Agency, 30 May 2005, Memorandum, in Cole, *The Torture Memos*, 225–74.

[117] Zelikow, 'Codes of conduct for a twilight war', 33–37.

[118] ibid, 39–40.

impact on its activities.[119] These Congressional efforts are the subject of the following section.

The official sanctioning by the US Government of state torture came to a halt with the inauguration of the new President, Barack Obama, in 2009. In an interview before taking office, the President-elect declared, 'I have said repeatedly that America doesn't torture. And I'm gonna make sure that we don't torture. Those are part and parcel of an effort to regain America's moral stature in the world'.[120] In one of President Obama's first acts, he signed executive orders that shut down the CIA's remaining detention centres, prohibited officials from subjecting detainees to interrogation techniques not listed in Field Manual 34–52, revoked the OLC torture memoranda and reaffirmed the Common Article 3 minimum standard of treatment for all detainees in US custody.[121]

Despite this, some of the changes instituted by the Bush Administration in the war on terror downgrading the rights of detainees became institutionalised under the Obama Administration.[122] For example, President Obama continued to rely for his counter-terrorism policies on the use of force resolution passed by Congress in 2001, preferring the war characterisation, with its expansive view of presidential discretion, over the criminal justice system, which would have circumscribed his powers.[123] President Obama promised to close the Guantánamo Bay detention facility.[124] However, a hostile Congress, which opposed the transfer of detainees to the US mainland for trial and incarceration, and used votes on appropriations bills to prohibit the use of funding for such purposes, stymied his efforts.[125] President Obama has continued the use of military commissions.[126] He also continued the policy of extraordinary rendition.[127] In May 2009, President Obama announced that he would continue to hold individual detainees, who could not be prosecuted but still posed a danger, indefinitely.[128]

President Obama also refused to engage in political accountability for state torture carried out during the war on terror, declining to prosecute any officials and maintaining that 'nothing will be gained by spending our time and energy laying

[119] Cole, *The Torture Memos*, 35.

[120] 'Obama on economic crisis, transition', *60 Minutes*, CBS, 16 November 2008 (Barack Obama).

[121] Executive Order No 13,491, 74 Fed Reg No 16, 22 January 2009.

[122] Jack Goldsmith, *Power and Constraint: The Accountable Presidency after 9/11* (New York, NY: WW Norton & Company, 2012) 5; Hafetz, *Habeas Corpus After 9/11*, 239–40.

[123] Goldsmith, *Power and Constraint*, 6.

[124] Charlie Savage, 'Guantánamo is leaving Obama with choices, neither of them simple', *New York Times*, 31 October 2015, http://www.nytimes.com/2015/11/01/us/politics/guantanamo-is-leaving-obama-with-choices-neither-of-them-simple.html?_r=0.

[125] Amy Davidson, 'Obama's flawed plan to close Guantánamo', *New Yorker*, 25 February 2016, http://www.newyorker.com/news/amy-davidson/obamas-flawed-plan-to-close-guantanamo.

[126] Barack Obama, 'Remarks by the President on national security', Washington, DC, 21 May 2009.

[127] Department of Justice, 'Special Task Force on interrogations and transfer policies issues its recommendations to the President', press release, 24 August 2009.

[128] Obama, 'Remarks by the President on national security'; see also Hafetz, *Habeas Corpus After 9/11*, 240–42.

blame for the past'.[129] This is despite the obligations of state parties to the CAT to start criminal investigations against alleged perpetrators of torture under Articles 5, 6 and 7. While in 2009 the Attorney General, Eric Holder, opened a preliminary inquiry into US interrogations of detainees, he limited the investigation to cases where officials acted outside the mandate afforded by the OLC legal memoranda.[130] Three years later the investigation was closed, with no prosecutions.[131] President Obama's Administration has also used national security arguments—the reliance on the state secrets privilege, in particular—to seek the dismissal of civil cases brought by detainees who were tortured.[132] President Obama's refusal to engage in any official accountability over the Bush Administration's torture policies means that 'a future president can, with the stroke of a pen, put the United States back in the torture business'.[133]

Congress

The above chronology documenting how torture became official US policy in the war on terror has focused almost exclusively on the conduct of the executive government. This is because the story of the US reaction to 9/11 is found in executive action.[134] The Bush Administration's response was one of unilateral executive action, supported by dubious and distorted claims of legality. A small coterie of powerful White House officials drove this approach, which was based on assertions of unfettered presidential power in dealing with the terrorist problem, founded in the wartime model. Kent Roach argues that the adoption of extra-legal means to achieve its detainee policies (torture and rendition) meant the executive was able to 'break the law in real or perceived emergencies', while maintaining the appearance of formal legal restraints.[135] This practice, which resonates powerfully with Carl Schmitt's idea of the state of exception and the suspension of law discussed

[129] Barack Obama, 'Statement of President Barack Obama on release of OLC torture memos', 16 April 2009.

[130] Eric Holder, 'Attorney General Eric Holder regarding a preliminary review into the interrogation of certain detainees', *Justice News*, 24 August 2009.

[131] Scott Shane, 'No charges filed on harsh tactics used by the C.I.A.', *New York Times*, 30 August 2012, 1.

[132] See *Mohamed v Jeppesen Dataplan, Inc*, 614 F 3d 1070 (9th Cir 2010) (en banc); see also Benjamin Bernstein, 'Over before it even began: Mohamed v Jeppesen Dataplan and the use of the state secrets privilege in extraordinary rendition cases', *Fordham International Law Journal* 34(5) (2011), 1400–429.

[133] Michael Ratner, 'From Guantánamo to Berlin: Protecting human rights after 9/11' in *The United States and Torture*, ed Cohn, 211.

[134] Kent Roach, *The 9/11 Effect: Comparative Counter-Terrorism* (New York, NY: Cambridge University Press, 2011) 162.

[135] ibid, 163.

in Chapter 2, freed the Bush Administration from having to seek Congressional approval for legislative changes. In this section, I consider what Congress was doing during this time, and why, especially in the first few years immediately following 9/11, it apparently had minimal impact on the conduct of the executive.

Congress's oversight role in the war on terror has been criticised as ineffective, though there are notable exceptions to its general reluctance to act.[136] Congress's typical response to President Bush's assertions of presidential authority was acquiescence.[137] This pattern commenced with Congress authorising a limitless war on terror, in approving the all-embracing 'use of force' Congressional resolution.[138] The Republicans, the President's party, controlled the House of Representatives in the US Congress on 11 September 2001. A lone Democratic Congressman in the House of Representatives, John Tierney, sought to limit the resolution by requiring the President to report to Congress every 60 days, but his efforts were rejected.[139] The Senate, narrowly controlled at that time by the Democrats, unanimously approved the resolution: OLC lawyers subsequently interpreted Congress's passage of the use of force resolution as demonstrating its acceptance of the President's unilateral war powers in an emergency such as that created by the 9/11 attacks.[140]

More specifically, a cowed Congress failed for many years to question or investigate growing evidence of detainee mistreatment.[141] Congress was silent in response to alarms raised by the media and civil liberties groups about detainee abuse, and left it to the courts to challenge the denial of habeas corpus rights to detainees.[142] According to the Constitution Project's Task Force on Detainee Treatment (a bipartisan watchdog group), Congress demonstrated great resistance to investigating the issue of detainee treatment on the basis that it would hinder intelligence collection and damage morale.[143] Concerns were not raised by members after they were privately briefed on the CIA's programs, and early attempts by members of Congress who did try to enforce US obligations with respect to torture through legislation were routinely thwarted.[144] It was not until revelations

[136] Constitution Project, *The Report of the Constitution Project's Task Force on Detainee Treatment*, 337.

[137] Owens, 'Congressional acquiescence to presidentialism in the US "war on terror"', 62.

[138] Parry, *Understanding Torture*, 168.

[139] Owens, 'Congressional acquiescence to presidentialism in the US "war on terror"', 42.

[140] John Yoo, Deputy Assistant Attorney General, to Timothy Flanagan, the Deputy Counsel to the President, 25 September 2001, memorandum, in *The Torture Papers: The Road to Abu Ghraib*, ed Greenberg and Dratel, 3-24.

[141] Jarmo Oikarinen, 'Parliamentary oversight of counter-terrorism policies' in *Counter-Terrorism: International Law and Practice*, ed Ana Maria Salinas De Frias, Katja Samuel and Nigel D White (New York, NY: Oxford University Press, 2012), 948.

[142] Owens, 'Congressional acquiescence to presidentialism in the US "war on terror"', 59–60.

[143] Constitution Project, *The Report of the Constitution Project's Task Force on Detainee Treatment*, 339.

[144] ibid, 340–41.

in the media about Abu Ghraib that Congress displayed any concern about the treatment of detainees in the war on terror.[145] At this time, however, there was no follow-through. The Senate Select Committee on Intelligence and the House Permanent Select Committee on Intelligence have very powerful statutory mandates over the US intelligence machine, yet for years they failed to conduct any serious or adequate investigations into the CIA rendition program.[146] This can be attributed to a lack of political will on the part of the leaders of the Congressional intelligence committees.[147] The first public hearings on rendition took place in 2007, and were arranged by the Subcommittees of the House Foreign Affairs and Judiciary Committees after the Republicans lost control of Congress.[148]

There are important exceptions to Congress's inaction on the Bush Administration's detainee policies. One concerns the Detainee Treatment Act. In July 2005, Republican Senator John McCain, a former prisoner of war in Vietnam and vocal opponent of torture, attempted to legislate changes to US interrogation and detention policies in the war on terror, to bring them into line with its international legal obligations regarding torture and cruel, inhuman and degrading treatment.[149] McCain proposed two amendments to a Defense Department authorisation bill. One stipulated that no person in the custody of the Defense Department could be subjected to any treatment not authorised by Field Manual 34-52, which prohibited torture and coercive interrogations. A second amendment prohibited the infliction of cruel, inhuman or degrading treatment upon any person in US custody, regardless of nationality or location. This amendment was intended to close a loophole opened by the Bush Administration in its interpretation of the CAT. The Bush Administration had argued that the prohibition on cruel, inhuman and degrading treatment of foreign nationals did not apply overseas because the definition of such treatment was linked to the Eighth Amendment ban on cruel and unusual punishment, which did not apply outside the US.[150] McCain's amendments had the support of some 28 former retired high-ranking military officers and the former Secretary of State, Colin Powell.[151]

The White House tried, unsuccessfully, to block Senator McCain's amendments.[152] The Detainee Treatment Act was eventually signed into law in December 2005, but came at a price. By then, it had been combined with further amendments, introduced by Republican Senators Lindsey Graham and Jon Kyle, and Democrat Senator Carl Levin, stripping the federal courts of jurisdiction to hear habeas corpus claims brought by Guantánamo Bay detainees, and replacing

[145] ibid, 339.
[146] Oikarinen, 'Parliamentary oversight of counter-terrorism policies', 947–48.
[147] Goldsmith, *Power and Constraint*, 104.
[148] Oikarinen, 'Parliamentary oversight of counter-terrorism policies', 948.
[149] Margulies, *Guantánamo and the Abuse of Presidential Power*, 239.
[150] Mayerfeld, 'Playing by our own rules', 121.
[151] Margulies, *Guantánamo and the Abuse of Presidential Power*, 240–41, 244.
[152] ibid, 242, 244.

it with limited review in the District of Columbia Court of Appeals.[153] This followed the US Supreme Court decision in *Rasul v Bush*, and the establishment of Combatant Status Review Tribunals (CSRTs) to determine whether Guantánamo Bay detainees were enemy combatants (prior to this there was no legal process for detainees at all).[154] *Rasul v Bush* is discussed below. The Graham/Kyle/Levin amendments meant that judicial review would be restricted to the question of whether the CSRTs had correctly followed their own procedures.[155] Further limiting the effect of McCain's amendments was an accompanying presidential 'signing statement', proclaiming that the President would obey the amendment only to the extent that it did not interfere with his decisions as Commander-in-Chief.[156]

A much later display of robust Congressional oversight of the executive's war on terror detainee policies came in 2009, with the decision by the US Senate Select Committee on Intelligence to conduct a review of the CIA's detention and interrogation program.[157] The Committee's 6,300-page report into the CIA's detention program was delivered to President Obama in December 2012, based on a documentary review of more than six million pages of CIA and other records.[158] An executive summary of the report was released in December 2014, after a year-long battle, led by Democrat Senator and Committee chairman, Dianne Feinstein, with the CIA and the Obama White House, which tried to obstruct its public release.

The Committee was scathing of the CIA's detention and interrogation program. It concluded that the CIA's 'enhanced interrogation techniques' were not an effective way to gather intelligence information; the CIA had provided extensive, inaccurate information about the program and its effectiveness to the White House, other parts of government and the public; the CIA's management of the program was deeply flawed; and the CIA program was far more brutal than previously believed.[159] The report completely discredited the existence of any 'ticking time bomb' scenario to justify the CIA's use of torture, and demonstrated that the use of coercive methods regularly resulted in fabricated information. It found that CIA officers who questioned aspects of the program were overruled by headquarters, and that the program itself was devised by two contract psychologists who had never conducted interrogations themselves or operated detention facilities. A minority report, issued by Republican members of the Committee, took issue

[153] Hafetz, *Habeas Corpus After 9/11*, 143.

[154] *Rasul v Bush*, 542 US 446 (2004); Margulies, *Guantánamo and the Abuse of Presidential Power*, 245.

[155] Margulies, *Guantánamo and the Abuse of Presidential Power*, 245.

[156] George W Bush, 'President's statement on signing of H.R. 2863, the "Department of Defense, Emergency Supplemental Appropriations to Address Hurricanes in the Gulf of Mexico, and Pandemic Influenza Act, 2006"', 30 December 2005; see also Margulies, *Guantánamo and the Abuse of Presidential Power*, 247.

[157] Dianne Feinstein, 'Feinstein, Bond announce Intelligence Committee Review of CIA detention and interrogation program', press release, 5 March 2009.

[158] Dianne Feinstein, 'Feinstein statement on CIA detention, interrogation report', 13 December 2012.

[159] Dianne Feinstein, 'Feinstein remarks on CIA report', press release, 9 December 2014.

with the majority report, criticising its 'flawed analytical methodology' and lack of objectivity.[160] The minority senators said they had 'no doubt' that the CIA's detention program saved lives and played a vital role in weakening Al-Qaeda.

The Courts

The ability to avoid judicial review was critical to the successful operation of the Bush Administration's detainee policies.[161] Over time, the US Supreme Court overruled the executive government, establishing that Guantánamo Bay was not a legal black hole, and that domestic and international law did apply there.[162] Overall, in contrast to Congress, the American judiciary's response to the Bush Administration's war on terror detainee policies was one of progressively firmer resistance, although, initially at least, it displayed a marked determination to rule as narrowly as possible on the issues before it. This progression can be traced through three key US Supreme Court decisions over six years: *Rasul v Bush* in 2004; *Hamdan v Rumsfeld* in 2006; and *Boumediene v Bush* in 2008.[163] Jack Goldsmith, who headed the OLC for two years in the Bush Administration's first term, wrote that the Supreme Court pushed back slowly, methodically and with increasing fortitude against the President, 'ultimately proving to be one of the most important agents for making the Constitution's checks and balances work'.[164] Others, however, have argued that the US Supreme Court decisions did not go far enough and actually aided presidential administrations in holding detainees indefinitely.[165]

While I focus on the Supreme Court in this section, the lower courts played a more mixed role in providing accountability for the executive's actions in the war on terror. For example, the US courts have declined to hear civil cases brought by former detainees in the war on terror on national security and 'state secrets' grounds, in decisions that have favoured the executive. In the case of Canadian citizen Maher Arar, discussed in Chapter 7, the US Court of Appeals for the Second Circuit dismissed his case seeking damages in relation to his extraordinary rendition to Syria, on the ground that Congress had not created a civil remedy for harms suffered in the context of extraordinary rendition.[166] Another case brought by UK

[160] United States Senate Select Committee on Intelligence, 'Minority views of Vice Chairman Chambliss joined by Senators Burr, Risch, Coats, Rubio, Coburn', *Committee Study of the Central Intelligence Agency's Detention and Interrogation Program*, 2014, 34.

[161] Hafetz, *Habeas Corpus After 9/11*, 27.

[162] Helen Duffy, *The 'War on Terror' and the Framework of International Law* (New York, NY: Cambridge University Press, 2005) 441.

[163] *Rasul v Bush*, 542 US 446 (2004); *Hamdan v Rumsfeld*, 548 US 577 (2006); *Boumediene v Bush*, 553 US 723 (2008).

[164] Goldsmith, *Power and Constraint*, 166.

[165] Mark Kende, 'The US Supreme Court, the war on terror, and the need for thick constitutional review', *Mississippi Law Journal* 80(4) (2011), 1–23.

[166] *Arar v Ashcroft*, 585 F 3d 559 (2d Cir 2009).

resident Binyam Mohamed and others against a company (Jeppesen DataPlan, Inc, a subsidiary of Boeing Company) involved in their extraordinary rendition was dismissed on the ground that continuing the litigation would create an unreasonable risk that state secrets would be exposed.[167] Mohamed's case is discussed in Chapter 6. These cases indicate a failure by the judiciary to hold the executive branch accountable.

Rasul v Bush

The first of the Supreme Court's decisions, *Rasul v Bush*, was delivered in June 2004. The case was brought by the Center for Constitutional Rights (CCR), a non-profit legal advocacy organisation based in New York, on behalf of a number of Guantánamo Bay detainees, including two UK citizens, Shafiq Rasul and Asif Iqbal, and an Australian, David Hicks.[168] *Rasul v Bush* concerned the issue of habeas corpus, and whether US courts had jurisdiction to hear detainees' applications challenging the basis of their detention at Guantánamo Bay. The Supreme Court found in the detainees' favour, on the basis that the Guantánamo Bay naval base is under the control of the US Government. However, the Court grounded its finding in statute (the Federal Habeas Corpus Statute), not the Constitution.[169] This left the door open to subsequent attempts by the Bush Administration to legislate away habeas corpus rights.

The Bush Administration responded to the *Rasul v Bush* decision by announcing the creation of CSRTs, which were an apparent attempt to create a habeas corpus substitute.[170] Based loosely on the status tribunals provided for by Article 5 of the Third Geneva Convention, a panel of three commissioned officers would determine whether detainees at Guantánamo Bay were enemy combatants (also known as unlawful combatants).[171] The Department of Defense defined 'enemy combatant' as 'an individual who was part of or supporting Taliban or al Qaeda forces, or associated forces that are engaged in hostilities against the United States or its coalition partners'.[172] The CSRTs were widely criticised as lacking every element of a fair process, and as being no more than 'mini show trials'.[173] For instance, evidence against the detainees was kept secret from them, evidence obtained through torture and coercion was admissible, detainees were denied access to lawyers and were not allowed to call witnesses.[174] Subsequently, Congress passed the Detainee

[167] *Mohamed v Jeppesen Dataplan, Inc*, 614 F 3d 1070 (9th Cir 2010) (en banc).
[168] Margulies, *Guantánamo and the Abuse of Presidential Power*, 145.
[169] *Rasul v Bush*, 542 US 446, 12–13 (2004).
[170] United States Department of Defense, 7 July 2004; see also Helen Duffy, 'Human rights litigation and the "war on terror"', *International Review of the Red Cross* 90(871) (2008), 576.
[171] Margulies, *Guantánamo and the Abuse of Presidential Power*, 159–60.
[172] Duffy, *The 'War on Terror' and the Framework of International Law*, 397.
[173] Hafetz, *Habeas Corpus After 9/11*, 130.
[174] Denbeaux and Hafetz, *The Guantánamo Lawyers*, 149.

Treatment Act of 2005, making it explicit there were no habeas corpus rights for Guantánamo Bay detainees.

Hamdan v Rumsfeld

The basis of Guantánamo Bay detentions was again challenged in the US courts, and in June 2006 the US Supreme Court delivered its decision in *Hamdan v Rumsfeld*. Salim Ahmed Hamdan, a Yemeni national captured in Afghanistan and transferred to Guantánamo Bay, was formally charged in July 2004 with conspiracy to commit war crimes, and was among the first detainees to be listed for trial by military commission.[175] Hamdan's lawyers challenged the validity of the military commissions process. The Supreme Court ruled that the military commissions suffered two fatal flaws.[176] They deviated from courts-martial procedures by, for example, denying detainees the right to be at their own trial and allowing the use of evidence obtained by coercion. Secondly, the Court ruled that the military commissions violated Common Article 3 of the Geneva Conventions. The Common Article 3 finding was a blow to the Bush Administration's post-9/11 global detention regime, which was premised on enemy combatants having no rights.[177] The Court disagreed with the Bush Administration's interpretation of the words 'conflict not of an international character', saying it was used in the Geneva Conventions 'in contradistinction to a conflict between nations', and Common Article 3 had to be read 'as wide as possible'.[178] The *Hamdan v Rumsfeld* decision had significant limitations, however. Importantly, it rested on the President's failure to seek appropriate authorisation from Congress for the military commissions, and it did not prevent Congress from creating new military commissions in the future.[179]

Following the *Hamdan v Rumsfeld* decision, the Bush Administration ordered the US military to comply with Common Article 3.[180] President Bush, for the first time, publicly acknowledged the existence of CIA 'black sites' and the Agency's use of an 'alternative set of procedures' in interrogations, and he announced that 14 of the CIA's detainees had been transferred to Guantánamo Bay where the ICRC would have access to them.[181] These policy decisions were contested inside the Administration, with Vice President Dick Cheney opposed to publicly

175 Hafetz, *Habeas Corpus After 9/11*, 138.
176 *Hamdan v Rumsfeld*, 548 US 577, 567 (Stephens J) (2006).
177 Hafetz, *Habeas Corpus After 9/11*, 148.
178 *Hamdan v Rumsfeld*, 548 US 577, 630–31 (Stephens J) (2006).
179 Hafetz, *Habeas Corpus After 9/11*, 149.
180 Gordon England, to Secretaries of the Military Departments, memorandum, 7 July 2006.
181 George W Bush, 'President discusses creation of military commissions to try suspected terrorists', remarks made at the White House, Washington, DC, 6 September 2006.

acknowledging the CIA's secret detention and interrogation program and formally adopting the Common Article 3 standard for detainees.[182]

President Bush also declared he would send legislation to Congress to specifically authorise the creation of military commissions. The Bush Administration began working with allies in the Congress to draft the Military Commissions Act, which became law in October 2006, and re-established military commissions to try foreign nationals in the war on terror.[183] While the new military commissions contained some improvements on the earlier version (giving defendants a partial right to be present at their trials, and affording them a greater opportunity to see and respond to the Government's evidence), they still had problematic features, such as allowing for the use of coerced evidence, as long as it was obtained before the passage of the Detainee Treatment Act.[184] The Military Commissions Act also sought to immunise interrogators in the war on terror by redefining grave breaches of the Geneva Conventions, and thus limiting the ambit of war crimes subject to prosecution in a US court (narrowing the definition of torture and excluding humiliating and degrading treatment entirely).[185]

Boumediene v Bush

The final US Supreme Court decision on detainees was delivered in June 2008. *Boumediene v Bush* went further than previous rulings, as the Court found a constitutional basis for the detainees' rights to habeas corpus.[186] The decision, resting on a narrow 5:4 margin, has been hailed as 'one of the most important Supreme Court decisions in recent years'.[187]

The *Boumediene v Bush* decision answered two key questions. First, it found that the US Constitution's guarantee of habeas corpus provided in Article I (known as 'the suspension clause') applied to aliens outside the formal territory of the US.[188] In so doing it rejected one of the central ideas underpinning the post-9/11 global detention system: that foreign nationals could be denied habeas corpus review, as long as they were held outside the US.[189] Secondly, it found that the military commissions established by the Military Commissions Act did not

[182] Condoleezza Rice, *No Higher Honor: A Memoir of My Years in Washington* (New York, NY: Crown Publishers, 2011) 498.

[183] Margulies, *Guantánamo and the Abuse of Presidential Power*, 259.

[184] Hafetz, *Habeas Corpus After 9/11*, 152.

[185] Jonathan Hafetz, 'Resisting accountability: Transitional justice in the post-9/11 United States', *The International Journal of Human Rights* 19(4) (2014), 429–46, 433.

[186] *Boumediene v Bush*, 553 US 723, 725 (Kennedy J) (2008).

[187] Ronald Dworkin, 'Why it was a great victory', *New York Review of Books*, 14 August 2008.

[188] United States Constitution, Art I, § 9, cl 2.

[189] Hafetz, *Habeas Corpus After 9/11*, 164.

provide an adequate habeas substitute, given the many deficiencies in the CSRT process. Justice Kennedy, delivering the Court's majority opinion, said:

> [T]he writ of habeas corpus is itself an indispensable mechanism for monitoring the separation of powers. The test for determining the scope of this provision must not be subject to manipulation by those whose power it is designed to restrain.[190]

While acknowledging the importance of this decision, its timing—six years after the establishment of the Guantánamo prison camp—has been criticised. It has been suggested, for example, that the judicial process overall in the US has been characterised by 'undue constitutional avoidance, as well as excessive judicial deference to the executive and congressional decision-making role'.[191] It has also been argued that the decision, the most assertive by the Supreme Court in the war on terror, must be seen in the context of there being greater distance from 9/11 and a lessening terrorist threat.[192] The decision also leaves unresolved a number of issues, including what procedural rights a military tribunal must afford to non-citizen detainees in determining whether they can be held as enemy combatants, perhaps indefinitely, without trial for any crime.[193]

Together, the Supreme Court's increasingly forceful decisions provide a backdrop for debates around the legitimacy of US detainee treatment policies that occurred in Australia, Canada and the UK. In Australia, for example, the *Hamdan v Rumsfeld* decision increased domestic political pressure on the Howard Government, which was in secret diplomatic negotiations with the US in relation to Hicks's detention and military commission trial at Guantánamo Bay.[194] In the UK, members of both houses of the UK Parliament filed an amicus curiae brief in support of the detainees in *Rasul v Bush*.[195] The Supreme Court decisions thus afforded important points of leverage for civil society overseas, as well as in the US.

Civil Society

Civil society organisations in the US played a crucial role in challenging core aspects of the Bush Administration's detainee policies. This reflects America's

[190] *Boumediene v Bush*, 553 US 723, 766 (Kennedy J) (2008).

[191] Duffy, 'Human rights litigation and the "war on terror"', 578.

[192] Baher Azmy, 'An insufficiently accountable presidency: some reflections on Jack Goldsmith's power and constraint', *Case Western Reserve Journal of International Law* 45(1&2) (2012), 38.

[193] Richard H Fallon, 'The Supreme Court, Habeas Corpus, and the war on terror: An essay on law and political science', *Columbia Law Review* 110(2) (2010), 357.

[194] Leigh Sales, *Detainee 002: The Case of David Hicks* (Melbourne: Melbourne University Press, 2007) 189.

[195] Ahmed and Others, 'Brief of 175 members of both houses of the Parliament of the United Kingdom of Great Britain and Northern Ireland as amici curiae in support of petitioners', submission in *Rasul v Bush*, Nos 03-343, 03-334, 14 January 2004.

strong human rights civil sector, which comprises many active human rights NGOs, civil liberties groups, immigrants' rights groups, ethnic and religiously identified groups, lawyers' professional organisations and grassroots organisations, and is buttressed by reasonably strong investigative media.[196] In this section, I provide an overview of civil society's role in pushing back against, or publicly backing, the Government's detainee policies. I do not analyse civil society's behaviour through the framework of enabling and constraining factors influencing human rights activism as is the case in the chapters on the US allies, where my concern is with understanding why those countries responded as they did when their own citizens were tortured in the war on terror. Rather, I outline here by way of background some of the key civil society actors who mobilised in the US on the issue of foreign nationals detained overseas, and note their role in either supporting or challenging the US Government.

American civil society actors engaged in many different forms of activism during the war on terror, including issuing critical reports, holding press conferences, launching lawsuits, lobbying Congress and publishing media reports exposing details of the human rights abuses of detainees. Goldsmith, the former Bush Administration official, has argued that the 'distributed forces' of actors beyond the traditional institutions such as Congress were critical in checking presidential power in the war on terror.[197] Their efforts 'shaped the public's view of presidential action and informed Congressional responses, lawsuits, and mainstream media reporting'.[198] Goldsmith's view has been criticised as flawed and overly rosy.[199] Not all sections of civil society contested the Government's detainee policies, including on torture, with some providing support for the Bush Administration's approach.

The US legal profession, which includes individual lawyers, legal advocacy organisations, professional legal organisations and legal academics, led civil society in challenging the Bush Administration's detainee policies. This was most apparent in the Guantánamo Bay litigation, where a few legal advocacy organisations took on the Bush Administration soon after 9/11, despite the unpopularity of the detainees' cause. America's legal profession has historically engaged in strategic litigation.[200] Another example of legal activism was that of the American Bar Association, which declared 'we must defend those whom we dislike or even despise' and urged Congress and the President to ensure that all military commission defendants had access to civilian lawyers.[201]

196 David Cole and Jules Lobel, *Less Safe, Less Free: Why America is Losing the War on Terror* (New York, NY: The New Press, 2007) 263.

197 Goldsmith, *Power and Constraint*, xiii.

198 ibid, xii.

199 Azmy, 'An insufficiently accountable presidency', 25.

200 Richard L Abel, 'Contesting legality in the United States after September 11' in *Fighting for Political Freedom: Comparative Studies of the Legal Complex and Political Liberalism*, ed Terence C Halliday, Lucien Karpik and Malcolm M Feely (Oxford: Hart Publishing, 2007) 361.

201 Jonathan Glater, 'ABA urges wider rights in cases tried by tribunals', *New York Times*, 13 August 2003, 18.

The *Rasul v Bush* case was launched by the CCR, an organisation founded by lawyers representing civil rights movement activists in the 1960s. Michael Ratner, one of the CCR lawyers involved, wrote that his organisation was the first, and for a long time the only, human rights organisation willing to take on Guantánamo Bay cases.[202] Lawyers and human rights groups were afraid of two things: the likelihood that they would lose, and the national outrage that would be directed against them for getting involved.[203] Joseph Margulies, another of the *Rasul v Bush* legal team, wrote that despite this general reluctance, the detainees' lawyers had the support of several retired federal judges (Democrats and Republicans), a number of current and former military lawyers, and a group of former American prisoners of war.[204] The amicus curiae briefs filed in the 2004 US Supreme Court detainee litigation (*Rasul v Bush*, *Hamdi v Rumsfeld* and *Rumsfeld v Padilla*) reflect this support from America's legal establishment. For example, briefs filed by law professors for detainees outnumbered those for government more than 20:1.[205] This underscores the role played by legal academics on the detainee issue, whose efforts also included producing influential reports on the Guantánamo Bay detention regime and giving Congressional testimony.[206]

The Guantánamo cases also highlight the way in which successful litigation can encourage new civil society actors to take up a contentious human rights cause. Successive US Supreme Court rulings in the detainees' favour led to the further mobilisation of other sections of civil society, generating confidence and spurring new actors into taking a stand. For example, following the *Rasul v Bush* decision, other US law firms came forward to offer their pro bono services to represent Guantánamo Bay detainees in bringing habeas corpus petitions.[207] By the time of the *Boumediene v Bush* decision, the Guantánamo Bay lawyers had built a network of lawyer-activists around the US, who lobbied tirelessly on the habeas corpus issue. What 'was initially a little band of habeas lawyers—that later grew into a brigade—took on two branches of government, over a seven-year period, and won the fight to preserve habeas corpus'.[208]

Other civil society groups dedicated to constitutional and rule-of-law values played an important role in checking the executive government. They include the

[202] Ratner, 'From Guantánamo to Berlin', 204.

[203] ibid, 206. Even the CCR hesitated before taking on the Guantánamo cases. Goldsmith writes that staff were worried about the effect on fundraising; how it fit with CCR's objectives to promote progressive social change; and whether it would be personally dangerous: Goldsmith, *Power and Constraint*, 162.

[204] Margulies, *Guantánamo and the Abuse of Presidential Power*, 147–48.

[205] Abel, 'Contesting legality in the United States after September 11', 394–95.

[206] See, eg, Mark Denbeaux et al, 'Report on Guantánamo detainees: A profile of 517 detainees through analysis of Department of Defense data', *Seton Hall Law*, 8 February 2006; Testimony of David Cole, 'Hearing: Torture and the case of Maher Arar', US House Committee on the Judiciary; Subcommittee on The Constitution, Civil Rights, and Civil Liberties and US House Committee on Foreign Affairs; Subcommittee on International Organizations, Human Rights and Oversight, 18 October 2008.

[207] Ratner, 'From Guantánamo to Berlin', 207.

[208] Denbeaux and Hafetz, *The Guantánamo Lawyers*, 218.

American Civil Liberties Union (ACLU), the Bill of Rights Defense Committee (a grassroots advocacy organisation promoting popular constitutionalism), the Constitution Project, the Muslim Public Affairs Council and the Council on American Islamic Relations. American constitutional scholar David Cole argues that such civil society groups helped to inculcate and reinforce a culture of legality, and provided a critically important voice for rule-of-law values. He argues, 'Absent that voice, it is far from clear that legality would have been restored to the extent that it was, or that the Supreme Court's opinions in the military detention and trial cases would have been as strong as they were.'[209]

Transnational NGOs such as Human Rights Watch and Amnesty International became more active on Guantánamo Bay and CIA interrogation over time. Such was the political climate after 11 September 2001 that human rights organisations reported government pressure on themselves and their funders 'to downplay their reporting of America's own human rights abusers'.[210] When the Secretary General of Amnesty International, Irene Khan, described Guantánamo Bay in 2005 as 'the gulag of our times', the Bush Administration criticised her for being anti-American.[211]

Certain sections of the US media scrutinised the Bush Administration's human rights abuses in the war on terror, ultimately forcing it to change some of its policies. This included the reporting, noted above, on Abu Ghraib prisoner abuse.[212] *Washington Post* journalist Dana Priest's 2005 exposé of the CIA's network of black sites is another example.[213] The impact of Priest's reporting on the CIA's detention and interrogation program was significant. Goldsmith credited Priest's journalism with bolstering Congressional efforts to pass the Detainee Treatment Act; causing outrage and recriminations among US allies in Europe, leading to the closure of a number of the CIA's secret prisons; and 'almost certainly' influencing the US Supreme Court's decision in *Hamdan v Rumsfeld*.[214] The Senate Select Committee on Intelligence similarly attributed great influence to Priest's journalism.[215] Media freedom in the US is protected by the First Amendment, which may help explain the important role of investigative journalism in exposing Bush Administration torture.[216]

209 David Cole, 'Where liberty lies: Civil society and individual rights after 9/11', *Wayne Law Review* 57(4) (2011), 1267.

210 Julie A Mertus, 'Human rights and civil society in a new age of American exceptionalism' in *Human Rights in the 'War on Terror'*, ed Richard Ashby Wilson (New York, NY: Cambridge University Press, 2005) 319.

211 Kate Nash, *The Cultural Politics of Human Rights: Comparing the US and UK* (New York, NY: Cambridge University Press, 2009) 88–89.

212 'Abuse of Iraqi POWs by GIs probes'; Hersh, 'Torture at Abu Ghraib'.

213 Dana Priest, 'CIA holds terror suspects in secret prisons', *Washington Post*, 2 November 2005, 1.

214 Goldsmith, *Power and Constraint*, 56.

215 United States Senate Select Committee on Intelligence, *Committee Study of the Central Intelligence Agency's Detention and Interrogation Program*, 151–53.

216 Roach, *The 9/11 Effect*, 229.

As noted, other sections of civil society, including some media, supported the Bush Administration's detainee policies, including the use of torture. Various journalists reinforced the executive's narrative that human rights, including the ban on torture, would hinder the successful prosecution of the war on terror. A senior journalist with *Newsweek* wrote after 9/11 that 'we need to keep an open mind about certain measures to fight terrorism, like court-sanctioned psychological interrogation'.[217] Another influential columnist wrote in the *Weekly Standard* that there were circumstances in which, 'by any rational moral calculus',[218] torture would not only be permissible but required.

There were also instances of conservative legal associations and prominent academics supporting the US Government's treatment of detainees. The Washington Legal Foundation accused the US Supreme Court, after its *Rasul v Bush* decision, of issuing, at the urging of 'radical' legal activists, 'sweeping decisions which extended new rights to enemy combatants and opened up the federal courts to a terrorist litigation explosion'.[219] In addition, there was a number of cases of high-profile legal academics providing justificatory arguments for the use of torture against terrorist suspects. Alan Dershowitz from Harvard Law School advocated using 'torture warrants' in rare situations in which torture was determined by a judge to be justified to prevent an imminent terrorist attack.[220] Jean Bethke Elshtain, a professor of social and political ethics at the University of Chicago Divinity School, argued that 'Torture 2', modest physical pressure or coercive interrogation, might, 'with regret, be used' to save innocent lives.[221]

Conclusion

In this chapter, I have documented the story of America's panic after 11 September 2001 and the shift that followed in the US attitude to a basic principle of international human rights: the norm against torture. The Bush Administration and its supporters employed a powerful discourse, and claimed the threat posed by Al-Qaeda terrorists was novel and unprecedented, requiring a new approach. This entailed casting off the old restrictive rules governing detainee treatment, in favour of more aggressive methods, underpinned by contorted interpretations of existing laws prohibiting torture. The executive confronted resistance, some internal, but

[217] Jonathan Alter, 'Time to think about torture', *Newsweek* (New York), 4 November 2001.

[218] Charles Krauthammer, 'The truth about torture: It's time to be honest about doing terrible things', *Weekly Standard* (Washington, DC), 5 December 2005.

[219] Abel, 'Contesting legality in the United States after September 11', 391.

[220] Alan M Dershowitz, *Why Terrorism Works: Understanding the Threat, Responding to the Challenge* (New Haven, CT: Yale University Press, 2002) 158–59.

[221] Jean Bethke Elshtain, 'Reflection on the problem of "dirty hands"' in *Torture: A Collection*, ed Sanford Levinson (New York, NY: Oxford University Press, 2004) 87.

most external, emanating largely from sections of civil society, the US Supreme Court, whose decisions became more assertive over time, and to a lesser extent from the Congress. Gradually, through these collective efforts, the Bush Administration was forced to conform more closely to its human rights obligations.

This narrative provides an important backdrop to the responses of US allies to the torture of their citizens in the war on terror. The US war on terror defined and shaped the foreign and domestic policies of other states, with events in America playing into the domestic politics of Australia, the UK and Canada around these issues. The influence of US detainee policies can be thought of in two, interrelated ways: realpolitik and moral leadership. Nine days after the 9/11 attacks, President Bush declared that every state faced a choice: 'Every nation, in every region, now has a decision to make. Either you are with us, or you are with the terrorists.'[222] For US allies at that traumatic moment, this was not a difficult choice. It became more complicated over time, however, as details of the Bush Administration's war on terror policies unfolded.

From a realist perspective, America after 9/11 was the world's only superpower. This condition of unipolarity had profound effects on the nature of contemporary alliances. This 'gross distribution of capabilities', as Stephen Walt described America's position, inevitably shaped the alliance choices that were available to different states.[223] As junior allies, Australia, Canada and the UK were reliant on US friendship for different reasons, ranging from geographic insecurity (Australia), to trade (Canada), to a desire to exercise global influence (the UK). The three states threw their support behind America and joined its war on terror launched in Afghanistan. They were thus implicated in the Bush Administration's detainee policies as alliance partners fighting in the same war. When their own citizens became caught up in that war as detainees and terrorist suspects, the allies were faced with the prospect of their own nationals being cast as enemies of America.

The US and its liberal allies are members of the Anglosphere, an informal grouping of states united by a common British heritage and identity based on shared human rights commitments.[224] When the US took a path after 11 September 2001 that involved the clear undermining of human rights, the allies confronted the choice—to follow the Bush Administration's lead, or reject the downgrading of the norm against torture. The question became whether these allies would tolerate their citizens being subjected to the legally dubious detention regime constructed by the Bush Administration for dealing with prisoners captured in the war on terror. How Australia, the UK and Canada, in terms of their executive governments, parliaments, courts and civil societies, responded to this challenge is the subject of the following three chapters.

[222] George W Bush, 'Address to a Joint Session of Congress and the American people', US Congress, Washington, DC, 20 September 2001.

[223] Stephen M Walt, 'Alliances in a unipolar world', *World Politics* 61(1) (2009), 86.

[224] Peter Katzenstein, 'The west as Anglo-America' in *Anglo-America and its Discontents: Civilizational Identities Beyond West and East*, ed Peter Katzenstein (New York, NY: Routledge, 2012) 1.

5

Australia

Introduction

No country was quicker to support the US-led war on terror than Australia. It pledged military backing to America on the day of the 9/11 attacks—the first ally to do so.[1] Australia displayed an unwillingness to challenge any aspect of the US conduct of the war. The unquestioning nature of its support was evident in its response to the detention and treatment of the two Australian citizens at Guantánamo Bay, David Hicks and Mamdouh Habib. Both Australians claimed they were tortured in detention. The Liberal-National Coalition Government of Prime Minister John Howard was slow to intervene in their cases, and only stepped in when their detention became a source of political liability. In Hicks's case, no official public inquiry was ever held into his allegations of mistreatment and torture. In the case of Habib, who was subject to extraordinary rendition to Egypt, it took until late 2010 for the Labor Government of Prime Minister Julia Gillard to order a closed inquiry into his detention by the Inspector-General of Intelligence and Security.[2]

I argue that for years an indifferent Australian Government faced little pressure at home on the need for accountability regarding the alleged torture of citizens detained in the war on terror. This lack of pressure was due partly to a range of constraints in the country's political and legal context that inhibited human rights activism, especially on the issue of torture.

In this chapter I outline Australia's involvement in the war on terror and the Hicks and Habib cases, including the men's claims of mistreatment and torture. I examine the responses of key actors to the citizens' cases, beginning with the executive government and including efforts by Parliament, the judiciary and civil society to check the executive. I then analyse the behaviour of domestic actors, particularly civil society, through the framework of the enabling and constraining

[1] Paul Kelly, *The March of the Patriots: The Struggle for Modern Australia* (Melbourne: Melbourne University Press, 2009) 583.

[2] Vivienne Thom, *Inquiry into the actions of Australian Government Agencies in relation to the arrest and detention overseas of Mr Mamdouh Habib from 2001 to 2005*, December 2011, https://www.igis.gov.au/sites/default/files/files/Inquiries/docs/habib-inquiry.pdf.

features of Australia's domestic legal and political context that influenced human rights activism around the issue of torture after 11 September 2001.

Australia and the War on Terror

The Australia–US Relationship

Australia's alliance with the US is underpinned by the formal architecture of the ANZUS treaty, the 1951 security pact between Australia, New Zealand and the US.[3] The Australia–US relationship contains functional and sentimental dimensions.[4] That is, it is built on Australia's long-standing perception of geographic vulnerability, but also a strong sense of cultural affinity with the US. In a speech a month before the 9/11 attacks, Prime Minister Howard described Australia's relationship with the US as 'the most important we have with any single country'.[5] This, he reasoned, was partly because of American strategic, economic and diplomatic power, but mostly because of shared values and aspirations. The 9/11 attacks provided Prime Minister Howard with an opportunity to demonstrate Australia's commitment to the alliance relationship. According to political commentator, Paul Kelly, 'Having pondered about how to bring Australia and America into a closer strategic partnership Howard got his answer in the most brutal manner. The 9/11 attack enabled Howard to realise his strategy.'[6]

Prime Minister Howard was in Washington on 11 September 2001 for talks marking the 50th anniversary of ANZUS, and reacted emotionally and instinctively to the terrorist attacks.[7] The attacks were not just an assault on the US, they were 'an assault on the way of life that we hold dear in common'.[8] Prime Minister Howard agreed with the Bush Administration's characterisation of 9/11 as having changed the world forever.[9] He grasped that 'the rules and norms that had governed international behaviour would change'.[10] In a 2004 terrorism White Paper,

[3] Security Treaty Between Australia, New Zealand and the United States of America.

[4] David MacDonald and Brendan O'Connor, 'Special relationships: Australia and New Zealand in the Anglo-American world' in *Anglo-America and its Discontents: Civilizational Identities Beyond West and East*, ed Peter Katzenstein (New York, NY: Routledge, 2012) 176.

[5] John Langmore, *Dealing with America: The UN, the US and Australia* (Sydney: UNSW Press, 2005) 68–69.

[6] Kelly, *The March of the Patriots*, 580.

[7] John Howard, *Lazarus Rising: A Personal and Political Autobiography* (Sydney: Harper Collins Publishers, 2010) 382.

[8] John Howard, 'Transcript of the Prime Minister the Hon John Howard MP press conference—Ambassador's residence, Washington DC', Washington, DC, 12 September 2001.

[9] 'The Prime Minister the Hon John Howard MP interview with Ray Martin on 60 Minutes Channel Nine, Sydney', *60 Minutes*, Channel Nine, 16 September 2001.

[10] Kelly, *The March of the Patriots*, 587.

the Howard Government emphasised the unprecedented nature of the post 9/11 terrorism threat, which demanded 'new and innovative forms of response'.[11]

Following 9/11, Prime Minister Howard pledged 'all support that might be requested of us by the United States in relation to any action that might be taken', and his Government invoked the ANZUS treaty for the first time in its history.[12] In October 2001, the Government committed Australian troops to the war in Afghanistan.[13] More controversially, in 2003 Australia—along with the UK, but not Canada—joined the US invasion of Iraq, launched without United Nations Security Council sanction.[14] The Iraq decision, unlike that concerning Australia's military involvement in Afghanistan, did not have bipartisan support.[15]

Australia's Detained Citizens

David Hicks

David Hicks, an Australian citizen, was captured by the Northern Alliance in Afghanistan in December 2001.[16] There are conflicting accounts as to what Hicks was doing in Afghanistan. Hicks maintains he was there under the command of the Taliban, while Australia and the US claim he received training with Al-Qaeda.[17] Hicks was transferred into US custody in Afghanistan, and was held by the US in various detention facilities and on board US naval vessels.[18] Hicks was then transported to Guantánamo Bay, and was among the first group of prisoners to arrive in January 2002.[19]

Hicks claims he was subject to various forms of ill-treatment while in US custody, including on US warships and aircraft, and at Guantánamo Bay. Hicks's claims of ill-treatment include: assaults; sexual abuse and humiliation; repeated threats with weapons; being forced into painful stress positions; prolonged

[11] Department of Foreign Affairs and Trade, *Transnational Terrorism: The Threat to Australia* (PP No. 196, 2004).

[12] Howard, 'Transcript of the Prime Minister the Hon John Howard MP press conference—Ambassador's residence, Washington DC'.

[13] John Howard, 'Transcript of the Prime Minister the Hon John Howard MP press conference, Parliament House, Canberra', Canberra, 4 October 2001.

[14] Robert Garran, *True Believer: John Howard, George Bush and the American Alliance* (Sydney: Allen & Unwin, 2004) 151.

[15] Phil Larkin and John Uhr, 'Bipartisanship, partnership and bicameralism in Australia's "war on terror": Forcing limits on the extension of executive power' in *The 'War on Terror' and the Growth of Executive Power*, ed John E Owens and Riccardo Pelizzo (New York, NY: Routledge, 2010) 142.

[16] Leigh Sales, *Detainee 002, The Case of David Hicks* (Melbourne: Melbourne University Press, 2007) 5.

[17] David Hicks, *Communication to the United Nations Human Rights Committee*, Individual Communication Under the First Optional Protocol to the ICCPR in *Hicks v Australia*, 23 August 2010, 6; *Hicks v United States of America*, CMCR 13-004 (18 February 2015).

[18] Hicks, *Communication to the United Nations Human Rights Committee*, 6.

[19] Sales, *Detainee 002*, 69; Donald Rumsfeld, 'Secretary Rumsfeld joint media availability with Australian Defense Minister', press conference, Washington, DC, 10 January 2002.

hooding and blindfolding; frequent tight handcuffing and shackling; enforced medication or drugging; sleep disruption and sleep deprivation; prolonged exposure to bright lighting and excessive continual noise; and prolonged solitary confinement.[20] Hicks says he agreed to everything interrogators put to him in order to avoid abuse.[21]

Hicks was detained at Guantánamo Bay for more than five years. He returned to Australia in May 2007, after making a plea deal in the US military commission process.[22] Hicks was charged earlier that year with attempted murder in violation of the law of war and providing material support for terrorism.[23] This followed an earlier attempt to charge him in 2004 that was thwarted by the US Supreme Court ruling in *Hamdan v Rumsfeld*, discussed in Chapter 4.[24] Hicks pleaded guilty to the material support charge and was sentenced to seven years' imprisonment, with six years and three months suspended.[25] He served the remainder of his sentence in Adelaide's Yatala Labour Prison and was released in December 2007. As a part of his plea deal at Guantánamo Bay, Hicks agreed to a number of additional terms, including that he was never illegally treated while in US custody and that he would not talk to the media for a year about his ordeal.[26] Hicks agreed to this in order 'to get out of Guantánamo and return to Australia'.[27] In 2012, the US Court of Appeals ruled the material support for terrorism charge was retrospective and therefore invalid.[28] Following this, in 2015, the US Court of Military Commission Review set aside Hicks's guilty plea and sentence.[29]

Mamdouh Habib

Mamdouh Habib, a dual Australian-Egyptian citizen, was arrested in Pakistan in October 2001.[30] Habib says he was in Pakistan pursuing new business opportunities.[31] The Australian Government alleged he had attended jihad training camps in Afghanistan.[32] Having recently crossed the Afghanistan border with Pakistan,

[20] Hicks, *Communication to the United Nations Human Rights Committee*, 61–62, 66.

[21] David Hicks, *Guantánamo: My Journey* (Sydney: William Heinemann, 2010) 278.

[22] Hicks, *Communication to the United Nations Human Rights Committee*, 7.

[23] United States Department of Defense, 'US Department of Defense charge sheet (February 2007)', 2 February 2007 in Sales, *Detainee 002*, 261–70.

[24] *Hamdan v Rumsfeld*, 548 US 557 (2006).

[25] Hicks, *Communication to the United Nations Human Rights Committee*, 7.

[26] David Hicks, 'Hicks's pretrial agreement (full transcript), 2 April 2007', Pretrial agreement in *United States v Hicks*, 26 March 2007, in Sales, *Detainee 002*, 270–76, 274–75.

[27] Hicks, *Guantánamo*, 388.

[28] *Hamdan v United States* (DC Circuit, No 11-1257, 6 December 2012).

[29] *Hicks v United States of America* CMCR 13-004 (18 February 2015).

[30] Mamdouh Habib with Julia Collingwood, *My Story: The Tale of a Terrorist Who Wasn't* (Melbourne: Scribe, 2008) 82–83.

[31] ibid, 45.

[32] Evidence to Senate Legal and Constitutional Affairs Committee, Additional Estimates, Parliament of Australia, Canberra, 15 February 2005, 7 (Mick Keelty).

Habib was on a bus from Quetta to Karachi when he was arrested with two German nationals.[33] Habib was detained in Quetta and visited by Australian Federal Police (AFP) and Australian Security Intelligence Organisation (ASIO) agents.[34] The two Germans were soon repatriated after the German Government protested their detention.[35] Habib was subjected to extraordinary rendition to Egypt—the extra-judicial process used by the US to secretly transfer prisoners to countries known to torture.[36] In April 2002, Habib was taken back to Pakistan, then Afghanistan and eventually Guantánamo Bay, where he arrived in May 2002.[37]

Habib's allegations of torture span his time in Pakistan, Egypt and Guantánamo Bay. According to an account, in a 2005 US District Court judgment, while in Egypt, Habib was allegedly routinely beaten to the point of unconsciousness; was locked in a room that would fill with water to a level just below his chin as he stood for hours on the tips of his toes; and was suspended from a wall with his feet resting on the side of a large electrified cylindrical drum which applied electric shocks to his feet.[38] Habib was made to listen to noises that sounded like his wife being raped and his children being beaten, and was deprived of sleep and drugged.[39] He also claims he endured sexual assault, electric shocks to his testicles, being burnt with cigarettes and threatened with dogs.[40] While at Guantánamo Bay, Habib alleges he was kept in isolation, drugged, sleep deprived, beaten, given electric shocks, injected repeatedly, left naked in freezing cold rooms for long periods, threatened with rape, urinated on and had 'menstrual blood' thrown in his face.[41]

Habib was designated eligible for military commission at Guantánamo Bay in July 2004.[42] The US allegations against Habib were based on confessions obtained in Egypt, including that he trained the 9/11 hijackers in martial arts and had prior knowledge of the terrorist attacks.[43] Late in 2004, Habib's American lawyer, Joseph Margulies, became aware of the Egyptian Government's interest in

[33] Habib with Collingwood, *My Story*, 84–86; Thom, *Inquiry into the Actions of Australian Government Agencies in Relation to the Arrest and Detention Overseas of Mr Mamdouh Habib from 2001 to 2005*, 28.

[34] Evidence to Senate Legal and Constitutional Affairs Committee, Additional Estimates, Parliament of Australia, Canberra, 15 February 2005, 5–6 (Mick Keelty).

[35] Christopher Kremmer, 'Second man linked to al-Qaeda', *Sydney Morning Herald*, 19 January 2002, 6.

[36] Joseph Margulies, *Guantánamo and the Abuse of Presidential Power* (New York, NY: Simon & Schuster Paperbacks, 2006) 188.

[37] Thom, *Inquiry into the Actions of Australian Government Agencies in Relation to the Arrest and Detention Overseas of Mr Mamdouh Habib from 2001 to 2005*, 66.

[38] *In re Guantanamo Detainee* Cases, 355 F Supp 2d 443, 473.

[39] Thom, *Inquiry into the Actions of Australian Government Agencies in Relation to the Arrest and Detention Overseas of Mr Mamdouh Habib from 2001 to 2005*, 79.

[40] Habib with Collingwood, *My Story*, 118–20.

[41] ibid, 155–56.

[42] Thom, *Inquiry into the Actions of Australian Government Agencies in Relation to the Arrest and Detention Overseas of Mr Mamdouh Habib from 2001 to 2005*, 95.

[43] Margulies, *Guantánamo and the Abuse of Presidential Power*, 182.

repatriating Habib, and filed a request to block this from occurring with the US Justice Department.[44] The document, which contained details of Habib's torture in Egypt, was cleared for public filing on 4 January 2005.[45] That same day, the US told Australia there was insufficient evidence to charge Habib.[46] One week later, the Australian Government announced Habib would be returning to Australia.[47] He was repatriated the same month, released immediately and never charged.[48]

The Executive

Australia had three different governments during the period under study. The Howard Government was in power from 1996 until November 2007, by which time Hicks and Habib had returned to Australia. The Rudd Government was in power from 2007 until June 2010, and the Gillard Government from June 2010 until 2013.

The Howard Government

The Howard Government's attitude towards Hicks and Habib was, for a long time, one of unreserved support for their detention at Guantánamo Bay and disregard for their allegations of torture. I highlight a number of features of this position, including the Government's willingness to ascribe guilt without any judicial process; its failure to question the conditions of the men's treatment or the fairness of the military commissions; and its ambivalence towards the men's torture claims.

Immediately following Hicks's transfer to Guantánamo Bay, the Federal Attorney-General, Daryl Williams, declared that all the individuals held there were guilty of terrorism. 'They have been trained to be terrorists and to act in accordance with the objective of al-Qaida', he said. 'That makes them about as dangerous as a person can be in modern times.'[49] A similar move to pronounce guilt without any judicial process was evident in government statements after Habib was repatriated to Australia and released. Although Habib was never charged by the US, Williams's successor, Attorney-General Philip Ruddock, and the Foreign Affairs

[44] ibid, 193.

[45] ibid.

[46] Thom, *Inquiry into the Actions of Australian Government Agencies in Relation to the Arrest and Detention Overseas of Mr Mamdouh Habib from 2001 to 2005*, 101.

[47] Alexander Downer and Philip Ruddock, 'Statement on Mamdouh Habib', joint media release, 11 January 2005.

[48] Alexander Downer, 'Mamdouh Habib arrives in Australia', media release, 28 January 2005.

[49] Daryl Williams, 'Detention of David Hicks doorstop interview Perth', 14 January 2002, http://pandora.nla.gov.au/pan/21248/20030501-0000/www.ag.gov.au/www/attorneygeneralHome.nsf/Web+Pages/F7B4712B843C3436CA256B650077666F02ec.html?OpenDocument.

Minister, Alexander Downer, noted in a press release, 'It remains the strong view of the United States that, based on information available to it, Mr Habib had prior knowledge of the terrorist attacks on or before 11 September 2001'.[50] The Howard Government's continued support for Habib's detention until 2005 is surprising when considered alongside the views of Australian intelligence and security agencies. The AFP told the Howard Government in August 2002 there was insufficient evidence to prosecute Habib, while ASIO formed the view in March or April 2002 that 'there was no legitimate reason for Habib [to be] anywhere but in Australia'.[51]

Another feature of the Howard Government's position on Hicks and Habib was an ongoing failure to question the harsh conditions of their detention at Guantánamo Bay. For example, the Government did not object to US decisions to withhold Geneva Conventions protections and not allow consular access.[52] For many years the Howard Government also supported the indefinite nature of Hicks's and Habib's detention. Prime Minister Howard agreed with a radio journalist's proposition in 2002, for instance, that it was 'fair' that Hicks be held in indefinite detention, 'given the circumstances of Afghanistan'.[53] Neither the Attorney-General nor the head of his department expressed concern about the denial of access to legal representation.[54] In 2004, when Habib still had not had access to a lawyer, Robert Cornall, Secretary of the Attorney-General's Department, observed under questioning in a parliamentary committee that this was 'because defence lawyers are only appointed after people are nominated for eligibility for prosecution'. Cornall did not know what the criteria for eligibility for prosecution were.[55]

The Howard Government also offered unquestioning support of the US military commissions at Guantánamo Bay; indeed, it was argued that no other government was so willing to endorse their legitimacy.[56] When the US Defense Department named Hicks in July 2003 as one of the first six detainees to be tried under the new process, the Prime Minister reacted with indifference. 'The question of who may or may not be facing trial in the United States is a matter for the United States to announce because the United States has these people in custody', he said.[57] The Howard Government did eventually seek and win some concessions in relation to Hicks's military commission, including a guarantee that the death penalty would

[50] Downer and Ruddock, 'Statement on Mamdouh Habib.'

[51] Thom, *Inquiry into the Actions of Australian Government Agencies in Relation to the Arrest and Detention Overseas of Mr Mamdouh Habib from 2001 to 2005*, 58.

[52] 'Hicks among fighters detained by US', *7.30 Report*, ABC, 17 January 2002 (Daryl Williams).

[53] 'The Prime Minister the Hon John Howard MP interview with Neil Mitchell, 3AW', 3AW, 2 August 2002.

[54] Williams, 'Detention of David Hicks doorstop interview Perth'.

[55] Evidence to Senate Legal and Constitutional Affairs Committee, Budget Estimates, Parliament of Australia, Canberra, 24 May 2004 (Robert Cornall) 17–18.

[56] Timothy McCormack, 'David Hicks and the charade of Guantánamo Bay', *Melbourne Journal of International Law* 8(2) (2007), 291.

[57] John Howard, 'Transcript of the Prime Minister the Hon John Howard MP doorstop interview, Roma', 4 July 2003.

not apply to Australians. However, when other requests were rejected—such as a more independent review process—Australia accepted this, unlike the UK.[58] Even when the governments, militaries and judiciaries of its war on terror allies rejected military commissions on the basis that they were fundamentally flawed, Australia continued to publicly back them. When the UK Attorney-General announced that his Government believed the military commissions did not afford sufficient guarantees of a fair trial according to international standards, Prime Minister Howard commented that it had been years 'since an Australian Attorney-General felt automatically bound to accede to the views of a British Attorney-General'.[59] When correspondence between US military commission prosecutors was published in 2005 disclosing that they held serious reservations that the process was 'rigged', Attorney-General Ruddock said the concerns had 'no substance'.[60] When the US Supreme Court ruled in *Hamdan v Rumsfeld* that the military commissions were illegal, Prime Minister Howard defended his Government's support for the process, saying 'our advice had been … that it was lawful'.[61] The Howard Government was similarly dismissive of domestic legal concerns about the military commission process. For example, barrister Lex Lasry QC was appointed independent observer of Hicks's military commission by the Law Council of Australia (LCA), and issued a critical report stating that the proceedings were flawed and a miscarriage of justice was highly likely.[62] Ruddock's response was to accuse Lasry of 'chauvinism' and remark that the report 'could have been written without in fact travelling to Guantánamo Bay'.[63]

A further feature of the Howard Government's position on the detention of Hicks and Habib concerned their claims of abuse and torture. The Government's attitude on the broader issue of the use of torture in the war on terror was one of ambivalence, bordering at times on endorsement. For instance, in response to the Abu Ghraib torture revelations, Prime Minister Howard made a moral distinction between torture committed by the Americans and by Saddam Hussein's regime. The latter, he implied, was worse. 'The prisoner abuse thing is terrible. But it is being dealt with and that is the difference', the Prime Minister said.[64]

[58] Sales, *Detainee 002*, 97.

[59] 'The Prime Minister The Hon John Howard MP interview with Tony Jones, Lateline, ACT TV', *Lateline*, ABC, 1 July 2004.

[60] 'News Focus', *Sydney Morning Herald*, 4 August 2005, 4.

[61] 'The Prime Minister the Hon John Howard MP interview with Neil Mitchell, Radio 3AW, Melbourne', 3AW, 30 June 2006.

[62] Lex Lasry QC, 'United States v David Matthew Hicks first report of the independent legal observer for the Law Council of Australia—September 2004', Law Council of Australia, 30 August 2004, http://www.lawcouncil.asn.au/lawcouncil/images/LCA-PDF/a-z-docs/Hicks_first_report.pdf.

[63] Cynthia Banham, Cosima Mariner and Penelope Debelle, 'No justice for Hicks in flawed trial: QC', *Sydney Morning Herald*, 16 September 2004, 3.

[64] 'The Prime Minister the Hon John Howard MP interview with Tracey Grimshaw, Today Show, Channel Nine,' *Today Show*, Channel Nine, 20 May 2004.

Similarly, Attorney-General Ruddock stated that he did not regard sleep deprivation as torture.[65]

With regard to the particular torture allegations of Hicks and Habib, the Howard Government cast doubt on the men's claims. In 2004, when the lawyers for Hicks and Habib aired claims about their clients' possible abuse, Prime Minister Howard suggested they should be taken 'with a grain of salt'.[66] 'I find it strange that these allegations of abuse against Mr Hicks and Mr Habib have arisen only since the prisoner abuse scandal erupted in relation to the American forces', Prime Minister Howard said. It was subsequently revealed that the Government had known about their abuse claims since at least 2002.[67] When Habib returned to Australia and described his torture in a television interview, the Government cast aspersions over his credibility and character.[68] The AFP Commissioner, Mick Keelty, told a parliamentary committee that Habib had concocted allegations of kidnapping and torture as a cover 'for the period of time that he had been in Afghanistan with al Qaeda'.[69]

The Howard Government professed ignorance of the circumstances surrounding Habib's rendition to Egypt, shirking responsibility for what happened to him. At first the Government suggested that Habib had been sent to Egypt at the Egyptian Government's request.[70] Then, in 2004, the Pakistani Interior Minister disclosed that Habib was transferred at the behest of the Americans.[71] A journalist asked Foreign Affairs Minister Downer whether Habib's rendition was raised with the US. 'Well, I don't have all—I don't have all the details of that. I don't have any evidence that the Americans took him there ... There are a lot of different ways you can get from Pakistan to Egypt', Downer said.[72] The Howard Government also used the fact that Egypt never officially acknowledged it had Habib in its custody to evade answering questions about his treatment.[73] Downer said, 'for all I know he may have been badly treated in Egypt but we don't know because the Egyptians have still not conceded to us that they held him'.[74]

While the Howard Government maintained it had no knowledge of plans for Habib's rendition to Egypt, Australia was consulted on a number of occasions in

[65] 'Quick trial for Hicks essential: Ruddock', *Insiders*, ABC, 1 October 2006.

[66] The Prime Minister the Hon John Howard MP interview with Tracey Grimshaw, *Today Show*, Channel Nine.

[67] Thom, *Inquiry into the Actions of Australian Government Agencies in Relation to the Arrest and Detention Overseas of Mr Mamdouh Habib from 2001 to 2005*, 68, 87.

[68] 'Interview: Alexander Downer', *Sunday*, Channel Nine, 13 February 2005.

[69] Evidence to Senate Legal and Constitutional Affairs Committee, 15 February 2005, 7.

[70] Robert Hill, 'Transcript press conference Commonwealth Parliamentary Offices Adelaide', 19 February 2002, http://pandora.nla.gov.au/pan/33784/20030619-0000/www.minister.defence.gov.au/ HillSpeechtpl0eb7.html?CurrentId=1403.

[71] 'The trials of Mamdouh Habib', *Dateline*, SBS, 7 July 2004 (Bronwyn Adcock).

[72] 'Interview: Alexander Downer', *Sunday*, Channel Nine, 13 February 2005.

[73] Evidence to Senate Legal and Constitutional Affairs Committee, Budget Estimates, Parliament of Australia, Canberra, 24 May 2004 (Robert Cornall), 17.

[74] 'Interview—2UE IV with John Laws—Habib', 2UE, 14 February 2005 (Alexander Downer).

October and November 2001. Habib's possible transfer was discussed at an informal meeting of senior government officials in Canberra on 24 October 2001.[75] An ASIO intelligence report of this meeting noted that after consulting with other government agencies, it had advised a foreign government that 'we could not knowingly agree to Habib being sent to Egypt given that there is no warrant for his arrest and given Egypt's poor human rights record'.[76] The Inspector-General subsequently described ASIO's formulation of words as 'an unfortunate choice' that 'risks being misinterpreted as Australia possibly being willing to turn a blind eye to the transfer'.[77]

Another way the Howard Government avoided questions over Hicks's and Habib's torture allegations was to rely wholly on the results of US investigations into the men's claims, refusing to conduct its own independent inquiry. The US investigations cleared American personnel of wrongdoing.[78] When the independence and reliability of the US investigations were questioned, the Howard Government took exception. Downer suggested, '[I]f that's someone's view of America I suppose nothing will help those people.'[79] Howard labelled such questions 'cynical'.[80]

The Inspector-General of Intelligence and Security, Vivienne Thom, noted the Government's reluctance to examine Habib's allegations of torture in Egypt in her report.When Habib reported his torture to Australian officials visiting Guantánamo Bay in 2002, it was 'not apparent that the Australian Government undertook further liaison with the US, Pakistan or Egyptian Governments at this time with respect to Mr Habib's allegations'.[81] The Howard Government's disregard for accountability over claims that an Australian citizen was tortured was again evident in 2005. Attorney-General Ruddock, asked by a journalist whether it was time to ask the US about Habib's rendition, replied, '[W]hat would be the value of it? To make it public?'[82]

The Howard Government's indifference towards the welfare of citizens at Guantánamo Bay came under challenge in 2006, when a discernible shift occurred

[75] Thom, *Inquiry into the Actions of Australian Government Agencies in Relation to the Arrest and Detention Overseas of Mr Mamdouh Habib from 2001 to 2005*, 47–48.

[76] ibid, 34.

[77] ibid, 35.

[78] Alexander Downer, 'Investigation into allegations of mistreatment of Guantánamo Bay detainees', media release, 26 August 2004, www.foreignminister.gov.au/releases/2004/fa126_04.html; John Howard, 'Transcript of the Prime Minister the Hon John Howard MP doorstop interview, the Willard Intercontinental Hotel, Washington DC', 16 July 2005, http://pandora.nla.gov.au/pan/10052/20050821-0000/www.pm.gov.au/news/interviews/Interview1465.html.

www.foreignminister.gov.au/releases/2004/fa126_04.html.

http://pandora.nla.gov.au/pan/10052/20050821-0000/www.pm.gov.au/news/interviews/Interview1465.html.

[79] Alexander Downer, 'Doorstop Adelaide', 26 August 2004.

[80] Howard, 'Transcript of the Prime Minister the Hon John Howard MP doorstop interview, the Willard Intercontinental Hotel, Washington DC'.

[81] Thom, *Inquiry into the Actions of Australian Government Agencies in Relation to the Arrest and Detention Overseas of Mr Mamdouh Habib from 2001 to 2005*, 79.

[82] 'The extraordinary rendition of Mamdouh Habib', *Dateline*, SBS, 9 March 2005 (Bronwyn Adcock).

in the public mood over the treatment of Hicks. The change in Australian public sentiment was signalled by the number of government backbenchers voicing concerns about Hicks, first in the party room and eventually publicly. The backbenchers reflected the growing concerns of their constituents.[83] Some were also influenced by the sustained advocacy of Hicks's American military lawyer, Major Mori.[84] The MPs were accompanied by a chorus of high-profile Australians who, during 2006 and early 2007, vented concerns over Hicks's continuing detention without trial—concerns that deepened when the *Hamdan v Rumsfeld* decision threw the military commission system into chaos.[85] These public figures included former High Court justices, diplomats, state premiers and a prime minister, as well as current State attorneys-general, church leaders, a State director of public prosecutions, military lawyers and the AFP Commissioner.[86]

At the close of 2006, a poll commissioned by the grassroots political group GetUp! found that 71 per cent of Australians believed that Hicks should be returned home, even if he was not charged.[87] With a federal election looming in 2007, the media reported that Hicks had become a political problem for Prime Minister Howard.[88] Howard acknowledged this, calling Hicks's ongoing detention without trial a barnacle—an issue 'which really aggravated sections of the electorate for no long-term policy gain and where no important principle was at stake'.[89] With this political realisation, the Government's rhetoric on Hicks changed.[90] Having previously blamed Hicks's lawyers for delays in bringing him to trial because of legal appeals against the fairness of the military commission system, in January 2007 the Prime Minister's focus turned sharply to the Bush Administration. Prime Minister Howard demanded that the US charge Hicks under the new post-*Hamdan v Rumsfeld* military commissions, saying the 'acceptability of him being kept in custody diminishes by the day'.[91]

In February 2007, with government MPs insisting that Prime Minister Howard bring Hicks home 'like the Brits did', and as polls showed voter dissatisfaction over the Government's handling of Hicks at 60 per cent, the US issued Hicks with new charges.[92] Hicks's military commission commenced on 26 March 2007, and

[83] David Marr, 'Australia's most wanted', *Sydney Morning Herald*, 13 January 2007, 21.
[84] Liberal MP, telephone interview, 9 January 2013.
[85] Sales, *Detainee 002*, 206.
[86] ibid, 212–13.
[87] Jonathan Pearlman, 'Most want Hicks to return—poll', *Sydney Morning Herald*, 14 December 2006, 4.
[88] Phillip Coorey, 'A new voice lifts an old story', *Sydney Morning Herald*, 15 December 2006, 13.
[89] Howard, *Lazarus Rising*, 634.
[90] Sales, *Detainee 002*, 213.
[91] John Howard, 'Press conference Parliament House, Canberra', 23 January 2007; Cynthia Banham, 'Federal police chief adds his voice to chorus demanding fair go for Hicks', *Sydney Morning Herald*, 5 January 2007, 5.
[92] Phillip Coorey and Cynthia Banham, 'I could free Hicks, but won't: PM', *Sydney Morning Herald*, 7 February 2007; Phillip Coorey, 'Prime Minister feeling the heat over Hicks', *Sydney Morning Herald*, 12 February 2007, 7; Sales, *Detainee 002*, 254.

his plea deal was finalised the same day.[93] Hicks has since complained of political interference by Australia in the decision by the US to prosecute him, a claim backed by the chief prosecutor at his trial, Colonel Morris Davis.[94]

The Rudd and Gillard Governments

The Rudd Government maintained some aspects of its predecessor's approach towards Hicks and Habib. For example, it placed Hicks under a control order in accordance with the Australian Criminal Code Act 1995 (section 104.4) for a year when he was released from prison in Australia, effectively legitimising his military commission plea deal.[95] The Rudd Government also continued to fight a Federal Court claim Habib brought against the Commonwealth after his return to Australia.[96] Habib alleged that officers of the Commonwealth aided, abetted and counselled his torture by foreign officials in Pakistan, Afghanistan, Egypt and Guantánamo Bay.[97] The Rudd Government resisted calls for an independent inquiry into Habib's allegations of torture, despite new evidence emerging from Senate committee hearings about the Australian Government's prior knowledge of his rendition to Egypt.[98] Instead, it pointed to the findings of the US Naval Criminal Investigative Service (NCIS) inquiry that, it noted, had found 'no evidence of maltreatment or abuse' of Hicks or Habib.

In December 2010, the Gillard Government settled Habib's Federal Court case against the Commonwealth for an undisclosed sum.[99] Following the settlement, Prime Minister Gillard asked the Inspector-General of Intelligence and Security to conduct an inquiry into the actions of Australian intelligence agencies in relation to Habib's arrest and detention overseas from 2001 to 2005.[100] An unclassified version of the Inspector-General's report was released in March 2012.

Thom made a number of findings that were critical of Australian government agencies over their handling of Habib's case, but ultimately found that no Australian officials knew where in Egypt he was detained, nor attended his place

[93] Sales, *Detainee 002*, 254.

[94] Hicks, *Communication to the United Nations Human Rights Committee*, 40; Josh White, 'Politics of Guantánamo exposed', *Sydney Morning Herald*, 30 April 2008, 8.

[95] Independent National Security Legislation Monitor, 'Declassified Annual Report', 20 December 2012, 21.

[96] Joel Gibson, 'Lawyer tells court Habib case outside its jurisdiction', *Sydney Morning Herald*, 15 September 2009, 2.

[97] *Habib v Commonwealth of Australia* [2010] FCAFC 12 [2] (Black CJ).

[98] Deborah Snow and David Marr, 'Sitting alone on our hands', *Sydney Morning Herald*, 16 May 2009, 6.

[99] Media reported that the Government settled Habib's claim after the emergence of new witness statements, including from a former Egyptian military intelligence officer, allegedly implicating Australian officials in his torture in Egypt. See Sally Neighbour, 'Mamdouh Habib's story is backed by evidence', *Australian*, 15 January 2011, 12.

[100] Thom, *Inquiry into the Actions of Australian Government Agencies in Relation to the Arrest and Detention Overseas of Mr Mamdouh Habib from 2001 to 2005*, 12–13.

of detention, nor were present during his interrogations.[101] Thom found, however, that ASIO should have made enquiries about how he would be treated in Egypt before providing information for use in his questioning there.[102] She also found that although Australian officials 'gave strong and consistent messages' to foreign governments that they would not agree to his transfer to Egypt, the head of ASIO did not take sufficient action to advise relevant ministers or the Department of Foreign Affairs and Trade that there was an urgent need for Australia to escalate its objections to this occurring.[103] In addition, Thom said, once Habib was at Guantánamo Bay, Australia had 'insufficient regard' to the fact he was held without charge and without access to any legal process for a significant period of time.[104]

In July 2011, with the Gillard Government still in power, the Commonwealth Director of Public Prosecutions (DPP) launched proceedings against Hicks under the Proceeds of Crime Act 2002 for royalties received from his memoirs, published in 2010.[105] The laws used to prosecute Hicks contained amendments made by the Howard Government in 2004 that were specifically aimed at Hicks and Habib and at hindering their capacity to reveal details of their treatment once released.[106] The DPP discontinued the proceedings against Hicks in July 2012 when new evidence was produced by Hicks's legal team concerning the reliability of his admissions in the US military commission.[107]

Parliament

The Australian Parliament provided modest accountability of the executive's actions on Hicks and Habib. This occurred mainly through the Senate, with its strong committee system. The federal opposition was largely ineffective in challenging the Howard Government's position on the treatment of Australians detained at Guantánamo Bay.

In the immediate aftermath of 9/11, the Labor Party, the largest federal opposition party, was demoralised and divided, experiencing five leadership changes in 11 years. Labor's confidence was shattered by its defeat at the 2001 federal election—an election fought over asylum seekers and national security—and the federal parliamentary party was racked by fear of being viewed by voters as

[101] ibid, 6.
[102] ibid, 7.
[103] ibid, 7–8.
[104] ibid, 8.
[105] Verity Edwards and Paul Maley, 'Prosecutors move on Hicks royalties,' *Australian*, 21 July 2011, 1.
[106] Anti-Terrorism Act 2004 (Cth); Jenny Hocking, 'Academic freedom in Australia in an age of terror,' in *Free Speech in Fearful Times: After 9/11 in Canada, the US, Australia and Europe*, ed James L Turk and Allan Manson (Toronto: James Lorimer and Company Ltd, 2007): 223.
[107] Commonwealth Director of Public Prosecutions, 'Statement in the matter of David Hicks', 24 July 2012, https://www.cdpp.gov.au/sites/g/files/net391/f/MR-20120724-David-Hicks.pdf.

weak on terrorism.[108] The issue of preserving civil liberties in the war on terror caused internal divisions inside Labor, with those advocating for human rights a distinct minority.[109] This attitude extended to Hicks and Habib, who were commonly viewed within the ALP as 'electoral poison'.[110] To be seen advocating for their rights in the years immediately after 9/11 would 'have been seen to be defending terrorists—that would have been an explosive position to have been held by the leadership'.[111] As a result, for most of Hicks's and Habib's detention at Guantánamo Bay, the Labor Party remained quiet, sharing the Government's assessment that most Australians had no sympathy for the men.[112]

The Opposition's approach towards Hicks and Habib was distinct from that of the Government in a couple of ways. One was that Labor lacked a consistent policy. Its position with respect to Australia's obligations to stand up for its citizens' rights was influenced by the views of the party leader at the time. Labor's leader from 2001 to 2003, Simon Crean, repeatedly called for Hicks and Habib to be returned to Australia and tried at home.[113] By contrast, the Labor leader from 2003 to 2005, Mark Latham, agreed with the Government that Habib's torture allegations should be treated with suspicion.[114] Latham's successor, Kim Beazley, who led the Opposition from 2005 to 2006, disregarded Habib's torture allegations completely. Following Habib's return to Australia, Beazley declared that the Senate 'should not waste a minute' seeking his testimony about his detention.[115] This was at odds with the position of his Shadow Attorney-General, Nicola Roxon, who labelled Habib's torture allegations 'very serious'.[116]

Labor's attitude towards Hicks was also characterised by opportunism. Labor became more critical of the Government's position on Hicks in 2006, as public concern over the length of his detention without trial intensified. Rudd, who was then Opposition leader, called for the closure of Guantánamo Bay and a fair trial for Hicks.[117] However, once the plea deal was announced, Rudd advocated

108 David Marr and Marian Wilkinson, *Dark Victory* (Sydney: Allen & Unwin, 2003); David Wright-Neville, 'The politics of fear: Counter-terrorism and Australian democracy', Working Paper No 27/2006, *Real Instituto Elcano*, 19 October 2006, 13.

109 MP, tel interview, 10 January 2013.

110 MP, tel interview, 15 January 2013.

111 Labor Senator, tel interview, 17 January 2013.

112 Sales, *Detainee 002*, 220.

113 Carol Altmann, Robert Garran, Rebecca Digirolamo and Andrew McGarry, 'The Taliban the army rejected', *Australian*, 14 December 2001, 1; Mark Riley and Brad Norrington, 'We're not against you: Labor', *Sydney Morning Herald*, 24 October 2003, 6; 'Hicks deserves fair trial: Labor', *Lateline*, ABC, 8 February 2002 (Daryl Melham).

114 Martin Chulov and John Kerin, 'Terrorist suspect "tortured"', *Australian*, 21 May 2004, 1.

115 'Habib granted right of reply', *PM*, ABC, 18 February 2005 (Kim Beazley).

116 Cynthia Banham, 'Government failed to protect a citizen, say human rights groups', *Sydney Morning Herald*, 13 January 2005, 7.

117 Matthew Franklin and Dennis Shanahan, 'Rudd follows mentor's mantra', *Australian*, 16 December 2006, 1.

allowing the US military commission system, which he had previously described as unfair, to unfold without impediment.[118]

The Howard Government did, however, come under more scrutiny regarding its position on detainees in the Senate. The Senate usually wields considerable power in Australia's federal parliamentary system.[119] Australia's Senate is elected by a different voting system from the government-dominated House of Representatives, and the minority parties often hold the balance of power. While the House of Representatives is the scene of partisan clashes, the Senate tends to be a more considered forum for scrutinising government legislation and policy through its robust committee system. Harry Evans, a former clerk of the Australian Senate, argued that the Senate plays a critical role in constraining arbitrary political power and that, without it, governments would be 'freer to practise malfeasance and concealment'.[120] The effectiveness of the Senate, however, depends on its not being under government control (the Howard Government achieved a majority in the Senate in 2005).[121]

One of the Senate's most important roles in checking the executive is its inquiry function, which gives it the power to compel governments to provide information and explain themselves in ways that would otherwise not be required.[122] Parliamentary committee systems often serve as the only forum in which civil servants can be questioned and speak publicly about governmental policy and actions, since they are not able to speak freely to the media.[123] Australia's Senate committee system is praised for providing locations for strengthening government–citizen connections and broadening participation in the deliberative process.[124]

The Senate inquiry system facilitated executive accountability on the Hicks and Habib cases during Howard's prime ministership and beyond, particularly in terms of obtaining information from the Government that would otherwise have remained secret. Senators from Labor, the Australian Greens and the Australian Democrats used Senate Estimates hearings, the specific role of which is to scrutinise government expenditure, to pursue departmental and agency officials for information about Hicks and Habib. After Habib's repatriation, for example, senators obtained details from public officials about Australia's involvement in and

[118] Coorey, 'Prime Minister feeling the heat over Hicks'; Phillip Coorey, 'Plea fails to legitimise trial, rights group say', *Sydney Morning Herald*, 29 March 2007, 8.

[119] Larkin and Uhr, 'Bipartisanship, partnership and bicameralism in Australia's "war on terror"', 136.

[120] Harry Evans, 'The case for bicameralism' in *Restraining Elective Dictatorship: The Upper House Solution?*, ed Nicholas Aroney, Scott Prasser and JR Nethercote (Crawley: University of Western Australia Press, 2008) 77.

[121] ibid, 71.

[122] ibid, 75.

[123] Philip Norton, *Parliament in British Politics* (London: Palgrave MacMillan, 2005) 120.

[124] David Smith, *The Canadian Senate in Bicameral Perspective* (Toronto: University of Toronto Press, 2003) 124.

knowledge of his rendition to Egypt. In hearings in 2005, the heads of the AFP and ASIO revealed for the first time that their officers and agents interviewed Habib in Pakistan in 2001; that he made allegations of mistreatment in 2001 and 2002; and that ASIO established that Habib was 'definitely' in Egypt by 2002.[125] In 2008, Australian officials confirmed in the Senate Estimates process that the US had consulted the Australian Government before sending Habib to Egypt.[126]

The Senate committee process was important for accountability on Habib's case partly because it was easier (more politically acceptable) for the federal Opposition to pursue such issues in that forum. A senator explained:

> The Senate committees, I think, have got their potential to highlight issues in a way that the House of Representatives doesn't, and in a way that is actually acceptable to the broader community. So I didn't have to say 'Habib needs to be let free', but I could ask questions about his treatment in a way that agencies were starting to worry about what the opposition knew.[127]

The Senate inquiry process was also useful for advocates of Hicks and Habib, some of whom worked with senators from the minority parties to directly question government agencies.[128]

The Courts

Australian courts ultimately played a small role in checking executive government policies on Hicks and Habib, though they displayed a readiness to scrutinise the Government's actions regarding the citizens' treatment. The men launched litigation suing the Federal Government over its failure to protect their rights only after a number of years had passed.

Habib launched an action in the High Court after his return to Australia, alleging that Commonwealth officers were complicit in his torture by foreign states while detained overseas (the matter was transferred to the Federal Court).[129] The Gillard Government settled Habib's claim in 2010. Hicks's legal team launched an action in the Federal Court in 2006, arguing that the Commonwealth was responsible for his ongoing wrongful internment.[130] His case was discontinued when

[125] Evidence to Senate Legal and Constitutional Affairs Committee 15 February 2005, 5–7 (Keelty); ibid, 31 (Richardson).

[126] Paul O'Sullivan, Director-General, Australian Security Intelligence Organisation, to Senator Patricia Crossin, Chair Senate Standing Committee on Legal and Constitutional Affairs, 23 June 2008.

[127] Labor senator, tel interview, 17 January 2013.

[128] Greens senator, tel interview, 9 January 2013.

[129] *Habib v Commonwealth of Australia* [2006] HCA Trans 202 (26 April 2006).

[130] *Hicks v Ruddock* [2007] FCA 299.

the Howard Government brought him home. Despite this, the Australian courts demonstrated a greater willingness to examine the executive government's actions with respect to Hicks's and Habib's treatment and detention than, arguably, courts in the US or UK.[131]

In both men's cases, the Federal Court rejected the Government's argument that it lacked jurisdiction because of the 'act of state doctrine' (the principle that courts will not make findings about the unlawfulness of an act of a foreign state) and agreed to hear the men's claims.[132] In *Hicks v Ruddock*, the Court determined that the area of law regarding the act of state doctrine was one where principles were still developing and there were no clear authorities justifying judgment against Hicks. Justice Tamberlin, in rejecting the Government's application seeking summary judgment on the basis of the act of state doctrine, also noted:

> It must be kept firmly in mind that this case concerns the fundamental right to have cause shown as to why a citizen is deprived of liberty for more than five years in a place where he has not had access to the benefit of a duly constituted court without valid charge.[133]

Justice Tamberlin observed that if Hicks were to succeed in his Statement of Claim, his military commission trial at Guantánamo Bay 'may be found to be contrary to the requirements of international law'.[134] This indicates that the *Hicks* case had the potential to subject Guantánamo Bay and the use of military commissions to trial in Australian courts.[135] Justice Tamberlin also considered the UK case of *Abbasi v Secretary of State*, discussed in Chapter 6, in which a UK citizen at Guantánamo Bay sought a court order forcing the Blair Government to make representations on his behalf to the US.[136] The UK Court of Appeal, though critical of the Guantánamo Bay detention regime, declined to issue such an order on the grounds that courts should not interfere in the conduct of foreign relations by the executive. Justice Tamberlin distinguished the two cases, saying that at the time of the *Abbasi* decision, internment had lasted for only eight months and there was the prospect of appellate review in the US courts. In Hicks's case, the injustice 'could be seen to be substantially greater', given the internment had now lasted for over five years with no similar prospect of any alleviation of the detainee's predicament.[137]

The Federal Court's boldness in being prepared to review executive action, even when courts overseas were not willing to do so, was also evident in the *Habib* litigation. In *Habib v Commonwealth of Australia*, the Government again tried unsuccessfully to dispose of the claim by seeking summary judgment relying

[131] Kent Roach, 'Substitute justice? Challenges to American counterterrorism activities in non-American courts', *Mississippi Law Journal* 82(5) (2013), 923, 926.
[132] *Hicks v Ruddock* [2007] FCA 299 [5].
[133] ibid, [90].
[134] ibid.
[135] Roach, 'Substitute justice?', 923.
[136] *Abbasi v Secretary of State* [2002] EWCA Civ 1598.
[137] *Hicks v Ruddock* [2007] FCA 299 [86].

on the act of state doctrine. The Court found that neither the common law nor domestic torture legislation supported the application of the act of state doctrine where grave breaches of human rights were affected. The 'heart of the matter', Justice Perram said, was the allegation that Commonwealth officers acted outside the law:

> The justiciability of such allegations is axiomatic and could not be removed by Parliament still less the common law. No doubt comity between the nations is a fine and proper thing but it provides no basis whatsoever for this Court declining to exercise the jurisdiction conferred on it by Parliament.[138]

This view contrasts with that of the US courts which, as noted in Chapter 4, were more deferential to executive claims of 'state secrets' in cases involving extraordinary rendition.[139] Chief Justice Black also remarked upon the gravity of the acts in which the Commonwealth was alleged to have been complicit, namely torture. He noted, 'the status of the prohibition against torture as a peremptory norm of international law from which no derogation is permitted and the consensus of the international community that torture can never be justified by official acts or policy'.[140]

The Federal Court's position in the *Habib* case is consistent with that taken by the UK courts in the *Binyam Mohamed* litigation, discussed in the next chapter.[141] In both cases, courts were unwilling to accept the presumption that national security concerns should automatically trump the public interest in open justice, especially as concerned allegations about state use of or complicity in torture.[142] Habib's Federal Court case contributed to the Gillard Government's decision not only to settle his claim, but also to order the Inspector-General's inquiry.[143] It demonstrates how, even when lawsuits are settled by governments wishing to avoid revealing state secrets, they may still help create the conditions under which accountability in some other form is demanded.[144]

Hicks and Habib found a receptive judicial forum in which to pursue their legal claims against the Australian Government for their treatment in detention in the war on terror, despite Australia—unlike other liberal democracies—not having a bill of rights. While this did not inhibit the courts' resolve to scrutinise executive action in the war on terror, I argue below that the same cannot be said of the impact that the absence of a bill of rights had on civil society activism.

138 *Habib v Commonwealth of Australia* [2010] FCAFC 12 [37] (Perram J).

139 See, eg, *Arar v. Ashcroft*, 585 F 3d 559 (2d Cir 2009).

140 *Habib v Commonwealth of Australia* [2010] FCAFC 12 [9] (Black CJ).

141 *The Queen on the Application of Binyam Mohamed v Secretary of State for Foreign and Commonwealth Affairs* [2010] EWCA Civ 65.

142 Roach, 'Substitute justice?' 927.

143 Labor MP, tel interview, 24 January 2013.

144 Roach, 'Substitute justice?', 928.

Civil Society

Civil society in Australia in the early years after 9/11 exerted little pressure on the Howard Government over the treatment of the two Australians detained at Guantánamo Bay. While this changed over time, particularly in relation to Hicks's detention as it extended into a sixth year, civil society never mobilised to any significant extent around the issue of torture and the need for a public inquiry into the men's claims. In this section, I describe civil society in Australia and outline the main actors involved in the detainee cases, as well as some features of civil society's behaviour in relation to the Hicks and Habib cases. These include its delayed start, the influence of victim likeability on campaigning, and its focus on legal process.

The Actors

Australia's human rights non-governmental sector was poorly organised after 9/11. Australia had no national human rights NGO.[145] Australian civil society, broadly speaking, did not have the large numbers or the sophistication of human rights NGOs in the UK, nor did it have the reputation for effectiveness on international human rights of Canadian civil society (see Chapters 6 and 7). Australia's modest human rights sector also confronted an overwhelmingly high volume of human rights issues after 9/11, including the Federal Government's draconian new counter-terrorism laws and harsh asylum-seeker policies. Compounding the sector's limited resources was the panic engendered by 9/11, similar to the situation across different liberal democracies. It meant that any issue linked to national security was easily and readily politicised, which created risks for NGOs advocating on human rights in the war on terror. For example, one lawyer said those advocating for the rights of Australians at Guantánamo Bay were 'treated as apologists for terrorism', and those prepared to do such work were 'very much in the minority'.[146]

I identify five categories of civil society actors involved in the Hicks and Habib cases, and examine their actions across the period 2001 to 2010. Among the legal profession the most prominent was the peak national body, the Law Council of Australia (LCA), with other active groups including the International Commission of Jurists Australian section (ICJ) and the Human Rights Law Centre (HRLC) (established in 2005, previously the Human Rights Law Resource Centre). A small number of human rights and other NGOs were active. They included the New South Wales Council for Civil Liberties (NSWCCL), GetUp!, a web-based political movement also set up in 2005, and Amnesty International's Australian section.

[145] Simon Rice and Scott Calnan, *Sustainable Advocacy: Capabilities and Attitudes of Australian Human Rights NGOs* (Sydney: Australian Human Rights Centre, 2007) 20.

[146] Lawyer, tel interview, 8 January 2013.

Muslim community groups included the Australian Federation of Islamic Councils, the country's umbrella Muslim organisation, and the Lebanese Muslim Association, which runs Australia's largest mosque. I also consider the role of media, and closely examine two major Australian broadsheets, the *Australian* (owned by News Limited) and the *Sydney Morning Herald* (owned by Fairfax Media). In addition, I look at the role of personal supporters, including family members, among whom three individuals stand out for their advocacy: Hicks's father, Terry, and his US military lawyer, Major Mori, and Habib's wife, Maha.

As in the US case, not all members of civil society defended the rights of detainees in the war on terror, with some publicly supporting the use of torture. For example, Melbourne legal academics Mirko Bagaric and Julie Clarke argued that torture was morally defensible.[147] They were not isolated in this view, with their position finding support from a former chairman of the National Crime Authority.[148] Support for torture also came from some sections of the media. The *Sydney Morning Herald* supported the prohibition absolutely;[149] the *Australian* argued that there were circumstances in which a democratic government could be obliged to torture. An editorial opined that 'it is possible—possible—to argue that there can be cases in the age of terror where torture is an act democratic governments could be obliged to undertake'.[150] News Limited, which owns the *Australian*, represents 65 per cent of the total metropolitan and daily newspaper market in Australia, and wields substantial influence over public opinion.[151] Its stance on torture illustrates that while media have the potential to play a powerful mobilising role in favour of human rights, media that condone rights abuses can contribute to the reverse outcome.[152]

A Delayed Start

A noticeable feature of civil society's approach towards the situation of Australians at Guantánamo Bay was that, in general, it was slow to organise. Activism only gathered momentum in 2006, a year after Habib had returned home and two years after the UK began repatriating its nationals. In Australia, public opinion often led civil society activism, rather than the other way around. Human rights campaigners talk about the convergence of a number of indirectly connected issues

[147] Mirko Bagaric and Julie Clarke, 'Not enough official torture in the world? The circumstances in which torture is morally justifiable', *University of San Francisco Law Review* 39(3) (2005), 581–616.

[148] Angela O'Connor, 'QC uses Dirty Harry to defend torture', *Age* (Melbourne), 23 May 2005, 3.

[149] 'The torture time bomb' (editorial), *Sydney Morning Herald*, 8 March 2005, 10.

[150] 'Time to ask a very difficult question' (editorial), *Australian*, 18 June 2007, 15.

[151] Ray Finkelstein and Matthew Ricketson, 'Report of the independent inquiry into the media and media regulation', 28 February 2012, 58.

[152] Zehra F Kabasakal Arat, 'Looking beyond the state but not ignoring it' in *Non-State Actors in the Human Rights Universe*, ed George Andreopoulos, Zehra F Kabasakal Arat and Peter Juviler (Bloomfield, CT: Kumarian Press, 2006) 14.

that ultimately turned public opinion as regards Hicks's situation in 2006. They include two high-profile wrongful immigration detention cases, in addition to the protracted length of time Hicks had spent at Guantánamo Bay without trial.[153] One lawyer says it took until Hicks had been in custody for five years without a trial, or much prospect of one, for Australians to begin thinking, 'whatever he's done, this just doesn't seem fair'.[154] Although individuals and organisations in civil society aired concerns over the detention of Hicks and Habib before then, media reporting of the cases in the *Australian* and the *Sydney Morning Herald* prior to 2006 makes it clear this did not occur with any intensity. The churches, for instance, only publicly criticised Australian government policy on Hicks from late 2006 and did not touch the torture issue.[155]

An exception to this delayed civil society response was the LCA, which ran a sustained campaign from 2003. As was the case in the US and the UK, lawyers and legal organisations were the most organised in criticising Australian government policy on detainees, compared to other NGOs. The LCA was highly critical of the Australian Government over its treatment of Hicks and Habib, and issued some 56 press releases on the subject. The organisation was mentioned in at least 26 news articles in the *Sydney Morning Herald* and 18 in the *Australian*—more than any other NGO in the same period (2001–10).[156] Reflecting how sustained its advocacy was, the Howard Government admonished the LCA for its work on Hicks. Attorney-General Ruddock, for example, accused it of 'imperial overreach' and said, 'For the nation's peak professional body to have so little to say about the profession and so much to say about fashionable issues is surprising.'[157]

Apart from the LCA, it took much longer for other parts of civil society to mobilise on the detainee issue. Elsewhere in the legal sector, the ICJ expressed concerns about the Australians at Guantánamo Bay in 2002.[158] However, the ICJ's campaign over Hicks began in earnest in 2006, with the drafting of an open letter to the Prime Minister containing 76 signatories, including four former Supreme Court and Federal Court judges.[159] An ICJ official says by this time Hicks's treatment 'had become a significant electoral image damaging the government, so that a number of us formed the view that we could force Howard's hand by raising the issue'.[160] The timing of the open letter points to the delayed response by Australia's judicial

[153] Civil liberties activist, tel interview, 31 January 2013. The cases involved permanent resident Cornelia Rau in 2005 and Indian national Dr Mohmaed Haneef in 2007.

[154] Lawyer, tel interview, 8 January 2013.

[155] Cameron Stewart, 'The making of a terrorist', *Australian*, 10 March 2007, 1.

[156] Based on a search using the Factiva database.

[157] Philip Ruddock, 'Some lawyers ignore their profession's core values', *Australian*, 3 November 2006, 14.

[158] Cynthia Banham and Gay Alcorn, 'US detention sparks call to protect citizens', *Sydney Morning Herald*, 12 January 2002, 7; Cynthia Banham, Gay Alcorn, Mike Seccombe and Peter Fray, 'A few bad men', *Sydney Morning Herald*, 19 January 2002, 24.

[159] Richard Kerbaj, 'Judges seek fair trial for Hicks', *Australian* (Sydney), 3 June 2006, 2.

[160] ICJ official, tel interview, 20 February 2013.

sphere to the situation of citizens at Guantánamo Bay. At least two former High Court justices had publicly criticised the treatment of detainees before 2005—but five more former and sitting High Court justices did in 2005 and 2006.[161] In 2003, an editorial in the *Sydney Morning Herald* criticised the failure of Australia's judiciary to speak out earlier, drawing a contrast with the UK, where Lord Steyn had publicly condemned the Guantánamo Bay military commissions: 'It is a pity that in Australia, all too few jurists are speaking out in this way.'[162]

The delayed mobilisation of civil society is further illustrated by an examination of the timeline of activism of some of the other more involved civil society groups on Australian detainees. Amnesty International Australia issued some 19 press releases on Hicks and Habib between 2001 and 2010.[163] Its main focus in Australia from 2001 to 2005 was refugees. Its campaign on Hicks accelerated in 2006, a shift coinciding with the visit of the organisation's Secretary-General, Irene Khan, to Australia in that year.[164] One of Amnesty International's most high-profile campaign events following this shift involved touring the eastern States of Australia with a replica of Hicks's cell at Guantánamo Bay.[165] Tellingly, this tour launched in March 2007.

From 2005, GetUp! played an important role in pushing for the release of Hicks. GetUp! is described as 'an independent, not-for-profit campaigning organisation using new technologies to inform, connect and empower Australians to have a voice on a range of national issues'.[166] Hicks's case was one of GetUp!'s core foundation issues. The decision to take it up was driven by member concerns and pressure from Hicks's family and its lobby group, Fair Go For David.[167] It was mid-2006, when GetUp! officials realised that the Hicks case had progressed from being a 'niche' human rights issue into a mainstream political concern. That moment of realisation came when GetUp! organised a public candlelight vigil for Hicks in central Adelaide.[168] It was attended by approximately 2,000 people, of whom an official said, 'I'm not talking ratbag activists but families, mums and dads with grandmothers and kids.'[169]

In the case of the Muslim community, its advocacy for Hicks and Habib remained restrained.[170] The community's reluctance to become associated with the men's cases must be viewed in the context of the suspicion and hostility

[161] For example, see Murray Gleeson, 'A core value', speech delivered at the Judicial Conference of Australia Annual Colloquium, Canberra, 6 October 2006.

[162] 'Guantánamo: Two views of justice' (editorial), *Sydney Morning Herald*, 27 November 2003, 12.

[163] This is based on the Amnesty International website, and the provision by Amnesty International Australia of its records of all press releases on the Hicks and Habib cases.

[164] Amnesty International official, tel interview, 18 January 2013.

[165] Jano Gibson, '1.8m x 2.4m: Living like Hicks', *Sydney Morning Herald*, 19 March 2007.

[166] GetUp!, *Annual Report 2005–2006*, 2006, 5.

[167] GetUp! official, tel interview, 21 February 2013.

[168] 'Hundreds in candlelight vigil for Hicks,' *ABC News*, ABC, 23 August 2006.

[169] GetUp! official, tel interview, 21 February 2013.

[170] Trudy Harris, 'Habib "owes Muslims an explanation"', *Australian*, 16 February 2005, 1. Analysis of Australian media reveals that in 2004, the year before Habib's return to Australia, there were no

Australian Muslims encountered in the wake of 9/11, similar to that in other Western countries. Muslims in Australia felt singled out by the Howard Government's counter-terrorism rhetoric and laws.[171] One Muslim community activist said, 'The political climate immediately following September 11 was very, very tense and certainly many Muslims in Australia were made to feel either unwelcome or to feel that we were under a very huge spotlight.'[172] A Muslim community leader said, 'At that time to show yourself as a leader and to articulate for the Muslim interests or to try and calm the situation you had to be very, very courageous.'[173] Muslim community leaders feared that taking up Hicks's and Habib's causes would invite suspicion. One said that his community 'did not do as much as we could in trying to organise the civil society around what was their incarceration and what was going on'. He explained that the reason 'was we didn't know enough about what their involvement was ... To go and support somebody, you can't do it blindly.'[174] In addition, the key Muslim organisations before 9/11 were divided and plagued by infighting, which diminished their ability to form a united front on political issues.[175] Habib's case stands in contrast to that of Canadian citizen, Maher Arar, who was also subjected to extraordinary rendition: Arar's case became a focal point around which Muslim organisations could mobilise, as discussed in Chapter 7.

Australia's major broadsheet newspapers, the *Australian* and the *Sydney Morning Herald*, displayed little interest in the need for accountability for the alleged torture of Australian detainees in the war on terror. For almost a decade, neither newspaper pushed for an independent commission of inquiry into Hicks's and Habib's allegations.[176] The position of these two publications is especially noteworthy when considered against the background of the Australian newspaper industry's being the most concentrated in the developed world.[177]

The Influence of Victim Likeability

A second feature of Australian civil society activism on Hicks and Habib was that support for the men was often influenced by their personal attributes and the

mentions of Australian Muslim organisations in the *Sydney Morning Herald* in connection with Hicks or Habib. In the *Australian*, two articles mentioned Australian Muslim organisations; one attributed only negative comments about Habib to such organisations. See Cameron Stewart and Trudy Harris, 'Habib recruited for jihad: Cleric', *Australian*, 17 July 2004, 4. See also Cameron Stewart and Louise Perry, 'Australia tarred by US brush in Iraq: Sheikh', *Australian*, 25 May 2004, 3.

[171] Wright-Neville, 'The politics of fear'.

[172] Muslim community activist, tel interview, 14 January 2013.

[173] Muslim community leader, tel interview, 18 January 2013.

[174] ibid.

[175] ibid.

[176] This shifted momentarily in 2011 with respect to Habib. See 'Leaks reveal terrorism concern' (editorial), *Australian*, 28 April 2011, 13.

[177] Finkelstein and Ricketson, 'Report of the independent inquiry into the media and media regulation', 59.

popularity of their family members and close advocates. Hicks became a more popular cause over time through the sustained efforts of his sympathetic father, Terry, and the much admired US military lawyer, Major Mori, while Habib, a divisive figure in the Muslim community, remained an unpopular figure. Habib's Middle Eastern-born Muslim wife, with accented English and head covering, was unable to connect in the same way with the broader Australian public.

Terry Hicks and Mori were sympathetic and articulate figures who engaged frequently with the media. They humanised David Hicks through their careful portrayal of him as a 'naive young man' and 'somebody's son', and because of their loyalty and support, which remained unswerving despite the terrorist accusations against him.[178] Terry Hicks and Mori connected with mainstream Australia for different reasons. Terry Hicks was white, working class, unassuming and unworldly. Political elites described him as 'a quintessential Aussie bloke' and 'a real salt of the earth character' who 'looked like everyone else'.[179] A civil society actor described Terry Hicks as 'everybody's dad … he was so transparent in his love and transparent in the way he communicated'.[180] Hicks's father demonstrated an unconditional love for his wayward son that resonated with the public. His willingness to plunge himself into a deeply unfamiliar world to help David—for instance, standing in a cage and orange jumpsuit on Broadway in New York to raise awareness of his son's plight—ultimately won over many Australians, and earned him sympathetic media coverage.[181] An MP reinforced this view of Terry Hicks, 'Here was the father, like any parents of teenagers, on the airwaves, on the television, pleading for his son, and it brings it home graphically to people.'[182] A civil liberties activist describes the impact the father had in popularising his son's cause over time:

> You had a public sentiment at the time where, frankly, the public couldn't care less if you tortured somebody if they were accused of terrorism. And then it sort of went from one extreme to another where, once David Hicks was humanised by the work his father did, explaining what sort of a person he was, how he was still an idiot, he'd got himself involved in this but did he really deserve to be in Guantánamo Bay and so on, then public sentiment shifted to the other extreme.[183]

Mori's appeal stemmed from his courage, as a relatively junior US marine, in taking on the mighty American Government to defend the rights of his Australian client.[184] The military lawyer's daring advocacy was evident from his first public

[178] Stewart, 'The making of a terrorist', *Australian*, 10 March 2007.
[179] Greens Senator, tel interview, 9 January 2013; Labor Senator, tel interview, 17 January 2013.
[180] GetUp! official, tel interview, 21 February 2013.
[181] Sales, *Detainee 002*, 89.
[182] Liberal MP, tel interview, 9 January 2013.
[183] Civil liberties activist, tel interview, 31 January 2013.
[184] Sales, *Detainee 002*, 221.

press conference in January 2004, when he accused the Australian Government of accepting a lower standard of justice than the UK Government had for its citizens.[185] Mori made frequent trips to Australia to lobby parliamentarians and attend public speaking events.[186] Political elites and civil society actors spoke in reverent terms of his impact. 'Mori was just such a charismatic fellow and such a good advocate', said one.[187] Another noted that 'people were very much inspired by his independence and his capacity to stand up to his own masters'.[188] A third commented that 'his preparedness to be outspoken, given that he was a military lawyer, was very powerful in the end in getting things progressing'.[189]

Compared to Terry Hicks and Mori, who were transformative in moving public opinion around David, Habib's wife faced significant obstacles in attracting similar sympathy for her husband. Though Maha Habib tried to raise awareness of her husband's situation, she was isolated in her advocacy.[190] The *Sydney Morning Herald* described Maha Habib as a 'lonely voice of protest'.[191] Her husband was a polarising figure, unpopular in his local Sydney Muslim community, some of whom described him as 'interfering' and 'aggressive'.[192] The result was that Maha Habib was ostracised both from the Muslim community, because of its dislike of her husband, and from the wider Australian community, because she and Mamdouh were foreign-born Muslims. A Greens Senator who worked closely with Maha Habib and pursued her husband's case in Senate Estimates hearings, says the public response to Habib's wife 'was about not relating to her … People in the Australian community don't connect with Maha in same way because of who she is and her experience in life'.[193] Maha Habib's relationship with the media was more complicated than that of Terry Hicks due to cultural differences. A lawyer says Maha 'didn't have the same comprehension of how the Australian community perceives things as someone born here'.[194] Once he was released from Guantánamo, Habib's Muslim identity, personal attributes and difficulties in communicating alienated him further from the broader public and civil society. 'Terry was able to communicate in a language that people understood and I don't think Mamdouh was able to do that', said a GetUp! official.[195] A Labor MP said, 'We

[185] Marian Wilkinson and Jonathan Pearlman, 'Military trial only option for Hicks, says Ruddock', *Sydney Morning Herald*, 23 January 2004, 6.

[186] Michael Gawenda, 'Tell it to the marine', *Sydney Morning Herald*, 19 November 2005, 30.

[187] Labor MP, tel interview, 24 January 2013.

[188] GetUp! official, tel interview, 21 February 2013.

[189] Torture survivors NGO official, tel interview, 10 April 2013.

[190] Steve Lewis, Patricia Karvelas and Matt Price, 'Defiant Greens vow further disruptions,' *Australian*, 24 October 2003: 3.

[191] Linda Morris, 'From housewife to a freedom fighter,' *Sydney Morning Herald*, 13 January 2005: 13.

[192] 'Worst of the worst?' *Four Corners*, ABC, 20 July 2004 (Sally Neighbour); Stewart and Harris, 'Habib recruited for Jihad: Cleric.'

[193] Greens senator, tel interview, 9 January 2013.

[194] Lawyer, tel interview, 19 January 2013.

[195] GetUp! official, tel interview, 21 February 2013.

regarded him as a bit of a lunatic.'[196] One civil society activist observed that Habib 'didn't endear himself to the broader population. Certainly from the kind of more activist side of civil society there was just as much commitment to his issue, but maybe not as much commitment to him as a person.'[197]

The Habib family's failure to establish a connection with Australians is apparent from the views of parliamentarians and activists, who spoke of Mamdouh Habib's lack of high-profile advocates compared to Hicks. 'I'm not conscious of someone clearly articulating his case the way it was articulated in Hicks's case', said one civil society actor.[198] Habib 'never really had any major supporters in the broader community, so this guy was very much on his own', said a Labor senator.[199] Maha Habib's experiences were also different from those of Monia Mazigh, the wife of Canadian citizen, Arar, despite their common Muslim foreign-born identity. Mazigh's broad public appeal was a critical factor in her husband's case, as discussed in Chapter 7. Mamdouh Habib's unpopularity among the Muslim and broader Australian communities helps explain this disparity in the two wives' experiences. The failure of Habib to connect with the Australian public ultimately affected attitudes towards his torture allegations, which—unlike in Arar's case—were not taken seriously by either political elites or the Australian public. For one Muslim community activist, Habib's religion and background directly contributed to the reluctance of the public and civil society to back his demands for accountability on torture:

> There's an attitude that seems to come across very regularly, and it is really perpetuated through some of the mainstream media, that Muslims are not to be trusted. With respect to the issue of torture, for a long time the comments from the Australian government and comments from some of the more right-wing commentators was that these claims should not be believed.[200]

The contrasting experiences of Hicks's and Habib's inner circles indicate that Australian civil society's willingness to mobilise around the Guantánamo detainee issue depended, to an extent, on the saleability of the individual victim to the wider public. This aspect of civil society's approach illustrates the idea, discussed in Chapter 3, of issue selection by human rights NGOs, where, in the face of harsh political and economic imperatives, some organisations resort to opportunistic behaviour, choosing concerns or cases that are more likely to attract public support. A comparison of the experiences of Terry Hicks and Mori, who both received significantly more media attention than Maha Habib, exemplifies this feature of civil society's activism.[201] An Amnesty International official acknowledged the

[196] Labor MP, tel interview, 24 January 2013.
[197] Civil society activist, tel interview, 2013.
[198] ICJ official, tel interview, 20 February 2013.
[199] Labor senator, tel interview, 17 January 2013.
[200] Muslim community activist, tel interview, 14 January 2013.
[201] Hicks's family and close advocates received greater media attention than Habib's, in part because Hicks was detained for longer. Nevertheless, the disparity is sizeable. At least 69 news articles that

link between the individual's public likeability and the willingness of civil society to take up their causes:

> It really did come down to whether or not a sympathetic and normal picture was able to be painted of that particular individual, so that the ordinary Australian could actually relate to this person and not see them as something completely outside normal … If that was able to be achieved, then it is certainly true to say civil society was much more readily able to get behind that person.[202]

Other actors in the sector did not view this dimension of civil society behaviour as surprising. A lawyer commented that 'I think it's just a quirk of human nature that people like to have someone they can feel sorry for before they can make any emotional investment.'[203] An HRLC official suggested that although civil society often takes up cases where it can get traction, 'they're not necessarily taking it up because they think it's more important or compelling—but because it may be the case through which they can effect change, which then becomes more systemic change'.[204]

The fact that Habib's wife found it more difficult to connect with the broader Australian public than Hicks's personal advocates also suggests that the notion of the 'Other' was at play.[205] David and Terry Hicks, as white men from traditional working-class backgrounds, were familiar and therefore non-threatening to Australians. Their stories—the forgiving father from the suburbs, his prodigal son who came to grief seeking adventure in the wrong places—resonated more readily with the wider Australian public, whose members could identify themselves in those narratives. In a country with a history of institutional racism, including white-only immigration policies, the last vestiges of which were only removed in the 1970s, Habib and his wife were too different.[206] Not only were they Muslim, but they were Muslims who had not assimilated into Australian society. This was evidenced by their imperfect English and the fact that Habib was arrested in Pakistan while seeking opportunities overseas for bringing up his children in a Muslim country.[207] The idea that the Habibs were regarded as 'Other' is evident in the comments of different political elites and civil society actors. For example, a Labor senator noted that 'the media and the public didn't want to know about Habib. He was one of them, [Hicks] was very much one of us'.[208] A civil society

mentioned Terry Hicks appeared in the *Sydney Morning Herald*, and 77 in the *Australian* between 2001 and 2010. For Mori, the volume was also significant: at least 51 in the *Sydney Morning Herald* and 44 in the *Australian*. This compares to some 21 articles in the *Sydney Morning Herald* and 26 in the *Australian* that mentioned Habib's family.

202 Amnesty International official, tel interview, 18 January 2013.
203 Lawyer, tel interview, 8 January 2013.
204 HRLC official, tel interview, 19 June 2013.
205 Edward Said, *Orientalism* (London: Penguin Books, 2003) xii.
206 Commonwealth of Australia, *Fact Sheet 8—Abolition of the 'White Australia' Policy* (2009), Department of Immigration and Border Protection.
207 Habib with Collingwood, *My Story*, 37.
208 Labor senator, tel interview, 17 January 2013.

official observed that 'Hicks being a white Australian, from a working class family, with a senior lawyer from the US military representing him, had a very different presentation to Habib.'[209] The different public attitudes towards Hicks and Habib are a reminder that, after 9/11, not all citizens were necessarily considered equal.

A Focus on Legal Process

A third feature of civil society activism in relation to the Australian detainees is that it concentrated on securing the releases of the Australians and on ensuring they received fair trials—not on torture. Most of these efforts centred on Hicks, since he was detained for longer. Civil society applied no sustained pressure on the Government to hold an independent inquiry into the men's allegations, and the torture issue was rarely mentioned once the men's releases were secured.

The work of the LCA, the most active civil society organisation on the issue of Australians detained at Guantánamo Bay, exemplifies this focus on due process and the US military commissions. Of the 56 press releases produced by the LCA, three mentioned torture and none referred to Habib after January 2005, when he was released from Guantánamo Bay.[210] The bulk of the LCA's interest in the Hicks and Habib cases, and most of its criticism of the Australian Government, was directed at the men's rights to a fair legal hearing. The LCA's busiest year for press releases was 2004, the year it appointed Lasry QC independent observer of Hicks's military commission.[211] Non-governmental organisations issued some calls for an official torture investigation, particularly in relation to Habib's experiences, but this pressure was not sustained.

Similarly, the HRLC, which formed in 2005, produced a legal opinion co-authored by six eminent jurists, barristers and legal academics that focused on the illegality of the military commission process. It argued that Hicks's US military commission breached international and Australian law, and could constitute a war crime under the Criminal Code Act 1995 (which incorporates the Rome Statute of the International Criminal Court into domestic law).[212]

Overall, NGOs were pessimistic about the impact of lobbying over torture accountability in Australia, believing it to be futile. A common attitude expressed by NGO officials was that no government (whether Liberal–National Coalition

[209] Torture survivors NGO official, tel interview, 10 April 2013.

[210] Law Council of Australia, 'Law Council alarmed at Guantánamo Bay torture allegations', media release, 8 October 2003; 'Inquiry into mistreatment of Guantánamo Bay detainees long overdue', media release, 6 May 2004; 'Latest Law Council Report highlights more hurdles for Hicks', media release, 21 July 2005.

[211] This is based on press releases listed on the Law Council of Australia website at www.lca.asn.au.

[212] Alistair Nicholson, Peter Vickery, Hilary Charlesworth, Andrew Byrnes, Gavan Griffith and Tim McCormack, 'David Hicks—Military Commissions Act 2006—Compliance with Common Article 3 of the Geneva Conventions, the *Hamdan* decision and Australian law' (opinion, Human Rights Law Centre, 9 November 2006).

or Labor) would hold a torture inquiry, and arguing for a fair trial and repatriation were more achievable goals. An ICJ official said, 'Issues like that [torture] are murky and people switch off ... there's no point in trying to get the press excited about complicated issues because the press like it simple.'[213] The Amnesty International official said no one in government wanted or saw the need for a torture inquiry:

> The reality is, it is fair to say once David Hicks came home, within a year of coming home, the Australian public went 'yeah, cool, done', so it just wasn't an issue that was ever going to get traction with politicians.[214]

A civil liberties activist said that the sense that lobbying for accountability on torture was pointless was not limited to the Howard Government. His organisation pushed Labor for an inquiry, but 'they just ruled it out and said "we're not going to do it is the answer"'.[215] Meanwhile, Habib had taken his own action and sued the Government, and the activist said, 'at that stage we thought well, it will come out in court'.

Tellingly, when the Gillard Government ordered the Inspector-General of Intelligence and Security inquiry into Habib's case, it was not precipitated by civil society pressure (given that activists were not specifically pushing for a torture inquiry).[216] Rather, it came about because civil servants followed the 'logic of appropriateness' characteristic of formal democratic institutions.[217] Bureaucrats from the Attorney-General's Department were concerned about being 'proper about process and procedure'. They recommended that, because Habib had raised allegations in court about the Australian Government's complicity in his torture that would not be tested with the settlement of his claim, an inquiry should be held to 'tie off the ends'.[218] I explore the reasons for civil society's pessimism regarding demands for accountability for torture in the next section.

Enabling and Constraining Activism

Australia responded with indifference to the torture allegations of citizens detained in the war on terror. Australia had an executive government deeply committed to the US alliance and the war on terror, determined to support both even when international human rights principles were undermined.

[213] ICJ official, tel interview, 20 February 2013.
[214] Amnesty International official, tel interview, 18 January 2013.
[215] Civil liberties activist, tel interview, 31 January 2013.
[216] Labor MP, tel interview, 24 January 2013.
[217] James G March and Johan P Olsen, 'The logic of appropriateness' in *The Oxford Handbook of Public Policy*, ed Michael Moran, Martin Rein and Robert Goodin (Oxford: Oxford University Press, 2008) 689.
[218] Labor MP, tel interview, 24 January 2013.

Alliance-based explanations would also suggest that Australia's choices were constrained as a junior partner with fewer capabilities in the war on terror.[219] This realist account, however, fails to explain many dimensions of the executive's behaviour on the torture issue. For example, once the Hicks matter became a damaging election issue, the Howard Government had no compunction about demanding that the US return the Australian citizen without delay. The Australian case poses other questions that alliance-based explanations do not help answer. For instance, why did the Hicks case become a difficult political issue for the Howard Government only in 2006, and then only for a brief period, until he was brought home? Why did Habib's case, with its compelling narrative of torture at the hands of a foreign regime, never become a political issue for any Australian government?

To understand how the Government was able to sustain its position of indifference on Hicks and Habib over such a long period, we must look to the lack of pressure it faced from domestic actors. This includes a weak federal Opposition, the minimal involvement of courts in checking executive action, and civil society's delayed activism that focused not on torture but on due process issues. In this section I ask: How do we explain this lack of pressure, particularly from civil society?

Australia had only two detainees at Guantánamo, unlike the UK which had nine plus residents. We might assume, therefore, that the detainee issue did not have as high a profile in Australia as it did in the UK. However, civil society activism was influenced by more than just the number of detained citizens in the war on terror. In Chapter 3 I suggested that liberal international theory offers a useful starting point for understanding state behaviour on global human rights issues, by directing attention to local conditions for mobilisation of domestic actors. Even across liberal democracies, where states are committed to upholding international human rights and democratic institutions that support government accountability, the national political and legal context can be important for understanding why domestic actors might robustly challenge their states' behaviour in some polities, but not in others.

Here I ask, what were the particular features of Australia's domestic context that may have influenced activism around the torture of citizens? I employ the framework of enabling and constraining factors—political culture, political and legal institutions, and political opportunity structure—that can affect human rights activism to analyse Australian civil society's behaviour on the Hicks and Habib cases.

Political Culture

A nation's political culture can enable or constrain civil society in mobilising on a contentious human rights issue. It influences the way members of a polity think about themselves as rights-bearing individuals, and can help determine their

219 Stephen M Walt, 'Alliances in a unipolar world', *World Politics* 61(1) (2009), 86.

willingness to act with respect to new experiences of rights infractions. Australia does not have a strong rights culture. This point was underscored when a National Human Rights Consultation Committee, established to consider the need for a bill of rights in Australia, reported that 'Australians know little about their human rights—what they are, where they come from and how they are protected'.[220] Human rights are taken for granted by the majority of Australians, who do not regard their lack of legal or constitutional protection to be a concern—or, at least, are unaware of how few safeguards there actually are.[221] Insights into Australia's political rights culture can be gleaned through two, interconnected features: historical legacies and experiences around rights and political violence, and current domestic debates about rights.

The Australian polity has a utilitarian view of rights that is preoccupied with ensuring the rights of the majority, rather than with identifying minority interests.[222] This outlook reflects dominant ideas in nineteenth-century Britain and the fact that the Australian colony gained its independence without violent struggle.[223] Because of its past, Australia takes an instrumental view of the state, one not averse to big government, that readily sanctions governments taking an interventionist role and which is less concerned with protecting individual freedoms.[224] Australia's history and utilitarian rights culture help explain why the country does not have a bill of rights. When the Constitution was drafted in the 1890s, there was no apparent reason not to trust the British traditions of the common law and responsible government.[225] There was also a desire by framers to give the Federal and State parliaments the power to pass racially discriminatory laws, a result of which is that Australia's modern constitutional framework entrenches racist legacies.[226] Prime Minister Howard articulated in contemporary terms the utilitarian underpinning of Australia's lack of constitutionally guaranteed rights, saying 'a Bill of Rights … would reduce the power of the citizens to control their own lives by handing political decision-making authority to judges'.[227]

[220] National Human Rights Consultation, *National Human Rights Consultation Report*, September 2009, v, http://pandora.nla.gov.au/pan/94610/20100324-0000/www.humanrightsconsultation.gov.au/www/nhrcc/RWPAttach.nsf/VAP/(4CA02151F94FFB778ADAEC2E6EA8653D)_NHRC+Report+(Prelims).pdf/$file/NHRC+Report+(Prelims).pdf.

[221] George Williams, *A Charter of Rights for Australia* (Sydney: UNSW Press, 2007) 67.

[222] Hilary Charlesworth, *Writing in Rights: Australia and the Protection of Human Rights* (Sydney: UNSW Press, 2002); Louis Pauly and Christian Reus-Smit, 'Negotiating Anglo-America: Australia, Canada and the United States' in *Anglo-America and its Discontents*, ed Katzenstein.

[223] Richard N Rosecrance, 'The radical culture of Australia' in *The Founding of New Societies: Studies in the History of the United States, Latin America, South Africa, Canada and Australia*, ed Louis Hartz (New York, NY: Harcourt Brace Jovanovich, 1964) 275; John Hirst, *Sense and Nonsense in Australian History* (Melbourne: Black Inc Agenda, 2005) 293.

[224] David Kinley and Christine Ernst, 'Exile on Main Street: Australia's legislative agenda for human rights', *European Human Rights Law Review* 1 (2012), 59; Hugh V Emy and Owen E Hughes, *Australia Politics: Realities in Conflict* (Melbourne: Macmillan Company of Australia, 1988) 38.

[225] Williams, *A Charter of Rights for Australia*, 53.

[226] Charlesworth, *Writing in Rights*, 32–33.

[227] Howard, *Lazarus Rising*, 587.

Another factor that influences rights awareness among the Australian polity is that it does not have significant historical experience of terrorism. Like America prior to 9/11, Australia was less familiar with terrorism, more easily frightened by it and more unrealistic in its beliefs that it could be permanently eradicated—even if that meant a significant curtailment of civil liberties. For most of their history, 'white Australians considered terrorism to be a phenomenon that happened elsewhere'.[228] Australia's most high-profile experience of domestic terrorism before 11 September 2001 was a bombing outside the Hilton Hotel in Sydney in 1978 during a Commonwealth Heads of Government Regional Meeting, which killed three people.[229] While Australia, like Canada, did not experience a terrorist attack in the post-9/11 period at home, it lost 88 citizens in terrorist bombings in Bali, Indonesia, in October 2002.[230]

Australia's inexperience of terrorism was reflected in its hyper-legislative response to the attacks. Australia had a larger legislative output than countries facing greater threats.[231] Before 9/11, only the Northern Territory in Australia had laws relating to terrorism. Australia's new counter-terrorism laws, it is argued, do more to undermine democratic freedoms than the laws of any comparable nation.[232] Australia's legislative exuberance after 9/11 reflected a tough-on-terrorism political agenda, integral to which was a readiness to sacrifice individual liberties for the sake of national security. This is illustrated by a 2005 speech on national security, where the Secretary of the Attorney-General's Department, Robert Cornall, argued that the recent increase in terrorism threats to Australia necessitated a change in the way Australians thought about rights.[233] 'There was not much need to think about community rights in the 20th century because they were not under any obvious challenge', he said. 'This allowed individual rights to flourish without regard to the broader setting of community rights … But things are a bit different now.'

In Australia, there is a noticeable lack of debate on relations between citizen and state, or over the proper nature and limits of political authority.[234] International human rights standards, in particular, are marginal to political debate and policy development in Australia.[235] An example of post-9/11 political discourse in Australia that typifies prevalent attitudes around ideas of rights and the role of government involves the issue of a national rights charter. The National Human

[228] Wright-Neville, 'The politics of fear', 2.

[229] Kent Roach, *The 9/11 Effect: Comparative Counter-Terrorism* (New York, NY: Cambridge University Press, 2011) 314.

[230] Wright-Neville, 'The politics of fear', 6.

[231] George Williams, 'A decade of Australian anti-terror laws', *Melbourne University Law Review* 35(3) (2011), 1145.

[232] ibid, 1171.

[233] Robert Cornall, 'A strategic approach to national security', speech delivered at the Security in Government Conference, Canberra, 10 May 2005.

[234] Emy and Hughes, *Australia Politics*, 41.

[235] Rice and Calnan, *Sustainable Advocacy*, 10.

Rights Consultation Committee, established by the Rudd Government in 2009, ascertained a 'need to create in Australia a culture in which human rights are better understood and are respected, protected, and promoted', and recommended the introduction of a legislative charter of rights.[236] The Government, however, rejected its recommendation in the face of widespread political opposition to such a move.[237] A dominant theme running through the anti-bill of rights discourse at the time was that rights are best protected by elected officials. A former New South Wales State premier argued, for example, that 'common sense' tells Australians they are free, and a charter 'would increase litigation, not rights'.[238] In 2013, Australia's incoming Attorney-General in the new Coalition Government (led by Liberal Party Prime Minister Tony Abbott) announced a return to a more traditional Australian minimalist approach to human rights. Senator George Brandis's view was that Australians would be 'much better protected' by existing common law rights and freedoms than by any charter of rights.[239]

The concept of an Australian rights culture is, necessarily, a very general one. It does not reflect the country's complex histories of its indigenous people and different migrant populations, whose encounters with Australian politics and society have involved human rights transgressions. In this sense, the idea of an Australian rights culture assumes a dominant (white) narrative, a part of which is a lack of familiarity with terrorism or widespread human rights abuses. This is most certainly not the experience of all Australians, particularly indigenous Australians.[240]

Australia's traditionally ambivalent attitude towards rights is significant for understanding why civil society was swamped by a reactive Government after 9/11 and was slow to mobilise on the detainee torture issue. Australia's human rights NGOs are hampered by powerful domestic political constraints, notably a weak national rights culture and the lack of any federal legislative guarantee of human rights standards, the absence of which limits community understandings and commitments about rights. A former Australian Human Rights Commissioner, Chris Sidoti, spoke in 2005 about the demoralisation of the Australian human rights community, and 'a lack of focus, a lack of leadership, and a lack of co-ordination' in the sector.[241] A 2007 study of Australian human rights NGOs noted that many were limited in their capacity to deal with human rights issues, and human rights issues in Australia were not being addressed sufficiently or at all.[242]

[236] National Human Rights Consultation, *National Human Rights Consultation Report*, 131.

[237] Robert McClelland, 'Launch of Australia's Human Rights Framework', address to the National Press Club of Australia, Canberra, 21 April 2010.

[238] Bob Carr, 'Bill of Rights is the wrong call', *Australian*, 9 May 2009, 20.

[239] Chris Merritt, 'George Brandis to reclaim rights agenda', *Australian*, 30 August 2013, 29.

[240] See, eg, Australian Human Rights and Equal Opportunity Commission, *Bringing them Home: Report of the National Inquiry into the Separation of Aboriginal and Torres Strait Islander Children from their Families*, Commonwealth of Australia, 1997.

[241] Chris Sidoti, 'Seeking a right way', keynote address to Revitalising Human Rights and Social Justice Conference, Geneva, 20 January 2005.

[242] Rice and Calnan, *Sustainable Advocacy*, 8.

Human rights activists supported the idea that Australia's human rights sector was ill-equipped to deal with events after 9/11. A civil liberties activist said, for example, 'At the time a lot of NGOs just sort of threw their hands up and said "what do we do, we can't argue for anything at the moment".'[243] An HRLC official said 'more should have been done' on the issue of the lack of accountability for international torture alleged by Hicks and Habib, but 'this would have meant forgoing work on some other human rights issue'.[244] The fact that Australian human rights NGOs did not organise around the issue of torture accountability in their domestic advocacy partly reflected the limited size and capacity of the sphere. According to the HRLC official, some of the reason there was more focus in the UK on torture accountability was because 'it's a bigger society, it's a bigger civil society, and there are larger and also more specifically focused organisations'.[245]

The formation in 2005 of two NGOs that became involved in advocating for Hicks further supports the suggestion that civil society struggled to deal with the high volume of issues after 11 September 2001. Both NGOs formed to fill a perceived gap in the Australian human rights sphere. The HRLC was set up out of the recognition that legal advocacy and strategic litigation, useful tools for human rights change, were not being used as fully or effectively in Australia as they could be. While the Hicks case itself did not drive the establishment of the HRLC, an official said 'it was a relevant factor in identifying the need for such an organisation and the kinds of strategies it might use'.[246] GetUp! was formed partly in response to the dejection afflicting Australian civil society, which worsened after the Howard Government won control of the Senate in the 2004 federal election.[247] Hicks's case was one of GetUp!'s core foundation issues. A GetUp! official said the organisation formed at a time when 'civil society and particularly the progressive side of civil society was extremely despondent, there was no political momentum, there was a series of failed campaigns'.[248]

Political and Legal Institutions

A state's political and legal institutions, particularly its national human rights framework, can also have an enabling or a constraining effect on activism. The organisational structures of the state, shaped by historical forces, affect the degree of power that different actors have over policy outcomes, and influence how they define their interests. Australia's political institutions have a limited capacity to

[243] Civil liberties activist, tel interview, 31 January 2013.
[244] HRLC official, tel interview, 19 June 2013.
[245] ibid.
[246] ibid.
[247] GetUp! official, tel interview, 21 February 2013.
[248] ibid.

protect human rights, especially at a time of high community fear of a terrorist attack.[249]

Australia's human rights framework has a number of glaring inadequacies, the most obvious being that Australia is the only democratic country without a federal constitutional or legislative rights charter.[250] Human rights, George Williams has argued, 'do not have a firm foothold' in Australia's political and legal system, and lack political effectiveness in part because they lack legal force.[251] In addition, on 11 September 2001 Australia's laws with respect to the prohibition of torture, in particular, were piecemeal. Australia had ratified the CAT. However, the Howard Government had refused to sign the Optional Protocol to the Convention Against Torture and Other Cruel, Inhuman or Degrading Treatment or Punishment (OPCAT), which would have allowed international inspections of Australian detention facilities.[252] There existed no Commonwealth offence against torture—a fact criticised by the UN Committee Against Torture.[253] The Crimes (Torture) Act 1988 only outlawed torture committed outside Australia. While the lack of a Commonwealth offence against torture did not directly affect the cases of Hicks and Habib, it did indicate a broader failure by Australia to fulfil its commitments under the CAT (Article 4 of which requires states to 'ensure that all acts of torture are offences under its criminal law').

The inadequacy of human rights protections in Australia undermined civil society members' views of their capabilities and interests, and their beliefs about what was possible in terms of holding the executive accountable for the treatment of citizens detained in the war on terror. This is clear from the views of different civil society actors, many of whom viewed advocating for a torture inquiry as futile. Why was civil society so despondent about the prospects of accountability on torture? Certainly, there was less concrete evidence of Australian complicity in torture compared to the UK. But an HRLC official also cited the absence of a specific federal torture offence or a constitutional prohibition on torture in Australia as a reason why advocates framed their claims around due process guarantees, rather than torture. It was, in part, about 'the legal hooks we had available to us'.[254] He said:

> To the extent that the Australian legal framework and particularly the constitutional framework provides hooks, it tends to be around due process, a fair trial, and rule of

[249] George Williams, 'Balancing national security and human rights: Lessons from Australia', *borderlands: new spaces in the humanities e-journal* 4(1) (2005), para 25.

[250] Williams, *A Charter of Rights for Australia*, 16.

[251] Williams, 'Balancing national security and human rights', para 33.

[252] Joint Standing Committee on Treaties, Parliament of Australia, *Report 58: Optional Protocol to the Convention Against Torture and Other Cruel, Inhuman or Degrading Treatment or Punishment*, 2004, http://www.aph.gov.au/Parliamentary_Business/Committees/House_of_Representatives_Committees?url=jsct/reports.htm.

[253] Committee Against Torture, *Consideration of Reports Submitted by States Parties Under Article 19 of The Convention—Concluding Observations of the Committee Against Torture, Australia*, 40th sess, UN Doc CAT/C/AUS/CO/3 (22 May 2008).

[254] HRLC official, tel interview, 19 June 2013.

> law issues, rather than around human rights and human dignity, and in particular the prohibition against torture or ill-treatment … In comparable liberal democracies like Canada with its Charter of Rights and Freedoms, and the UK domestically incorporating the European Convention on Human Rights through the Human Rights Act, there are constitutionally or legislatively enshrined rights to life, rights to liberty and security of the person, and prohibitions against torture and ill-treatment.[255]

Australian civil society was restricted in its campaigning on the detainee torture issue by not having a bill of rights. Its absence meant civil society was directed by the state's institutional settings to frame claims in terms of due process, rather than human dignity or torture. This factor may also assist in understanding why Hicks and Habib, particularly in the early years of their detention, had little recourse to the domestic courts. Most of Australian civil society's calls for accountability on torture were instead made in the international forum of the UN Committee Against Torture. The NSWCCL, the HRLC and Amnesty International all urged Australia to conduct a public inquiry in shadow reports made in the context of the Committee's third periodic report of Australia in 2008.[256] These NGOs invoked Australia's obligations under the CAT in their submissions, with respect to the state's failing to act on allegations of torture.

After 2007, Labor governments sought to rectify some of the legislative inadequacies with respect to Australia's human rights framework, including on torture. The Rudd Government introduced legislation in 2009 (passed the following year) specifically creating a Commonwealth torture offence, which outlawed torture committed both within and outside Australia.[257] The Rudd Government also signed OPCAT in 2009, although Australia has yet to ratify the Protocol. These reforms and actions reflected the prominence of torture in the war on terrorism, including in the Hicks and Habib cases.[258] In addition, the Human Rights (Parliamentary Scrutiny) Act 2011, enacted by the Gillard Government, brought Australia into line with Canada and the UK in enhancing Parliament's role in ensuring that human rights considerations are part of the process of policy and legislative development.[259]

[255] ibid.

[256] Amnesty International Australia, 'A briefing for the Committee Against Torture', Submission to the Committee Against Torture, October 2007; New South Wales Council for Civil Liberties, *Shadow Report Prepared for the United Nations Committee Against Torture on the Occasion of its Review of Australia's Third Periodic Report Under the* Convention Against Torture and other Cruel, Inhuman or Degrading Treatment or Punishment, Submission to the Committee Against Torture 27 July 2007; Human Rights Law Resource Centre, *Australia's Compliance with the* Convention Against Torture*: Report to the UN Committee Against Torture*, Submission to the Committee Against Torture, April 2008.

[257] Crimes Legislation Amendment (Torture Prohibition and Death Penalty Abolition) Act 2010 (Cth).

[258] Greg Carne, 'Is near enough good enough?—Implementing Australia's international human rights torture criminalisation and prohibition obligations in the criminal code (Cth)', *Adelaide Law Review* 33(1) (2012), 241–42; see also Robert McClelland, 'Human rights: A moral compass', speech to the Lowy Institute for International Policy, Sydney, 22 May 2009.

[259] Kinley and Ernst, 'Exile on Main Street', 63.

Then again, Australia, as noted, has a robust Senate committee system, which provides an effective parliamentary forum for investigating human rights issues involving executive government processes. Habib's wife worked with Greens senators, who pressed public officials for information about Habib's extraordinary rendition in Senate Estimates hearings.[260] The committee process was thus important in providing one of the few official forums for accountability on the Hicks and Habib cases, into which civil society was able to tap.

Political Opportunities

Changing political opportunities also offer incentives for or discouragement of activism. Increasing political opportunities can communicate crucial information for movement formation, revealing allies and exposing the vulnerabilities of enemies, in so doing affecting activists' expectations for success. In Australia, political opportunities were scarce after 9/11. This shifted five years later, and the spaces within which individuals and groups perceived they could legitimately make claims noticeably expanded. I trace this development through three kinds of political opportunities relating to the political party in power, the unity of the government and the electoral cycle.

I noted in Chapter 3 that the relationship between government and civil society can vary according to the political party in power. The Howard Government looked unfavourably upon the role of the non-government sector, particularly groups advocating for human rights issues, in the democratic process.[261] Its ideological position encompassed a belief that NGOs engaging in advocacy for the rights of minorities—what the Prime Minister disparagingly labelled 'the narrower agendas of elites and special interests'—lacked representative legitimacy.[262] This marginalisation of NGOs had a demobilising effect on movement actors that arguably resulted in reduced government accountability.[263] The Howard Government's position was exemplified by the Attorney-General's attacks on the Law Council for its advocacy on Hicks. The Government chided the LCA for spending too much time on 'fashionable issues'. It implied that civil society actors had no proper role in criticising government policies on the treatment of citizens detained in the war

[260] Greens senator, tel interview, 9 January 2013.

[261] Marian Sawer, 'Populism and public choice in Australia and Canada: Turning equality-seekers into "special interests"' in *Us and Them: Anti-Elitism in Australia*, ed Marian Sawer and Barry Hindess (Perth: Curtin University of Technology, 2004) 40.

[262] John Howard, 'The liberal tradition: The beliefs and values which guide the Federal Government', 1996 Sir Robert Menzies Lecture, Melbourne, 18 November 1996.

[263] Sarah Maddison and Greg Martin, 'Introduction to "Surviving neoliberalism: The persistence of Australian social movements"', *Social Movement Studies: Journal of Social, Cultural and Political Protest* 9(2) (2010), 108.

on terror.[264] The Government's efforts to delegitimise the engagement of domestic advocacy groups in public debate also extended to international forums. In 2000, for example, Foreign Affairs Minister Downer said that UN committees were losing credibility because they were too accepting of NGO submissions.[265]

This closed feature of Australia's political environment for activism immediately after 9/11 was further compounded by Prime Minister Howard's tight control over his Government. Howard emerged from his Government's 2001 federal election victory strong, popular and newly emboldened to pursue his policy agenda, including national security.[266] A result was that Howard ran a ministry and backbench with few public dissenters. This minimised opportunities for civil society actors to identify disaffected and sympathetic political elites to target for lobbying. Prime Minister Howard's power over the political process increased further after the 2004 election, when his Government won control of the Senate. Ironically, however, this consolidation of political power also served as a trigger for the formation of a new grassroots political movement, GetUp!.[267] This illustrates another idea from social movement theory: the apparent paradox that while state toleration of contention provides a low-risk environment for protest, it also deprives organisers of the potent weapon of outrage.[268] The Howard Government's takeover of the Senate, which undermined the power of the upper house to scrutinise executive power, provided a reason for outrage that was harnessed by civil society groups.

This shift in Australia's protest environment is connected to another kind of political opportunity: the electoral cycle. Elections can sometimes offer critical points of pressure, providing opportunities to influence the executive in the course of ongoing human rights campaigns. This occurred in Australia in 2006, where civil society groups concerned about the Hicks case were able to exploit two parallel political developments: a shift in public opinion on his ongoing detention, and the impending 2007 federal election. The work of two NGOs in particular demonstrate this: GetUp! and NSWCCL.

GetUp! employed a number of grassroots tactics specifically designed to demonstrate growing public disquiet over Hicks's ongoing detention and, in so doing, exploit the Howard Government's fear of electoral defeat in 2007.[269] Examples of GetUp!'s tactics included positioning billboards at the entrance of the Sydney Harbour Bridge so that commuters and politicians would see them on their drive to work (including the Prime Minister and Attorney-General, who lived in

[264] Ruddock, 'Some lawyers ignore their profession's core values'.

[265] Alexander Downer, 'Keeping the United Nations relevant: International peace and security, and reform', statement by the Hon Alexander Downer MP Minister for Foreign Affairs to the 55th Session of the General Assembly of the United Nations, New York, 18 September 2000.

[266] Kelly, *The March of the Patriots*, 625.

[267] GetUp! official, tel interview, 21 February 2013.

[268] Sidney Tarrow, *Power in Movement: Social Movements and Contentious Politics* (New York, NY: Cambridge University Press, 1998) 84.

[269] GetUp! official, tel interview, 21 February 2013.

Sydney); placing full-page advertisements in national newspapers; holding public rallies in Adelaide, the home of Hicks and the Foreign Affairs Minister; and conducting public opinion polling. The polling, a GetUp! official said, was designed 'to take the temperature of what the Australian people wanted, and to demonstrate that the position was actually inconsistent with the government's position and also was a risk to them'.[270] Other tactics included campaigning in Prime Minister Howard's seat in the NSW State election, held in early 2007. GetUp! handed out postcards demanding Hicks's release to all voters in Howard's Bennelong electorate. More than 11,000—representing 12 per cent of all voters—were endorsed, returned and forwarded to the Prime Minister.[271]

The NSWCCL was concerned with a different issue: legislative reform with respect to torture. Its goals were broader and longer-term, and bring to mind the briefcase image mentioned in Chapter 3, where ideas for social change initiatives are sometimes carried around for years until the right opportunity presents.[272] After 9/11, the NSWCCL was concerned that human rights would be wound back in Australia.[273] In particular, it was worried about the re-emergence of the death penalty, banned only at the Commonwealth level, where some public figures were calling for its reintroduction against terrorists. The organisation wrote to federal MPs and an all-party parliamentary working group was established, among whose members was a future Labor Attorney-General, Robert McClelland. According to some accounts, the group also worked on the torture issue, specifically the need for legislation implementing a Commonwealth offence of torture and the ratification of OPCAT.[274] By the time McClelland became Attorney-General, public opinion on the war on terror had shifted in favour of protecting human rights, and his department, alert to his interest in strengthening institutional protections against torture, presented him with a number of recommendations.[275] The Rudd Government went on to legislate against torture (and the death penalty) and signed OPCAT, without controversy.[276] A civil liberties activist described what occurred in terms of political opportunity:

> We just find often [with] these things that it's a matter of opportunity, where suddenly something will happen where you might get a change of government, or you might get dramatic overreach, and then you've got to take that opportunity, and you've got to have done the ground work to be in a position to change that, because you get very few

[270] ibid.

[271] According to the Australian Electoral Commission, 92,700 votes were cast in Bennelong in 2007: Australian Electoral Commission, *NSW Division—Bennelong* (11 December 2007).

[272] Julie A Mertus, *Bait and Switch: Human Rights and US Foreign Policy* (New York, NY: Routledge, 2008) 182.

[273] Civil liberties activist, tel interview, 31 January 2013.

[274] ibid.

[275] See Geoffrey Barker, 'Iraq: A point of departure', *Australian Financial Review* (Sydney), 16 November 2007, 22.

[276] Crimes Legislation Amendment (Torture Prohibition and Death Penalty Abolition) Act 2010 (Cth).

> opportunities. You know it might come along once in a generation, so if you're not ready, you miss it.[277]

This example demonstrates how human rights transformation can sometimes be the result of collective effort, as well as of the ability of individuals, groups and, in some cases, institutions to recognise and act upon fleeting openings in the political system. Here, there was a convergence of diverse actors with common long-term goals, including a persistent civil liberties NGO and public servants prepared to pursue human rights policy objectives at the first signals of enthusiasm from elected officials.

The success of GetUp! and the NSWCCL in using a federal election and the arrival of a new government to achieve their human rights objectives is a powerful demonstration of how, given the right domestic conditions, Australian civil society effectively exploited political opportunities to effect change.

Conclusion

For almost a decade, Australian governments appeared indifferent to the torture allegations of Australian citizens detained at Guantánamo Bay. While initially the US alliance might explain Australia's apparent disregard for its citizens' international human rights, to understand the sustained nature of that response, domestic political factors must be examined.

Australian governments faced few demands at home over the need for accountability on torture allegedly carried out overseas. The Howard Government confronted minimal pressure from the legislature, particularly the weak federal Opposition, or the judiciary, with Hicks and Habib only resorting to litigation many years after they were first detained. Civil society was slow to mobilise on the cases, escalating its efforts in 2006 and 2007. The civil society activism that did occur was focused on legal process issues, rather than on the need for accountability on torture. Where domestic legal organisations and human rights NGOs referenced Australia's international legal obligations on torture, it was generally in shadow reports submitted to the UN Committee Against Torture, rather than in advocacy at home. Treaties provide focal points for civil society activism where deficiencies exist in domestic human rights structures. Where such lacunae occur, as Australia's case illustrates, they can also direct the efforts of citizenries overseas. There, outside the realm of domestic politics, their impact on national governments is weaker.

The enabling and constraining features of Australia's national political context for human rights activism help explain the lack of domestic pressure on the

[277] Civil liberties activist, tel interview, 31 January 2013.

Government over the issue of accountability for the torture of Hicks and Habib. A domestic NGO sector, overwhelmed after 11 September 2001, was constrained by a weak human rights culture, which reflected the country's historical apathy towards the need for rights protections against government, as well as its lack of experience of terrorism. An inadequate national human rights framework further inhibited and discouraged civil society, particularly in relation to making claims about torture. Hicks's and Habib's supporters and advocates saw agitating about torture as futile. Civil society was also impeded by a relatively closed political system for the first five years of Hicks's and Habib's detention, where the highly disciplined Howard Government challenged the legitimate role of NGOs in public debate, especially in critiquing its human rights policies. When the political system eventually presented cleavages, as the popularity of the Howard Government waned and public concerns about the treatment of Hicks increased, civil society was able to organise, agitate and inspire political change on human rights. However, this did not occur on the issue of accountability for torture, where the legal hooks for framing claims were not available.

Where domestic actors do not demonstrate that they care about international human rights transgressions in ways that affect domestic politics, the state has little impetus to act. In Australia, a range of constraints for mobilisation on international human rights issues meant that activism on Hicks's and Habib's behalf was limited, and this made it easier for the Government to avoid responding to human rights breaches by a dominant ally.

6

The United Kingdom

Introduction

At first glance, the United States (US) had no closer friend in the war on terror than the United Kingdom (UK). Tony Blair's Labour Government, at pains to influence America's war on terror policies, provided the most substantial political and military backing of any of the alliance partners.[1] This was demonstrated by the UK's actions on Iraq, including its diplomatic efforts to secure international support for the US invasion.[2] Yet on the issue of torture, and its use against Britons detained in the war on terror, the UK did not stay in step with the US. A number of UK citizens and residents were detained at Guantánamo Bay, and alleged they were mistreated and tortured. The UK Government refused to allow UK citizens to be tried by US military commissions and brought them home by 2005. Its approach to UK residents was different, with the Government initially arguing that it had no legal responsibility for the men. However, beginning in 2007, residents too were repatriated. In 2010, the Conservative–Liberal Democrat Coalition Government led by David Cameron ordered a public inquiry into the UK's complicity in the torture of UK nationals and residents detained at Guantánamo Bay.[3]

I argue that the UK Government's initial reluctance to stand up for citizens and residents tortured in the war on terror gave way relatively quickly under sustained domestic pressure. While different factors contributed to the Government's vulnerability to pressure on this issue, human rights activism was facilitated by a range of features of the national political and legal context that were enabling of mobilisation on torture.

In this chapter I discuss the UK's role in the war on terror, and describe the torture allegations of the UK citizens and residents detained at Guantánamo Bay. I outline the response of the executive government to the men's claims, and the roles of Parliament, the judiciary and civil society in holding the executive accountable for its actions and policies. I then apply the framework of enabling

[1] David Coates and Joel Krieger, with Rhiannon Vickers, *Blair's War* (Cambridge: Polity, 2004); John Kampfner, *Blair's Wars* (London: Free Press, 2004).

[2] Tony Blair, *A Journey* (London: Hutchinson, 2010) 415–40.

[3] Detainee Inquiry, *The Report of the Detainee Inquiry*, December 2013, http://www.parliament.uk/business/news/2013/december/statement-on-detainee-inquiry-19-december-2013/.

and constraining features affecting human rights activism on torture in order to analyse the behaviour of domestic actors on the issue of the mistreatment of the UK's detainees.

The UK and the War on Terror

The UK–US Relationship

The UK's alliance with the US is often described as the 'Special Relationship', a notion that embodies two central ideas.[4] One is that the countries share many values and a common identity.[5] The other is that it is in the UK's interests, as a former imperial power, to stay as close as possible to the US in order to continue to exercise a global influence beyond its current position. Prime Minister Blair was a strong supporter of the Special Relationship and arrived in office resolved to rebuild it.[6] His resolve was grounded in the conviction that the UK, using the levers of its historical alliances, could once again be an international player with a moral purpose, using its influence to promote the values and aims it believed in.[7] The events of 11 September 2001 provided Prime Minister Blair with an opportunity to realise this vision.[8]

Prime Minister Blair's inflated rhetoric regarding the significance of the terrorist attacks closely matched that of the Bush Administration. For example, according to the Prime Minister, 9/11 was 'the worst terrorist attack in human history'; left unchallenged 'this could threaten our way of life to its fundamentals'; it signalled the start of a war 'unlike any other'; and it was an opportunity to 're-order the world around us'.[9] For Prime Minister Blair, it was imperative that the UK work as closely as possible with the US so that it might shape the Bush Administration's response to 9/11.[10]

The UK's international response to the war on terror included the deployment of significant military forces to Afghanistan in October 2001.[11] Prime Minister Blair also threw himself into the task of helping the US build a case for war in Iraq,

[4] WM Roger Louis and Hedley Bull, *The Special Relationship: Anglo-American Relations Since 1945* (Oxford: Clarendon Press, 1986).

[5] Tim Dunne, '"When the shooting starts": Atlanticism in British security strategy', *International Affairs* 80(5) (2004), 898.

[6] Inderjeet Parmar, '"I'm proud of the British Empire": Why Tony Blair backs George W Bush', *The Political Quarterly* 76(2) (2005), 226.

[7] Dunne, '"When the shooting starts"', 904.

[8] Philip Stephens, *Tony Blair: The Price of Leadership* (London: Politico's, 2004) 272.

[9] Blair, *A Journey*, 345; Peter Riddell, *Hug Them Close: Blair, Clinton, Bush and the 'Special Relationship'* (London: Politico's, 2003) 145.

[10] Blair, *A Journey*, 352.

[11] Kampfner, *Blair's Wars*, 129.

and committed substantial UK military forces to the conflict in March 2003, at significant personal political cost.[12] Critics, internal and external, viewed the Prime Minister's unflinching support for the US war on terror, particularly the invasion of Iraq, as servile to Washington.[13]

The UK's Detained Citizens and Residents

UK Citizens

Nine UK citizens were held at Guantánamo Bay. Rhuhel Ahmed, Shafiq Rasul, Asif Iqbal, Jamal Udeen Al-Harith and Tarek Dergoul were UK-born. Taken into custody in Afghanistan in late 2001, they were transferred to Guantánamo Bay in early 2002, and were eventually released and returned to the UK in March 2004.[14] Ahmed, Rasul and Iqbal, known as the Tipton Three after their home town, claim they travelled to Pakistan and Afghanistan for a wedding.[15] They were detained in Afghanistan by Afghan forces and turned over to the American military.[16] Al-Harith claims he was imprisoned by the Taliban on suspicion of being a British spy while travelling in northern Pakistan.[17] From his Kandahar jail he made contact with UK diplomats and the International Committee of the Red Cross (ICRC), who were working on plans for his evacuation when he was taken by US forces. Dergoul claims he was on an extended holiday in Pakistan in 2001 when he decided to travel to Afghanistan and buy cheap property after the war started.[18] The villa he was staying in was bombed, and Dergoul was found by Northern Alliance troops, who turned him over to the US military for a US$5,000 bounty. The men allege they were subjected to ill-treatment and abuse in Afghanistan, including hooding, beatings, threats and sexual humiliation.[19] They gave similar accounts of brutal treatment at Guantánamo Bay, which they allege amounted to torture. This included subjection to extreme temperatures, stress positions, loud music, beatings by the 'ERF' (Extreme Reaction Force) teams, forced injections, short shackling and long periods in isolation.[20] In addition, Dergoul claimed he

[12] John Dumbrell, 'Working with allies: The United States, the United Kingdom, and the war on terror', *Politics & Policy* 34(2) (2006), 462.

[13] Alex Danchev, 'Accomplicity: Britain, torture and terror', *The British Journal of Politics and International Relations* 8(4) (2006), 588; House of Commons Foreign Affairs Committee, United Kingdom Parliament, *Global Security: UK–US Relations* (HC 2009–10, 537).

[14] Detainee Inquiry, *The Report of the Detainee Inquiry*, 14.

[15] Danae Brook, 'Back home, but still imprisoned: The shadow of Guantánamo', *Independent*, 9 March 2006.

[16] Shafiq Rasul, Asif Iqbal and Rhuhel Ahmed, 'Composite statement: Detention in Afghanistan and Guantánamo Bay', statement, Centre for Constitutional Rights, 26 July 2004.

[17] Tim Reid, 'Traveller who called Kandahar Prison "home"', *The Times*, 11 March 2004, 6.

[18] David Rose, 'They tied me up like a beast and began kicking me', *Observer*, 16 May 2004, 8.

[19] Rasul, Iqbal and Ahmed, 'Composite statement: Detention in Afghanistan and Guantánamo Bay'; Rose, 'They tied me up like a beast and began kicking me'.

[20] Rasul, Iqbal and Ahmed, 'Composite statement: Detention in Afghanistan and Guantánamo Bay'; Shafiq Rasul, Asif Iqbal, Rhuhel Ahmed and Jamal al-Harith, 'Complaint', Submission in *Rasul*

was pepper-sprayed, had his eyes poked, his head flushed in a toilet, was kneeled on and kicked and punched.[21]

A second group of UK citizens, including Feroz Abbasi, Moazzam Begg, Richard Belmar and Martin Mubanga, was released from Guantánamo Bay in January 2005. Begg and Belmar were UK-born, Abbasi was born in Uganda and Mubanga in Zambia. Abbasi was captured by the Northern Alliance in Afghanistan in December 2001, reportedly fighting with the Taliban, and handed over to the Americans, who took him to Guantánamo Bay.[22] Begg was living with his family in Pakistan while he worked on a school project in Afghanistan, and was arrested at his home in January 2002 by a group of American and Pakistani officials.[23] He was interrogated by MI5 before being sent to Afghanistan, where he was again questioned by UK agents, and in February 2003 he was transported to Guantánamo Bay.[24] Belmar recounts how, having travelled to Afghanistan in July 2001 to study at a religious school, he fled to Pakistan after the start of the war and was arrested by Pakistani intelligence officials at a house in Karachi in February 2002.[25] Belmar was sent to Afghanistan and, in October 2002, to Guantánamo Bay.[26] Mubanga, a dual UK-Zambian national, was arrested in March 2002 in Zambia by Zambian security officers.[27] By Mubanga's account, he was visiting relatives on his way home to the UK from Pakistan and Afghanistan, where he had been since late 2000 studying Islam and Arabic.[28] He was questioned by US and UK agents, and was sent to Guantánamo Bay in April 2002.[29]

Abbasi, Begg, Belmar and Mubanga also allege ill-treatment and torture before and during their detention at Guantánamo Bay. In Afghanistan this included, for Begg, being hooded, shackled, kicked, kept in isolation, subjected to sleep deprivation and loud music, having his family threatened, and witnessing the deaths of other detainees.[30] Belmar's alleged mistreatment in Afghanistan included being hooded, shackled in stress positions, sexually assaulted, kicked, hung by his wrists and witnessing the murder of another detainee.[31] The four men claim they were

v Rumsfeld, Case 1: 04-cv-01864-RMU, 27 October 2004; Tania Branigan, 'Briton accuses American captors', *Guardian*, 13 March 2004, 6.

[21] Rose, 'They tied me up like a beast and began kicking me'.

[22] Ian Cobain, 'Guantánamo Bay files: Profiles of the 10 released British prisoners', *Guardian*, 25 April 2011, 2; *The Queen on the Application of Abbasi v The Secretary of State for Foreign and Commonwealth Affairs* [2002] EWCA Civ 1598 [1].

[23] Moazzam Begg, *Enemy Combatant: The Terrifying True Story of a Briton in Guantánamo* (London: Pocket Books, 2006) 1–2, 8, 90, 106.

[24] ibid, 108–12; Detainee Inquiry, *The Report of the Detainee Inquiry*, 13.

[25] David Rose, 'Beatings, sex abuse and torture: How MI5 left me to rot in US jail', *Observer*, 27 February 2005, 11.

[26] Detainee Inquiry, *The Report of the Detainee Inquiry*, 12.

[27] Intelligence and Security Committee of Parliament, United Kingdom Parliament, *Rendition* (Cm 7171, 2007) 31.

[28] David Rose, 'How I entered the hellish world of Guantánamo Bay', *Observer*, 6 February 2005, 4.

[29] Detainee Inquiry, *The Report of the Detainee Inquiry*, 12.

[30] Begg, *Enemy Combatant*, 155–58, 170, 172, 183.

[31] Rose, 'Beatings, sex abuse and torture'.

treated in a brutal manner at Guantánamo Bay similar to the other UK citizens.[32] Mubanga also alleges he was mopped with his own urine.[33]

UK Residents

At least nine UK residents were detained at Guantánamo Bay.[34] The UK Government ultimately requested the repatriation of six. Bisher Al Rawi, an Iraqi national resident in the UK since 1983, was the first of the UK residents to be released and returned to the UK, in March 2007.[35] Al Rawi had worked as an informant for MI5, acting as an intermediary with the alleged extremist (and Jordanian citizen) Abu Qatada. Al Rawi was arrested with his friend Jamil El Banna, a Jordanian refugee and UK resident since 1994, in November 2002 by Gambian Intelligence while on a business trip to The Gambia.[36] A month after their arrests, Al Rawi and El Banna were taken to Afghanistan, where the men were kept in the CIA's 'dark prison' in Kabul and later at Bagram airbase.[37] They allege they were subjected to abuse and torture in Afghanistan, including being kept in continual darkness, shackled, kicked and beaten, being subject to very loud music, sleep deprivation, sexual humiliation and death threats.[38] Al Rawi and El Banna were taken to Guantánamo Bay in early 2003 where they alleged further mistreatment.[39]

El Banna, along with two other UK residents, Omar Deghayes and Abdennour Sameur, were repatriated to the UK in December 2007.[40] Deghayes was a Libyan national who fled the Gaddafi regime, coming to the UK in 1986.[41] He was in Afghanistan studying the Taliban in 2001, but moved that year to Pakistan. In April 2002 Deghayes was arrested by bounty hunters and turned over to Pakistani

[32] Begg, *Enemy Combatant*, 33, 195; David Rose, *Guantanamo Bay: The War on Human Rights* (New York: The New Press, 2004); Rose, 'How I entered the hellish world of Guantánamo Bay'; 'Beatings, sex abuse and torture'; Severin Carrell, 'Guantánamo account: "I was shackled, beaten, suffocated by a plastic bag and deprived of sleep. This is how they forced my confession"', *Independent*, 30 January 2005; Vikram Dodd, Richard Norton-Taylor and Rosie Cowan, 'Isolation, breakdowns and mysterious injections', *Guardian*, 26 January 2005, 1.

[33] Rose, 'How I entered the hellish world of Guantánamo Bay'.

[34] House of Commons Foreign Affairs Committee, United Kingdom Parliament, *Visit to Guantánamo Bay* (HC 2006-07, 44) 28.

[35] REDRESS, *The United Kingdom, torture and anti-terrorism: Where the problems lie*, Report, Redress Trust, December 2008, 42–44.

[36] David Rose, 'I helped MI5. My reward: Brutality and prison', *Observer*, 29 July 2007.

[37] REDRESS, *The United Kingdom, torture and anti-terrorism*, 43.

[38] Human Rights Council, *Joint Study on Global Practices in Relation to Secret Detention in the Context of Countering Terrorism of the Special Rapporteur on the Promotion and Protection of Human Rights and Fundamental Freedoms While Countering Terrorism, Martin Scheinin; the Special Rapporteur on Torture and Other Cruel, Inhuman or Degrading Treatment or Punishment, Manfred Nowak; the Working Group on Arbitrary Detention Represented by its Vice-Chair, Shaheen Sardar Ali; and the Working Group on Enforced or Involuntary Disappearances Represented by its Chair, Jeremy Sarkin*, UNGA, 13th sess, Agenda Item 3, A/HRC/13/42, 19 February 2010, 60.

[39] Andrew Tyrie, Roger Gough and Stuart McCracken, *Account Rendered: Extraordinary Rendition and Britain's Role* (London: Biteback Publishing, 2011) 82.

[40] Detainee Inquiry, *The Report of the Detainee Inquiry*, 19.

[41] *Al Rawi v The Secretary of State* [2006] EWCA Civ 1279 [10].

authorities.[42] He was visited by US and UK officials in Pakistan.[43] Deghayes's mistreatment in Pakistan included beatings, whippings, electrocution, threats of rape, snakes and threats to his family, stress positions and near drownings in a large drum.[44] Deghayes was moved to Afghanistan, where he was subjected to stress positions, starved, held in a dark room for days, locked in boxes with no air, tied in the 'strappado' hanging position, was beaten, kept naked and witnessed rapes and guards forcing petrol into prisoners' anuses. Finally, in Guantánamo Bay, Deghayes was 'ERFed', his face was smeared with faeces, his head was flushed in the toilet, he was shackled and beaten up, he had water forced up his nose with a high pressure hose until nearly suffocating, was slammed onto concrete, kept in isolation and humiliated. Deghayes is blind in one eye, the result, he says, of guards at Guantánamo trying to gouge out his eyes with their fingers.[45] Sameur was an Algerian national who was granted asylum in the UK in 2000.[46] He had travelled to Afghanistan in 2001 to 'experience life in an Islamic country' and was captured by the Pakistani army, having travelled to Pakistan after the start of the war, subsequently getting shot by soldiers in both knees and one hand. He was handed over to the US military and, while in Kandahar, was kicked and denied medical treatment for his infected legs unless he made false confessions. He was then taken to Guantánamo.

Binyam Mohamed was released from Guantánamo Bay in February 2009. An Ethiopian national who came to the UK in 1994, he was detained in Pakistan in April 2002 while trying to leave on a passport that was not his.[47] Mohamed claims he had travelled to Afghanistan in 2001, the year he converted to Islam, to overcome a drug habit; the US claimed he was there fighting anti-Taliban forces.[48] UK intelligence was informed of his capture and he was interrogated by the FBI in Pakistan.[49] According to the findings of a US District Court judge, Mohamed was beaten by Pakistani officials with a leather strap and subjected to staged mock executions.[50] He was taken to Morocco, where he endured sustained beatings, was hung from a wall, and where interrogators cut his chest and penis with a scalpel. He was burnt with liquids, blasted with loud music, given mind-altering substances and sexually humiliated. In January 2004, US soldiers moved Mohamed to Afghanistan. There, in the 'dark prison', his head was repeatedly beaten against a wall, he was hung up for days, sleep deprived, subjected to loud music and scary

[42] Center for the Study of Human Rights in the Americas, *Deghayes: The 'Torture Dossier'*, 30 March 2005.

[43] Tyrie, Gough and McCracken, *Account Rendered*, 97–98.

[44] Center for the Study of Human Rights in the Americas, *Deghayes: The 'Torture Dossier'*.

[45] Patrick Barkham, 'How I fought to survive Guantánamo', *Guardian*, 21 January 2010, 4.

[46] European Parliament, *Parliamentary Questions*, 22 June 2007, E-3203/07 (Sajjad Karim (ALDE)).

[47] Reprieve, *'Human Cargo': Binyam Mohamed and the rendition frequent flier programme*, 10 June 2008, 3.

[48] 'Profile: Binyam Mohamed', *BBC News*, 12 February 2010.

[49] Reprieve, *'Human Cargo'*, 6.

[50] *Mohammed v Obama* (DDC, Civ No 05-1347, 19 November 2009) slip op 48–57, 49–55.

sounds, and given inadequate and inedible food. The judge noted that the US Government did not 'challenge or deny the accuracy of Binyam Mohamed's story of brutal treatment'.[51] Mohamed was taken to Guantánamo Bay in September 2004.[52]

Shaker Aamer, a Saudi Arabian-born man resident in the UK since 1996, whose wife and children are UK citizens, was the last UK resident released from Guantánamo, in 2015.[53] Aamer moved his family to Afghanistan in June 2001 to work, he says, for Islamic charities building schools in remote regions; the US says he went to train and fight with Al-Qaeda.[54] Aamer was captured by the Northern Alliance trying to flee Afghanistan in late 2001, and was sold to the Americans who took him to Bagram air base and Guantánamo Bay. Aamer alleges he was tortured in Afghanistan, including in the presence of UK intelligence officials, when he was subjected to 'walling': his head was smashed against a wall while he sat shackled in a chair.[55] He was also beaten, sleep deprived, 'hog-tied', put in stress positions, subjected to extreme temperatures, and threatened with the rape of his five-year-old daughter.[56] At Guantánamo, where Aamer was held for 13 years without charge, he engaged in hunger strikes over his brutal treatment.[57] Many have speculated as to why Aamer was held for so long, despite having been cleared for release by the Bush Administration in 2007 and the Obama Administration in 2009. It is suggested that UK officials witnessed Aamer's mistreatment; that Labour governments wanted him to be released to Saudia Arabia; and that he had knowledge of the torture in Afghanistan of Ibn al-Shaykh al-Libi, whose coerced confessions about a link between Saddam Hussein and Al-Qaeda were relied on by the US and its allies to justify the 2003 Iraq invasion.[58]

The Executive

The Labour Party held power in the UK between 1997 and 2010, first under Blair and then, from 2007, under Gordon Brown. Following a General Election in 2010, David Cameron became Prime Minister after his Conservative Party formed a

[51] ibid, 58.

[52] Reprieve, '*Human Cargo*', 40–41.

[53] Sam Greenhill, David Jones and Emine Sinmaz, 'A great day for justice', *Daily Mail*, 31 October 2015.

[54] Guy Adams, 'Troubling questions that may never be answered', *Daily Mail*, 31 October 2015.

[55] David Rose, 'Journey to torture: Aamer tells of how he went from working for the US army to being savagely abused in an American base under the noses of British intelligence officers', *Mail on Sunday*, 12 December 2015.

[56] ibid; 'Shaker Aamer: "No plans to sue" over Guantánamo', *BBC News*, 14 December 2015.

[57] David Rose, '"They don't want me to see the sun again": Shaker Aamer—the last Briton held in Guantánamo Bay—gives searing account of his 14-year ordeal', *Mail on Sunday*, 4 October 2015.

[58] David Rose, '"They don't want me to see the sun again"'; 'David Miliband faces new torture questions', *Daily Mail*, 23 December 2014, 14.

coalition government with the Liberal Democrats, led by Nick Clegg. In 2015, the Conservatives won a parliamentary majority.

The Blair and Brown Governments

Prime Minister Blair was a close supporter of the war on terror, and his successor, Gordon Brown, remained committed.[59] The Blair and Brown Governments also maintained a consistent approach as to UK detainees at Guantánamo. The Blair Government reversed position relatively quickly after initially accepting US treatment of UK citizens.

In relation to more public aspects of US detainee policies, at first the UK was openly supportive of the Bush Administration's approach, with Prime Minister Blair describing Guantánamo Bay as 'unusual' but necessary for intelligence gathering.[60] The UK also defended the US decision not to apply Geneva Conventions protections to detainees.[61] Much is still unknown about how far the UK's support extended to the US practice of extraordinary rendition. The Blair and Brown Governments strongly denied any involvement with the program until, in 2008, a series of investigations by the media, NGOs and the UK Parliament forced the Foreign Secretary, David Miliband, to admit that the UK territory Diego Garcia was used for rendition flights.[62] The UK Government continues to obfuscate over the extent of its involvement in rendition, including whether Diego Garcia hosted an actual CIA prison.[63]

In the months following 9/11, the Blair Government supported the transfer of UK citizens to Guantánamo Bay. In January 2002, according to an internal Foreign and Commonwealth Office (FCO) memorandum, the Government decided that this was 'the best way to meet our counter-terrorism objective', since the citizens would have to be released if returned home.[64] In the case of one citizen, Mubanga, the Blair Government prevented its embassy officials in Zambia from offering consular assistance to the dual national, to ensure that he could not be returned to the UK.[65] The Blair Government also dismissed as 'completely false' early allegations that detainees at Guantánamo were being mistreated.[66] The Government

[59] Mark Shephard, 'Parliamentary scrutiny and oversight of the British "war on terror": Surrendering power to parliament or *plus ça change*?' in *The 'War on Terror' and the Growth of Executive Power*, ed John E Owens and Riccardo Pelizzo (New York: Routledge, 2010) 89.

[60] Steven Kettell, *New Labour and the New World Order: Britain's Role in the War on Terror* (Manchester: Manchester University Press, 2011) 41.

[61] United Kingdom, HC Deb 14 February 2002, vol 380, col 333 (Geoff Hoon).

[62] Tyrie, Gough and McCracken, *Account Rendered*, 70–73.

[63] Ian Cobain and Richard Norton-Taylor, 'Files on UK role in CIA rendition accidentally destroyed, says Minister', *Guardian*, 10 July 2014, 2.

[64] Tyrie, Gough and McCracken, *Account Rendered*, 93.

[65] ibid, 96.

[66] Michael White, Richard Norton-Taylor and Ian Black, 'War in Afghanistan—Ministers dismiss Cuba jail concerns', *Guardian*, 22 January 2002, 5.

supported its citizens' remaining in US military detention, even after UK intelligence officials in Afghanistan raised concerns that British detainees were being abused and possibly tortured.[67] MI5 and MI6 agents were subsequently informed by their superiors in London that, since the men were not in their custody or control, 'the law does not require you to intervene to prevent this'.[68]

By mid-2003, the Blair Government's view of the detention of UK citizens at Guantánamo began to change. Various factors contributed to the shift in position. Inside the Government, according to former Labour Foreign Secretary, Robin Cook, many of Blair's colleagues were 'perplexed' at his lack of concern over the treatment of detainees.[69] A significant turning point came with a UK Court of Appeal ruling in November 2002, in a case brought by the mother of a citizen, seeking judicial review to compel the FCO to make representations to the US on her son's, Abbasi, behalf.[70] While the Court ruled in the Government's favour, it issued a scathing critique of Guantánamo Bay.[71] A second turning point occurred in July 2003, when the US listed Begg and Abbasi for trial by military commission.[72] This event emboldened MPs to speak out, with Foreign Office Minister Chris Mullin telling the House of Commons that the Government had 'strong reservations about the military commission'.[73] A further factor contributing to the pressure on the Government over detainees was growing concern over Prime Minister Blair's handling of the Iraq war.[74]

With momentum building for the Blair Government to change its policy on Guantánamo Bay, the Prime Minister publicly called on the US to ensure that the military commissions were fair, and the cases against Begg and Abbasi were suspended as the UK Attorney-General, Lord Goldsmith, began talks with US officials about the trial rules.[75] In early 2004 the Foreign Minister, Jack Straw, announced that Lord Goldsmith's negotiations had reached a stalemate. The military commissions, he said, 'as presently constituted, would not provide the type of process which we would afford UK nationals'.[76] Straw also announced the repatriation of five UK citizens. Once home, the returned men described their experiences and said that the Blair Government had known about their abuse while they were in

[67] Ian Cobain, *A Secret History of Torture* (Berkeley, CA: Counterpoint, 2012) 218, 221.

[68] ibid, 218.

[69] Robin Cook, *The Point of Departure: Why One of Britain's Leading Politicians Resigned over Tony Blair's Decision to go to War in Iraq* (London: Simon & Schuster, 2003) 82.

[70] *The Queen on the Application of Abbasi v The Secretary of State for Foreign and Commonwealth Affairs* [2002] EWCA Civ 1598.

[71] ibid [64].

[72] United States Department of Defense, 'President determines enemy combatants subject to his military order', News Release, No 485-03, 3 July 2003.

[73] Nicholas Watt and Vikram Dodd, 'MPs' fury at secret US trials of "terror" Britons—Minister passes Commons protest to Americans', *Guardian*, 8 July 2003, 2.

[74] Riddell, *Hug Them Close*, 280.

[75] Nicholas Watt, 'Keep to the law, Blair tells Bush', *Guardian*, 10 July 2003, 11; 'Bush aids Blair by halting trial of Britons in Guantánamo Bay', *Guardian*, 19 July 2003, 8.

[76] Jack Straw, 'Straw's statement in full', 19 February 2004, http://news.bbc.co.uk/2/hi/uk_news/politics/3504501.stm.

detention, a fact it eventually admitted.[77] In June 2004, as the Australian Government continued to support US military commissions, Lord Goldsmith announced that the UK Government had been unable to accept that they offered 'sufficient guarantees of a fair trial in accordance with international standards'.[78] Prime Minister Blair asked the US for the remaining four UK citizens to be sent home.[79]

The Blair and Brown Governments were more reluctant to take responsibility for residents at Guantánamo Bay, only shifting their position in 2006. Until this time, their approach remained that, as non-nationals, the UK Government was unable to act on residents' behalf.[80] This was spelt out in correspondence from the FCO to the men's families, advising them to contact authorities in their countries of birth.[81] In Al Rawi's case, this was Iraq, which at the time of the correspondence was about to be invaded by allied forces; in Deghayes's case, this was Libya, whose Gaddafi regime had allegedly murdered his father. The UK Court of Appeal, in a case brought on behalf of Al Rawi, El Banna and Deghayes seeking to force the UK Government to request their release, described the FCO letters as 'crass and inappropriate'.[82] The Court, however, upheld the legal basis for the UK Government's refusal to take up the men's cases with the US (I return to this below).[83]

Although the UK Government now had a solid legal basis for refusing to help residents, a series of embarrassing revelations in the courts and media implicating the UK in the detainees' mistreatment ultimately forced it to reverse its position. In 2005, Al Rawi gave evidence to the Combatant Status Review Tribunal (CSRT) at Guantánamo that MI5 had urged him to remain close to Qatada so he could inform on the alleged extremist.[84] In addition, the *Al Rawi* litigation in the UK disclosed a series of documents implicating MI5, forcing admissions from the UK Government about the agency's role in providing inaccurate information to the Gambians and Americans that led to the arrests of Al Rawi and El Banna.[85] In March 2006, Foreign Secretary Straw announced that the Government would seek Al Rawi's release from Guantánamo Bay.[86] Other events put pressure on the

[77] Tania Branigan and Vikram Dodd, 'Britons held in Cuba say MI5 knew of abuse', *Guardian*, 15 May 2004, 4; Vikram Dodd, 'Foreign Office admits Guantánamo Briton has alleged ill treatment', *Guardian*, 27 August 2004, 11.

[78] Lord Goldsmith, 'Lord Goldsmith's speech in full', 25 June 2004, http://news.bbc.co.uk/2/hi/uk_news/politics/3839153.stm.

[79] Vikram Dodd, 'Blair makes secret plea to Bush on Guantánamo: Court papers reveal PM's effort to persuade US to send back four British prisoners', *Guardian*, 26 June 2004, 1.

[80] Vikram Dodd, 'The UK businessmen trapped in Guantánamo—arrested in Gambia, interrogated in Afghanistan, abandoned in Cuba', *Guardian*, 11 July 2003, 1.

[81] *The Queen on the Application of Al Rawi v The Secretary of State for Foreign and Commonwealth Affairs* [2006] EWCA Civ 1279 [19]–[20].

[82] ibid [19].

[83] ibid [89].

[84] Vikram Dodd, 'Guantánamo Briton claims he spied for MI5: Detainee says agents urged contact with Islamic cleric', *Guardian*, 22 March 2005, 6.

[85] Richard Norton-Taylor, Stephen Grey and Vikram Dodd, 'MI5 tip-off to CIA led to pair's rendition to Guantánamo', *Guardian*, 28 March 2006, 5.

[86] Richard Norton-Taylor, 'Straw pledges to intercede for UK resident in Guantánamo', *Guardian*, 23 March 2006, 4.

Blair and Brown Governments over the remaining residents. Mullin, now a former minister, publicly stated that the UK Government had a 'moral obligation' to help Al Rawi and El Banna because of its involvement in their predicament.[87] Conservative Member of Parliament Andrew Tyrie formed an All Party Parliamentary Group on Extraordinary Rendition (APPG).[88] The Council of Europe released a report implicating MI5 in the extraordinary renditions of UK residents.[89] Al Rawi returned home and spoke out about his experiences, including his torture and involvement with MI5.[90] In July 2007, the High Court gave the Government two weeks to disclose whether it would accept El Banna's return to the UK.[91] A week later, the Government called on the US to release the five remaining UK residents from Guantánamo.[92] Three of the men, El Banna, Deghayes and Sameur, were released in December 2007.

Mohamed, who the US claimed was 'particularly dangerous', was released in February 2009.[93] Leading up to his release, Mohamed was charged in the military commission system with offences carrying the death penalty.[94] Mohamed claimed the charges were based on false confessions procured through torture, and his lawyers launched a case in the High Court seeking the release of documents in the UK Government's possession that would prove this.[95] Mohamed won a series of legal victories, in the course of which highly embarrassing information was revealed about the extent of the UK's knowledge of, and involvement in, his torture.[96] In October 2008, the charges against Mohamed were dropped, and the Home Secretary asked the Attorney-General to investigate possible criminal wrongdoing by MI5.[97]

Throughout 2009 and 2010, demands for a public inquiry into UK complicity in torture grew. This included from parliamentary committees, the UK's

[87] Richard Norton-Taylor, 'Britain helped us seize pair held in Guantánamo, says ex-minister', *Guardian*, 19 December 2005, 7.

[88] All Party Parliamentary Group on Extraordinary Rendition, 'MPs and peers from all parties come together to demand that the government comes clean over "torture flights"', press release, 4 December 2005.

[89] Council of Europe Committee on Legal Affairs and Human Rights, *Alleged secret detentions and unlawful inter-state transfers of detainees involving Council of Europe member states*, 2006, http://assembly.coe.int/CommitteeDocs/2006/20060606_Ejdoc162006PartII-FINAL.pdf.

[90] Sean O'Neill, 'MI5 betrayed me, says Guantánamo man', *The Times*, 30 July 2007, 11.

[91] ibid.

[92] Vikram Dodd and Richard Norton-Taylor, 'Government requests return of British residents from Guantánamo Bay', *Guardian*, 8 August 2007, 12.

[93] Ed Pilkington and Alexandra Topping, 'And then there was one: Four British residents freed from Guantánamo', *Guardian*, 8 December 2007, 3; Detainee Inquiry, *The Report of the Detainee Inquiry*, 20.

[94] Tyrie, Gough and McCracken, *Account Rendered*, 85.

[95] *The Queen on the Application of Binyam Mohamed v Secretary of State for Foreign and Commonwealth Affairs* [2008] EWHC 2048 (Admin).

[96] Richard Norton-Taylor, 'Suspect tortured while MI5 visited Morocco: High Court papers seem to contradict agency account Binyam renditioned to Middle East from Pakistan', *Guardian*, 1 August 2009, 2.

[97] Tyrie, Gough and McCracken, *Account Rendered*, 85; Richard Norton-Taylor and Duncan Campbell, 'Smith orders inquiry into MI5 and CIA torture claims: Investigation into possible criminal wrongdoing Guantánamo campaigner welcomes decision', *Guardian*, 31 October 2008, 4.

Independent Reviewer of Terrorism Legislation and the Conservative Party leader, David Cameron.[98] Prime Minister Brown refused.

The Cameron Government

Within two months of the new Conservative–Liberal Democrat Government taking power, Prime Minister Cameron announced the establishment of the independent, judge-led Detainee Inquiry.[99] The Detainee Inquiry's terms of reference specified that it would examine whether, and to what extent, the UK Government and its security and intelligence agencies were involved in, or were aware of, the improper treatment or rendition of UK nationals and residents after 11 September 2001.[100] The Prime Minister insisted that the inquiry was 'not some political witch hunt to get at Ministers from a previous Government', though commentary at the time noted that it would place pressure on Labour.[101]

The Cameron Government gave various reasons for holding an inquiry into the UK's complicity in torture. Addressing Parliament, Prime Minister Cameron emphasised a moral imperative, noting 'we need to restore Britain's moral leadership in the world'.[102] More pragmatically, Prime Minister Cameron argued that UK intelligence services were unable to do their jobs properly, and were 'paralysed by paperwork as they try to defend themselves in lengthy court cases with uncertain rules'.[103] The Prime Minister was also responding to political pressure, including from the Liberal Democrats and some Conservative MPs, such as Tyrie, who were pushing hard for an inquiry.[104] The Government was also concerned to prevent more sensitive disclosures in court proceedings. In late 2010, it reached a confidential settlement with the Guantánamo Bay detainees, which avoided admissions of culpability and brought an end to further litigation.[105]

The Detainee Inquiry attracted extensive criticism from detainees, their lawyers and human rights NGOs, who argued that it lacked transparency and independence. The head of the Detainee Inquiry, Sir Peter Gibson, was a former Court of Appeal judge who had served as Intelligence Services Commissioner, prompting

[98] Ian Cobain, Richard Norton-Taylor and Deborah Summers, 'Cameron demands full inquiry into Intelligence Agencies' links to torture', *Guardian*, 12 March 2009, 4; Richard Norton-Taylor, 'Watchdog inquiry into UK's rendition role', *Guardian*, 2 March 2009, 18.

[99] United Kingdom, HC Deb 6 July 2010, vol 513, cols 175–90 (David Cameron), cols 175–76.

[100] HM Government, *The Detainee Inquiry Terms of Reference*, 2011 (Detainee Inquiry), http://www.detaineeinquiry.org.uk/wp-content/uploads/2011/06/20110706-The-Detainee-Inquiry-and-HM-Government-Terms-of-reference.pdf.

[101] United Kingdom, HC Deb 6 July 2010, vol 513, cols 175–90 (David Cameron), col 187; Patrick Wintour, 'Hague orders inquiry into torture claims: Judge will investigate allegations that UK was complicit in abuse of detainees', *Guardian*, 21 May 2010, 1.

[102] United Kingdom, HC Deb 6 July 2010, vol 513, col 175–90 (David Cameron), col 178.

[103] ibid, col 175.

[104] Tyrie, Gough and McCracken, *Account Rendered*, 2.

[105] United Kingdom, HC Deb 16 November 2010, vol 518, col 752 (Kenneth Clarke).

questions about his impartiality.[106] Other concerns stemmed from the Inquiry rules, which included that the Government had the final say as to what evidence should be disclosed to the public.[107] These concerns resulted in widespread boycotting of the Inquiry in August 2011, undermining its legitimacy.[108]

The Government abandoned the Detainee Inquiry in January 2012.[109] The official reason was the launch of a new police investigation into allegations of UK involvement in the extraordinary rendition of Libyan dissidents to Libya.[110] The Government told the UN Committee Against Torture that 'we fully intend to hold an independent judge-led inquiry', once police investigations were completed.[111] Gibson submitted a report of his preparatory work to the Cameron Government in June 2012, and it was released 18 months later.[112]

The Detainee Inquiry report was based entirely on documents.[113] It made no findings of fact, neither did it reach any conclusions, but it raised a number of issues the panel thought should be taken up by a future inquiry. Those issues were based around the themes of interrogation and treatment; rendition; training and guidance; and policy and communications. Documents examined by the Inquiry indicated that there were instances where UK intelligence officers were aware of 'inappropriate interrogation techniques and mistreatment or allegations of mistreatment of some detainees by liaison partners from other countries', and the UK Government or its agencies may have become inappropriately involved in cases of rendition.[114] Among questions the Inquiry wanted pursued were whether agencies inappropriately continued to engage with liaison partners in cases where treatment issues had been identified, and whether the Government responded adequately on becoming aware of renditions or proposed renditions of UK nationals and residents.

Upon releasing the Detainee Inquiry report, the Cameron Government announced that it was handing over the investigation of the issues raised by the panel to the Intelligence and Security Committee of Parliament (ISC)—a committee previously criticised over its lack of independence on the torture issue.[115] The

[106] Cobain, *A Secret History of Torture*, 269.

[107] HM Government, *Protocol for the Detainee Inquiry* (2011); Christian Khan Solicitors to Sara Carnegie, Solicitor to the Detainee Inquiry, 3 August 2011, http://www.detaineeinquiry.org.uk/wp-content/uploads/2011/06/20110706-The-Detainee-Inquiry-and-HM-Government-Protocol.pdf.

[108] Cobain, *A Secret History of Torture*, 270.

[109] Detainee Inquiry, 'Statement by the Chairman of the Detainee Inquiry', press release, 18 January 2012.

[110] United Kingdom, HC Deb 18 January 2012, vol 538, col 751 (Kenneth Clarke).

[111] United Kingdom, *List of Issues in Connection with the Consideration of the Fifth Periodic Report of the United Kingdom of Great Britain and Northern Ireland, adopted by the Committee at its Forty-Ninth Session (29 October–23 November 2012)—Addendum—Replies of the United Kingdom to the List of Issues (CAT/C/GBR/Q/5)*, Reply to List of Issues to Committee Against Torture, UN Doc CAT/C/GBR/Q/5/Add, 2 May 2013.

[112] Detainee Inquiry, 'Statement by the Inquiry—28 June', press release, 28 June 2012.

[113] Detainee Inquiry, 'Statement by the Detainee Inquiry on publication of its report on 19 December 2013', press release, 19 December 2013, 7.

[114] ibid, 89.

[115] Tyrie, Gough and McCracken, *Account Rendered*, 5.

Government said it would decide, following the ISC's report, if a further judicial inquiry 'still remains necessary'.[116] The Government's decision was met with widespread criticism, including from Detainee Inquiry panel members.[117] The secret ISC inquiry is ongoing.[118]

The release of the US Senate Select Committee on Intelligence report on CIA torture at the end of 2014 put renewed pressure on the Cameron Government to establish another judge-led inquiry into UK complicity.[119] This followed revelations that Cameron Government representatives met with US Senate Select Committee members and requested that information implicating the UK be kept out of the public version of its report on 'national security grounds'.[120] The Cameron Government, meanwhile, continued to pursue the release from Guantánamo Bay of the remaining UK resident, Aamer.[121]

Parliament

Parliamentary oversight of the torture issue under Labour governments was, for many years, secondary to the role played by the courts. The UK Parliament provided some accountability for the executive government's detainee policies in two ways: through parliamentary committees, though this was limited, and through the work of individual MPs.

Under the Blair Government, Parliament's role was marginalised as a result of the substantial size of Labour's House of Commons majority, the Prime Minister's unilateral attitude to governing and a passive Conservative Party.[122] Prime Minister Blair's Cabinet was weak, especially after he replaced Robin Cook as Foreign Secretary in 2001. The Prime Minister's attitude towards the Parliament and its committees was one of neglect.[123] Running counter to these developments were others, however, that bolstered Parliament's powers. This included the growing status of the UK's third political party, the Liberal Democrats, a party traditionally strong on civil liberties and which campaigned heavily on Guantánamo Bay. Its position was enhanced by 1999 reforms of the House of Lords, removing

[116] United Kingdom, HC Deb 19 December 2013, vol 572, col 913 (Kenneth Clarke).

[117] Ian Cobain, Richard Norton-Taylor and Nick Hopkins, 'MI5 and MI6 face questions over torture of terrorism suspects', *Guardian*, 20 December 2013, 12.

[118] Intelligence and Security Committee of Parliament, 'Intelligence and security committee—work priorities statement', statement, 29 October 2015.

[119] Richard Norton-Taylor and Ian Cobain, 'UK must reveal truth on torture, say critics', *Guardian*, 11 December 2014, 1.

[120] Tom McTague, 'Did torture stop UK terror attack? Al-Qaeda terrorist captured in London after CIA spies interrogated Guantanamo Bay detainees', *Daily Mail*, 12 December 2014.

[121] Ian Drury and Neil Sears, 'Bring torture victim to UK for trial, family of British man held in Guantanamo beg the government', *Daily Mail*, 12 December 2014, 2.

[122] Shephard, 'Parliamentary scrutiny and oversight of the British "war on terror"', 89.

[123] Philip Norton, *Parliament in British Politics* (London: Palgrave MacMillan, 2005) 243.

hereditary peers.[124] Another was the parliamentary backlash that occurred in Prime Minister Blair's third term of office over security policy, particularly the UK's involvement in extraordinary rendition.[125] This loss of trust in Prime Minister Blair arose primarily from his support of the Bush Administration's invasion of Iraq. The Conservatives supported military action against Hussein's regime and applied little pressure on Prime Minister Blair. However, the Prime Minister's lack of consultation with Parliament ahead of the invasion led to a backbench rebellion from his own party's ranks.[126] Compounding this, controversies surrounding the subsequent failure to find weapons of mass destruction in Iraq led to a loss of legitimacy for Prime Minister Blair, including from the public, Parliament and Labour MPs.[127]

The record of parliamentary committees in providing oversight of the executive on detainee treatment in the war on terror was mixed. The ISC, which oversees intelligence agencies, was criticised for its failure to robustly investigate allegations of complicity by UK intelligence in torture. The ISC's members are nominated by the Prime Minister, and critics argued that it believed too readily the Government's claims of ignorance of extraordinary rendition.[128] For example, in 2007 the ISC accepted the Prime Minister's (inaccurate) assurances that US rendition flights never used UK airspace after 9/11.[129] Conservative MP Andrew Tyrie accused the ISC of failing 'in its primary task of obtaining the truth on the public's behalf'.[130] The ISC was reformed by the Justice and Security Act 2013, which gave it slightly more independence.

The Joint Committee on Human Rights (JCHR) was more critical of the Government's policies with respect to torture, and became a vocal proponent of a public inquiry into complicity in torture. The JCHR was established after the passage of the Human Rights Act (HRA) in 1998, which gave effect to rights under the European Convention on Human Rights (ECHR), to which the UK is a party, as domestic statutory rights.[131] This meant that claimants could bring cases under the Convention in the UK courts, rather than having to go to the European Court of Human Rights (ECtHR) in Strasbourg. The role of the JCHR includes scrutinising the executive's record on human rights and its compliance with international treaties, and human rights scholars have praised its diligence in this regard since 9/11.[132] The JCHR tends to act in a consensual, non-partisan and independent

[124] Shephard, 'Parliamentary scrutiny and oversight of the British "war on terror"', 87, 90.

[125] ibid, 99.

[126] ibid, 93–95.

[127] ibid, 99.

[128] Cobain, *A Secret History of Torture*, 267–68.

[129] Intelligence and Security Committee of Parliament, United Kingdom Parliament, *Rendition*, 68–69.

[130] Tyrie, Gough and McCracken, *Account Rendered*, 5.

[131] Rayner Thwaites, *The Liberty of Non-Citizens* (Oxford: Hart Publishing, 2014) 137.

[132] Norton, *Parliament in British Politics*, 150–51; Janet L Hiebert, 'Parliamentary review of terrorism measures', *The Modern Law Review* 68(4) (2005), 676–80; Conor Gearty, '11 September 2001, Counter-terrorism, and the Human Rights Act', *Journal of Law and Society* 32(1) (2005), 32.

way, because there is generally no government majority on the committee and it employs outside legal advisers.[133] Although the JCHR's influence on legislative and judicial outcomes in the UK varies, there is evidence that it has had a positive impact on parliamentary debate around human rights.[134] This includes on torture.

In its 2006 report on the UN Convention Against Torture and Other Cruel, Inhuman or Degrading Treatment or Punishment (CAT), the JCHR criticised a number of UK government policies and actions, including its attempts to undermine a 1997 ECtHR ruling in *Chahal v UK*, and its reliance on diplomatic assurances before deporting non-nationals to countries where they could be tortured.[135] *Chahal v UK* established that a person may not be deported to a country where he faces a real risk of torture, and that the protection of Article 3 of the ECHR prohibiting torture was absolute, even in a time of public emergency.[136] The JCHR also voiced scepticism about the UK Government's assurances regarding the UK's lack of involvement in extraordinary renditions.[137] In its 2009 report into allegations of UK complicity in torture, it called on the Government to establish an independent inquiry, singling out Canada's Arar inquiry (see Chapter 7) as an appropriate model.[138]

Another way in which the UK Parliament provided executive accountability for government policy regarding Guantánamo Bay detainees was through the actions of individual MPs. For example, after Begg and Abbasi were listed for trial by military commission, more than 200 MPs signed a House of Commons motion calling for UK citizens at Guantánamo Bay to be given a fair trial.[139] The following year, 175 members of both houses of Parliament filed an amicus curiae brief in support of the petitioners in the US Supreme Court case *Rasul v Bush*, discussed in Chapter 4.[140] Andrew Tyrie's APPG on Extraordinary Rendition was another unusual show of cross-party unity.[141] Tyrie and his group worked closely with human rights NGOs and media to pressure the Government as regards its policy

[133] Aileen Kavanagh, 'The Joint Committee on Human Rights: A hybrid breed of constitutional watchdog' in *Parliament and Human Rights*, ed Murray Hunt, Hayley J Hopper and Paul Yowell (Oxford: Hart Publishing, 2015) 117–18.

[134] Michael C Tolley, 'Parliamentary scrutiny of rights in the United Kingdom: Assessing the work of the Joint Committee on Human Rights', *Australian Journal of Political Science* 44(1) (2009), 53.

[135] Joint Committee on Human Rights (JCHR), United Kingdom Parliament, *The UN Convention Against Torture (UNCAT)* (2005–06, HL 185, HC 701) 4, 14.

[136] *Chahal v United Kingdom* (1997) 23 EHRR 413.

[137] JCHR, *The UN Convention Against Torture (UNCAT)* (2005–06, HL 185, HC 701) 19.

[138] JCHR, United Kingdom Parliament, *Allegations of UK Complicity in Torture*, (2008–09, HL 152, HC 230) 3, 21, 35.

[139] Tania Branigan and Vikram Dodd, 'The bitterest betrayal—among the 680 men imprisoned at Camp Delta, Cuba, are nine Britons', *Guardian*, 19 July 2003, 25.

[140] Ahmed and Others, 'Brief of 175 members of both houses of the Parliament of the United Kingdom of Great Britain and Northern Ireland as amici curiae in support of petitioners', submission in *Rasul v Bush*, Nos 03-343, 03-334, 14 January 2004.

[141] All Party Parliamentary Group on Extraordinary Rendition, 'MPs and peers from all parties come together to demand that the government comes clean over "torture flights"', press release, 4 December 2005.

on residents at Guantánamo Bay, and to argue for an independent public inquiry into complicity in torture.[142] All-party parliamentary groups can provide a means of contact between outside organisations and MPs and ministers, and are attractive to interest groups because they operate outside the party context.[143] Local MPs of UK Guantánamo Bay detainees also built public awareness of their constituents' plights through parliamentary debates and the media.[144]

The Courts

The UK judiciary played an important role in reviewing executive action on Guantánamo Bay detainees.[145] In the course of hearing the cases of individual citizens and residents, the courts brought about significant changes to the UK Government's treatment of detainees. This often occurred indirectly. While the courts frequently ruled in favour of the Government, they provided moral accountability by denouncing official policy, forcing the release of embarrassing documents and raising public awareness of the issues. Three cases in particular put substantial pressure on the Government: *Abbasi v Secretary of State*, *Al Rawi v Secretary of State* and *Mohamed v Secretary of State*.[146]

The central issue in *Abbasi* was whether the Government could be compelled to make diplomatic representations on a citizen's behalf to a foreign government. The Court of Appeal rejected the Government's argument, based on the act of state doctrine, that it could not express a view on the legitimacy of a foreign state's actions.[147] The Court found that Abbasi had a very limited right, under the common law doctrine of legitimate expectations, to have the UK Government 'consider' making representations to the US.[148] It was inappropriate, the Court said, to order the Secretary of State to make such representations, as 'this would have an impact on the conduct of foreign policy' at a particularly delicate time.[149] The Court also found that Abbasi could not rely on his rights under the ECHR (including Article 3), which did not apply because the UK exercised no authority or control over

[142] Tyrie, Gough and McCracken, *Account Rendered*, ix, 2.

[143] Norton, *Parliament in British Politics*, 127.

[144] Examples are Labour's Geraint Davies, Abbasi's local MP; Liberal Democrat Edward Davey, Al Rawi's local MP; and Conservative Jane Ellison, Aamer's local MP.

[145] Kent Roach, *The 9/11 Effect: Comparative Counter-Terrorism* (New York, NY: Cambridge University Press, 2011) 239.

[146] *The Queen on the Application of Abbasi v The Secretary of State for Foreign and Commonwealth Affairs* [2002] EWCA Civ 1598; *The Queen on the Application of Al Rawi v The Secretary of State for Foreign and Commonwealth Affairs* [2006] EWCA Civ 1279; *The Queen on the Application of Binyam Mohamed v Secretary of State for Foreign and Commonwealth Affairs* [2008] EWHC 2048 (Admin); *The Queen on the Application of Binyam Mohamed v Secretary of State for Foreign and Commonwealth Affairs* [2010] EWCA Civ 65.

[147] *Abbasi v Secretary of State* [2002] EWCA Civ 1598 [53], [57].

[148] ibid [106].

[149] ibid [107].

its citizen at Guantánamo Bay.[150] Ultimately, the Court of Appeal offered Abbasi no effective remedy since it found that the UK Government had considered his request for diplomatic protection.[151] However, by criticising Guantánamo Bay, noting that Abbasi was 'arbitrarily detained in a "legal black hole"', the Court gave his campaign powerful ammunition to pressure the Blair Government.[152]

The issue of diplomatic representations was litigated in a subsequent case brought by UK residents Al Rawi, El Banna and Deghayes. The Court of Appeal ruled that while *Abbasi* established that a citizen had a right to expect that the UK Government would consider making diplomatic representations, a resident had no such right.[153] The Court rejected the claims of the residents (and their families) based on the Race Relations Act 1976 and ECHR rights, including the rights not to be discriminated against or tortured and the right to family life (Articles 8, 3 and 14).[154] The Court found that the non-nationals had been treated differently from nationals, 'not because of their race (nationality) but because one group is entitled to diplomatic protection and the other is not'.[155] However, once again, the Court of Appeal made its disapproval of Guantánamo Bay clear, outlining the harsh treatment authorised by the US Government against detainees.[156]

The UK courts were also instrumental in the campaigning of another resident, Mohamed, who sued the UK Government for access to information it had proving he was tortured. Mohamed relied on the *Norwich Pharmacal* principle, under which a third party involved (unwittingly) in wrongdoing to a person is obliged to assist that person by giving information to help the individual pursue the wrongdoer.[157] The UK Government opposed disclosure on the ground that it would 'cause significant damage to national security of the United Kingdom', as it would harm the UK–US intelligence-sharing relationship.[158] In its 2008 judgment, the High Court ruled that—subject to public interest immunity issues—the UK Government was bound to turn over to Mohamed's lawyers information in its possession that related to Mohamed's rendition and treatment.[159] The court attached 'particular significance to the prohibition on State torture'.[160] In reaching this decision the court made various findings about the involvement of MI5 and MI6 in Mohamed's case, including that the agencies knew about his detention in Pakistan and Morocco, and had supplied information and questions for his

[150] ibid [77].
[151] ibid [67], [107].
[152] ibid [64].
[153] *The Queen on the Application of Al Rawi v The Secretary of State for Foreign and Commonwealth Affairs* [2006] EWCA Civ 1279 [89].
[154] ibid [87], [114].
[155] ibid [78].
[156] ibid [25].
[157] *Norwich Pharmacal v Customs and Excise Commissioners* [1974] AC 133.
[158] *Mohamed v Secretary of State* [2008] EWHC 2048 (Admin) [3].
[159] ibid [147].
[160] ibid [142].

interrogations.[161] The UK's involvement 'was far beyond that of a bystander or witness to the alleged wrongdoing'.[162] In August 2009, the High Court was forced to revise its earlier judgment after it established that an MI5 agent had visited Morocco three times during Mohamed's detention, and MI5 had asked the CIA if it could interrogate him and provided it with a list of questions.[163]

In response to the High Court ruling, the UK Government once again sought to withhold documentation relating to Mohamed's torture, this time relying on the 'control principle', that only the provider of the intelligence (the US) could release it.[164] This resulted in protracted litigation, with the matter eventually making its way to the Court of Appeal. By this time, the disclosure sought related to seven paragraphs redacted from the High Court's original judgment that described Mohamed's torture and UK intelligence's knowledge that it was occurring (other relevant material had been disclosed already in US court proceedings).[165] In February 2010, the Court of Appeal ordered the disclosure of evidence the UK Government had fought to keep secret, ruling that the 'control principle' did not necessarily trump public interest in every case.[166] While this judgment was unanimous, two out of three judges based their decision on the fact that, prior to giving it, the US courts had already ruled that Mohamed had been tortured.[167]

The above cases resulted in mixed outcomes for detainees. Abbasi and Al Rawi and others lost their legal bids to force the UK Government to press for their release, while Mohamed won the disclosure of torture documents only because a US court had previously established his torture. Yet these cases were critical in the men's campaigning. The judges' reproachful comments on UK Government policy helped legitimise concerns raised by the detainees' supporters, and increased pressure on the Government to secure their release. The cases also led to compensation settlements for citizens and residents. Hence the power of war on terror litigation to provide state accountability on issues of detainee treatment can be understood in ways that go beyond any particular legal ruling. Litigation reasserts the principle of the rule of law in a highly politicised discourse, and can send a judicial message to the political branches.[168] It can secure access to secret information, make concepts like 'extraordinary rendition' less abstract and, ultimately, serve as a catalyst to change law or practice.

The cases raise issues about the extent to which courts can augment or curtail civil society power in human rights cases. Lawyers and families of detainees and

[161] ibid [87]–[88].

[162] ibid [88].

[163] Norton-Taylor, 'Suspect tortured while MI5 visited Morocco'.

[164] Adam Tomkins, 'National security and the due process of law', *Current Legal Problems* 64(1) (2011), 226.

[165] *Mohamed v Secretary of State* [2010] EWCA Civ 65 [2]; Tomkins, 'National security and the due process of law', 228.

[166] *Mohamed v Secretary of State* [2010] EWCA Civ 65 [290].

[167] ibid [191], [295].

[168] Helen Duffy, 'Human rights litigation and the "war on terror"', *International Review of the Red Cross* 90(871) (2008), 595–97.

human rights NGOs worked through the formal juridical structures of domestic courts to influence government policy and bring about improvements in their clients' situations. In the UK context, the ability of detainees' supporters and courts themselves to influence the executive government was enhanced by the HRA 1998. The Act empowered the judiciary to engage more robustly on human rights issues in cases brought by Guantánamo Bay detainees.[169] I discuss this below.

Civil Society

Civil society in the UK mobilised sooner on the issue of the treatment of detainees in the war on terror, compared to Australia. Individuals and groups used a range of tools and organised in a collaborative way to demand the release of UK detainees and a torture inquiry. This section gives a brief overview of UK civil society and the main actors involved in the detainee issue. I then outline some features of civil society behaviour, including its early activism, particularly by lawyers, the collaboration between different actors for a torture inquiry and the focus on impunity rather than individual victims.

The Actors

After 11 September 2001, UK civil society was in a more solid position than that in Australia. Following a long period of Conservative rule, including a challenging decade under Margaret Thatcher, who led an 'attack on … the associational basis of civil society', the sector was enjoying a resurgence.[170] The renewed interest in civil society can be seen against the background of the transition from Communism to democracy in Eastern Europe.[171] Other factors elucidate UK civil society's stronger position. London is the birthplace of Amnesty International, the transnational organisation founded in 1961 by a British lawyer.[172] Stephen Hopgood locates the impetus for Amnesty International in the tradition of radical English popular dissent stretching back to Thomas Paine.[173] The relatively large number of human rights organisations in the UK is also a consequence of the problems in Northern Ireland, which were most intense during the 1970s and 1980s.

[169] John Ip, 'The Supreme Court and House of Lords in the war on terror: Inter Arma Silent Leges?', *Michigan State Journal of International Law* 19(1) (2010), 41–42.

[170] John Dryzek et al, *Green States and Social Movements: Environmentalism in the United States, United Kingdom, Germany and Norway* (Oxford: Oxford University Press, 2003) 42, 50.

[171] Siobhan Daly and Jude Howell, *For the common good? The changing role of civil society in the UK and Ireland*, Carnegie UK Trust, June 2006, 12.

[172] Stephen Hopgood, *Keepers of the Flame: Understanding Amnesty International* (Ithaca, NY: Cornell University Press, 2006) 1, 7.

[173] ibid, 8.

This is not to say that civil society in the UK was fully prepared for the challenge to human rights associated with the war on terror. As in Australia, the political climate in the UK was toxic for Muslims. Lawyer Gareth Peirce, who acted for a number of detainees, noted at a Muslim community event in 2004, 'I have never known such venom and such hatred … as there has been against the Muslim community.'[174] This created an inhibiting environment for activism for Muslims. One Muslim human rights activist said 'there was absolute panic' by most Muslim organisations after 9/11, and a lack of 'a strategy or understanding of how to cope with what was going on'.[175]

As in the Australian case, in this section I consider five categories of actors. A small but active group of progressive human rights lawyers played a significant role in the detainee torture issue. These lawyers had the early backing of legal professional organisations, including The Law Society of England and Wales and The Bar Council. Numerous domestic and international NGOs also became involved with the detainee torture issue, though mainstream Muslim community organisations, including the Islamic Human Rights Commission (IHRC) and the Muslim Council of Britain (MCB), engaged in little public advocacy on it. Cage (formerly Cageprisoners) is an Islamic-based organisation specifically established to advocate for war on terror detainees. Sections of the UK media campaigned on torture. I analysed editorials published by two newspapers: the *Guardian*, a more liberal newspaper, and *The Times*, which is more conservative. Family members had a limited role in the torture issue, with some exceptions.

Early Activism

Human rights lawyers were the earliest and most forthright actors to take up the cases of Guantánamo detainees. A small number of UK lawyers appeared regularly in the media, challenging the Blair Government on its detainee policies, well before human rights NGOs and MPs went public with their concerns. Illustrating this, in 2003 the *Guardian* noted that the detainees' families' 'only real support has come from campaigning lawyers … and a handful of sympathetic MPs'.[176] This view was supported by the lawyers. One, who represented detainees, said:

> [T]he people who were most active really early on were the lawyers and a small section of the left wing press, but it took time for the mainstream media and for other NGOs and for the public generally to become aware of the issues.[177]

The lawyers included Peirce, a seasoned campaigner on Northern Ireland who had previously acted for the Guilford Four and Birmingham Six, two high-profile

[174] Colin Blackstock, 'Muslims face "dark age of injustice": Civil rights lawyer accuses police and press', *Guardian*, 1 April 2004, 4.

[175] Muslim human rights activist, tel interview, 5 March 2013.

[176] Branigan and Dodd, 'The bitterest betrayal'.

[177] Detainee lawyer, tel interview, 11 February 2013.

miscarriage of justice cases relating to IRA bombings in the 1970s.[178] According to media reports, Peirce was instrumental in the Government's decision to bring home UK citizens from Guantánamo.[179] Clive Stafford Smith was a US-trained death penalty lawyer who founded the legal charity Reprieve and took on Guantánamo cases, over time acting for some 85 detainees.[180] Another lawyer involved in the *Abbasi* litigation was Louise Christian, a former chair of Liberty, the national civil liberties organisation.[181] The lawyers were backed in their criticisms of UK Government policy on Guantánamo Bay by a few outspoken judges. Foremost among them was Lord Steyn, a member of the Judicial Committee of the House of Lords, whose comments made headlines around the world. In November 2003, while the Blair Government was in negotiations with the US over its military commission rules, Lord Steyn called the proposed trials a 'monstrous failure of justice'.[182]

Lawyers in the UK worked with legal professional organisations, the detainees' families and progressive media, as well as through the courts. It was clear from the beginning that acting for the detainees 'was very much going to be a case of campaigning', a lawyer said.[183] An early success was getting The Law Society of England and Wales and The Bar Council on board on the detainee rights issue in 2002, at a time when 'not a lot of people had a lot to say on it'. The organisations, representing more than 100,000 lawyers, demanded that Guantánamo detainees be given access to legal advice.[184] Litigation was a key component of the lawyers' arsenal for pressuring the UK Government on detainees, and the power of judicial rulings, as discussed, often went beyond legal outcomes. A lawyer described the effect of the *Abbasi* case in 2002 on campaigning in such terms:

> Officially we lost the case, but the Court also described his legal predicament in quite swingeing terms, that he was detained in a 'legal black hole' ... and this judgment went around the world. So in a way you can say that that view from the judiciary was also a real turning point.[185]

Engaging in public advocacy through the media was crucial to lawyers' campaigning. Lawyers used media to humanise detainees and exert moral pressure on the UK Government. Stafford Smith, shaped by his experiences working in the US,

[178] Gareth Peirce, *Dispatches from the Dark Side: On Torture and the Death of Justice* (London: Verso, 2010).

[179] Owen Bowcott, '*The Guardian* Profile: Gareth Peirce,' *Guardian*, 14 January 2005: 14.

[180] David Cole, *Engines of Liberty: The Power of Citizen Activists to make Constitutional Law* (New York: Basic Books, 2016): 176.

[181] Louise Christian, 'Comment and analysis: Letters: My tortured clients,' *Guardian*, 15 September 2004: 25.

[182] Clare Dyer, 'Law Lord castigates US justice: Guantánamo Bay detainees facing trial by "kangaroo court",' *Guardian*, 26 November 2003, 9.

[183] Detainee lawyer, tel interview, 11 February 2013.

[184] Clare Dyer, 'Camp X-Ray families threaten writ—Britain accused of aiding US in unlawful detention', *Guardian*, 26 February 2002.

[185] Detainee lawyer, tel interview, 11 February 2013.

was unafraid to use media in his campaigning for detainees.[186] He gave media interviews and wrote newspaper opinion pieces. A Muslim human rights activist said of Stafford Smith's 'media-centric approach':

> He understood the role straight away, that there was a narrative that was trying to come out that they [the UK and US Governments] needed to supress in whatever way they could, and so he did openly speak about the abuses that were taking place and that really helped.[187]

Stafford Smith's media advocacy was exemplified by his article for the *Guardian* regarding his first visit to Guantánamo Bay to see Begg. Stafford Smith questioned the UK's role in Begg's treatment, including his possible torture, and wrote, '[a]s a nation, our morality is defined by whether we join the gang that is casting stones, or stand between the mob and its target'.[188] Another lawyer, Christian, also in the *Guardian*, accused the UK Government of 'nothing less than a collusion in an international experiment in inhumanity' over its response to UK citizens detained at Guantánamo.[189]

Lawyers partnered with family members of detainees to lobby the UK and American Governments. Many families were afraid to speak out. An analysis of news articles in the *Guardian* and *The Times* over the period 2001 to 2010 suggests they were not a major force, especially initially, in pressuring the UK Government. The *Guardian* reported that families 'kept their heads down, fearing that anything they say could be used against their loved ones'.[190] Begg's father, Amzat, was an exception, described by the *Guardian* in 2004 as 'the most vocal campaigner among the UK families of Guantánamo prisoners'.[191] A Muslim human rights activist said Amzat 'literally didn't sleep for all those years, he made sure he kept on pushing, and it did eventually succeed'.[192] Amzat was a regular voice in the media. He lobbied at the European Parliament, helped launch the Guantánamo Bay Human Rights Commission, took part in a delegation to Washington to lobby US politicians and helped launch a new political party, Peace and Progress.[193] Abbasi's mother launched legal proceedings, gave media interviews and lobbied parliamentarians.[194]

[186] Vikram Dodd, 'The *Guardian* Profile: Clive is used to the US way, where people play things to the media', *Guardian*, 10 August 2007, 19.

[187] Muslim human rights activist, tel interview, 11 February 2013.

[188] Clive Stafford Smith, 'US censors silenced me over the Gitmo gulag', *Guardian*, 20 December 2004, 16.

[189] Louise Christian, 'Guantánamo Bay: A global experiment in inhumanity', *Guardian*, 10 January 2004, 24.

[190] Branigan and Dodd, 'The bitterest betrayal'.

[191] Vikram Dodd and Tania Branigan, 'Guantánamo families seek justice in US', *Guardian*, 9 March 2004, 4.

[192] Muslim human rights activist, tel interview, 5 March 2013.

[193] For example, see Tania Branigan, 'Guantánamo families to take fight to US: American Civil Liberties group to help British detainees', *Guardian*, 21 January 2004, 4.

[194] For example, see Dyer, 'Camp X-Ray families threaten writ', 2.

The families of UK residents, after some five years had passed, turned to the media to raise awareness and pressure the Government. The *Guardian* noted that in the early years after El Banna's disappearance, his wife 'tried to shield her children from the truth about their father's whereabouts. But now she has decided she must speak out to try to get Jamil home'.[195] The Deghayes family released a 'detailed dossier' of Omar's torture.[196] Al Rawi's mother went public after the Court of Appeal ruling against her son.[197] When the UK Government reversed its position on residents at Guantánamo Bay, the *Guardian* reported that 'Whitehall officials admitted the decision had come after relentless pressure from the men's families and lawyers'.[198]

Collaboration for an Inquiry

A second feature of UK civil society activism was the collaboration between different actors, including lawyers, media, NGOs and parliamentarians, in demanding the Government establish an inquiry into torture complicity.

The media's role was critical in raising public awareness in the UK of detainee treatment, in marked contrast to Australia. Andrew Tyrie, who led the APPG on Extraordinary Rendition, credited investigative journalists, along with NGOs, with having 'uncovered much of what is known about rendition and highlighted issues that became part of the APPG's campaign'.[199] An NGO lawyer noted that there was a period 'for a year or two when it was only the media who was exposing these things and a very limited number … of the big main human rights organisations just raising questions, criticising, saying this needed to be investigated'.[200] Two newspapers campaigned heavily on the issue of detainee torture: the *Guardian* and, subsequently, the *Daily Mail*.

The *Guardian* was consistently critical in editorials from 2002 of the Blair Government's 'sotto voce' approach to detainees at Guantánamo Bay.[201] The *Guardian* is known for its 'liberal journalism'.[202] It claimed credit for having helped to bring about the Detainee Inquiry through its investigative journalism.[203] The Leveson

[195] Diane Taylor, 'Family: Interview: Sabah Sunnoqrot's youngest child doesn't believe she has a father', *Guardian*, 18 March 2006, 3.

[196] Vikram Dodd, 'Guantánamo man's family release "torture" dossier', *Guardian*, 11 August 2007, 15.

[197] Diane Taylor, 'Guantánamo detainees: "I haven't stopped crying since I heard … I think they want to kill him"', *Guardian*, 13 October 2006, 11.

[198] Dodd and Norton-Taylor, 'Government requests return of British residents from Guantánamo Bay'.

[199] Tyrie, Gough and McCracken, *Account Rendered*, ix.

[200] NGO lawyer, tel interview, 30 January 2013.

[201] See, eg, 'Brought to injustice—Britain must challenge US lawlessness' (editorial), *Guardian*, 9 July 2003, 23.

[202] Lord Justice Leveson, *An Inquiry into the Culture, Practices and Ethics of the Press—Report* (Leveson Inquiry) (London: Stationery Office, 2012) vol I, 134.

[203] 'Four years of reports' (editorial), *Guardian*, 27 May 2009, 15.

Inquiry of 2012 into the 'Culture, Practices and Ethics of the Press' also paid tribute to the *Guardian* and journalist Ian Cobain. Cobain's reporting 'was one of the key factors leading to the Government's decision to order an inquiry into allegations of British complicity in torture'.[204] The *Guardian* worked with other civil society actors, including human rights lawyers, NGOs and Tyrie, in pushing for this outcome. An NGO lawyer described the relationship between the *Guardian* and Tyrie as 'symbiotic', because the two 'would feed into each other'. The lawyer explained: 'The *Guardian* would expose things, and Tyrie could pick up and report on it and raise it in Parliament'.[205] Likewise the *Guardian* would 'give publicity to what the NGOs were saying virtually whenever they said it because it also supported their own agenda. The *Guardian* definitely decided editorially this was fundamental, let's put all our resources into it'.[206] The *Guardian* also worked with families of detainees to humanise the men. In one article, the *Guardian* juxtaposed Begg's US military-issued identity, 'detainee JJEEH#00558', with his family's depiction of him as a 'deeply religious man and devoted father', who urged his children in his letters home 'to work on their English spelling'.[207]

For a long time, the *Guardian* was not typical of other UK media in campaigning strongly on detainee torture. A human rights NGO lawyer noted that 'popular opinion is not in the *Guardian*', though it is 'politically influential'.[208] A detainee lawyer described the majority of UK media as 'cowed'. She said, 'The *Guardian* obviously is an important media outlet on the left, but you have to win round more than the *Guardian* to get somewhere in a campaign.'[209] In contrast to the *Guardian*, the editorial position of *The Times*, a politically conservative newspaper owned by News Corporation, supported the Government on the torture issue.[210] Early on, *The Times* argued that the 'intelligence war is, of necessity, a campaign waged in the shadows', and described the allegations of torture at Guantánamo Bay as 'exaggerated'.[211] The attitude of *The Times* shifted, however, and from 2006 it called for Guantánamo Bay to close, and subsequently welcomed Prime Minister Cameron's announcement of a torture inquiry.[212]

Some civil society actors nominated the reporting of a conservative tabloid newspaper, the *Daily Mail*, on the Mohamed case as more significant for

204 Leveson Inquiry, vol II, 457.

205 NGO lawyer, tel interview, 30 January 2013.

206 ibid.

207 Branigan and Dodd, 'The bitterest betrayal'.

208 Human rights NGO lawyer, tel interview, 7 February 2013.

209 Detainee lawyer, tel interview, 11 February 2013.

210 Leveson Inquiry, vol I, 99, 105.

211 'Phase one (again)—the US must eliminate al-Qaeda in Afghanistan' (editorial), *The Times*, 5 March 2002, 23; 'Bay watch—the myths about Guantánamo are challenged' (editorial), *The Times*, 7 May 2003, 19.

212 'Strike camp. It is time to set a date for Guantánamo's closure' (editorial), *The Times*, 28 April 2006, 23; 'Emotional intelligence: Allegations of torture have damaged Britain's reputation. An inquiry is to be welcomed, as is an examination of how intelligence should be treated in court' (editorial), *The Times*, 7 July 2010, 2.

influencing public debate on the torture issue.[213] The *Daily Mail* in 2002 had a circulation of nearly 2.5 million; the *Guardian*'s was under 400,000.[214] The *Daily Mail* called for a 'full judicial inquiry' into allegations of UK complicity in the torture of detainees in 2009, after a series of reports about Mohamed's torture.[215] When Aamer, the last UK resident released from Guantánamo, arrived home, the *Daily Mail* quoted a 'US State Department source' as saying that the newspaper's campaign had 'absolutely made a difference' in the decision to release Aamer.[216] The *Daily Mail's* campaigning was widely praised by a range of actors, including MPs, lawyers, human rights activists and Aamer himself.[217]

The role of the *Guardian* and the *Daily Mail* in pushing for government accountability on the detainee torture issue is part of a wider tradition of the UK press in campaigning on issues considered to be of public importance. For example, the *Daily Mail* takes pride in its 'campaigning stance' and the fact that 'it is not afraid to expose the wrongs and shortcomings of people in power'.[218] Such a tradition is not as evident among newspapers in Australia and Canada. The campaigning of the *Guardian* and the *Daily Mail* on UK detainees at Guantánamo illustrates the media's potential to mobilise public opinion on human rights by documenting and reporting violations, increasing people's awareness and understanding of human rights.[219] It also highlights media's power to select issues and give space to particular actors in reporting. By determining which voices will be heard and which to give credibility to (detainees' families and lawyers, for example), the media set agendas and frame human rights issues in ways that influence outcomes.[220]

Human rights NGOs were slower than lawyers and the liberal media to take up the cause of UK Guantánamo detainees. Initially, Muslim organisations sensed that some transnational NGOs were reluctant to advocate for Guantánamo detainees because, in the words of one activist, 'there was almost a tacit acceptance that these are not really the type of people you want to advocate for'.[221] Despite this, over the course of the post-9/11 decade, spurred on by media revelations and developments in the detainees' court cases, a significant number of NGOs mobilised around the issue. Among them was Cage, a new NGO dedicated to the issue of detainees, and Reprieve, which before 2001 had focused on death penalty cases.

[213] Human rights lawyer, tel interview, 15 February 2013.
[214] Leveson Inquiry, vol I, 95.
[215] 'Daily Mail Comment', *Daily Mail*, 27 February 2009, 14.
[216] Ian Drury, David Jones and Jason Groves, 'Justice at last!', *Daily Mail*, 26 September 2015, 1.
[217] Greenhill, Jones and Sinmaz, 'A great day for justice'.
[218] Leveson Inquiry, vol I, 114.
[219] Thomas R Lasner, 'No empty vessel—media roles in human rights' in *Non-State Actors in the Human Rights Universe*, ed George Andreopoulos, Zehra F Kabasakal Arat and Peter Juviler (Bloomfield, CT: Kumarian Press, 2006) 249.
[220] Kate Nash, *The Cultural Politics of Human Rights: Comparing the US and UK* (New York, NY: Cambridge University Press, 2009) 52.
[221] Muslim human rights activist, tel interview, 5 March 2013.

A detainee lawyer noted, 'There are actually more NGOs now as a result of what's happened.'[222]

The activism of NGOs in the UK contributed to the pressure on the Government regarding detainees, and generated momentum around the need for a public inquiry. Their actions included giving evidence to parliamentary inquiries (Amnesty International, REDRESS, Human Rights Watch (HRW) and Liberty) and intervening in detainee litigation (Amnesty International, Liberty, Reprieve).[223] More generally, NGOs criticised the UK Government's detainee policy and called for a torture inquiry. Amnesty International released reports dealing with the impact of Guantánamo Bay on detainees and documenting cases of UK complicity.[224] Reprieve released a report detailing Mohamed's torture that was influential in convincing Prime Minister Brown to examine MI5's interrogation policy.[225] REDRESS published a report setting out UK detainees' torture allegations and calling for an inquiry.[226] Human Rights Watch released a number of reports criticising the UK's ambiguous torture policies.[227] Cage also published reports concerning the treatment of UK detainees at Guantánamo and UK complicity.[228] Some of these reports cited the UK's obligations under the CAT.[229] Others referenced the ECHR.[230]

By the time the Cameron Government announced the Detainee Inquiry in 2010, a group of 10 domestic and international NGOs had developed high profiles around the torture issue. They were: Liberty, Amnesty International, REDRESS, Cage, The AIRE Centre, Freedom from Torture, HRW, Justice (the International Commission of Jurists UK section), Reprieve and Rights Watch (UK) (formerly British Irish Rights Watch). These NGOs worked with detainee lawyers on the Inquiry, first cooperating with the Government and then boycotting it. The competitive pressures that exist between NGOs were discussed in Chapter 3. Some NGOs have argued that the HRA 1998 exacerbated this rivalry by making it easier

[222] Detainee lawyer, tel interview, 11 February 2013.

[223] See, eg, Intelligence and Security Committee of Parliament, United Kingdom Parliament, *Rendition*; Clare Dyer, 'Lords to rule on terror suspects held in jail: Detainees say opt-out from Human Rights Act unlawful', *Guardian*, 4 October 2004, 7.

[224] For example Amnesty International, *United Kingdom: Time for an inquiry into the UK's role in human rights violations overseas since 11 September 2001*, Report No EUR 45/001/2010, 23 March 2010.

[225] Reprieve, *'Human Cargo'*; Ian Cobain, 'Series of allegations that finally forced Brown to act: Brown asks ISC to look at interrogation policy again detainees claimed MI5 collusion as early as 2005', *Guardian*, 19 March 2009, 6.

[226] REDRESS, 'The United Kingdom, torture and anti-terrorism'.

[227] Human Rights Watch, *'No questions asked': Intelligence cooperation with countries that torture*, report, June 2010.

[228] See, eg, Asim Qureshi, *Fabricating terrorism: British complicity in renditions and torture*, report, Cageprisoners, 28 March 2006; *Fabricating terrorism II: British complicity in renditions and torture*, report, Cageprisoners, April 2009; *Fabricating terrorism III: British complicity in renditions and torture*, report, Cageprisoners, 19 January 2011.

[229] REDRESS, 'The United Kingdom, torture and anti-terrorism', 11; Human Rights Watch, *Cruel Britannia: British complicity in the torture and ill-treatment of terror suspects in Pakistan*, report, 24 November 2009; Qureshi, *Fabricating terrorism III: British complicity in renditions and torture.*

[230] Human Rights Watch, 'Cruel Britannia'.

and more profitable to argue about human rights in domestic courts.[231] Against this background, the alliance that formed between NGOs and lawyers on detainee torture was lauded by civil society actors as unusual—a case of putting principle before self-interest. A human rights NGO lawyer said that for such a group of 'high-profile, high-end NGOs, high-profile radical lawyers ... to come together on that single issue ... was unprecedented'.[232] An NGO lawyer made a similar observation:

> The NGOs here we work together, Amnesty, Human Rights Watch, Liberty, everybody, Reprieve—we're all on the same side basically, but there's a degree of competition to some extent and specialisation, and everybody is looking for funding from donors and so on. So we don't always work in a close coalition. But with the Detainee Inquiry, thanks to some individual NGOs including, especially, Amnesty, I think they realised how important this was.[233]

The decision by major UK and transnational human rights NGOs and lawyers to collectively boycott the Detainee Inquiry—having previously argued so vigorously for one—was, in some ways, surprising. The 10 NGOs wrote to the Detainee Inquiry in August 2011 advising that, due to the lack of credibility and transparency of the process, the organisations were ceasing their involvement.[234] The same day, the law firm Christian Khan, representing detainees, wrote to the Detainee Inquiry advising it of their clients' decisions not to give evidence.[235] Not all those involved were comfortable with the decision to boycott. One human rights lawyer indicated that some organisations only joined the boycott when it became untenable to do otherwise because other groups had already pulled out.[236] After Reprieve withdrew, 'then either civil society organisations had to speak with two or three different voices or just tacitly go along with non-cooperation, and that's what happened in the end'. Another human rights lawyer believed that some NGOs were 'much too eager to pull out and shut it down'.[237] This was 'because in any event it was a unique opportunity—I don't think any investigation into the secret services had ever been done before'. To see NGOs pulling out 'was a very sad moment'.

Cage was the only Muslim NGO in the informal coalition that developed around the issue of a torture inquiry. More established Muslim community organisations played negligible roles in the detainee torture debate in the UK, similar to the case in Australia (but unlike Canada). This was due to intimidation and fear caused by

[231] Richard J Maiman, '"We've had to raise our game": Liberty's litigation strategy under the Human Rights Act 1998' in *Human Rights Brought Home: Socio-Legal Studies of Human Rights in the National Context*, ed Simon Halliday and Patrick Schmidt (Portland, OR: Hart Publishing, 2004) 97–98.

[232] Human rights NGO lawyer, tel interview, 7 February 2013.

[233] NGO lawyer, tel interview, 30 January 2013.

[234] Liberty, Amnesty International, REDRESS, Cageprisoners, The AIRE Centre, Freedom from Torture, Human Rights Watch, JUSTICE, Reprieve and British Irish Rights Watch to Sara Carnegie, solicitor to Detainee Inquiry, 3 August 2011.

[235] Christian Khan Solicitors to Sara Carnegie, Solicitor to Detainee Inquiry, 3 August 2011.

[236] Human rights lawyer, tel interview, 5 February 2013.

[237] Human rights lawyer, tel interview, 15 February 2013.

the 'poisonous' political climate that existed for Muslims after 9/11.[238] An analysis of press releases published by the MCB illustrates the near absence of mainstream Muslim organisations from debate. It issued some seven press releases on Guantánamo Bay between 2001 and the end of 2010; only two pre-dated the return of the first UK citizens and none related to UK residents.[239] A Muslim human rights activist illustrated the high level of apprehension in the community with an anecdote. She recalled when the US Government released the first pictures of detainees at Guantánamo, in January 2002:

> [M]y husband … started ringing around people to say 'we need to mobilise and start campaigning, this is really unacceptable'. And people were saying 'no we can't do that, we can't associate ourselves, otherwise we will be tarnished, tarred with the same brush' and people were in that kind of panic—that was almost universal.[240]

The IHRC was alone among more established Muslim organisations in agitating on the Guantánamo detainee issue; but, overwhelmed by the high volume of Muslim civil liberties cases at the time, eventually it focused its advocacy on other areas. The IHRC did no original work on torture because other NGOs already were working on it, and there was a policy 'not to replicate work if somebody else is doing it and they know what they're doing'.[241] Another Muslim human rights activist said one of the reasons that Cage formed was that existing Muslim organisations were unwilling to get involved in these issues, and 'nobody was willing to stick their neck out'.[242]

More recently Cage, along with the IHRC and MCB, have been accused of being apologists for Muslim fundamentalist political movements that use or advocate violence.[243] The controversy around Cage intensified in 2014, when one of its officials, former Guantánamo Bay detainee, Begg, was arrested and charged with terrorism offences relating to Syria.[244] Begg was subsequently released from custody, and charges against him were dropped, after MI5 provided information about his case, prompting supporters of Cage to complain about attempts to criminalise the charity work of the Muslim community.[245] At the centre of these disagreements are contestations over Cage's (and other Muslim organisations') legitimate

[238] Muslim human rights activist, tel interview, 5 March 2013; see also Victoria Brittain, 'Besieged in Britain', *Race & Class* 50(3) (2009), 1–29.

[239] They were Muslim Council of Britain, 'British detainees at Guantánamo Bay must be repatriated', press release, 23 July 2003; 'MCB meets Attorney-General to express concerns over Guantánamo Bay detainees', press release, 9 September 2003.

[240] Muslim human rights activist, tel interview, 5 March 2013.

[241] ibid.

[242] Muslim human rights activist, tel interview, 11 February 2013.

[243] Karima Bennoune, *Your Fatwa Does Not Apply Here* (New York, NY: WW Norton & Company, 2013) 16.

[244] Cage, 'Press Release: Moazzam Begg arrested for uncovering western complicity in rendition and torture?', press release, 6 March 2014; Tracy McVeigh, 'Guantánamo detainee Moazzam Begg held again', *Observer*, 2 March 2014, 10.

[245] Richard Norton-Taylor, 'The strange case of Moazzam Begg', *Guardian*, 8 October 2014.

place in civil society. They illustrate Jai Sen's ideas, noted in Chapter 3, about the representativeness of civil society and attempts of some members to subjugate or tame those who do not conform to dominant ideas about what it means to be 'civilised'.[246] Similar debates occurred in Canada with respect to Muslim organisations advocating for the rights of detainees in the war on terror.

A Focus on Impunity

Another feature of civil society activism in the UK was that it tended to focus on state impunity in relation to complicity in torture, and was less influenced by the likeability of individual victims compared to Australia and Canada. Factors such as detainees' personal attributes, whether they seemed innocent or guilty and whether they had charismatic family members, did not appear to cause civil society to distinguish between victims. A human rights NGO lawyer explained civil society's approach as 'more about questioning the impunity of the state in relation to the victim than the victim themselves'.[247] Similarly, a Muslim human rights activist said, 'I can't recall anyone ever saying "this poor person trapped in Guantánamo" and singling out some more than others.'[248]

Civil society's non-discriminatory approach to detainees was further exemplified by the fact that that it did not, in general, accept the UK Government's attempts to distinguish between its obligations to citizens and residents at Guantánamo Bay. In 2003, for instance, Amnesty International criticised the Government's decision not to help Al Rawi and El Banna because they were not citizens as 'questionable morally and legally'.[249] Peirce, who acted for UK citizens and residents, commented after the court in the *Al Rawi* case found for the Government that '[t]his is not an area where the government is entitled to discriminate and it has discriminated between nationals and residents'.[250] Similarly, in NGO reports calling for UK Government accountability over the treatment of UK citizens and residents, the organisations did not differentiate between the two groups.[251] This attitude was also apparent from media reporting on residents, particularly in the *Guardian*, which first reported on the UK Government's abandonment of Al Rawi and El Banna in mid-2003.[252] UK civil society saw little difference in the state's responsibilities towards citizens or residents where their human rights were being transgressed overseas.

[246] Jai Sen, 'The power of civility: Some critical reflections on global civil society', paper presented at *Global Civil Society: More or Less Democracy?*, World Social Forum, Nairobi, Kenya, 22 January 2007, 54.

[247] Human rights NGO lawyer, tel interview, 7 February 2013.

[248] Muslim human rights activist, tel interview, 5 March 2013.

[249] Dodd, 'The UK businessmen trapped in Guantánamo.'

[250] Richard Norton-Taylor, 'Judges powerless over detainees at Guantánamo,' *Guardian*, 5 May 2006, 4.

[251] See, eg, Reprieve, '*Human Cargo*'; REDRESS, *The United Kingdom, torture and anti-terrorism*; Human Rights Watch, '*No questions asked*'.

[252] Dodd, 'The UK businessmen trapped in Guantánamo'.

Civil society actors based their challenge of UK Government policy differentiating between citizens and residents on moral, normative and legal grounds. Morally, UK intelligence services were closely involved in the original detention and early interrogations of some residents, particularly Al Rawi, El Banna and Mohamed. In addition, many residents had close connections to the UK. This was in terms of their lives and families being embedded in UK society, because of the length of time they had lived there, and because some had British wives and children. Media reporting of El Banna emphasised his family's UK links.[253] One human rights lawyer explained the connection of residents to the UK as follows:

> They were denizens, they were such embedded residents that they were a hop and skip away from being citizens. Their links with the UK were very strong without the technicality of citizenship. Some had British wives, British children—you were not looking at people who had just come off the boat or tourists, these were people who had been an integral part of British society for a long time.[254]

UK civil society's non-discriminating position on citizens and residents was also grounded in normative and legal arguments, notably in the universality that underpins international human rights law.[255] This universality is evident in the Universal Declaration of Human Rights (UDHR). As noted in Chapter 1, the universal application of international human rights law has influenced state practice on citizenship in the post-World War II era. A growing body of scholarship argues that the emergence of the international human rights regime has resulted in the corrosion of traditional notions of nation-based citizenship and the absolute distinction between citizens and non-citizens.[256] It is argued that a 'new and more universal concept of citizenship has unfolded, one whose organising and legitimising principles are based on universal personhood rather than national belonging'.[257]

The legal notion of universality refers to states having obligations to protect the international human rights of non-nationals within their jurisdictions.[258] It is arguable, however, that these ideas influenced civil society activism around the obligations of the UK towards its residents detained overseas in the war on terror with an obvious connection to the state. The literature on the modern expansion of understandings about citizenship draws attention to the role of global civil society in driving universalist ideas.[259] Contests between civil society and the state over

[253] Taylor, 'Family: Interview: Sabah Sunnoqrot's youngest child doesn't believe she has a father'.

[254] Human rights lawyer, tel interview, 5 February 2013.

[255] Duffy, 'Human rights litigation and the "war on terror"', 580.

[256] Yasemin Nuhoglu Soysal, *Limits of Citizenship: Migrants and Postnational Membership in Europe* (Chicago, IL: University of Chicago Press, 1994) 1; Saskia Sassen, *Territory Authority Rights: From Medieval to Global Assemblages* (Princeton, NJ: Princeton University Press, 2008) 307; Seyla Benhabib, *The Rights of Others: Aliens, Residents and Citizens* (New York, NY: Cambridge University Press, 2004) 144.

[257] Soysal, *Limits of Citizenship*, 1.

[258] Helen Duffy, *The 'War on Terror' and the Framework of International Law* (New York, NY: Cambridge University Press, 2005) 289.

[259] Sassen, *Territory Authority Rights*, 286.

the boundaries of citizenship were also occurring, I argue, at the domestic level in the UK with respect to the rights of residents not to be tortured. In the face of resistance from the UK Government, local civil society actors successfully pressed for more universal notions of citizenship with regards to the state's obligations to defend the human rights of residents.

Civil society's non-discriminating attitude towards citizens and residents was further influenced by a parallel issue playing out in the UK polity that concerned the detention without trial of foreign nationals suspected of involvement in terrorism. This presented a political opportunity for advocates of Guantánamo Bay detainees, as I explain.

Enabling and Constraining Activism

Having positioned itself closely to the US after 9/11, the UK Government's initial reluctance to stand up for the rights of UK detainees tortured in the war on terror gave way reasonably quickly. Within a year, the Government's approach towards detainees at Guantánamo Bay became more questioning of US policies and more protective of UK nationals' rights.

Alliance-based explanations suggest that the UK was in a stronger position, as a country with global influence (a permanent member of the UN Security Council), to stand up to the US than Australia. I argue, however, that such factors cannot adequately account for the early change in the UK's position on detainees. The UK was, at the same time, standing shoulder to shoulder with the US on the Iraq invasion, even though the majority of the British population was against it. So why did the UK, unlike Australia or Canada, tell the US that its system of detaining and trying detainees in the war on terror was unfair by international standards? The answer is more complex than alliance politics.

I have shown in previous sections that the Government came under sustained domestic political pressure over detainees, particularly from sections of civil society, including human rights lawyers and some media, who were assisted by moral, not necessarily legal, victories in the courts. Juxtaposed with Australia, where the Government did not come under such early pressure to stand up for citizens or face strong demands for accountability on torture, this gives rise to a series of questions: Why did UK civil society, especially lawyers, mobilise so early around the issue of the mistreatment of detainees in the war on terror? Why was a torture inquiry a central focus of UK civil society activism? Why was its activism not as influenced by the personal attributes of victims?

The UK had more detainees than Australia or Canada at Guantánamo Bay, and the issue may have had a higher profile. But I also locate some of the answers to these questions about UK civil society's strong engagement on the torture of detainees in the forces that shaped domestic activism on the issue in the UK. My focus on the local conditions for mobilisation is guided by liberal international theory, which, as discussed in Chapter 3, highlights the potential power of domestic actors to positively influence state behaviour on international human rights by altering national politics. In trying to understand differences in behaviours of liberal democracies sharing similar political systems and values, I argue that the domestic political and legal context can affect human rights activism. Here, I employ the framework of enabling and constraining factors that affect mobilisation on human rights, including political culture, political and legal institutions, and political opportunities, to analyse the role of domestic actors in the UK in the cases of citizens and residents detained in the war on terror.

Political Culture

A country's political culture is an historically transmitted pattern of meanings that helps define the range of acceptable possible options from which groups or individuals may choose a course of action.[260] In the context of human rights, these possibilities concern how to react when faced with violations by the state. I argue that the UK had a stronger rights culture—by which I mean a heightened human rights awareness, particularly in the context of terrorism and torture—compared to Australia. This influenced the readiness of some civil society actors to mobilise around the cases of Guantánamo Bay detainees. This was partly the result of historical factors, especially the UK's Northern Ireland experiences, as well as the more recent introduction of the HRA 1998.

The UK had more experience than Australia or Canada of political violence. In the years from 1970 to 1992, it experienced nearly 250 incidents of international terrorism at home and abroad.[261] Some of it was related to issues in the Middle East, but the most significant related to the Troubles in Northern Ireland. These latter experiences shaped the UK Government's broader response to terrorism, including its legislative response and the capability of intelligence services.[262] The UK also differs from Australia or Canada in experiencing, soon after 9/11, a major terrorist attack at home. In July 2005, terrorists inspired by Al-Qaeda ideologies staged a series of attacks on London's transport system, killing 56 people.[263]

The Northern Ireland conflict developed out of a 1960s civil rights movement led by the Province's Catholic minority, who sought equal rights with the

[260] Clifford Geertz, *The Interpretation of Cultures* (New York, NY: Basic Books, 1973); David Elkins and Richard Simeon, 'A cause in search of its effect, or what does political culture explain?', *Comparative Politics* 11(2) (1979), 127–45.

[261] Bruce W Warner, 'Great Britain and the response to international terrorism' in *The Deadly Sin of Terrorism: Its Effect on Democracy and Civil Liberty in Six Countries*, ed David Charters (Westport, CT: Greenwood Press, 1994) 13.

[262] ibid, 15.

[263] '7 July bombings—overview', *BBC News*, nd; Home Office, *Report of the official account of the bombings in London on 7 July 2005* (HC 1087 2005–06).

Protestant majority.[264] A violent conflict developed between Irish Republican paramilitaries seeking British withdrawal from Northern Ireland, Loyalist paramilitaries opposing this and the state's security forces. Security legislation applying to Northern Ireland existed before this time, including the Civil Authorities (Special Powers) Act (Northern Ireland) 1922 (the Special Powers Act), which permitted the imposition of curfews, the banning of printed materials and assemblies, and detention without charge or trial, known as internment.[265] In August 1971, under the Special Powers Act, the British Prime Minister, Edward Heath, authorised the use of internment, which continued until 1975. During this time, 1,981 people were detained without charge or trial, 1,874 of them Catholic Nationalists.[266] The oppressive and discriminatory internment policies were, in hindsight, widely viewed as a failure, leading to the detention and mistreatment of innocent people, the alienation of the Catholic population and the escalation of violence.[267]

Detainees interned by security forces during the political unrest in Northern Ireland in the 1970s were subject to a range of mistreatment.[268] The systematic use of the so-called 'five techniques' of interrogation became the subject of multiple inquiries, litigation in the ECtHR and world-wide condemnation. These five disorientation or sensory deprivation techniques included wall-standing, hooding, continuous 'white noise', sleep deprivation and the denial of food and drink.[269] The Government held two inquiries into the use of the techniques. One, the 1971 Compton Committee, found that they amounted to 'ill-treatment' but not torture.[270] The subsequent Parker Report found the five techniques to be necessary in security situations. A minority report, however, argued they were unethical and illegal, and in 1972 the UK Government discontinued their use.[271] Meanwhile, the Irish Government brought a case against the UK for breaching the ECHR. The European Commission of Human Rights in 1976 found that the UK's use of the five techniques amounted to torture.[272]

On appeal by the UK Government, the ECtHR found that the five techniques fell short of torture, though they did constitute 'inhuman and degrading treatment' and still breached Article 3 of the ECHR.[273] The ECtHR decision continues to be controversial. In 2005, the House of Lords said the 'five techniques' would be

[264] Robert W White and Terry Falkenberg White, 'Repression and the liberal state: The case of Northern Ireland, 1969–1972', *Journal of Conflict Resolution* 39(2) (1995), 334.

[265] Michael P O'Connor and Celia M Rumann, 'Into the fire: How to avoid getting burned by the same mistakes made fighting terrorism in Northern Ireland', *Cardozo Law Review* 24(4) (2003), 1664–65.

[266] ibid, 1678.

[267] ibid, 1678–79.

[268] Caroline Kennedy-Pipe and Andrew Mumford, 'Torture, rights, rules and wars: Ireland to Iraq', *International Relations* 21(1) (2007), 122–23.

[269] *Case of Ireland v The United Kingdom* (1978) 2 EHHR 25 [96].

[270] Kennedy-Pipe and Mumford, 'Torture, rights, rules and wars', 123.

[271] ibid.

[272] *Ireland v The United Kingdom* (1976) Y.B. EUR. CONV on HUMAN RIGHTS 512.

[273] *Case of Ireland v The United Kingdom* (1978) 2 EHHR 25 [167].

characterised as torture by contemporary standards.[274] In 2014, the Irish Government requested that the ECtHR re-open the case after Ireland's National Public Service Broadcaster uncovered evidence previously withheld from the Strasbourg Court, including correspondence indicating that the UK Government internally regarded the techniques to be torture.[275]

The UK's use of state torture goes further back than Northern Ireland, and has roots in counter-insurgency campaigns conducted in the pursuit and maintenance of the colonial empire.[276] Despite this, there persists a 'comforting myth', central to British national identity, that torture, like slavery, has always been alien to the operations of the British state, and is something done by other people, or by people in other places.[277] By way of illustration, Lord Bingham, in a 2005 House of Lords judgment, commented that 'the English common law has regarded torture and its fruits with abhorrence for over 500 years'.[278] While historically it is true that torture was never regularised within English criminal law procedure, it was used against prisoners and colonial subjects during and after World War II, in Kenya in the 1950s against the Mau Mau, in Cyprus during the same decade, and in Aden in the 1960s.[279] Torture also re-emerged in UK counter-terrorism and counter-insurgency practices after 9/11. The 2011 Baha Mousa Inquiry into the torture and killing of an Iraqi detainee by UK forces in Iraq found that the same five techniques employed in Northern Ireland had migrated to Iraq three decades later.[280]

The Northern Ireland conflict influenced UK political culture, making the public more familiar with terrorism and more aware of the potential for injustices associated with heavy state responses to the threat. On the one hand, the legacy of Northern Ireland has arguably impacted on the UK in negative ways for liberal democratic values, leading to public support for more draconian counter-terrorism measures and making the society less free.[281] The UK exhibited a readiness, manifest after 9/11 but present before that, to legislate to impose robust limits and derogations on rights.[282] This includes using administrative detention (non-transparent immigration law measures) and insisting on heavy secrecy in

[274] *A (FC) v Secretary of State for the Home Department* [2005] UKHL 71 [97] (Lord Bingham).

[275] Fiona De Londras, 'Revisiting the five techniques in the European Court of Human Rights', *EJIL: Talk!* 12 December 2014.

[276] Andrew Mumford, 'Minimum force meets brutality: Detention, interrogation and torture in British counter-insurgency campaigns', *Journal of Military Ethics* 11(1) (2012), 10–25.

[277] John Tulloch, 'Normalising the unthinkable: The British press, torture, and the human rights of terrorists suspects' in *Communication Ethics Now*, ed Richard Keeble (Leicester: Troubadour Publishing, 2008) 5; Tobias Kelly, *This Side of Silence: Human Rights, Torture, and the Recognition of Cruelty* (Philadelphia, PA: University of Pennsylvania Press, 2012) 44.

[278] *A (FC) v Secretary of State for the Home Department* [2005] UKHL 71 [51] (Lord Bingham).

[279] John H Langbein, *Torture and the Law of Proof: Europe and England in the Ancien Regime* (Chicago, IL: University of Chicago Press, 2006 [1976]) 73; Cobain, *A Secret History of Torture*.

[280] Baha Mousa Public Inquiry, *Report of the Baha Mousa public inquiry*, September 2011, http://webarchive.nationalarchives.gov.uk/20120215203912/http://www.bahamousainquiry.org/report/index.htm.

[281] Warner, 'Great Britain and the response to international terrorism', 37.

[282] Roach, *The 9/11 Effect*, 238–41.

relation to counter-terrorism operations. The most contentious of the UK's legislative response to the war on terror was the 2001 Anti-terrorism, Crime and Security Act, which was challenged in the House of Lords.[283] I examine this Act, which authorised the indefinite detention without trial of foreign nationals who could not be deported because of a risk of torture, in the context of the politics around Guantánamo Bay detainees.

On the other hand, I argue that there is evidence that the UK's Northern Ireland experiences meant that civil society was wary of governments using counter-terrorism responses as an excuse for violating civil liberties. It formed a prism through which lawyers and NGOs viewed the UK Government's responses to Islamic extremist terrorism after 2001, and meant they were less easily intimidated by the politics of national security surrounding 9/11. One human rights lawyer, for example, compared the London bombings in 2005 to the IRA bombings of the mid-1990s leading up to the 1998 Good Friday Agreement, and said the latter was 'much, much more significant' in creating a more hostile political environment for human rights NGOs working on terrorism.[284] This resonates with the idea, discussed in Chapter 3, that European countries, because of their histories of domestic terrorism, had more tolerance for vulnerability than states, like the US and Australia, with less experience.[285] UK civil society's less naive perspective on terrorism is an example of social learning, where past incursions on civil liberties can reduce the scope of violations being allowed to recur in a time of national emergency.[286]

Civil society actors familiar with Northern Ireland terrorism were therefore more ready to recognise signs of repressive laws and policies that targeted particular groups, in this case Muslims, in UK society. For example, a human rights NGO lawyer said the re-emergence of torture after 9/11 rekindled collective memories. 'People have started to re-engage and re-remember in that sense about what happened in Northern Ireland in terms of internment', he said.[287] Another human rights lawyer said, 'I think the Northern Ireland experience was very pertinent because we had a decade of familiarity with complicity in torture in the context of that situation, so it wasn't new.'[288] Similarly, a detainee lawyer noted, 'There is a tradition in this country of questioning government responses to terrorism, particularly because of Northern Ireland and what happened there, and that probably makes us more aware of the dangers of government overreaction to terrorism.'[289]

[283] *A v Secretary of State for the Home Department* [2004] UKHL 56.
[284] Human rights lawyer, tel interview, 15 February 2013.
[285] Philip Gordon and Jeremy Shapiro, *Allies at War America, Europe, and the Crisis over Iraq* (New York, NY: McGraw-Hill, 2004) 60.
[286] Mark Tushnet, 'Defending Korematsu? Reflections on civil liberties in wartime', *Wisconsin Law Review* 2 (2003), 273–307, 274.
[287] Human rights NGO lawyer, tel interview, 7 February 2013.
[288] Human rights lawyer, tel interview, 5 February 2013.
[289] Detainee lawyer, tel interview, 11 February 2013.

The UK's Northern Ireland experience meant there was a small band of lawyers well versed in issues of human rights and counter-terrorism, who were primed to act for Guantánamo Bay detainees. Lawyers 'had already seen the reintroduction of the same policies, the same types of laws that had happened with Northern Ireland—in a way they were ready for it'.[290] One such lawyer was Peirce, a seasoned campaigner on Northern Ireland civil rights issues, who acted for a number of Guantánamo Bay detainees. Peirce previously acted for the Guilford Four and the Birmingham Six, two high-profile miscarriage of justice cases relating to IRA bombings in the 1970s.[291] Peirce wrote after 9/11 about the striking parallels between the Irish and Muslim experience, describing Muslims as the 'new suspect community in this country'.[292] A Muslim human rights activist said, 'Gareth has so much experience with the Irish issue that for her, Guantánamo was readily identifiable, it wasn't something that was alien in any way. She understood the politics surrounding these things such as political violence.'[293]

Public discourse around rights can provide insights into a country's rights culture, which matters not just at the level of the citizen but throughout the whole polity, including its institutions. The debate around the introduction of the HRA 1998 by the Blair Government indicated a desire by political leaders to develop a stronger rights culture, where institutional attitudes towards rights were more alert and receptive to their existence and importance. Lord Irvine, the Lord Chancellor who oversaw the introduction of the 1998 Act, said it would 'create a more explicitly moral approach to decisions and decision-making', and would promote a 'culture where positive rights and liberties become the focus and concerns of legislators, administrators and judges'.[294] His successor, Lord Falconer, advocated a rights culture that encompassed a widely shared sense of entitlement to rights and respect for the rights of others, and that influenced institutional policies and practices.[295] The meaning of rights culture in the context of the HRA 1998, it is argued, embodies a 'culture of controversy', which emphasises that the identity and content of rights are not self-evident, that rights are a matter of political argument.[296] The 1998 Act achieved this by enhancing not only the judiciary's but also Parliament's role in the work of rights deliberations.

The discourse around the HRA 1998 points to the way in which political culture and institutions are interrelated and can be co-constitutive. In this case, political leaders saw the introduction of the Act as a means by which to build a stronger rights culture. Legal scholars have, however, expressed scepticism about its ability

[290] Muslim human rights activist, tel interview, 5 March 2013.

[291] Peirce, *Dispatches from the Dark Side*; Warner, 'Great Britain and the response to international terrorism', 20.

[292] Gareth Peirce, 'Was it like this for the Irish?', *London Review of Books*, 10 April 2008, 3.

[293] Muslim human rights activist, tel interview, 11 February 2013.

[294] Lord Irvine, *The development of human rights in Britain under an incorporated convention on human rights*, Tom Sargant Memorial Lecture, Law Society Hall, London, December 1997.

[295] Lord Falconer, 'Human rights and constitutional reform', speech to the Law Society and Human Rights Lawyers' Association, London, 17 February 2004.

[296] Danny Nicol, 'The Human Rights Act and the politicians', *Legal Studies* 24(3) (2004), 454.

to improve the UK's rights culture and the durability of such attempts.[297] Moreover, the future of the Act is tenuous. The Conservative Government, re-elected in 2015, announced its intention to scrap the HRA 1998 and replace it with a 'British Bill of Rights'.[298] This demonstrates how rights culture can be contested, unsettled and precarious.[299]

Political and Legal Institutions

The organisational structure of the state shapes the course of political battles, empowering and constraining actors, providing resources and advantages necessary to win.[300] The UK functions without a written constitution, a factor that affords the executive considerable power, particularly in the field of national security.[301] However, the UK's legal and political institutions were more robust than Australia's in a significant way after 9/11: they included the HRA 1998. The legislative bill of rights elevated the rights awareness of the courts and Parliament, and provided to civil society some legal levers around the prohibition on torture. Other torture-related legislation and jurisprudence in the UK is more equivocal.

An examination of legislation and common law suggests an ambiguity that reflects the UK's chequered historical practice with respect to torture. Internationally, the UK ratified the CAT and the Optional Protocol. Domestically, while the UK Criminal Justice Act 1988 creates an offence of torture (under section 134), it provides a defence if the perpetrator had 'lawful authority, justification or excuse for that conduct'. The UN Committee Against Torture has criticised the existence of this defence, calling it an 'escape clause' to the absolute prohibition of torture.[302] UK jurisprudence is similarly less than complete in disavowing torture. An important example is *A (FC) v Secretary of State for the Home Department*.[303] The House of Lords ruled that evidence obtained under torture by foreign agencies was not admissible in court, rejecting the Government's argument that the Special Immigration Appeals Commission should be able to receive such evidence where there was no UK complicity in the torture. However, the House of Lords went on to sanction the executive's use of intelligence obtained by foreign torturers. Lord

[297] David Kinley, 'Finding and filling the democratic deficit in human rights' in *Parliament and Human Rights*, ed Hunt et al, 34.

[298] David Feldman, 'Democracy, law, and human rights: Politics as challenge and opportunity' in *Parliament and Human Rights*, ed Hunt et al, 96. David Cameron was replaced as Prime Minister by the new leader of the Conservative Party, Theresa May, in July 2016, following the UK 'Brexit' referendum that voted in favour of the UK's leaving the European Union. See Owen Bowcott, 'Theresa May does not intend to trigger article 50 this year, court told', *Guardian*, 19 July 2016.

[299] Murray Hunt, 'Introduction' in *Parliament and Human Rights*, ed Hunt et al, 15.

[300] G John Ikenberry, 'Conclusion: An institutional approach to American foreign policy', *International Organization* 42(1) (1988), 219–43.

[301] Warner, 'Great Britain and the response to international terrorism', 17–18.

[302] Committee Against Torture, *Concluding Observations on the Fifth Periodic Report of the United Kingdom, Adopted by the Committee at its Fiftieth Session*, 50th sess, 6–31 May 2013.

[303] *A (FC) v Secretary of State* [2005] UKHL 71.

Nicholls remarked that it would be 'absurd' for the police to reject intelligence obtained by torture 'if use of such information might save lives'.[304] The House of Lords judgment has been widely criticised as seeming to be willing to defer to security imperatives that undermined the absolute prohibition against torture, 'so long as its judicial processes were not tainted'.[305] The UK Government has since relied on the House of Lords decision to justify practices undermining the absolute prohibition on torture, noting in a counter-terrorism policy paper that intelligence obtained under torture 'may still be used to investigate and to stop terrorist attacks'.[306]

While there are gaps in its legislative and common law framework prohibiting torture, as a member of the Council of Europe the UK is entrenched in the world's most effective regional human rights system. The UK, as noted, is a party to the ECHR, which prohibits torture, and the HRA 1998 gives UK courts clear authority from the UK Parliament to enforce ECHR rights.[307] I argue that the 1998 Act influenced activism around the issue of Guantánamo Bay detainees and torture in different ways. By making it easier for victims to bring claims against the UK Government in the domestic courts, the HRA 1998 increased the frequency of claims and the profile of the issue. It also raised the rights consciousness of the judiciary in hearing these claims. Convention rights were invoked in a number of cases previously discussed, and although detainees did not always win their legal arguments, the fact that they were able to argue their cases before the UK courts brought further pressure on the Government as regards accountability. Human rights NGOs in the UK emphasised the importance of the HRA 1998 in legal and campaigning strategies adopted by lawyers in the Guantánamo cases. An NGO lawyer said that the Act was 'crucial':

> As soon as the European Convention [on Human Rights] could be used directly by British courts, that gave a huge input or impetus—it gave a whole new arsenal to the lawyers … to argue that you had to look at the principles that had been laid down in the Convention. Particularly, there had to be proper inquiries into allegations of torture.[308]

The HRA 1998 provides one possible explanation for why lawyers played an early and prominent role on the issue of torture in the war on terror. The Act equipped lawyers with effective domestic legal levers by which to make rights claims on behalf of detainees, and positively influenced their expectations as to how claims would be received by the courts.

[304] ibid [68] (Lord Nicholls).

[305] Katja Samuel, 'The rule of law framework and its lacunae: Normative, interpretive, and/or policy created?' in *Counter-Terrorism: International Law and Practice*, ed Ana Maria Salinas de Frias, Katja LH Samuel and Nigel D White (New York, NY: Oxford University Press, 2012) 31.

[306] United Kingdom Secretary of State for the Home Department, *Pursue Prevent Protect Prepare: The United Kingdom's Strategy for Countering International Terrorism: Annual Report* (Cm 7547 2009) 76.

[307] Robert Wintemute, 'The Human Rights Act's first five years: Too strong, too weak, or just right?', *Kings College Law Journal* 17(2) (2006), 210.

[308] NGO lawyer, tel interview, 30 January 2013.

The impact of the HRA 1998 on legal activism around the detainee treatment issue was arguably evident in the way greater emphasis was placed on the ECHR than on UN conventions in pressing for state accountability on torture. Human rights lawyers involved in the detainee torture issue noted the preference for European law, with one commenting that international law outside the ECHR 'is hardly mentioned in the UK by lawyers'.[309] European torture law is more operational—and therefore influential—than the CAT.[310] Fionnuala Ní Aoláin describes a 'uniquely European approach to the prohibition on torture', with an unparalleled body of case law.[311] Despite this, human rights NGOs also used the UN treaty system to complain about the UK's conduct in relation to the alleged torture of Guantánamo detainees.[312]

The HRA 1998, as noted, was intended to promote greater rights awareness among the different branches of government. Prior to the Act, the UK's legal culture was described as one in which judges were 'remarkably conservative' and where parliamentary sovereignty was favoured 'to the nearly complete exclusion of judicial creativity' on issues of rights.[313] Following the enactment of the HRA 1998, the UK came closer to having a rights culture where human rights litigation plays a role in rights development through judicial interpretation.[314] Scholars have singled out the Act's effect in the war on terror in terms of giving confidence to judges to stand up to the executive on human rights matters. They argue that the HRA 1998 elevated the judiciary as an institution, giving it a firm mandate to act in cases involving human rights, and helping it to overcome the traditional judicial reluctance to act in cases involving national security.[315] This effect was evident in detainee litigation against the Government. Lord Neuberger, in *Mohamed v Secretary of State*, noted that the HRA 1998 'has enlarged the court's role for present purposes'.[316] A detainee lawyer attributed the increasing willingness of the courts to challenge the Government on human rights to the Act, saying it 'has had an enormous civilising impact on our courts'.[317] In addition, activists themselves, in using the HRA 1998 in campaigning for the rights of detainees, arguably enhanced the UK's rights culture, building rights awareness and making rights meaningful.

[309] Human rights lawyer, tel interview, 15 February 2013.

[310] John T Parry, *Understanding Torture: Law, Violence, and Political Identity* (Ann Arbor, MI: The University of Michigan Press, 2010) 44.

[311] Fionnuala Ní Aoláin, 'The European Convention on Human Rights and its torture prohibitions' in *Torture: A Collection*, ed Sanford Levinson (New York, NY: Oxford University Press, 2004) 218.

[312] See, eg, REDRESS, *Comments to the United Kingdom's 4th Periodic Report to the Committee Against Torture*, Submission to the Committee Against Torture, 15 October 2004; Birnberg Peirce & Partners, *Shadow Report—United Kingdom (UK) Non-Compliance with the United Nations Convention Against Torture (UNCAT) with Respect to Mr Shaker Aamer*, Submission to the Committee Against Torture, 17 April 2013.

[313] Charles R Epp, *The Rights Revolution: Lawyers, Activists, and Supreme Courts in Comparative Perspective* (Chicago, IL: University of Chicago Press, 1998) 111.

[314] Maiman, '"We've had to raise our game"', 87.

[315] Ip, 'The Supreme Court and House of Lords in the war on terror', 41–42.

[316] *Mohamed v Secretary of State* [2010] EWCA Civ 65 [180] (Lord Neuberger).

[317] Detainee lawyer, tel interview, 11 February 2013.

The HRA 1998 led the UK Parliament to establish the JCHR, which played an accountability role in the detainee torture issue, as previously discussed. The language of human rights embodied in the 1998 Act has provided a focus for parliamentarians, and has helped frame public discussion around the necessity to balance freedom and security.[318] The JCHR provides new opportunities for civil society to interact with parliamentarians and parliamentary processes, and has communicated and collaborated with a wide array of people and groups, including academics, the media and NGOs.[319]

Political Opportunities

More dynamic changes in the political environment in the form of new or disappearing opportunities can also facilitate or inhibit activism. The UK had a more open political system than Australia after 9/11, due to opportunities that emerged at different times, some of which were more significant than others for activism on detainees and accountability for torture. They included Labour's inclusive attitude towards NGOs, points of political vulnerability for the Blair Government regarding the Iraq War and its indefinite detention regime for non-national terrorist suspects, and the formation of a coalition government in 2010.

In contrast to the Howard Government in Australia, the Blair Government came to power espousing a philosophy that voluntary and community activity was fundamental to the development of a democratic, socially inclusive society.[320] Its views towards the voluntary and community sector were embodied in The Compact of 1998.[321] The Compact was a non-legally binding framework that explicitly recognised the sector's independence and right to campaign, comment on and challenge government policy.[322] While it is important not to overstate the significance of The Compact in relation to the detainee torture issue, it gave a level of legitimacy, and hence confidence, to civil society in publicly advocating on contentious government policy, including counter-terrorism, that was absent in Australia.

Another kind of political opportunity that emerged in the UK was based on related issues playing out concurrently in the polity that informed concerns about the treatment of detainees at Guantánamo Bay. These issues affected electoral politics and presented civil society activists with openings for pressuring the Blair

[318] Gearty, '11 September 2001, Counter-terrorism, and the *Human Rights Act*', 26–27, 32.

[319] Kavanagh, 'The Joint Committee on Human Rights', 117.

[320] Jeremy Kendall, 'The mainstreaming of the third sector into public policy in England in the late 1990s: Whys and wherefores', *Policy & Politics* 28(4) (2000), 541–62.

[321] United Kingdom Secretary of State for the Home Department, *Compact on Relations Between Government and the Voluntary and Community Sector in England*, Compact Voice, 1998.

[322] Jane Lewis, 'Reviewing the relationship between the voluntary sector and the state in Britain in the 1990s', *International Journal of Voluntary and Non-Profit Organizations* 10(3) (1999), 264.

Government. One was the Iraq War, a difficult issue politically for the Government not only because it was unpopular with the public, but because of serious allegations that arose of systematic abuse by the UK military of detainees inside Iraq after 2003. The public outrage at the UK's role in the Iraq War divided the Government and drew out potential parliamentary allies for civil society activists across the broad spectrum of politics.[323] It also contributed to broader unease across the polity that Prime Minister Blair's attitude towards the US was too deferential, which fed into concerns about the treatment of UK detainees at Guantánamo Bay. According to one human rights lawyer, by 2004/05, the notion that Prime Minister Blair was 'sacrificing British citizens' to the Bush Administration had currency.[324]

Allegations of the abuse of Iraqi detainees by the UK military influenced the way the public viewed the treatment of detainees at Guantánamo Bay. News of the death in UK military custody of Iraqi hotel employee, Mousa, surfaced in late 2003.[325] Following a highly criticised court martial and a House of Lords decision that the HRA 1998 applied to Mousa while he was in UK custody in Iraq, a public inquiry was held into his death and the army's detainee treatment practices.[326] The inquiry found that UK soldiers had subjected detainees to serious, gratuitous violence; there was widespread ignorance inside the army about the proper handling of prisoners of war; and the 1972 ban on the five techniques had been forgotten.[327] Investigations into allegations of abuse of detainees by UK military are ongoing, with the International Criminal Court announcing in May 2014 it was re-opening a preliminary investigation into allegations that UK officials were responsible for war crimes involving systematic detainee abuse in Iraq between 2003 and 2008.[328] Civil society actors emphasised the role that allegations of the torture and killing of Iraqis by UK forces had in increasing the pressure on the Blair Government over the treatment of detainees at Guantánamo Bay. One NGO lawyer said that 'the climate was all kind of intertwined'; 'I'm convinced that you cannot separate it [Guantánamo] from the huge furore which Iraq caused.'[329]

While, ultimately, disquiet over Iraq did not shift Prime Minister Blair's support for the war, it arguably contributed to his early reversal on the detention of UK citizens at Guantánamo Bay, which was a more palatable back-down to mollify public opinion. The Iraq War played out very differently in the UK for Prime Minister Blair, compared to Australia, where it was not a difficult political issue for Prime Minister Howard, and Canada, which did not join the invasion.

[323] Coates and Krieger with Vickers, *Blair's War*, 60; Kampfner, *Blair's Wars*, 273.

[324] Human rights lawyer, tel interview, 15 February 2013.

[325] AT Williams, *A Very British Killing: The Death of Baha Mousa* (London: Vintage Books, 2013) 175.

[326] ibid, 274; *Al-Skeini v Secretary of State for Defence* [2007] UKHL 26.

[327] William Gage, 'Statement by Chairman', The Baha Mousa Public Inquiry, 8 September 2011.

[328] International Criminal Court, 'Prosecutor of the International Criminal Court, Fatou Bensouda, reopens the preliminary examination of the situation in Iraq', statement, 13 May 2014, https://www.icc-cpi.int//Pages/item.aspx?name=otp-statement-iraq-13-05-2014.

[329] NGO lawyer, tel interview, 30 January 2013.

A second issue that presented an opportunity for activism, especially around the cases of residents detained at Guantánamo Bay, was the *Belmarsh* litigation. Belmarsh was the name of the prison where non-nationals suspected of terrorism were detained without trial under the 2001 Anti-terrorism, Crime and Security Act. The UK Government could not deport the men because they were at risk of torture in their own countries in contravention of the ECHR (under Article 3) and the ECtHR ruling in *Chahal v UK*.[330] The 2001 Act drew many comparisons with the UK Government's Northern Ireland internment policies of the 1970s, and fuelled the suspicions of activist lawyers involved in the Guantánamo cases about a 'growing disrespect for the rule of law'.[331] The Act was subject to legal challenge and, in 2004, the House of Lords ruled that the provisions permitting the indefinite detention of non-nationals were not compatible with the ECHR.[332] Specifically, they breached Article 5 (the right to liberty and security) and Article 14 (the right to non-discrimination). In striking down the laws, the House of Lords singled out the Government's differential and arbitrary treatment of citizens and non-citizens as the principal weakness in the Government's case.[333] Their Lordships found that the laws were predicated on the understanding that non-citizens had lesser liberty rights than citizens, with the Government failing to demonstrate why, if the detention measures were not necessary for citizens suspected of international terrorism, they were necessary for non-citizen suspects.[334]

The *Belmarsh* decision was a significant instance of judicial protection of individual liberty in the war on terror context, where states frequently relied on distinctions based on nationality as a basis for inferior treatment. Though the case related to domestic internment, it generated debates around the discriminatory treatment of non-citizens that informed the responses of civil society to the UK Government's differential treatment of residents at Guantánamo Bay. This occurred in two interconnected ways. The debates around the *Belmarsh* litigation created an opening in the UK's political system that meant it was easier for supporters of the residents detained at Guantánamo to find public support for their cases, as they could point to parallels with what was occurring domestically. In addition, developments in the *Belmarsh* litigation help to explain why civil society more broadly was non-discriminating in its approach to detainees, and why it pushed for accountability for the treatment not just of UK citizens detained at Guantánamo, but of residents too.

A final opportunity that emerged in the UK political system for activism on accountability for torture came with the 2010 Election, and the formation of a

[330] *Chahal v United Kingdom* (1997) 23 EHRR 413.

[331] Steve Hewitt, *The British War on Terror: Terrorism and Counter-Terrorism on the Home Front Since 9/11* (London: Continuum, 2008) 37; Human rights lawyer, tel interview, 15 February 2013.

[332] *A v Secretary of State* [2004] UKHL 56.

[333] ibid [76] (Lord Nicholls).

[334] ibid [65] (Lord Bingham).

minority Conservative Government in coalition with the Liberal Democrats. The Liberal Democrats had taken a strong position in the lead up to the election on the need for a torture inquiry, and as coalition partner had a say on government policy.[335] In an indication of how elevated the issue of torture had become in UK politics, the official coalition agreement contained the statement, 'We will never condone the use of torture'.[336] When Prime Minister Cameron established the Detainee Inquiry, it was reported that Deputy Prime Minister Clegg was instrumental in negotiating the terms, including that it would be judge-led.[337] While not wanting to overstate the role of the Liberal Democrats, the fact that the Conservatives had to rely for power on an agreement with a minor party that had firm views on the need for accountability on torture, presented a political opportunity for detainees, advocates and activists.

Conclusion

The UK case had complexities that were absent in Australia and Canada, including larger numbers of detainees at Guantánamo Bay, more cases of alleged state complicity and ongoing allegations that its military personnel tortured detainees in Iraq. As prefaced in Chapter 1, my intention is not to rank the human rights records of liberal democracies based on how they responded to the torture of citizens. Rather, I am interested in mapping the conditions under which individuals and groups are more or less likely to become engaged when fellow citizens are tortured. Acknowledging the complexities, the UK case demonstrates how certain features of the domestic political and legal context can support activism on international human rights issues, including torture, with consequences for the state's response.

United Kingdom governments were responsive to allegations that detained citizens and residents were mistreated and tortured in the war on terror. This was illustrated by the UK's early decision not to allow citizens to be tried by the US military commissions at Guantánamo Bay and to bring them, and subsequently residents, home. It was also evident in the decision to hold an independent inquiry into citizens' and residents' allegations of torture and UK complicity, though the inquiry was abandoned prematurely. The governments faced intensive political

[335] Ian Cobain, 'Torture and rendition,' *Guardian*, 21 May 2010, 4; Cobain, *A Secret History of Torture*, 269.

[336] HM Government, *The Coalition: Our Programme for Government* (2010), 20, https://www.gov.uk/government/uploads/system/uploads/attachment_data/file/78977/coalition_programme_for_government.pdf.

[337] Ian Cobain, 'Torture inquiry: Pressure from courts and victims forced government's hands', *Guardian*, 7 July 2010, 6.

pressure at home over their policies towards detainees from human rights lawyers, campaigning media and a large number of NGOs, which collaborated with each other and with parliamentarians. The courts were central to activism, lending moral (if not always legal) support to the campaigning, with the first judicial ruling on detained UK citizens being delivered as early as 2002. Civil society did not discriminate between victims based on whether they were likeable or appeared to be innocent, nor did it differentiate between citizens and residents. Its focus was on state impunity.

Civil society's sustained pressure on the UK Government can be understood through an examination of the domestic political context, various features of which facilitated activism on the torture issue. They include a rights culture that was informed by the state's experience of terrorism and torture in Northern Ireland. The HRA 1998 elevated the rights consciousness of the judiciary, and provided legal levers to detainees and supporters for bringing rights claims in UK courts, including on the right not to be tortured. Civil society groups did not emphasise the UK's obligations under international conventions because they did not need to, having sufficient regional and domestic mechanisms. Civil society also faced a relatively open political system, which was receptive to mobilisation on issues to do with human rights and the war on terror. This was because of the unpopularity of the Iraq War and ongoing high-profile claims of abuse by the UK military of Iraqi detainees, and because of debates at home over the Government's counter-terrorism laws, which UK courts said discriminated against non-citizens.

The combination of a cultural awareness of the need to balance security and rights, institutional levers to contest human rights transgressions, and apertures in the political system through which to gain a sympathetic hearing, meant that some civil society groups were ready and able to mobilise on the issue of accountability for the torture of detainees. This contributed to pressure on the UK Government to protect citizens' and residents' rights, and to engage in accountability for its complicity in transgressions of those rights, even if that process was ultimately incomplete.

7

Canada

Introduction

Canada's contribution to the war on terror was more limited than that of Australia or the United Kingdom (UK). Its involvement featured a robust military commitment to the conflict in Afghanistan, but a refusal to embroil itself in the United States (US) invasion of Iraq.[1] Canada's partial support for the US war on terror was reflected in its inconsistent responses to the alleged torture of citizens detained in the course of that war. It stood up to the US for the rights of one tortured citizen, while for another it did not. In the case of Maher Arar, whom the US subjected to extraordinary rendition to Syria, Canada undertook thorough accountability of its own involvement and issued a public apology.[2] Yet in Omar Khadr's case—first under Liberal Governments and then a Conservative Government—Canada refused to defend his human rights or accept responsibility for him for a decade, even though he was just 15 years old when detained.[3]

I argue that Canadian governments, for many years, faced intense domestic pressure to protect the rights of only one of these two detained and tortured citizens. Canada's domestic context had many features that were enabling of activism on international human rights. Ultimately, they were not strong enough to overcome the inhibitions of civil society members concerned for their own public image, who avoided Khadr because of his family's associations with terrorists.

I begin this chapter with an overview of Canada's role in the war on terror and its relationship with the US. I introduce the Arar and Khadr cases, and set out their torture allegations. I then outline the responses of executive governments to the cases, as well as those of the legislature, the judiciary and civil society. Lastly, I analyse the behaviours of domestic actors through the framework of enabling and constraining factors particular to Canada's national legal and political context, in order to better understand the state's inconsistent responses to the torture of its citizens.

[1] Janice Gross Stein and Eugene Lang, *The Unexpected War: Canada in Kandahar* (Toronto: Penguin Canada, 2007) 75.

[2] Stephen Harper, 'Prime Minister releases letter of apology to Maher Arar and his family and announces completion of mediation process', News Release, 26 January 2007.

[3] Alex Neve, 'Canada must bring Khadr home without further delay', *Globe and Mail*, 24 July 2012, 11.

Canada and the War on Terror

The Canada–US Relationship

Canada's response to 9/11 must be viewed against the background of its, at times, testy relationship with the US. Former US Secretary of State, Condoleezza Rice, called America's relationship with Canada 'the most complex we have with any country'.[4] The complexities stem in part from Canada's geographic proximity to such a powerful and overbearing ally—'the giant Republic', as Seymour Martin Lipset called it.[5]

Many of Canada's concerns about the US centre around two themes. The first is a preoccupation with retaining an identity distinct from that of its culturally similar neighbour. Alison Brysk writes about Canada as 'the so-called *moral* superpower of the Americas', where human rights promotion distinguishes it from the US to the world and its own citizens.[6] Liberal Prime Minister Paul Martin evoked this identity in his Government's 2005 international policy statement, noting Canada's 'doctrine of activism that over decades has forged our nation's international character'.[7] Examples of Canada's liberal internationalism include its work on the treaty to ban landmines, its promotion of the Responsibility to Protect norm, and the role of Canadian forces in UN peacekeeping operations.[8] The Conservative Harper Government challenged aspects of the 'liberal internationalist consensus' underpinning Canada's post-World War II foreign policy.[9] Canada's other concern is to maintain sovereignty, especially over its defence and foreign policy, a difficult mission given its strategic importance to Washington.[10] As a middle power, Canada has sought to achieve this objective through its embrace of multilateralism, its full participation in the evolving international system and its involvement in North American defence.[11]

[4] Paul Cellucci, *Unquiet Diplomacy* (Toronto: Key Porter Books, 2007) 235.

[5] Allan Kornberg and Harold D Clarke, *Citizens and Community: Political Support in a Representative Democracy* (Cambridge: Cambridge University Press, 1992) 18; Seymour Martin Lipset, *Continental Divide: The Values and Institutions of the United States and Canada* (New York, NY: Routledge, 1990) 5.

[6] Alison Brysk, *Global Good Samaritans: Human Rights as Foreign Policy* (New York, NY: Oxford University Press, 2009) 66.

[7] Government of Canada, 'Canada's international policy statement: A role of pride and influence in the world: Overview', International Policy Statement, Ottawa, 2005.

[8] Jennifer M Welsh, 'The 2005 international policy statement', *International Journal* 61(4) (Autumn 2006), 921; UN Convention on the Prohibition of the Use, Stockpiling, Production and Transfer of Anti-Personnel Mines and on their Destruction, opened for signature 3 December 1997, 2056 UNTS 211 (entered into force 1 March 1999).

[9] Roland Paris, 'Are Canadians still liberal internationalists? Foreign policy and public opinion in the Harper era', *International Journal* 69(3) (September 2014), 274–307.

[10] Donald Barry and Duane Bratt, 'Defense against help: Explaining Canada-US Relations', *American Review of Canadian Studies* 38(1) (2008), 63–89.

[11] Srdjan Vucetic, 'Why did Canada sit out of the Iraq war? One constructivist analysis', *Canadian Foreign Policy* 13(1) (2006), 142.

Canada had another, more immediate and pragmatic concern in the aftermath of 11 September 2001. This was to protect its economy from collateral damage arising out of the tightening of control of movements across its northern border by the US.[12] At the time, over 85 per cent of Canada's foreign trade relied on open access to the American market, which depended on the free flow of goods and people across the Canadian–US border.[13]

United States scepticism about Canada's supposedly lax border security stemmed partly from a 1999 incident in which an Algerian man, who had claimed refugee status in Canada, was arrested at the US border with explosives intended for use in an attack on the Los Angeles International Airport.[14] The Ahmed Ressam case took on added significance after 9/11, as some American politicians and commentators wrongly suggested that the hijackers had entered the US from Canada.[15] The US Ambassador to Canada, Paul Cellucci, said it was 'inevitable that terrorists would look to Canada as a potential launching pad to get into the US'.[16] A US State Department report noted, 'Terrorists and their supporters have capitalized on liberal Canadian immigration policies.'[17] Many Canadians, including Prime Minister Jean Chrétien, felt that Americans were using 9/11 as 'a convenient way' to attack Canada's multiculturalism and social and immigration policies.[18]

In order to reassure Washington of its diligence on terrorism and protect Canadian economic interests, the Chrétien Government took a number of quick policy decisions.[19] It established an ad hoc Cabinet Committee on Public Security and Anti-Terrorism, allocated C$8 billion to new security measures, signed the Smart Border Accord with the US (designed to secure and improve management of the border) and passed new counter-terrorism laws, including the Anti-terrorism Act 2001.[20] It also committed military forces to the war in Afghanistan.

Tensions between Canada and the US over identity and sovereignty surfaced again, however, over the US invasion of Iraq. Chrétien made it one of his top

[12] Frank P Harvey, 'Canada's addiction to American security: The illusion of choice in the war on terrorism', *The American Review of Canadian Studies* 35(2) (2005), 272.

[13] Joel J Sokolsky, 'Northern exposure? American homeland security and Canada', *International Journal* 60(1) (2004/2005), 35.

[14] Wesley Wark, 'Learning lessons (and how) in the war on terror: The Canadian experience', *International Journal* 60(1) (2004/2005), 73.

[15] Kent Roach, *September 11: Consequences for Canada* (Montreal: McGill-Queen's University Press, 2003) 5–6.

[16] Jason Ackleson, 'From "thin" to "thick" (and back again?): The politics and policies of the contemporary US–Canada border', *American Review of Canadian Studies* 39(4) (2009), 341.

[17] United States Department of State, Office of the Coordinator for Counterterrorism, 'Country reports on terrorism 2005', April 2006, 160.

[18] Jean Chrétien, *My Years as Prime Minister* (Toronto: Vintage Canada, 2008) 300; see also Roach, *September 11*, 6.

[19] Sokolsky, 'Northern exposure?', 36.

[20] Reg Whitaker, 'More or less than meets the eye? The new national security agenda' in *How Ottawa Spends 2003–2004: Regime Change and Policy Shift*, ed G Bruce Doern (Don Mills: Oxford University Press, 2003) 46–47; Kent Roach, *The 9/11 Effect: Comparative Counter-Terrorism* (New York, NY: Cambridge University Press, 2011) 361–62.

priorities, upon taking office in 1993, 'to reassert our independence and protect Canada from being seen as the fifty-first state of the United States'.[21] His decision not to support the Iraq invasion without the UN sanction exemplified this position. The decision played to domestic politics, particularly anti-Americanism most prominent in Québec, and fractured bilateral relations.[22] Chrétien's successors, Martin and Stephen Harper, both promised to improve the Canada–US relationship.[23] Harper, who supported the invasion of Iraq, envisioned a Canadian global identity based on proud membership of the 'Anglosphere' and the status of loyal ally of the US.[24]

Canada's Detained Citizens

I selected the Arar and Khadr cases for examination because they represent extremes in Canada's response to the international torture issue. They were not the only Canadian citizens tortured in the war on terror. Three others, Abdullah Almalki, Ahmad Abou-Elmaati and Muayyed Nureddin, were tortured in Syria and Egypt between 2001 and 2004. However, there was no direct US involvement in their cases in the form of extraordinary renditions (all were arrested upon arrival in Syria).[25] I discuss their cases briefly below.

Maher Arar

Arar was a Syrian-born Canadian citizen. He was detained at New York's John F Kennedy International Airport by US immigration officials on his way home from a family holiday in Tunisia in September 2002.[26] The FBI and New York Police questioned him about Osama bin Laden and Almalki, a Canadian under investigation by Canadian police. Arar was placed in chains and ordered to volunteer to go to Syria, which he refused to do. He was held for 12 days at the Metropolitan Detention Centre and permitted to see a Canadian consular official and a US lawyer. In early October, the US Immigration and Naturalization Service (INS) issued an order finding Arar to be a member of Al-Qaeda and directing he be removed

[21] Chrétien, *My Years as Prime Minister*, 42.

[22] Kim Richard Nossal, 'Defense policy and the atmospherics of Canada-US relations: The case of Harper Conservatives', *American Review of Canadian Studies* 37(1) (2007), 24–25.

[23] ibid, 25–26.

[24] Howard Cody, 'Stephen Harper, Michael Ignatieff, and Canada's politics of identity', *Southern Journal of Canadian Studies* 3(1) (2010), 20.

[25] Frank Iacobucci, 'Internal inquiry into the actions of Canadian officials in relation to Abdullah Almalki, Ahmad Abou-Elmaati and Muayyed Nureddin', October 2008, 269, 298, 323.

[26] Maher Arar, 'Maher Arar statement in Ottawa on November 4, 2003, less than one month after being released from prison in Syria', Syrian Human Rights Committee, 29 November 2003, http://www.shrc.org/en/?p=19801.

from the US.[27] Arar was flown to Jordan then driven to Syria.[28] The US Inspector General of Homeland Security subsequently found that the INS had originally decided to send Arar to Zurich, assessing he would face torture in Syria, but this was overridden by the Acting US Attorney General.[29] The Inspector General could not rule out the possibility that Arar was sent to Syria to be interrogated under torture.[30]

Upon his arrival in Damascus, Arar was taken to the Far Falestin detention centre, run by Syrian Military Intelligence.[31] Arar was questioned by the head of interrogation and threatened with torture.[32] He was taken to a cell, which was 'like a grave' and had no light, and which was three feet wide and six feet deep.[33] He spent 10 months inside this cell, which was cold, damp and infested with rats. Throughout the first two weeks of his detention, Arar was interrogated and subjected to severe beatings. He was struck with a two-inch thick electric cable all over his body and threatened with various forms of torture. The most intense beating lasted 18 hours. Arar heard other prisoners screaming and being tortured, and was beaten until he urinated on himself and made false confessions.

The Canadian embassy in Damascus obtained confirmation from Syrian authorities 12 days after his arrival that Arar was in Syria, and he received his first of nine consular visits two days later.[34] During his last consular visit in August 2003, with the head of Syrian Military Intelligence in the room, Arar told the Canadian consular official of his beatings.[35] Six days later, Arar was transferred to Sednaya Prison where conditions improved.[36] In October 2003, after signing a confession, Arar was released and returned to Canada. Stephen Toope, the Fact Finder to the Commission of Inquiry into Arar's case ('Arar Commission'), concluded

[27] Commission of Inquiry into the actions of Canadian officials in relation to Maher Arar, *Report of the events relating to Maher Arar: Analysis and recommendations*, 2006, ('Arar Commission') 139, http://epe.lac-bac.gc.ca/100/206/301/pco-bcp/commissions/maher_arar/07-09-13/www.ararcommission.ca/eng/index.htm.

[28] Arar, 'Maher Arar statement in Ottawa on November 4, 2003'.

[29] United States Department of Homeland Security, Office of Inspector General, *The removal of a Canadian citizen to Syria*, Report No OIG-08-18, Office of Inspector General, March 2008, 21–22.

[30] Evidence to Joint Hearing before the Subcommittee on the Constitution, Civil Rights, and Civil Liberties of the Committee on the Judiciary and the Subcommittee on International Organizations, Human Rights, and Oversight of the Committee on Foreign Affairs House of Representatives, US Congress, Washington, DC, 'US Department of Homeland Security Inspector General Report OIG-08-18, "The removal of a Canadian citizen to Syria"', 5 June 2008 (Richard Skinner, Office of the Inspector General, US Department of Homeland Security) 53.

[31] Arar Commission, 55.

[32] Stephen J Toope, *Report of Professor Stephen J Toope Fact Finder*, Commission of Inquiry into the actions of Canadian officials in relation to Maher Arar, 14 October 2005, 14, http://epe.lac-bac.gc.ca/100/206/301/pco-bcp/commissions/maher_arar/07-09-13/www.ararcommission.ca/eng/index.htm.

[33] Arar, 'Maher Arar statement in Ottawa on November 4, 2003'.

[34] Arar Commission, 184–85, 229.

[35] Monia Mazigh, *Hope and Despair: My Struggle to Free My Husband, Maher Arar* (Toronto: McClelland and Stewart, 2008) 220.

[36] Toope, *Report of Professor Stephen J Toope Fact Finder*, 17.

that Arar's treatment in Far Falestin prison 'constituted torture as understood in international law'.[37]

Omar Khadr

Khadr was a Canadian citizen by birth, and aged 15 when taken into custody by the US military in Afghanistan in July 2002.[38] Khadr was the son of Egyptian-born parents who met and married in Canada but frequently moved their family between Canada, Pakistan and Afghanistan.[39] The family had a history of associating with senior Al-Qaeda figures. His father, Ahmed Said Khadr, sent Omar's elder brothers to Al-Qaeda training camps in the mid-1990s, and the family lived in Osama bin Laden's compound in Afghanistan for a period.[40] In mid-2002, Omar Khadr was sent by his father on a trip into Afghanistan to be translator for a senior Al-Qaeda figure.[41] There, Khadr found himself in a firefight with the US military after they surrounded the compound where he was housed with various Al-Qaeda members.[42] According to the US military's version of events, which has been disputed, when US forces entered the compound Khadr threw a grenade, killing a medic.[43] Khadr himself was severely wounded. He was shot twice in the back and once through his left shoulder, struck with shrapnel in his left eye, and wounded in his left thigh, knee, ankle and foot.[44]

United States soldiers took the unconscious Khadr into custody. His interrogations began in hospital as soon as he regained consciousness a week later, and continued when he was moved to the US military camp at Bagram.[45] Khadr was considered to be 'an intelligence treasure trove' because of his father's connections to Al-Qaeda.[46] In an affidavit, he recounted crying during questioning as a result of his rough treatment, and told interrogators 'whatever I thought they wanted to hear'.[47] Interrogators covered his head with a bag, used barking dogs to scare him and poured cold water over him. While his wounds were still healing, Khadr was

[37] ibid.

[38] United States Department of Defense, Office of the Chief Prosecutor, Office of Military Commissions, 'Memorandum for Detainee Omar Amar Khadr 0766, Guantanamo Bay, Cuba, Subject: Notification of the Swearing of Charges', 2 February 2007.

[39] Michelle Shephard, *Guantánamo's Child* (Mississauga: John Wiley & Sons, 2008) 17, 19, 61–63.

[40] ibid, 44, 61–63.

[41] ibid, 82.

[42] United States Department of Defense, Office of the Chief Prosecutor, Office of Military Commissions, 'Memorandum for Detainee Omar Amar Khadr 0766, Guantanamo Bay, Cuba, Subject: Notification of the Swearing of Charges'.

[43] ibid. For alternative accounts see Shephard, *Guantánamo's Child*, 224–25; and Omar El Akkad, 'US Army altered Khadr report; First version said attacker was slain, Military Court told', *Globe and Mail*, 14 March 2008, 1.

[44] Omar Ahmed Khadr, 'Affidavit of Omar Ahmed Khadr', 22 February 2008.

[45] ibid.

[46] Shephard, *Guantánamo's Child*, 103.

[47] Khadr, 'Affidavit of Omar Ahmed Khadr'.

forced to clean the floors on his hands and knees, carry heavy buckets of water and pick up rubbish; he was not allowed to use the bathroom and urinated on himself, was threatened with rape, and had his hands tied to the top of a door frame or ceiling and made to stand in this position for hours.[48] After turning 16 in October 2002, Khadr was transferred to Guantánamo Bay, where American and Canadian officials interrogated him.[49] Khadr told the Canadians he had been tortured. He was subject to numerous forms of mistreatment at Guantánamo Bay, including sleep deprivation, isolation and cold temperatures.[50] He was short-shackled by his hands and feet to a bolt in the floor for hours, had his hair pulled, was spat on, kicked, dropped and grabbed in painful pressure points. He was kept with adult detainees and threatened with removal to Middle Eastern countries to be raped or tortured. On two occasions in 2003, military police used Khadr's body, with his hands and feet cuffed together behind him, to mop up his urine and cleaning fluid off the floor.[51]

Khadr was charged in the military commissions in November 2005 and again in April 2007 (following the US Supreme Court *Hamdan v Rumsfeld* ruling that the system was invalid).[52] His charges included murder in violation of the law of war, attempted murder in violation of the law of war, conspiracy, providing material support for terrorism and spying. Khadr's lawyers unsuccessfully sought rulings in the military commission that incriminating statements he made during interrogations be struck out because they were procured using torture and because of his age.[53] His lawyers, again unsuccessfully, sued the US Government in the American courts to stop his torture and interrogation, and sought his transfer into a juvenile detention facility.[54] In October 2010, Khadr entered a plea agreement with the US, admitting guilt to all charges in exchange for an eight-year sentence on top of time already spent in US detention.[55] He returned to Canada in September 2012 and was incarcerated in a 'maximum security' prison, was granted bail in April 2015

[48] ibid; United States of America, 'Defense motion to suppress statements procured using torture, coercion and cruel, inhumane, and degrading treatment', Submission in *United States of America v Khadr*, Military Commission, 7 November 2008, 5c(9).

[49] Khadr, 'Affidavit of Omar Ahmed Khadr'.

[50] ibid; United States of America, 'Defense motion to suppress statements procured using torture, coercion and cruel, inhumane, and degrading treatment,' 5d(5).

[51] Khadr, 'Affidavit of Omar Ahmed Khadr.'

[52] Shephard, *Guantánamo's Child*, 177, 204.

[53] United States of America, 'Defense motion to suppress statements procured using torture, coercion and cruel, inhumane, and degrading treatment'; United States of America, 'D-094 Government response to the defense's motion to suppress statements allegedly procured using torture, coercion and cruel, inhumane, and degrading treatment', Submission in *United States of America v Khadr*, Military Commission, 12 December 2008.

[54] *O.K. v Bush*, 377 F Supp 2d 102 (DDC, 2005) and *Khadr v Bush* (DDC, Civ No 04-1136 (JBD) 24 November 2008).

[55] Omar Khadr, 'Offer for pre-trial agreement', *United States of America v Khadr*, 13 October 2010.

and released a month later.[56] Khadr is challenging his US military commission convictions in the US Court of Appeals.[57]

The Executive

This section considers the responses of different Canadian governments to the Arar and Khadr cases. They are the centre-left Liberal Governments of Chrétien (1993–2003) and Martin (2003–06), and the Conservative Harper Government (2006–15).

The Chrétien and Martin Governments

Arar's detention in Syria occurred under the Chrétien Government. The behaviour of the executive throughout Arar's imprisonment was marked by the over-zealous actions of security agencies (the Canadian Security Intelligence Service (CSIS) and the Royal Canadian Mounted Police (RCMP)), as well as discord between different parts of the Government as to how the case should be handled.[58] Questions have been raised about whether Canadian security officials may have been trying to make up for their embarrassment over the 1999 Ressam case in responding to the Arar case.[59]

Arar's arrest came about as a result of the RCMP's post-9/11 counter-terrorism operation, Project A-O Canada, established amid pressure from the US over fears of a second wave of terrorist attacks.[60] Arar became a 'person of interest' when he met with Almalki, the focus of Project A-O Canada, in Ottawa in October 2001.[61] Canadian investigators provided information to American agencies about Arar that overstated his importance in the investigation and was inaccurate—including a description of him as an 'Islamic Extremist … suspected of being linked to the al Qaeda terrorist movement'.[62] Canadian investigators asked Canada Customs and US Customs to place 'border lookouts' for Arar and his wife.[63]

[56] Michelle Shephard, 'Omar Khadr walks free on bail after 13 years in custody', *Toronto Star*, 7 May 2015.

[57] Michelle Shephard, 'US court decision bodes well for Omar Khadr case, his lawyers say', *Toronto Star*, 12 June 2015.

[58] Roach, *The 9/11 Effect*, 374–75.

[59] Kent Roach, 'Uneasy neighbors: Comparative American and Canadian counter-terrorism', *William Mitchell Law Review* 38(5) (2012), 1730.

[60] Arar Commission, 65–66.

[61] ibid, 78.

[62] ibid, 101, 113.

[63] ibid, 19.

From the time Canada's Department of Foreign Affairs and International Trade (DFAIT) confirmed Arar's presence in Syria with the Syrian Government, Canadian officials worked at cross-purposes on his case. For example, some DFAIT officials downplayed the likelihood that Arar was tortured and took actions that implied Canada condoned his torture. Canada's Ambassador to Syria, Franco Pillarella, who met with the head of Syrian Military Intelligence, and consular official, Leo Martel, who visited Arar, failed to report on or acknowledge obvious signs of his mistreatment.[64] This meant that the Foreign Affairs Minister was never informed of the likelihood of Arar's torture, which led to his making inaccurate public statements, including that Arar had rejected allegations of torture.[65] Pillarella also requested from the Syrians a 'bout de papier', summarising the results of their interrogations of Arar, and distributed it to various government agencies without warnings that torture was likely to have been used to obtain it.[66] This action 'could have been viewed as condoning the use of torture and even encouraging it in other cases', according to Justice Dennis O'Connor, who carried out the public inquiry into Arar's case.[67] After receiving the 'bout de papier', CSIS officials travelled to Syria to obtain further information from Syrian Military Intelligence about Arar, which they shared with other agencies, again without warnings about torture.[68]

The Canadian agencies informed the Syrians they did not want Arar returned to Canada, and baulked when a DFAIT consular official sought a joint letter from the Foreign Affairs Minister and the Solicitor General (responsible for the RCMP and CSIS) seeking his release.[69] In July 2003 Prime Minister Chrétien wrote to the Syrian President asking for Arar's release. He stated, 'I can assure you that there is no Canadian government impediment to his return.'[70]

Canadian security agencies and DFAIT continued to work against Arar's interests after he returned home in October 2003. For example, anonymous officials leaked damaging information to the media.[71] In addition, Martel, who accompanied Arar back to Canada, provided an incorrect account to the Foreign Affairs Minister about Arar's treatment, wrongly reporting that his Syrian jailers had not beaten him.[72] A month after returning to Canada, Arar made a public statement outlining his torture.[73] The most explosive official leak against Arar occurred four days later.[74] *Ottawa Citizen* journalist, Juliet O'Neill, wrote an article containing

[64] ibid, 185, 190.
[65] ibid, 240.
[66] ibid, 192.
[67] ibid, 195.
[68] ibid, 197–98.
[69] ibid, 221–22.
[70] ibid, 228.
[71] ibid, 251.
[72] ibid, 253.
[73] Mazigh, *Hope and Despair*, 233.
[74] Arar Commission, 259.

previously classified material, including that Arar told Syrian Military Intelligence 'minute details' of seven months of training at a camp in Afghanistan with the Mujahadeen in 1993; that the RCMP had caught Arar in their sights while investigating the activities of members of an alleged Al-Qaeda logistical support group in Ottawa; and that the existence of this Al-Qaeda cell explained why the Canadian Government opposed a public inquiry into his case.[75]

Meanwhile, Prime Minister Chrétien resisted increasing calls for a public inquiry into Arar's deportation and treatment, some from government MPs.[76] Chrétien's successor and rival, Martin, who became Prime Minister in December 2003, was more open to a public inquiry.[77] In January 2004, the RCMP raided the home of O'Neill, ostensibly as a part of its investigation into whether the journalist had breached the Security of Information Act, and calls for a public inquiry intensified.[78] This act of agency overreach was the trigger for Prime Minister Martin to order a public inquiry.[79] Its head, O'Connor, had a reputation for fierce independence, and his terms of reference were broad.[80] The inquiry would examine the actions of Canadian officials dealing with Arar's deportation and detention.[81]

In contrast with the Arar case, the Liberal Governments adopted a tougher, more rigid, position on Khadr, whose allegations of torture and pleas for Canada to help in his case went largely ignored for a decade. The Chrétien Government's immediate response to Khadr's capture in Afghanistan was one of concern for his welfare and age. At first, the Government sought consular access, which the Americans refused.[82] The DFAIT publicly suggested that Khadr could have been recruited into terrorism as a child soldier, noted Canada's work on the child soldier issue, and implored the US to take his age into account in determining treatment.[83] Canada had ratified the 1989 UN Convention on the Rights of the Child (CRC), which states that children should not be subjected to torture or other cruel, inhuman or degrading treatment or punishment (Article 37(a)). It was also one of

[75] Juliet O'Neill, 'Canada's dossier on Maher Arar: The existence of a group of Ottawa Men with alleged ties to al-Qaeda is at the root of why the government opposes an inquiry into the case', *Ottawa Citizen*, 8 November 2003, 1.

[76] Jeff Sallot, 'Backbenchers call for Arar inquiry; Liberals jump on Easter about RCMP role in year-long jailing of Canadian in Syria', *Globe and Mail*, 8 October 2003, 7; Steven Chase and Drew Fagan, 'Prime Minister scorns call for probe: If there is a Canadian link in deportation of Arar, Powell will tell us, Chretien Says', *Globe and Mail*, 6 November 2003, 4.

[77] Paul Martin, *Hell or High Water: My Life In and Out of Politics* (Toronto: Emblem/McClelland and Stewart, 2009) 228, 230.

[78] Reg Whitaker, 'Arar: The affair, the inquiry, the aftermath', *IRPP Policy Matters* 9(1) (2008), 23.

[79] Martin, *Hell or High Water*, 405.

[80] Whitaker, 'Arar: The affair, the inquiry, the aftermath', 11.

[81] Anne McLellan, 'Deputy Prime Minister issues terms of reference for the public inquiry into the Maher Arar matter', press release, 5 February 2004.

[82] Clark Campbell, 'Red Cross visits captured teenager Canada still denied access to 15-year-old', *Globe and Mail*, 16 September 2002, 8.

[83] Allan Thompson, 'Toronto teen held for terror role', *Toronto Star*, 6 September 2002, 1.

the first countries to ratify the Optional Protocol to the Convention on the Rights of the Child on the Involvement of Children in Armed Conflict (OPCRC). The OPCRC sets the minimum age of military involvement at 18 years, and requires states to accord former child soldiers 'all appropriate assistance for their physical and psychological recovery and their social reintegration' (Article 6).

The Government's concern for Khadr's welfare was short-lived. The DFAIT's legal advisor asked that in future public communications on Khadr, diplomatic officials 'claw back on the fact that [Omar] is a minor'.[84] After Khadr's transfer to Guantánamo Bay, the Chrétien Government's attitude hardened further. While it protested the US failure to consult it before transferring Khadr, once at Guantánamo Bay, Prime Minister Chrétien publicly rebuked MPs who questioned the treatment of detainees.[85]

The Chrétien Government was anxious for Canadian intelligence officials to gain access to Khadr at Guantánamo Bay, which they obtained in February 2003.[86] Their interrogations of Khadr continued for two years. One Canadian intelligence official noted in a report following an interrogation in 2004 how 'thoroughly screwed up' Khadr was: 'All those persons who have been in positions of authority over him have abused him and his trust for their own purposes.'[87] Khadr's lawyers sued the Canadian Government over its interrogations.[88] In 2005, the CSIS admitted to the Canadian Federal Court that it had shared information obtained from Khadr with the US, without seeking guarantees that it would not be used in any future prosecution.[89] Defending his agency, CSIS Deputy Director, Jack Hooper, said, '[We] have the choice, talk to Omar, don't talk to Omar. Well, excuse me if my decision falls on the side of the greater good and the greater good is for the majority of Canadians.'[90] In August 2005, Khadr's lawyers obtained a Federal Court injunction preventing Canadian officials from further interrogating him on the basis that continuing to do so risked causing irreparable harm, given that any intelligence collected might be used by the US in military proceedings.[91]

When the first US military commission charges were laid against Khadr in 2005, the Martin Government made little comment beyond noting its support for his right to legal representation.[92] It also obtained the US assurance that it would not seek the death penalty against Khadr.[93]

[84] Shephard, *Guantánamo's Child*, 117.
[85] ibid, 119, 121; Colin Freeze, 'Canada will have access to teen in Cuba, US says', *Globe and Mail*, 1 November 2002, 6.
[86] Shephard, *Guantánamo's Child*, 113.
[87] ibid, 126.
[88] ibid, 165.
[89] Colin Perkel, 'CSIS admits sharing Khadr information with US', *Globe and Mail*, 11 April 2005, 8.
[90] Shephard, *Guantánamo's Child*, 167.
[91] *Khadr v Canada* [2006] 2 FCR 505.
[92] Alan Freeman and Colin Freeze, 'Canadian charged in US soldier's death', *Globe and Mail*, 8 November 2005, 1.
[93] Shephard, *Guantánamo's Child*, 178.

The hard-line position of successive Liberal Governments on Khadr must be viewed through the lens of what is termed in Canadian politics 'the Khadr effect'.[94] This refers to an episode in the mid-1990s when Prime Minister Chrétien, unaware of the terrorist links of Ahmed Said Khadr (Omar's father), intervened in his case following his arrest in Pakistan in connection with the 1995 bombing of the Egyptian embassy in Islamabad.[95] Chrétien's intervention was seen as 'an appalling political error', and thereafter served as a warning to Canadian officials and politicians not to get involved in cases that could embarrass them.[96] No Canadian Government wanted to risk its reputation with voters by defending 'Canada's first family of terrorism', as the Khadrs were known.[97]

The Harper Government

By the time the Arar Commission issued its findings in September 2006, the Harper Government was in power. The inquiry marked a significant milestone in government accountability in the war on terror.[98] The Arar Commission provided the first officially documented description of the US practice of extraordinary rendition, and inspired subsequent investigations, including one conducted by the Council of Europe.[99] It also drew another clear line of demarcation between Canada and the US in the war on terror, following the rupture over Iraq. O'Connor cleared Arar of involvement in terrorism, and criticised the RCMP, DFAIT and CSIS for the roles they played in his ordeal.[100] Among his findings was that the RCMP provided inaccurate information to the Americans about Arar without caveats, which they relied upon. Canadian officials also took actions that could have prolonged Arar's detention in Syria, and leaked confidential, sometimes inaccurate, information to the media for the purposes of damaging his reputation or protecting their interests or those of the Government. O'Connor made 23 recommendations, including that the Canadian Government should compensate Arar.[101]

In response to some of O'Connor's recommendations, the Harper Government formally apologised to Arar and paid him C$11.5 million compensation.[102] It also

[94] Audrey Macklin, 'From cooperation, to complicity, to compensation: The war on terror, extraordinary rendition, and the cost of torture', *European Journal of Migration and Law* 10(1) (2008), 20.

[95] Shephard, *Guantánamo's Child*, 54.

[96] ibid, 58. This had implications for Arar's case: see Colin Freeze, 'Mounties warn against release of Arar', *Globe and Mail*, 27 November 2004: 1; Mazigh, *Hope and Despair*, 108.

[97] Shephard, *Guantánamo's Child*, xiii.

[98] Macklin, 'From cooperation, to complicity, to compensation', 12.

[99] Whitaker, 'Arar: The affair, the inquiry, the aftermath,' 9.

[100] Arar Commission, 9, 13–16.

[101] ibid, 364–69.

[102] Jeff Sallot, 'Arar given $11.5 million in compensation: Canadian engineer tortured in Syria laments life he lost four long years ago', *Globe and Mail*, 27 January 2007, 4.

ordered another (internal) inquiry into the treatment of the three other Canadians tortured in Syria (Almalki, Elmaati and Nureddin), headed by Justice Frank Iacobucci.[103] Iacobucci reported in 2008 and found that the men were tortured, and that Canadian officials contributed indirectly to their mistreatment.[104] (The Harper Government refused to apologise to or compensate the men, who are now suing Canada for redress.)[105] Following the release of O'Connor's report, the Canadian House of Commons voted unanimously to apologise to Arar, as did the RCMP Commissioner, who later resigned for reasons connected to the case.[106] It is suggested that the Harper Government was so responsive to O'Connor's findings because they enabled the Conservatives to highlight the Liberals' failings.[107] Harper's apology did contain a pointed reference to previous Liberal Governments, noting, '[a]lthough these events occurred under the last government, please rest assured that this government will do everything in its power to ensure that the issues raised by Commissioner O'Connor are addressed'.[108] Irrespective of political motives, the Arar torture inquiry—where an investigation was followed by compensation and an unqualified apology—is hailed as a model for other countries.[109] The Harper Government also lodged a formal protest with the US over its treatment of Arar.[110] The US refused to apologise to Arar or remove him from its terrorist 'watch list'.[111] As noted in Chapter 4, Arar's attempt to seek damages from the American Government failed after his case was dismissed by US courts.[112]

On the Khadr case, the Harper Government also continued with the approach of previous Liberal Governments in demonstrating no concern for his welfare and refusing to request his repatriation from Guantánamo Bay. It fought efforts by Khadr's lawyers in the Supreme Court of Canada to force it to intervene in his situation.[113] By 2008, with Khadr's military commission underway, the Harper Government had refined the three 'talking points' to justify its hands-off approach: Khadr's charges were serious; the Government had been assured he was being

[103] Iacobucci, 'Internal inquiry into the actions of Canadian officials in relation to Abdullah Almalki, Ahmad Abou-Elmaati and Muayyed Nureddin'.

[104] ibid, 35–39.

[105] Tonda MacCharles, 'Liberals back CSIS in torture lawsuit', *Toronto Star*, 7 February 2016, 1.

[106] Jeff Sallot and Colin Freeze, 'House apologizes for Arar's treatment', *Globe and Mail*, 21 September 2006, 1; Jeff Sallot, '"Mr Arar, I wish to take this opportunity to express publicly to you, to your wife and to your children how truly sorry I am"', *Globe and Mail*, 29 September 2006, 1; Daniel Leblanc, 'Zaccardelli takes the fall', *Globe and Mail*, 7 December 2006, 1.

[107] Member of Parliament, tel interview, 12 January 2013.

[108] Harper, 'Prime Minister releases letter of apology to Maher Arar and his family and announces completion of mediation process'.

[109] Helen Duffy and Stephen A Kostas, '"Extraordinary rendition": A challenge for the rule of law' in *Counter-Terrorism: International Law and Practice*, ed Ana Maria Salinas de Frias, Katja LH Samuel and Nigel D White (New York, NY: Oxford University Press, 2012) 577–78.

[110] Jeff Sallot, '"Come clean" on Arar, Harper tells Bush', *Globe and Mail*, 7 October 2006, 1.

[111] Paul Koring, 'US snubs Canada's Arar plea', *Globe and Mail*, 22 December 2006, 1; Paul Koring and Gloria Galloway, 'US erred on Arar file, Rice says', *Globe and Mail*, 25 October 2007, 1.

[112] *Arar v Ashcroft*, 585 F 3d 559 (2d Cir 2009).

[113] *Canada (Justice) v Khadr* [2008] 2 SCR 125; *Canada (Prime Minister) v Khadr* [2010] 1 SCR 44.

treated humanely; and any effort to act on his case while he was still before the courts would be premature.[114] The Harper Government's position was backed by a majority of public opinion. A July 2010 poll found that 52 per cent of Canadians had 'no sympathy at all' for Khadr.[115] The lack of public support for Khadr was strongly linked to the widespread dislike of his family, some of whom had appeared in a CBC documentary expressing support for the 9/11 terrorist attacks.[116]

While the Harper Government displayed little interest in Khadr's military commission plea deal in October 2010, the Obama Administration began lobbying Canada to allow Khadr to serve his prison sentence at home.[117] Later that month, the Canadian Government exchanged diplomatic notes with the US in which it agreed to 'favorably consider' any request by Khadr, following his completion of one more year at Guantánamo Bay, to serve the remainder of his sentence in Canada.[118] By July 2012 the Harper Government had failed to repatriate Khadr to Canada, and his lawyers commenced action in the Canadian Federal Court to bring him home.[119] One media commentator opined that Harper's Government had done 'everything in its legal power, short of a diplomatic breach with the US government, to keep him interned at Guantánamo Bay'.[120]

Finally, in September 2012, the Harper Government reluctantly allowed Khadr to return to Canada to continue his sentence. The Minister of Public Safety, Vic Toews, issued a statement noting that Khadr was a 'known supporter' of Al-Qaeda, who idealised his dead father.[121] When Khadr was granted bail by the Alberta Court of Queen's Bench in April 2015, pending a legal challenge of his US military commission convictions in the US courts, the Harper Government's reaction was indignant.[122] It appealed the bail decision, calling Khadr's crimes 'heinous'.[123] The Court of Appeal of Alberta upheld the decision to grant Khadr bail, and the Harper Government appealed to the Supreme Court of Canada.[124] Commentary at the time suggested that the Harper Government's consistently hard-line attitude

[114] Omar El Akkad, 'Don't persecute a child soldier, Dallaire tells MPs', *Globe and Mail*, 14 May 2008, 4.

[115] Chris Selley, 'Spinning Omar Khadr: No matter what Ezra Levant says, the term "child soldier" applies to anyone under 18', *National Post*, 16 July 2010, 13.

[116] 'We are an al-Qaeda family', *CBC News*, 4 March 2004.

[117] Daniel Leblanc, 'US pushes Canada to take Khadr', *Globe and Mail*, 23 October 2010, 11.

[118] Stephen D Mull, Executive Secretary, United States Department of State, to Michael L Bruhn, Executive Secretary, Department of Defense, 24 October 2010.

[119] Colin Perkel, 'Canadian government's foot-dragging in Omar Khadr transfer "unprecedented"', *Canadian Press*, 19 July 2012.

[120] John Ibbitson, 'The US dumps a problem on Ottawa, with Omar Khadr's return', *Globe and Mail*, 29 September 2012.

[121] Vic Toews, 'In the matter of Omar Ahmed Khadr and the International Transfer of Offenders Act', statement, 28 September 2012, https://www.publicsafety.gc.ca/cnt/cntrng-crm/crrctns/_fl/lttr-20120929-eng.pdf.

[122] *Khadr v Bowden Institution* [2015] ABQB 261.

[123] Tristin Hopper, 'Khadr wins taste of freedom', *National Post*, 25 April 2015, 1.

[124] *Bowden Institution v Khadr* [2015] ABCA 159.

towards Khadr was part of a 'tough-on-terrorists' political agenda.[125] The new Liberal Government of Justin Trudeau, elected in October 2015, announced that it would not pursue the Harper Government's Supreme Court appeal.[126]

Parliament

The Canadian Parliament played a limited role in checking the executive on the Arar case, and for many years an even lesser role in Khadr's. Committees were mostly inactive, and while Arar found a few important parliamentary allies, it took until 2008 for a lone senator to start lobbying for Khadr's rights.

Canada's Parliament does not have a significant tradition of providing oversight in relation to security issues. Such scrutiny has historically been left to judicial commissions rather than parliamentary inquiries—a pattern described as '"fire alarm" oversight driven by scandal and partisan fishing, rather than sustained in-depth "police patrol" inquiry'.[127] Judicial commissions in Canada tend to be powerful; this was case with the Arar Commission, which had stronger powers than the UK Detainee Inquiry discussed in Chapter 6.[128] Legal scholars and parliamentarians have criticised the absence of parliamentary oversight of national security, arguing that there are insufficient safeguards around the activities of agencies.[129] They have recommended the establishment of a parliamentary committee with access to secret information.[130] Canada is almost alone among Western democracies in not permitting parliamentary committees access to secret information.[131]

In addition, Canada's Senate is often criticised as lacking political legitimacy because it is unelected.[132] Despite this, the Senate has a positive record of protecting the rights of unpopular minorities against arbitrary procedure by ministers or officials, precisely because its members are not directly answerable to voters.[133]

[125] Ian MacLeod, 'Court rejects bid to treat Khadr as adult', *Ottawa Citizen*, 15 May 2015, 9.

[126] Colin Perkel, 'Ottawa drops appeal over Khadr's bail', *Toronto Star*, 19 February 2016, 10.

[127] Jonathan Malloy, 'Canada's "war on terror", parliamentary assertiveness and minority government' in *The 'War on Terror' and the Growth of Executive Power*, ed John E Owens and Riccardo Pelizzo (New York, NY: Routledge, 2010) 159.

[128] Roach, 'Uneasy neighbors,' 1737.

[129] Craig Forcese and Kent Roach, 'Bridging the national security accountability gap: A three-part system to modernize Canada's inadequate review of national security', Forcese/Roach/01/16 working draft, 11 January 2016.

[130] House of Commons Standing Committee on Public Safety and National Security, *Review of the Findings and Recommendations Rising from the Iacobucci and O'Connor Inquiries*, June 2009, 16–17, http://www.parl.gc.ca/Committees/en/SECU/Work?show=reports&parl=40&session=2.

[131] Forcese and Roach, 'Bridging the national security accountability gap', 13.

[132] Malloy, 'Canada's "war on terror", parliamentary assertiveness and minority government', 175.

[133] David E Smith, *The Canadian Senate in Bicameral Perspective* (Toronto: University of Toronto Press, 2003) 110.

Members of Parliament are subject to popular pressures that senators do not experience, putting the latter in a position 'to speak as the conscience of Parliament'.[134] A more recent development in Canadian politics marginally increased Parliament's influence over the executive in the war on terror. This was the emergence of a less firmly majoritarian party system, which meant that governing parties did not for many years (from 2004–11) control a majority of seats in the House of Commons.[135]

Viewed against these general features, some observations can be made about Parliament's actions on the Arar and Khadr cases. Parliamentary committees were mostly ineffective in pressuring the executive over the cases. Parliament's two human rights committees—the House of Commons Standing Committee on Justice and Human Rights and the Senate Standing Committee on Human Rights—held no inquiries and issued no reports into the men's cases. This was despite the Senate Standing Committee on Human Rights' conducting significant work on the issue of children's rights during Khadr's detention at Guantánamo Bay.[136] While Parliament played some part in drawing attention to Arar's plight, its role has been described as 'at best supplementary'.[137] The House of Commons Standing Committee on Foreign Affairs and International Trade heard testimony from Arar's wife.[138]

The first parliamentary committee hearing on Khadr occurred in 2008, when the House of Commons Standing Committee on Foreign Affairs and International Development held an inquiry into his detention and prosecution.[139] The majority, controlled by opposition and minor parties, found that Khadr should be considered a 'child involved in armed conflict' and be given special protection as outlined in the OPCRC.[140] It recommended the Harper Government demand the immediate termination of the military commission proceedings against Khadr and seek his release from US custody. Conservative government MPs on the committee

[134] ibid, 111.

[135] Malloy, 'Canada's "war on terror", parliamentary assertiveness and minority government', 157.

[136] Senate Standing Committee on Human Rights, Parliament of Canada, *Children: The Silenced Citizens: Effective Implementation of Canada's International Obligations with respect to the Rights of Children*, April 2007, http://www.parl.gc.ca/sencommitteebusiness/CommitteeReports.aspx?parl=39&ses=1&Language=E&comm_id=1077.

[137] Malloy, 'Canada's "war on terror", parliamentary assertiveness and minority government', 168.

[138] Evidence to House of Commons Standing Committee on Foreign Affairs and International Trade, Parliament of Canada, Ottawa, 25 September 2003, 1215 (Monia Mazigh); House of Commons Standing Committee on Foreign Affairs and International Trade, Parliament of Canada, *Public Enquiry into the Maher Arar Case*, 2003, http://www.parl.gc.ca/Committees/en/FAIT/Work?parl=37&session=2&show=reports.

[139] Michell Shephard, 'Canada is Khadr's "only hope"; accused war criminal wouldn't be a risk if returned, his US military lawyer tells Commons committee', *Toronto Star*, 30 April 2008, 4.

[140] House of Commons Standing Committee on Foreign Affairs and International Development, Subcommittee on International Human Rights, Parliament of Canada, *Omar Khadr—Report of the Standing Committee on Foreign Affairs and International Development*, 2008, 4, 6, http://www.parl.gc.ca/Committees/en/FAAE/Work?parl=39&session=2&show=reports.

dissented, and accused the opposition and minor parties of downplaying Khadr's alleged crimes and links to terrorism. Khadr, they said, 'could become a litmus test on Canada's commitment to impeding global terrorism'.[141]

A number of individual MPs were active on the Arar case. Three in particular were close allies of Arar's wife, Monia Mazigh, during her husband's imprisonment. They were the minority New Democratic Party (NDP) leader, Alexa McDonough, and Liberal MPs Marlene Catterall and Irwin Cotler. McDonough introduced Mazigh to key parliamentarians and members of the Muslim community who became important supporters of Arar's cause.[142] Catterall visited Arar in his Syrian prison, lobbied the Syrian authorities and organised meetings with senior Liberal government ministers.[143] Cotler, an international human rights lawyer, acted pro bono for Arar and lobbied his Government.[144] One MP believes that Parliament's role in Arar's case was significant. The MP says:

> By and large the parliamentary system was responsive at a micro level of this compelling crisis for this family and this particular individual. But also on a kind of macro level, on a public policy level, I think it worked the way it was supposed to work.[145]

In Khadr's case, Parliament's role was negligible until six years into his detention at Guantánamo Bay. Khadr's case 'never seemed to be as compelling for people' as Arar's, the MP said.[146] One factor influencing a shift in 2008 was that the Liberal Party became more critical of the war on terror after it lost power in 2006.[147] In 2008, a number of former Liberal Government ministers, including former Prime Minister Martin, expressed regret for not having acted while in power to bring Khadr home.[148] In February 2008, the three federal opposition and minor parties—the Liberal Party, the NDP and the Bloc Québécois—issued a joint call on the Harper Government to bring Khadr home, admitting they had previously failed to protect his rights.[149]

Khadr also acquired a staunch parliamentary ally in 2008: Liberal Senator Roméo Dallaire. Dallaire, a retired Canadian Army Lieutenant-General, became an advocate on child soldiers after his experience as Force Commander of the UN Assistance Mission in Rwanda.[150] No other parliamentarian was as consistent or willing to risk the political ramifications involved in supporting Khadr as

[141] ibid, 15.
[142] Mazigh, *Hope and Despair*, 32, 71, 82, 107, 109, 145.
[143] ibid, 29, 102, 127, 140.
[144] ibid, 136, 174.
[145] MP, tel interview, 12 January 2013.
[146] ibid.
[147] Malloy, 'Canada's "war on terror", parliamentary assertiveness and minority government', 170.
[148] Colin Freeze, 'Bring back Khadr now, ex-PM says he should have worked to repatriate prisoner while in office', *Globe and Mail*, 21 July 2008, 4; Martin, *Hell or High Water*, 407.
[149] Omar El Akkad, 'Opposition parties call for Khadr's return', *Globe and Mail*, 26 February 2008, 7.
[150] Michelle Shephard, 'Dallaire vows to agitate for Omar Khadr', *Toronto Star*, 1 May 2008, 4.

Dallaire.[151] From 2008, he was an outspoken critic of the Harper Government's position on Khadr, and said that Canada's treatment of him 'makes us look like a damn bunch of hypocrites'.[152] In 2012, Dallaire launched an online petition to pressure the Harper Government to bring Khadr home from Guantánamo Bay.[153] The petition was framed in terms of Khadr's rights under the CRC and the OPCRC.[154]

The Courts

Canadian courts played virtually no role in the Arar case. With the help of a large number of influential allies in civil society and Parliament, Arar secured his freedom and a public inquiry reasonably quickly without having to rely on the courts. He sued the Canadian Government for damages, but his case was settled within months of the release of the Arar Commission report.[155] However, Khadr had few allies in Parliament, or anywhere else. Canada's judiciary, for a long time, afforded Khadr his only forum for contesting Canada's involvement in his abusive treatment. His lawyers brought a number of legal actions against the Canadian Government to enforce his rights under the Canadian Charter of Rights and Freedoms, Canada's constitutional bill of rights. I focus here on the Supreme Court of Canada, which heard three of Khadr's cases and demonstrated a willingness to hold the executive to account—though within limits.

The first Supreme Court decision on Khadr was delivered in 2008. The Court found that Khadr's Charter rights (in particular, section 7, which guarantees the 'right to life, liberty and security of the person') and his rights under international law (the Geneva Conventions) were violated when Canadian officials shared the results of their interrogations of Khadr with the US.[156] The Court took a more diplomatic approach on Guantánamo Bay than did the UK Court of Appeal in *Abbasi v Secretary of State*, which called it a 'legal black hole'.[157] The Supreme Court of Canada held that it did not need to pronounce on the legality of Guantánamo because the US Supreme Court had already done so, in *Rasul v Bush* and *Hamdan v Rumsfeld*.[158] The Court also ordered the Government to release

[151] Michelle Shephard, tel interview, 21 February 2013.

[152] Shephard, 'Dallaire vows to agitate for Omar Khadr'.

[153] 'Petition to bring home Omar Khadr draws thousands', *CBC News*, 17 July 2012.

[154] Roméo Dallaire, 'Petitioned Minister Towes—bring back Omar Khadr from Guantánamo Bay'—victory', *Change.org*, September 2012.

[155] Kent Roach, 'Substitute justice? Challenges to American counterterrorism activities in Non-American courts', *Mississippi Law Journal* 82(5) (2013), 931.

[156] *Canada (Justice) v Khadr* [2008] 2 SCR 125 [26].

[157] *The Queen on the Application of Abbasi v The Secretary of State for Foreign and Commonwealth Affairs* [2002] EWCA Civ 1598 [64].

[158] *Canada (Justice) v Khadr* [2008] 2 SCR 125 [21]; *Rasul v Bush*, 542 US 446 (2004); *Hamdan v Rumsfeld*, 548 US 577 (2006).

information relating to Canada's interrogations of Khadr. These disclosures revealed that ahead of interrogations by Canadian intelligence officials, Khadr was placed in a 'frequent flyer program'.[159] He was moved from cell to cell every three hours, 24 hours a day, and was placed in isolation for three weeks to make him more susceptible to interrogation. Video footage of the 2003 interrogations by Canadian intelligence agents showed a 16-year-old Khadr sobbing, rocking back and forth, and calling for his mother.[160]

In the second case, in 2010, the Supreme Court of Canada overturned two decisions of lower courts that had ordered the Harper Government to seek Khadr's repatriation.[161] The Supreme Court agreed with the lower courts that Khadr's Charter rights (under section 7) had been violated. However, it ruled that because of the separation of powers and the well-grounded reluctance of courts to intervene in matters of foreign relations, the appropriate remedy was to grant Khadr a declaration that his Charter rights had been infringed and leave the Government 'a measure of discretion in deciding how best to respond'.[162] On the violation of Khadr's rights, it found that Canada had actively participated in a process contrary to its international human rights obligations and contributed to his ongoing detention so as to deprive him of his Charter rights. It said:

> The interrogation of a youth detained without access to counsel, to elicit statements about serious criminal charges while knowing that the youth had been subjected to sleep deprivation and while knowing that the fruits of the interrogations would be shared with the prosecutors, offends the most basic Canadian standards about the treatment of detained youth suspects.[163]

Despite its strong condemnation of Khadr's treatment, the Supreme Court was criticised for its failure to issue a meaningful remedy for a citizen who was tortured and indefinitely detained.[164]

A more recent decision by the Supreme Court of Canada concerned the Harper Government's treatment of Khadr after his return home. The Government wanted to imprison Khadr as an adult in a federal penitentiary; his lawyers argued that he should be held in a provincial jail, given that his sentence related to crimes committed as a juvenile. The Supreme Court found for Khadr.[165]

Canada's courts play a strong role in holding governments to account through the interpretive power they exercise via the Charter.[166] Canadian courts were

[159] Colin Freeze and Omar el Akkad, 'Canada's secret documents on Khadr's treatment revealed', *Globe and Mail*, 10 July 2008, 1.

[160] Michelle Shephard, 'Omar Khadr's lawyers had fought for years for this moment', *Toronto Star*, 16 July 2008, 14.

[161] *Canada (Prime Minister) v Khadr* [2010] 1 SCR 44.

[162] ibid, 44, 50.

[163] ibid, 46–47.

[164] Audrey Macklin, 'Comment on *Canada (Prime Minister) v. Khadr* (2010)', *Supreme Court Law Review* 51 (2010), 329.

[165] *Bowden Institution v Khadr* [2015] 2 SCR 325.

[166] FL Morton and Rainer Knopff, *The Charter Revolution and the Court Party* (Toronto: Broadview Press, 2000) 13.

bolder than those in the UK in not accepting at face value the executive government's claims that disclosing documents relating to the torture of citizens would harm national security interests.[167] It is also arguable that in the war on terror, despite the Charter, Canada's judiciary showed too much deference to the executive, as with its denial of a remedy for Khadr.[168] In Khadr's case, where he had few allies, the ability of his lawyers to bring claims under the Charter in domestic courts was crucial to challenging the Canadian Government's treatment of him and for building wider support for his case, though this took many years. I discuss the enabling role of the Charter on civil society activism below.

Civil Society

Civil society in Canada was engaged and effective in demanding accountability for one citizen, Arar, detained and tortured in the war on terror. In relation to the plight of another citizen, however, Canadian civil society was virtually absent for five years into his detention. By the time civil society overcame its reticence about Khadr, a government was in place whose attitude towards him was resolute in its disregard for his rights. In this section I describe civil society in Canada and outline the main actors involved in the two cases. I highlight some distinguishing features of civil society's behaviour, including its inconsistency, the important influence of family members and the prominent role of international actors.

The Actors

Canada's human rights NGO sector was in a stronger position after 9/11 compared to that in Australia, though it still faced a sensitive political atmosphere for rights activism around the war on terror. Historically, Canadian NGOs have a positive record of organising around and influencing global human rights issues.[169] Brysk extols Canadian civil society as the 'best case' for human rights promotion. Canada's civil society is 'dense, internationalist, and well connected to channels of influence on foreign policy'; its NGOs are 'plentiful, rights-oriented, [and] globalist'.[170] This position is underpinned by various factors: multiculturalism, social equity, the dominance of the Liberal Party, the Francophone dimension and general public

[167] See, eg, *The Queen on the Application of Binyam Mohamed v Secretary of State for Foreign and Commonwealth Affairs* [2010] EWCA Civ 65.

[168] Kent Roach, 'The role and capacities of courts and legislatures in reviewing Canada's anti-terrorism law', *Windsor Review of Legal and Social Issues* 24 (2008), 52; Macklin, 'Comment on *Canada (Prime Minister) v. Khadr* (2010)', 298.

[169] Richard Price, 'Reversing the gun sights: Transnational civil society targets land mines', *International Organization* 52(3) (1998), 625.

[170] Brysk, *Global Good Samaritans*, 87.

opinion, which guides policy makers 'to prioritize humane internationalism'.[171] Similar to other liberal democracies after 9/11, the political climate in Canada was difficult for activism around respecting the rights of terrorist suspects, especially for Muslim organisations. One human rights NGO official said, '[T]he space in which to express a human rights view about events was tenuous.'[172] Muslim organisations 'did not want to be out there publicly associated with a case that had the words "Muslim terrorist", even if the word "accused" might be there'.

Among civil society actors, I focus on five categories that were active in the Arar and Khadr cases. Arar's wife was an exceptional advocate for her husband, the opposite of Khadr's family. Khadr's staunchest allies were his Canadian lawyers, Dennis Edney and Nate Whitling, who took on his case in 2003. Otherwise, lawyers and legal groups played a minor role in either case. The Canadian Bar Association (CBA) joined calls for a public inquiry into Arar's case, but only spoke out on Khadr's situation in 2007.[173] A number of legal academics, among them University of Toronto law professor, Audrey Macklin, were active in Khadr's case from 2007, as were lawyers' advocacy groups.[174] Human rights NGOs pressured the Government from early on over Arar's case, including Amnesty International Canada. Kerry Pither, an activist backed by her trade union-funded NGO, the Solidarity Network, played a central role. A range of other NGOS were active in the Arar case, including the International Civil Liberties Monitoring Group (a Canadian coalition of civil society organisations established after 11 September 2001), the London-based Syrian Human Rights Committee, the New York-based Center for Constitutional Rights, and Human Rights Watch (HRW). Domestic NGOs were engaged in the Arar Commission, including the British Columbia Civil Liberties Association (BCCLA) and the Canadian Civil Liberties Association (CCLA) (both founded in the 1960s).[175] The BCCLA and CCLA became involved in the Khadr case only after 2008. Few human rights NGOs engaged in any significant advocacy on Khadr's case before 2007, although from 2008 a large number of transnational actors became involved.[176] Muslim organisations were vocal about Arar's case, but slow to take up Khadr's cause. The Council on American-Islamic Relations Canada (CAIR-CAN, now the National Council of Canadian Muslims), the Canadian Arab Federation, and Muslim women's organisations such as the Canadian Council of Muslim Women and the Ottawa Muslim Women's Organization, were active in the Arar case. The media played significant roles in the Arar

[171] ibid, 88–90.

[172] Human rights NGO official, tel interview, 21 February 2013.

[173] Canadian Bar Association, 'CBA calls for full public inquiry into case of Maher Arar', press release, 24 November 2003; 'CBA calls for Omar Khadr to be released from Guantánamo Bay and turned over to Canada', press release, 12 August 2007.

[174] Audrey Macklin, 'The rule of law, the force of law, and the rule of force' in *Omar Khadr, Oh Canada*, ed Janice Williamson (Montreal: McGill-Queen's University Press, 2012) 222.

[175] Charles R Epp, 'Do bills of rights matter? The Canadian Charter of Rights and Freedoms', *American Political Science Review* 90(4) (1996), 769.

[176] Human Rights Watch, Human Rights First, Coalition to Stop the Use of Child Soldiers and Amnesty International to Stephen Harper, Prime Minister of Canada, 1 February 2008.

and Khadr cases, though in contrasting ways. I examined the editorials of two major Canadian newspapers to ascertain media attitudes towards accountability for the torture of Canadian citizens: the *Globe and Mail*, a newspaper with centrist views owned by Globe and Mail Inc, and the more conservative *National Post*, owned by Postmedia Network Inc.[177]

Inconsistency

The most striking feature of Canadian civil society's activism on Arar and Khadr was its different responses to the two cases. Arar's wife, Monia Mazigh, amassed a large collective of local activists during the first 10 months of her husband's detention, who were vital to her success in mobilising public support for freeing and returning him home from Syria and in calling for an inquiry.[178] By comparison, for the first five years of Khadr's detention, civil society was largely absent.[179]

Among Mazigh's supporters were a number of key activists backed by different organisations across the spectrum of Canadian civil society. One of Mazigh's first allies was Riad Saloojee from CAIR-CAN (as it was then known), who facilitated her communications with journalists a fortnight after Arar's arrest.[180] Following this, Amnesty International Canada's Secretary General Alex Neve agreed to launch an emergency campaign on Arar's case after just one conversation with Mazigh.[181] Still in October 2002, NDP leader McDonough called Mazigh.[182] She introduced Mazigh to Nazira Tareen, President of the Ottawa Muslim Women's Organization.[183] Five months later, a human rights academic, Bill Skidmore, contacted Mazigh and promised to put her in touch with an activist who had worked on East Timor, Kerry Pither.[184] A Liberal MP, Catterall, whom Mazigh had contacted soon after Arar's arrest, rang to say she was visiting Syria as part of a delegation.[185] Meeting Pither was a turning point.[186] By then, Arar's story was disappearing from the news. Beyond Saloojee and Tareen, Mazigh had little support from the Muslim community and was struggling financially to raise two small children.[187] Pither had experience working with the political media and Canadian foreign policy issues, and with building alliances between social justice

[177] Canadian Newspaper Association and the Canadian Community Newspaper Association, *Ownership: Daily Newspapers* (May 2014), Newspapers Canada.
[178] Mazigh, *Hope and Despair*.
[179] Lawyer, tel interview, 16 January 2013.
[180] Mazigh, *Hope and Despair*, 27.
[181] ibid, 32.
[182] ibid.
[183] ibid, 63.
[184] ibid, 114–15.
[185] ibid, 117.
[186] ibid, 114.
[187] Human rights activist, tel interview, 28 January 2013.

movements from around the country.[188] Most crucially, her organisation's board voted to allow her to work full-time on the Arar case.

When news of Arar's case first emerged, many members of the Muslim community were too nervous to get involved. One Muslim human rights activist said, '[P]eople were very reluctant … simply because of the accusations surrounding him.'[189] Another human rights activist who worked on the Arar case noted the Muslim community 'stayed scared for a long time':[190] 'A lot of people were just terrified and were being harassed by the security and intelligence services here.' Over time, however, Arar's case became a focal point for Muslim groups, who used it as a platform on which to speak more confidently about wider human rights issues affecting the community. As was the case in Australia before 9/11, Canada's Muslim community was fractured and diverse. Unlike in Australia, however, Arar's case helped unify it, educating members and providing, through its resolution, 'a type of collective and popular struggle to some of the challenges around 9/11'.[191] Arar's case 'epitomised some of the challenges the community would face after 9/11', a Muslim human rights activist said.[192] It 'exemplified many of those nagging issues that kept cropping up … in terms of security visitations … the curtailment of certain basic rights, cross border travel, racial profiling, the idea of loyalty to Canada'.

For many years into his detention at Guantánamo Bay, Khadr's only advocates were his lawyers, Edney and Whitling. A journalist recalls from the early days of reporting that 'you could not get comments from grass roots groups', and 'some of even the most strident groups were unwilling to touch the Khadr case and people would tell me "off the record" they just didn't want to go near it'.[193] Similarly, a lawyer says there 'was no organisation, no group, willing to step up and advocate for Omar Khadr' other than Edney and Whitling.[194] A search of relevant newspaper articles on Amnesty International, so active on the Arar case, is instructive. Across all newspapers for the period July 2002 to the end of 2006, the NGO's name appeared in 10 articles about Khadr; for the same period, its name appeared in 209 about Arar.[195] CAIR-CAN's website revealed that the first press release the organisation issued on Khadr was in March 2004, and its purpose was to distance itself from the Khadr family.[196] By comparison, its first press release on Arar was

[188] ibid.
[189] Muslim human rights activist, tel interview, 13 January 2013.
[190] Human rights activist, tel interview, 28 January 2013.
[191] Muslim human rights activist, tel interview, 13 January 2013.
[192] ibid.
[193] Shephard, tel interview, 21 February 2013.
[194] Lawyer, tel interview, 16 January 2013.
[195] Based on a search using the Factiva database.
[196] Council on American-Islamic Relations Canada, 'Canadian Muslims condemn recent Khadr comments', press release, 5 March 2004.

issued in October 2002 and demanded his release.[197] The organisation's earliest press release protesting Khadr's treatment at Guantánamo Bay was issued in March 2006.[198] Newspaper editorials commented on civil society's reticence, with the *Globe and Mail* observing in 2007,

> It is not just the government that has been mute. Until recently, most of civil society was silent. The Canadian Bar Association … took four years before denouncing Guantánamo, and another year before it mentioned Mr Khadr by name.[199]

One of Khadr's lawyers, Edney, has spoken of the failure of Canada's legal profession to offer any assistance on the case.[200]

Civil society attitudes towards Khadr began to shift noticeably in 2007, and by 2008 became more forceful in pressing for his return and critical of the Canadian Government's treatment of him.[201] For example, in 2009, when CAIR-CAN wrote to Prime Minister Harper demanding Khadr's repatriation, it had the backing of 185 organisations and individuals.[202] A number of factors help to explain the change in civil society's behaviour on Khadr. One was the time that had elapsed since 9/11. A Canadian journalist said, 'I think all cases picked up the further we got away from 9/11.'[203] Another was limited resources, with civil society preoccupied with the Arar case for many years.[204] Additional factors included the Supreme Court of Canada decisions in favour of Khadr and developments at Guantánamo Bay. As Australian detainee David Hicks was repatriated to Australia after making a plea deal in 2007, Khadr's military commission was embroiled in chaos.[205]

Khadr's US military lawyers, observing the impact Hicks's Pentagon-appointed lawyer, Major Michael Mori, had on public opinion in Australia through his intensive campaigning, launched a similar offensive in Canada. Lieutenant Commander William Kuebler, one of Khadr's US military lawyers, addressed the annual meeting of the CBA in August 2007.[206] The impact of Kuebler's advocacy was immediate: the CBA, which until then had been silent, wrote to Prime Minister Harper the next day and called on him to negotiate Khadr's release.[207] In 2008, after hearing

[197] Council on American-Islamic Relations Canada, 'CAIR-CAN demands release of Canadian citizen deported by US to Syria', press release, 12 October 2002.

[198] Council on American-Islamic Relations Canada, 'CAIR-CAN calls on Prime Minister to speak out against Guantánamo Bay', press release, 6 March 2006.

[199] 'To release Khadr from Guantánamo' (editorial), *Globe and Mail*, 21 August 2007, 14.

[200] Colin Freeze, 'Khadr legal team puts opposing styles on full display', *Globe and Mail*, 20 May 2015, 5.

[201] Shephard, tel interview, 21 February 2013.

[202] Council on American-Islamic Relations Canada, '185 organizations and individuals write PM to repatriate Omar Khadr', press release, 3 February 2009.

[203] Shephard, tel interview, 21 February 2013.

[204] ibid.

[205] Paul Koring, 'US terror trials in doubt as Khadr case crumbles', *Globe and Mail*, 5 June 2007, 1.

[206] Shephard, *Guantánamo's Child*, 215.

[207] Canadian Bar Association, 'CBA calls for Omar Khadr to be released from Guantánamo Bay and turned over to Canada'.

Edney speak, a group of university students and academics from Alberta mobilised to advocate for Khadr and organise lessons for him at Guantánamo Bay.[208] Other law professors contributed to amicus curiae briefs, and intervened in litigation involving Khadr in the US and Canada.[209]

The role of Canada's media on the Arar and Khadr cases reflected the broader civil society approach to the two detainees in some ways, though not others. In general terms, the *Globe and Mail* and *National Post* supported an unequivocal ban on torture.[210] They also called for an inquiry into Arar's detention and treatment.[211] These calls intensified when journalists became the target of the RCMP, following the raid on O'Neill, demonstrating the role that self-interest can play in determining the media agenda.[212] The morning after the raid, wrote Pither, '[A]nyone who hadn't already been calling for a full public inquiry was, and pretty much every journalist and media outlet in the country made it their mission to win one.'[213] On the Khadr case, by comparison, the positions of the *Globe and Mail* and *National Post* differed. The *Globe and Mail* was firm in warning from the outset that Khadr's family history 'did not automatically confer guilt' on his part, and from 2005, in criticising the Canadian Government over its treatment of him.[214] The *National Post*, however, supported Khadr's harsh treatment. In a 2008 editorial, for example, it noted that despite his Canadian citizenship, he had 'little connection to our country', and it urged the Harper Government to keep Khadr 'where he is'.[215]

The Arar and Khadr cases demonstrate the complex role that the media can play in the area of security and intelligence, which can range from collaborative to oppositional.[216] In Arar's case, the media were implicated in attempts by security agencies to avoid accountability for their involvement in his human rights breaches.[217] One commentator accused the Canadian media of being 'complicit in destroying the lives' of Arar and the other detainees who were the subject of Iacobucci's

[208] Sheila Pratt, 'Khadr's Canadian defence: Two Edmonton lawyers, a professor, and the rule of law' in *Omar Khadr, Oh Canada*, ed Williamson, 217.

[209] Macklin, 'The rule of law, the force of law, and the rule of force', 223.

[210] 'The harm the US does in rationalizing torture' (editorial), *Globe and Mail*, 12 June 2004, 26; 'Zero tolerance on torture' (editorial), *National Post*, 23 October 2008, 18.

[211] 'Hold an inquiry into the Arar case' (editorial), *Globe and Mail*, 5 November 2003, 4; 'What happened to Arar?' (editorial), *National Post*, 11 October 2003, 19.

[212] See, eg, 'Freedom of the press' (editorial), *National Post*, 22 January 2004, 17.

[213] Kerry Pither, *Dark Days: The Story of Four Canadians Tortured in the Name of Fighting Terror* (Toronto: Viking Canada, 2008) 324.

[214] 'The case of Omar Khadr' (editorial), *Globe and Mail*, 5 November 2002; 'Omar Khadr's limbo' (editorial), *Globe and Mail*, 11 August 2005, 14.

[215] 'Keep Khadr where he is' (editorial), *National Post*, 17 July 2008, 12.

[216] Vian Bakir, 'News, agenda building, and intelligence agencies: A systematic review of the field from the discipline of journalism, media, and communications', *The International Journal of Press/Politics*, 20(2) (2015), 138.

[217] For example, see Robert Fife, 'Officials Link Arar to Al Qaeda camp: Family says claim is part of smear campaign by anonymous officials, demand inquiry', *National Post*, 30 December 2003, 1.

inquiry, by recycling 'tainted information supplied by unnamed sources'.[218] An activist blamed journalistic ambition, saying there was 'this campaign of reaching out to the journalists who were ambitious and using them to portray Maher Arar as something scary'.[219] Yet, at the other extreme, the media kept attention on the Arar and Khadr cases when the public's interest waned. According to activists in Arar's case, one of the reasons for the campaign's success was 'continued and sustained media activism'.[220] Frequent media engagement was central to Mazigh's strategy, and Pither's media expertise was vital to the Arar campaign. An activist noted that Pither was 'constantly on the media case 24 hours a day with Maher's case before he was released'.[221] Similarly, with respect to the Khadr case, a lawyer called *Toronto Star* reporter, Michelle Shephard, a 'hero' for her unceasing coverage:[222] 'Without the media's persistence, the Omar Khadr story may have gotten lost.' The media's reporting on Khadr shows how, in documenting and reporting violations, journalists can increase the public's awareness and understanding of human rights.[223]

The Influence of Victims' Families

A second feature of Canadian civil society activism was that it was heavily influenced by the personal attributes of the particular victim and his family. Civil society groups were drawn to Arar's case because of his likely innocence and appealing wife, but were repelled by Khadr because of the nature of his alleged crime (killing a US soldier) and widespread public dislike of his family.[224]

Arar's wife, Monia Mazigh, was a sympathetic figure and savvy in her advocacy for her husband. She was highly educated, holding a doctorate in finance, articulate, and trilingual in English, Arabic and French.[225] Her command of French was important politically given Canada's bilingual status, and it meant she was able to write newspaper opinion articles in English and French.[226] One activist remarked, 'I can't tell you enough how much language matters here because Québec and French-speaking Canadians have a lot of power, especially for the Liberals who were in power at the time.'[227]

218 Haroon Siddiqui, 'Prejudice in a post 9/11 world: It bears repeating that all Canadians, born or naturalized, are entitled to equal treatment', *Toronto Star*, 26 October 2008, 19.

219 Human rights activist, tel interview, 28 January 2013.

220 Muslim human rights activist, tel interview, 13 January 2013.

221 ibid.

222 Lawyer, tel interview, 16 January 2013.

223 Zehra F Kabasakal Arat, 'Looking beyond the state but not ignoring it' in *Non-State Actors in the Human Rights Universe*, ed George Andreopoulos, Zehra F Kabasakal Arat and Peter Juviler (Bloomfield, CT: Kumarian Press, 2006) 14.

224 Macklin, 'The rule of law, the force of law, and the rule of force', 224.

225 Mazigh, *Hope and Despair*, 53.

226 ibid, 101.

227 Human rights activist, tel interview, 28 January 2013.

Mazigh was the mother of an eight-month-old son and a five-year-old daughter.[228] One MP noted the effect this had in winning sympathy, saying 'this is a human interest story of a young mother with two small children who is desperate at what has happened'.[229] A result was that other women wanted to help Mazigh, including parliamentarians and Muslim women's organisations. Tareen, an active member of the Muslim community, became an important ally to Mazigh, and arranged government lobbying opportunities for her.[230] According to an MP, although Muslim women had not engaged in much activism before Arar's case, they were perceptive about using the most effective tactics given the sensitive times.[231] At one particular meeting the women agreed to hold a candlelight vigil, which was 'all about peace and calm and trying to move towards the light'. They ruled out a noisy demonstration, because it might precipitate fears about violence and the eruption of hostilities.

Mazigh was not afraid to engage the media, believing that 'for me, the media was my only hope of ever seeing Maher again'.[232] The media warmed to her, with an MP describing her as 'a media dream'.[233] A Muslim human rights activist echoed this:

> She was a very sensitive media figure because of her articulate person, because of the fact that she could speak both languages, so she was able to keep that fire burning, the fire of interest in Maher's case at every level: at the social level within the Muslim community, she was able to communicate more broadly with Canadians at the media level, she was able to do media interviews and speak intelligently to the issue and she was able to liaise with public officials as well.[234]

Mazigh was not intimidated by government and, in the face of obvious disapproval from the DFAIT over her high media profile, ran a tireless campaign on her own terms: 'I would speak out to the media, I would hold vigils, I would keep writing letters, I would visit human rights organizations, I would do everything I could to see justice done', she recalled.[235]

Mazigh was always measured and dignified in her statements and lobbying—a tactic that won over wary civil society actors. For instance, when asked why Amnesty International was so quick to support Mazigh, a human rights NGO official says:

> It always struck me how even from the early days, she wasn't out there screaming about the fascist US government, and wasn't even out there necessarily insisting on her husband's innocence, even though I'm sure there was never any doubt of that in her heart.[236]

[228] Mazigh, *Hope and Despair*, 1.
[229] MP, tel interview, 12 January 2013.
[230] Mazigh, *Hope and Despair*, 129.
[231] MP, tel interview, 12 January 2013.
[232] Mazigh, *Hope and Despair*, 28.
[233] MP, tel interview, 12 January 2013.
[234] Muslim human rights activist, tel interview, 13 January 2013.
[235] Mazigh, *Hope and Despair*, 85.
[236] Human rights NGO official, tel interview, 21 February 2013.

As the NGO official implies, Mazigh's framing of the issues was judicious. She was cautious not to direct her anger and frustration at Canada, but rather emphasised her faith and pride in being Canadian. Mazigh framed her claims in ways that appealed to Canada's national and international identity as rights-respecting, ideas particular to the country's political culture as I discuss in the next section. For example, in the evidence she gave to the House of Commons Standing Committee, Mazigh appealed to Canadian values of justice and citizenship. She told the Committee, 'I believe in the Canadian values of justice. I will try to educate my children to believe in them, and I hope that one day they will be proud to see Canada doing all it can to bring their father back home.'[237] It helped, too, that Arar did not appear to be guilty. An MP notes that there 'was such a strong sense that he just was a completely, totally innocent, uninvolved—not even a bystander on anything—he was just an innocent victim of fabricated identity by accusers.'[238]

Mazigh's impact on her husband's case is apparent in public commentary at the time. For instance, MPs honoured her work in the House of Commons; the *Globe and Mail* nominated Mazigh as a 'Nation Builder of the Year'; and the NDP approached her to enter politics.[239] Civil society actors maintain that Arar would have died if not for his wife. An MP, for instance, says, 'I'm almost prepared to say if Maher Arar hadn't had Monia Mazigh for a wife, or somebody close to her magnificence, he probably would have died in that hell hole.'[240] After Arar's return from Syria, the husband and wife kept up the campaign for a public inquiry and continued to attract civil society support.[241] A human rights NGO official described their impact: 'Both Maher and Monia were so inspiring and irresistible that I think … there was just never any question that we would do everything we could to back them in that call.'[242]

By contrast, Khadr's campaign lacked sympathetic family figures and a narrative of innocence.[243] A Canadian MP said of Khadr's case, 'There were some worrisome events there, and whether people were willing to buy the idea that he was just really a kid or not—it was just a very different set of circumstances.'[244] Because of its well-documented history of associating with terrorists, and its ongoing sympathy for Al-Qaeda, the Khadr family alienated the Canadian public and had a repellent effect on Canadian civil society. A journalist describes the role of Khadr's family in shaping Canada's response to Omar's case as 'huge':

[237] Evidence to House of Commons Standing Committee on Foreign Affairs and International Trade, Parliament of Canada, Ottawa, 25 September 2003, 1215 (Monia Mazigh).

[238] MP, tel interview, 12 January 2013.

[239] Pither, *Dark Days*, 302; 'Meet the class of 2003', *Globe and Mail*, 6 December 2003, 4; Steven Chase, 'Arar's wife approached to enter politics', *Globe and Mail*, 11 February 2004, 4.

[240] MP, tel interview, 12 January 2013.

[241] Mazigh, *Hope and Despair*, 213.

[242] Human rights NGO official, tel interview, 21 February 2013.

[243] The same might be said of other three Canadians tortured in Syria (Almalki, Abou-Elmaati and Muayyed Nureddin), whose cases also failed to capture the public imagination in the way Arar's did. See Pither, *Dark Days*.

[244] MP, tel interview, 12 January 2013.

> I think a lot of people, when they look at the case on its facts, question why Canada acted as it did. Because of his age, and Canada's strong stance on child soldiers, people ask why Canada wasn't more forceful in advocating for him at various stages. But, really, it has so much to do with the family, because Canadians just loathe … the family.[245]

A Muslim human rights activist says Khadr's case was 'very difficult … to bring forward into the media' because of his unsympathetic family, who was 'almost seen at that time as a family of outcasts, and even casting them as Canadian Muslims was extremely difficult'.[246] This activist said it 'seemed as though the activism for them could not really get off the ground … There really wasn't anyone in the family to actually bring the case forward in the way that Maher had Monia'.

A critical event that cemented the Canadian public's dislike of the Khadrs was the airing in 2004 of the CBC documentary, *Al Qaeda Family*.[247] In the program, Khadr's brother, Abdurahman, revealed that he was sent to Afghanistan by his father 'to become an al-Qaeda' and 'was raised to become a suicide bomber'.[248] Khadr's mother and sister made incendiary comments about terrorism. Asked about their reactions to the 9/11 attacks, Khadr's mother responded, 'I said, "let them have it"', while his sister said 'you just sort of think, well, they deserve it'.[249] Khadr's mother was also disparaging of Canadian society, saying, 'You would like me to raise my child in Canada and by the time he's twelve or thirteen he'll be on drugs or having some homosexual relation?' Many Canadians regarded the Khadrs as Canadians of convenience, rejecting those aspects of Canada's progressive society that did not fit with their fundamentalist religious beliefs, yet availing themselves of Canada's generous welfare system.[250] An activist says the television appearances of Khadr's mother and sister 'turned Canada against him':[251] 'They weren't reaching out to the public and trying to make friends with the public. His mother and sister went on national television and essentially just really screwed up his case.' After the documentary, wrote Shephard, even Canadian Muslim and Arab civil rights groups 'would not utter Omar's name'.[252]

Khadr's lawyers despaired of the impact his family had on his case in Canada. The first time one of his US military lawyers, Lieutenant Colonel Colby Vokey, met the family he told them to stop speaking publicly because '[e]very time you open your mouths … you hurt Omar's case'.[253] Vokey contrasted Khadr's case with that of Australian citizen David Hicks, whose father's influence on public opinion

[245] Shephard, tel interview, 21 February 2013.

[246] Muslim human rights activist, tel interview, 2013.

[247] Shephard, *Guantánamo's Child*, 137.

[248] 'We are an al-Qaeda family.'

[249] Shephard, *Guantánamo's Child*, 146–47.

[250] Lee Greenbery, 'Khadrs will get medical, social benefits, McGuinty says: Province's "responsibility"', *National Post*, 14 April 2004, 4.

[251] Human rights activist, tel interview, 28 January 2013.

[252] Shephard, *Guantánamo's Child*, 147.

[253] ibid, 196.

was critical: 'Hicks's dad never stood up and said, "I'd rather my son be a suicide bomber than sell drugs in the streets of Melbourne".'[254] Another lawyer said, 'The fundamental problem for Omar Khadr was the fact that he was branded with the same reputation as his family.'[255]

Different individuals and groups acknowledged the effect the Khadr family had in frightening away civil society activists. In 2007, Neve noted, 'There has been some nervousness about the dynamic associated with the Khadr family.'[256] Similarly, in a 2007 letter urging Prime Minister Harper to intervene in Khadr's case, over 100 signatories, including current and former parliamentarians, domestic, international and transnational NGOs, lawyers and legal academics, recognised the negative influence of the family.[257] The letter, one of the first examples of collective civil society mobilisation on the Khadr case, noted that 'it was plainly unjust to punish the son for the sins of the father'. A human rights NGO official said the reluctance of civil society to get behind Khadr's cause initially 'was more the family effect than anything else, they were pretty notorious, and every once in a while they did or said something in the media that only made things worse'.[258] A journalist says Muslim community groups were worried to speak out about the Khadr case 'for the same reason that the NGOs were—it was seen as such a hot potato with such unlikeable relatives of his that no one wanted to get involved'.[259]

The impact that the citizens' families had on their abilities to attract allies illustrates the literature on civil society and issue selection examined in Chapter 3.[260] This is where the survival imperative for some NGOs can manifest in opportunistic behaviour, leading organisations to choose cases more likely to find support from the public, donors and media.

The Role of International Actors

The role of international actors in the Khadr case, particularly in demanding that the Harper Government protect his rights as a child soldier, is another notable feature of civil society activism in Canada. Their role was more prominent than in the cases of Australian and UK detainees in the war on terror. This again highlights how dramatic Canada's abandonment of its citizen was—especially given his age—and brings into sharper relief the failure of domestic civil society to take up his cause for so long.

[254] ibid, 206.
[255] Lawyer, tel interview, 16 January 2013.
[256] Shephard, *Guantánamo's Child*, 215.
[257] Lloyd Axworthy et al to Prime Minister Stephen Harper, 14 June 2007.
[258] Human rights NGO official, tel interview, 21 February 2013.
[259] Shephard, tel interview, 21 February 2013.
[260] Clifford Bob, *The Marketing of Rebellion: Insurgents, Media, and International Activism* (New York, NY: Cambridge University Press, 2005).

A large number of international actors became engaged in the Khadr case from 2007. For example, the US-based Center for Constitutional Rights, HRW and Physicians for Human Rights were all signatories to a June 2007 letter to Prime Minister Harper.[261] In another letter to Prime Minister Harper the following year, HRW, Human Rights First, the Coalition to Stop the Use of Child Soldiers and Amnesty International appealed to Canada's 'global leadership regarding children and armed conflict', and asked it to intervene to 'prevent the continued mistreatment of its own citizen and former child soldier'.[262] In January 2008, under the headline 'Campaign to Free Khadr Escalates', the *Toronto Star* published comments from David Crane, the former Chief Prosecutor of the Special Court for Sierra Leone, who described Khadr's military commission as 'horrific' and said it was the first time in history that a child had been prosecuted for war crimes.[263] The same month, five UK legal organisations, including the General Council of the Bar, The Law Society, the Commonwealth Lawyers' Association and the Bar Human Rights Committee, wrote to Prime Minister Harper.[264] They called on Canada to secure Khadr's release, saying the lengthy detention and war crimes trial of 'someone who appears to be a "child soldier"' was contrary to international laws regarding the protection of children. In February 2008, five senior UK parliamentarians wrote to Prime Minister Harper pointing out that Khadr's military commission was in breach of US international legal obligations under the CRC and OPCRC, and urged him to intervene in Khadr's case.[265]

In addition, Canadian NGOs used international forums such as the Committee Against Torture and the Human Rights Council extensively in their activism on the Khadr case. For example, NGOs raised his case with the Human Rights Council at the Universal Periodic Review of Canada in 2009. Khadr was 'an example of a child soldier who under international law should be considered a victim', a number of groups noted.[266] Amnesty International, Lawyers Rights Watch Canada, the International Civil Liberties Monitoring Group and the CCLA used the Committee Against Torture to raise awareness of Khadr's case during its consideration of Canada's sixth periodic report in 2012.[267] The Harper Government

[261] Lloyd Axworthy et al to Prime Minister Stephen Harper, 14 June 2007.

[262] Human Rights Watch, Human Rights First, Coalition to Stop the Use of Child Soldiers and Amnesty International to Stephen Harper, Prime Minister of Canada, 1 February 2008.

[263] Michelle Shephard, 'Campaign to free Khadr escalates', *Toronto Star*, 7 January 2008, 1.

[264] 'Our deafening silence' (editorial), *Globe and Mail*, 2 January 2008, 14.

[265] Lord Carlile of Berriew, QC, Rt Hon Kenneth Clarke, Rt Hon The Lord Goldsmith QC, Chris Mullin MP and Andrew Tyrie MP to Prime Minister Stephen Harper, 7 February 2008.

[266] Human Rights Council, *Summary Prepared by the Office of the High Commissioner for Human Rights, in Accordance with Paragraph 15 (C) of the Annex to Human Rights Council Resolution 5/1*, HRC Res 5/1, 4th sess, UN Doc A/HRC/WG.6/4/CAN/3, 24 November 2008, 11.

[267] Amnesty International, *Canada Briefing to the UN Committee Against Torture*, 48th Session, May 2012, Submission to the Committee Against Torture, April 2012; Lawyers Rights Watch Canada and the International Civil Liberties Monitoring Group, *Canada Briefing to the Committee Against Torture, 48th Session, May 2012 on the Omar Khadr Case from Lawyers Rights Watch Canada and the International Civil Liberties Monitoring Group*, 18 February 2012; International Civil Liberties Monitoring Group,

was irritated by the criticisms of the Committee Against Torture, which in its Concluding Observations urged Canada to repatriate Khadr and provide him with 'appropriate redress for human rights violations'.[268] 'When there are serious concerns regarding human rights violations across the world, it is disappointing that the UN would spend its time decrying Canada', said the Minister of Public Safety, Toews.[269] Frequent appeals to Canada's international legal obligations were made by NGOs, including the CBA, in lobbying Prime Minister Harper (under the OPCRC), and the BCCLA, which intervened in Khadr's 2008 Canadian Supreme Court case (its submission referenced the Geneva Conventions).[270] Despite Canada's having a constitutional bill of rights, international law became important in Khadr's campaign in the face of an intransigent national government.

Enabling and Constraining Activism

On Arar, Canada's record in seeking accountability for the international human rights breaches of its citizen was exemplary.[271] On Khadr, Canada achieved global condemnation as the last Western nation to bring its citizen—a 15-year-old—home from Guantánamo Bay, having never examined, nor pressed the US for a full investigation into, his torture allegations.[272]

Alliance-based explanations fall short in explaining Canada's inconsistent treatment of nationals. Traditional analyses of the country's behaviour on international human rights protection view it through the US relationship, where, as discussed, to differentiate itself Canada has carved out a global identity as a 'good international citizen'.[273] Proponents of such a view dismiss the actions of

Submission of Information by the ICLMG to the Committee Against Torture (CAT) for the Examination of Canada's 6th Report in May 2012, 16 April 2012; Canadian Civil Liberties Association, *Report to the UN Committee Against Torture 48th Session, May 2012, Regarding List of Issues to be Considered in Connection of the Sixth Periodic Report of Canada (CAT/C/CAN/6)*, April 2012.

[268] Committee Against Torture, *Consideration of Reports Submitted by States Parties Under Article 19 of the Convention—Concluding Observations of the Committee Against Torture, Canada*, 48th Sess, UN Doc CAT/C/CAN/CO/6, 25 June 2012, 5.

[269] Catherine Morris, 'Undermining the rule of law: The case of Omar Khadr', *Toronto Star*, 10 October 2012, 27.

[270] Canadian Bar Association, 'CBA calls for Omar Khadr to be released from Guantánamo Bay and turned over to Canada'; British Columbia Civil Liberties Association, '*Khadr v Canada (Minister of Justice)*', press release, 20 January 2008; British Columbia Civil Liberties Association, Criminal Lawyers' Association (Ontario) and University of Toronto, Faculty of Law—International Human Rights Clinic and Human Rights Watch, 'Factum of the Intervener British Columbia Civil Liberties Association', submission in *Minister of Justice v Khadr*, SCC File No 32147, 21 February 2008.

[271] Duffy and Kostas, '"Extraordinary rendition"', 577.

[272] Shephard, *Guantánamo's Child*, xiv; Maxime Bernier, Foreign Affairs Minister, to Audrey Macklin, Associate Professor University of Toronto, 17 October 2007.

[273] Vucetic, 'Why did Canada sit out of the Iraq war?', 142.

Canadian intelligence and security agencies in cooperating in Arar's extraordinary rendition, and successive governments' policies regarding Khadr's situation, as post-9/11 aberrations, the result of bilateral pressures and counterterrorism challenges.[274] However, such explanations are too generalised for understanding the policy continuity of successive Liberal and Conservative governments in holding a public inquiry into Arar's torture and apologising to and compensating him, and their wholesale abandonment of Khadr.

An alternative explanation might rely on electoral politics. Fear of political embarrassment, referred to sometimes as the 'Khadr effect', and consistent public opinion polls confirming the family's unpopularity in Canada meant that governments shied away from helping the country's only citizen detained at Guantánamo Bay. However, I argue that civil society's behaviour in Canada also demonstrates in a striking way its importance for shaping government behaviour on human rights. Arar was a popular and safe cause for Canadian civil society to back, and inspired a strong and well-organised campaign that succeeded, in a relatively short time, in demanding better treatment for him. Khadr was risky, and for many years few actors in Canadian civil society pushed for his rights to be protected. Despite eventually winning two Supreme Court of Canada cases, he was left in Guantánamo Bay for a decade.

There were some obvious reasons why it was easier for different domestic actors to support Arar over Khadr. Arar did not stand accused of killing an American soldier and his torture claims were directed against Syria, an authoritarian state known to torture prisoners, not the US, a liberal democracy and Canadian ally. Here, I explore some of the less obvious effects that Canada's domestic political and legal context had on shaping civil society activism. I use the framework of enabling and constraining features than can affect human rights activism, including the interrelated factors of political culture, institutions and opportunity structures, to analyse Canada's domestic circumstances and offer a deeper understanding of civil society's different engagement on the two cases.

Political Culture

Political culture can affect civil society activism by influencing the way members of a polity think about rights in the context of their relationship to the state. Canada has an aspirational rights culture. Rights have featured prominently in domestic political attempts to unify a nation that, because of its dual English and French heritage, has faced uncertainty about its future.[275] Claims about Canada's moral superpower identity tend to gloss over deep cleavages within the Canadian polity that have had important consequences for the development of a common political culture and understandings about rights.

[274] Brysk, *Global Good Samaritans*, 83.

[275] Michael Ignatieff, *The Rights Revolution* (Toronto: House of Anansi Press, 2007) 6, 78.

In Chapter 3 I mentioned Louis Hartz's concept of the liberal fragment, or colonial offshoot, that once 'hurled outward onto new soil', loses the stimulus toward change that the whole provides.[276] His ideas are insightful for understanding the way in which a nation's historical experiences confer upon its people a shared consciousness through which current human rights issues are commonly interpreted. Canada is a 'two-fragment society'.[277] The country was born out of two sets of counter-revolutionary forces: the earlier fragment of conservative Catholics escaping the French Revolution, joined later by conservative English Tories, loyal to the monarchy and the empire, who were fleeing the American Revolution.[278] As a result of these historical legacies, Canadian society tends to be law-abiding, deferential to authority, statist, conservative, communitarian and collectivity-orientated.[279] The ready manipulation of the media by security and intelligence agencies that occurred in Arar's case is suggestive of this element of Canadian political culture, in particular the deference to authority and the laudatory treatment of police, though this should not be overstated.[280]

Political culture refers to general understandings that are predominant across a broad section of a nation's population. However, the cultural norms that it comprises are never equally shared by all members of a polity but are always partial and exclusionary.[281] The experiences of Canada's indigenous people, including a long history of human rights violations by the state, are very different from those of the broader population.[282] This example shows how political culture is a generalised concept, and that the shared histories on which it is based are often contested.

An important legacy of Canada's dualism is that, historically, the country has confronted difficult divisions.[283] Canada has two dominant and distinct cultural groupings: the Francophone community, based mostly in Québec; and the majority English-speaking Canadians. Divisions between the two groups have affected the way Canadians think about their country and rights, two preoccupations that are intertwined. The growing concerns of the minority Québécois in the second half of the twentieth century with preserving their language and distinct cultural

[276] Louis Hartz, 'The fragmentation of European culture and ideology' in *The Founding of New Societies: Studies in the History of the United States, Latin America, South Africa, Canada and Australia*, ed Louis Hartz (New York, NY: Harcourt Brace Jovanovich, 1964) 3.

[277] Kenneth D McRae, 'The structure of Canadian history' in *The Founding of New Societies*, ed Hartz, 219.

[278] Lipset, *Continental Divide*, 10.

[279] Charles R Epp, *The Rights Revolution: Lawyers, Activists, and Supreme Courts in Comparative Perspective* (Chicago, IL: University of Chicago Press, 1998) 157; Charles Taylor, *Reconciling the Solitudes: Essays on Canadian Federalism and Nationalism* (Montreal: McGill-Queen's University Press, 1993) 158.

[280] Lipset, *Continental Divide*, 90–91.

[281] David Schneiderman, 'Property rights and regulatory innovation comparing constitutional cultures', *International Journal of Constitutional Law* 4(2) (2006), 374.

[282] Truth and Reconciliation Commission of Canada, *Honouring the Truth, Reconciling for the Future: Summary of the Final Report of the Truth and Reconciliation Commission of Canada*, 2015.

[283] Ignatieff, *The Rights Revolution*, 9.

heritage meant that Canadians have struggled to develop a single national identity and a unifying political culture.[284] Canada, wrote Lipset, is 'almost alone among modern developed countries' in continuing to debate its self-conception.[285] These fractures and differences have left Canadians feeling deeply uncertain about the future of their nation and Québec's place in it.[286]

The same divisions also led to an awakening, from the 1960s onwards, about the importance of human rights, initially among Québécois, and subsequently among newer immigrant and indigenous groups.[287] The Federal Government seized on this new rights awareness and actively cultivated it as a part of its strategy to counteract the separatist forces in Québec.[288] This was the motivation behind Prime Minister Pierre Trudeau's early push in the late 1960s and early 1970s for a constitutional bill of rights.[289] One of his hopes was to encourage the development of rights-based loyalties that would unite Canadians across provincial boundaries. This history forms the basis for arguments today that, despite Canada's dual ancestry, common ground should, and can, be found in a commitment to rights. A proponent of this view is Michael Ignatieff, Canadian scholar and former leader of the Liberal Party. He argues that because 'the principles of national unity cannot be found by joint appeal to common origins … Canada has no choice but to gamble on rights'.[290] Rights, not roots, 'are what will hold us together in the future'.[291]

The 1982 Canadian Charter of Rights and Freedoms was an attempt by political leaders to use rights to unify the Canadian polity.[292] It came about as a result of the failed 1980 referendum on granting Québec political sovereignty, and fulfilled a promise that Prime Minister Trudeau made to the people of that province for voting in the negative.[293] It has, however, been contentious among Québécois, who have questioned its legitimacy.[294] Canadian philosopher Charles Taylor, while arguing that over time the Charter has become 'not just an additional bulwark of rights' but 'part of the indispensable common ground on which all Canadians ought to stand', also acknowledges that the primacy it affords individual rights over collective rights clashes with basic Québec policy and values.[295] The Charter shines a light on what Taylor calls a genuine difference in philosophy concerning the bases of a liberal society.[296] On one side sits the Anglo-American view that individual rights must always come first; on the other sit the views of Québec

[284] Taylor, *Reconciling the Solitudes*, 100; Kornberg and Clarke, *Citizens and Community*, 16.
[285] Lipset, *Continental Divide*, 42.
[286] Ignatieff, *The Rights Revolution*, 6.
[287] Epp, *The Rights Revolution*, 158–59.
[288] ibid, 159.
[289] ibid, 160.
[290] Ignatieff, *The Rights Revolution*, 129.
[291] ibid, 130.
[292] ibid, 77.
[293] Kornberg and Clarke, *Citizens and Community*, 1.
[294] Ignatieff, *The Rights Revolution*, 77.
[295] Taylor, *Reconciling the Solitudes*, 162, 173.
[296] ibid, 174.

governments, prioritising the fundamental collective goal of the survival and flourishing of French culture.[297] Despite the Charter's focus on individual rights, it preserves the principles of parliamentary sovereignty and retains the traditional Canadian emphasis in favour of collective or group rights, as, for example, with respect to language rights.[298] These complexities within the Canadian polity provide a more nuanced perspective on common assumptions made about the country's strong global identity based on a national commitment to human rights.

The Charter has, through its existence, altered Canada's political culture and demonstrated the way culture and institutions are interlinked and can influence the other. Canadian legal academic, Kent Roach, argues that as a result of the Charter, generalisations about Canada's collectivist emphasis on peace, order and good government in contrast to the more individualist US pursuit of life, liberty and happiness, no longer hold true.[299] This is because the Charter has made Canadian courts less deferential to executive and legislative action that infringes individual rights. Others, however, argue that the effect the Charter has on the Supreme Court of Canada agenda is overstated.[300]

A country's previous history of political violence also influences how a polity thinks about rights and the relationship between the citizen and the state. Canada's history of terrorism, while less extensive than the UK's, is also linked in part to its legacy of the dual fragments. Canada's pre-9/11 terrorism experiences were limited to two events. The first was the October crisis of 1970, in which the extremist separatist organisation Front de libération du Québec (FLQ) kidnapped a British diplomat and killed a Québec provincial cabinet minister.[301] The Trudeau Government responded by invoking the 1914 War Measures Act and sending 6,000 troops into Montreal. This response was later viewed by Canadians as excessive, providing a lesson in the dangers of over-reacting to threats and increasing support for the Charter.[302] A second terrorist event was the 1985 bombing of an Air India jet by Sikh terrorists, which killed 329 people, most of them Canadians.[303] Despite these experiences, neither the Canadian Parliament nor the public had considered counter-terrorism a high priority before 2001.[304]

Lastly, Canadians see themselves as a cultural mosaic, where diverse ethnic groups exist in an environment more protective of their distinct cultures than America's melting pot, which insists on assimilation.[305] This cultural mosaic has been identified as important for relatively recent developments in Canada's

[297] ibid, 175.
[298] Lipset, *Continental Divide*, 3, 103–05.
[299] Roach, 'Uneasy neighbors', 1709.
[300] Epp, 'Do bills of rights matter?', 765–67.
[301] Roach, *The 9/11 Effect*, 366.
[302] Roach, 'Uneasy neighbors', 1714, 1716.
[303] Roach, *The 9/11 Effect*, 369.
[304] David Charters, 'The (un)peaceable kingdom? Terrorism and Canada before 9/11', *IRPP Policy Matters* 9(4) (2008), 3.
[305] Lipset, *Continental Divide*, 172.

'rights-focused' legal culture.[306] It has also been a source of misunderstanding between Canada and the US, particularly in the context of counterterrorism.[307]

Underpinning Canadian understandings of multiculturalism, however, are notable limits about what kind of individuals are acceptable members of the cultural mosaic. These limits came to the fore in the Arar and Khadr cases. Arar's wife, Monia Mazigh, though a migrant and a Muslim, was non-threatening. She demonstrated, including through her testimony to Parliament, that she had bought into Canadian culture and integrated into its society. As an MP explained, Mazigh was, along with her husband, 'part of the Canadian model of immigrants, who were engaged in building the country and building constructive lives'.[308] Khadr, by contrast, was a 'figure on the margins', whose right to Canadian citizenship—despite being born in Canada—was constantly questioned.[309] Many Canadians regarded Khadr's family as having 'wantonly disavowed liberal democratic values', and because of this it was situated 'outside the boundaries of belonging and citizenship in the public and national imaginary'.[310] Khadr's treatment, like Mamdouh Habib's discussed in Chapter 5, recalls Leti Volpp's discussion of how racial identity, post-9/11, disrupts citizenship.[311]

Canada's political culture is complex and understandings of rights are contested. An exposition of Canada's rights culture does not, alone, explain why activism was so different across the Arar and Khadr cases, but it does provide a deeper understanding of the norms that informed the actions of domestic actors.

Political and Legal Institutions

A state's institutional structures can influence human rights activism by providing resources to civil society actors and shaping their interests about taking such action. The Canadian case shows that political and legal levers are no guarantee that civil society will take up a particular human rights cause, nor that they will be effective in campaigning when they do. Canada was the only country of the three studied here to have a constitutional bill of rights. Khadr's lawyers employed the Charter in litigation demanding the state protect him. Supreme Court of Canada rulings upholding his Charter rights came late, however, and their mobilising effect on civil society had limited effects for Khadr's campaign because of the Harper Government's intransigence on his case. As well as analysing the Charter's effect

306 Epp, *The Rights Revolution*, 159.
307 Roach, 'Uneasy neighbors', 1791–92.
308 MP, tel interview, 12 January 2013.
309 Yasmin Jiwani, 'Omar Khadr, The carceral net, and the Muslim body' in *Omar Khadr, Oh Canada*, ed Williamson, 379.
310 Jasmin Zine, 'Stolen youth: Lost boys and imperial wars,' in *Omar Khadr, Oh Canada*, ed Janice Williamson, 391.
311 Leti Volpp, 'The citizen and the terrorist', *UCLA Law Review* 49(5) (2002), 1595–96.

on civil society activism in the Arar and Khadr cases, I consider other institutional factors, including torture legislation and jurisprudence, and parliamentary mechanisms on human rights.

Canada's legal and policy positions with respect to torture are permissive in some respects. However, 'cruel and unusual treatment or punishment' is prohibited under the Charter (section 12), and Canada's Criminal Code bans the use of torture in and outside Canada (section 269.1). Canada ratified the UN CAT, though it has not signed or ratified the OPCAT. Also relevant to Khadr's case is the CRC, which prohibits the torture of children, defined as every human being below the age of 18 (Article 1). However, Canadian jurisprudence on torture is more ambivalent. For example, in the 2002 case *Suresh v Canada (Minister of Citizenship and Immigration)*, the Supreme Court of Canada ruled that in 'exceptional circumstances', where there was a high risk to national security, the Government could deport individuals to places where they faced a risk of torture.[312] The *Suresh* decision has been widely criticised, including by the UN Committee Against Torture and a Canadian parliamentary Senate Committee.[313] The Canadian Government's tolerance of torture was also displayed in evidence to the Iacobucci inquiry, where it argued that while not practising or condoning torture, it did not believe that the CAT was an impediment to sharing information with countries that did.[314] Combined, these different features of Canada's position on torture point to an incomplete commitment to its absolute prohibition, similar to the situation in the UK.

As noted, the Canadian Parliament's capacity to hold the executive to account on human rights, particularly in the context of national security matters, is limited. Parliamentary committees in Canada are not well staffed, and there is no equivalent of the UK's Joint Committee on Human Rights.[315] This matters for activism, and hampers the ability of civil society actors to work with parliamentarians through committees to press ministers and bureaucrats for accountability on human rights issues, including on individual cases (as occurred in Australia). Arar's wife was able to use the Parliament to a limited extent because she found willing parliamentary allies. The legislature offered little opportunity for Khadr's campaign, which relied much more heavily on the courts through litigation based on the Charter.

[312] *Suresh v Canada (Minister of Citizenship and Immigration)* [2002] 1 SCR 3.

[313] Committee Against Torture, *Consideration of Reports Submitted by States Parties Under Article 19 of the Convention*, 2; Special Senate Committee on the *Anti-terrorism Act*, Parliament of Canada, *Fundamental Justice in Extraordinary Times: Main Report of the Special Senate Committee on the Anti-terrorism Act*, February 2007, 110.

[314] Tonda MacCharles, 'Information-sharing rules defended: Ottawa can't rule out sending intelligence to regimes that torture, lawyer tells inquiry', *Toronto Star*, 9 January 2008, 14.

[315] Kent Roach, 'The varied roles of courts and legislatures in rights protection' in *Parliament and Human Rights*, ed Murray Hunt, Hayley J Hopper and Paul Yowell (Oxford: Hart Publishing, 2015) 408.

The Charter operated in Khadr's case in two distinct ways. It provided a judicial mechanism to Khadr and his lawyers to challenge the executive's intractable position in the courts. Through successful court rulings, it also gave much-needed confidence to a timid civil society to support his cause. The Charter was also invoked in campaigning on the Arar case in different ways. This included by legal activists arguing for an inquiry; by Arar's lawyers, who unsuccessfully sought to sue Jordan and Syria in the Canadian courts; and by the media, who also demanded an inquiry, though they were more concerned with violations of the right to press freedom rather than Arar's Charter rights (section 2).[316] The influence of the Charter in civil society activism was most prominent, however, in Khadr's case.

Civil society actors acknowledged the Charter's important role in Khadr's case. A human rights NGO official credited the Charter with opening up innovative legal strategies to Khadr's lawyers.[317] A lawyer emphasised the way the Charter empowered Canadian courts in the case: 'It talks about fundamental rights, it's a young Charter, it's a young Constitution, and therefore the Canadian courts are alive to the development of its Constitution.'[318] The lawyer praised the Canadian courts for being 'stellar in carrying out [their] duty to uphold the rule of law'. The human rights NGO official emphasised the mobilising effect the Supreme Court's decisions had on the rest of civil society, saying judicial rulings on the breaches of Khadr's Charter rights gave civil society organisations more focus and fuel in their campaigning for Khadr: '[A]ll of that gave greater confidence to organisations', he said; 'more and more organisations I think started to come forward as we got more and more court rulings, but the court rulings themselves also became real focal points for activism'.[319] This was particularly evident after the Supreme Court ordered the release of documents and videos from Khadr's interrogations by Canadian officials. Media reports noted that Amnesty International was prompted by the disclosures to write to Prime Minister Harper about the Government's extensive knowledge of Khadr's ill-treatment, and that his lawyers finally felt they were improving his case 'in the court of Canadian public opinion'.[320]

By the time this shift in public opinion and civil society campaigning occurred in 2008, the Harper Government, so firmly opposed to defending Khadr's rights, had won a second federal election by an increased margin. Civil society groups had waited too long, and political opportunities for activism had closed.

[316] Audrey Macklin, 'Mr Easter, we need a probe in the Arar case', *Globe and Mail*, 14 November 2003, 23; Colin Freeze, '*Canada failed him, Arar suit says: Contends courts must let him sue Syria because he lacked protection from torture*', *Globe and Mail*, 29 November 2003, 19; Bruce Garvey, 'Raids evoke outrage at "police state" tactics', *Ottawa Citizen*, 22 January 2004, 1.

[317] Human rights NGO, tel interview, 21 February 2013.

[318] Lawyer, tel interview, 16 January 2013.

[319] Human rights NGO official, tel interview, 21 February 2013.

[320] Michelle Shephard, 'Omar Khadr's lawyers had fought for years for this moment', *Toronto Star*, 16 July 2008, 14; Colin Freeze, 'Family's lawyers working court of Canadian public opinion', *Globe and Mail*, 16 July 2008, 11.

Political Opportunities

The opening and closing of political opportunity structures, though their effects may be fleeting, can influence civil society activism on human rights. The Arar and Khadr cases clearly demonstrate the dynamic nature and potentially important effects of changing political opportunities. This includes how they can appear seemingly accidentally, how they can reveal new allies, and how detrimental for individual victims it can be if they are not exploited when they present, for such opportunities may soon be gone.

Political opportunities can appear unexpectedly. Whether they prove decisive in human rights campaigning depends on activists being prepared—having done the groundwork on a particular issue—and identifying them as they arise. The raid by the RCMP on a journalist's house was an unexpected event in the course of the Arar campaign that had huge repercussions in terms of bringing the full weight of the media and others behind calls for a public inquiry. Activist Pither writes that 'everything changed' on the day of the raid.[321] Arar's campaign was, by that time, intense. Mazigh writes that in the weeks leading up to the raid, she and Arar were calling for an inquiry from 'every tribune, in the newspapers, before the most diverse audiences'.[322] The couple was continuing a letter-writing campaign to Prime Minister Chrétien, and more and more politicians and human rights NGOs were joining the calls for an inquiry.[323]

Before the raid, another unexpected event occurred: Martin became Prime Minister, and appointed Irwin Cotler, an MP who had acted as Arar's lawyer and supported an inquiry into his case, as Justice Minister.[324] This event highlights another feature of political opportunity, where government disunity and a sudden change in leader revealed new allies in the course of a continuing human rights campaign. Not only was Prime Minister Martin keen to differentiate himself from his predecessor, who was opposed to calling an inquiry, he also chose a sympathetic, international human rights lawyer as the Government's chief law officer (who, however, had to distance himself from Arar's case).[325] Mazigh and Arar were ready to capitalise on the public outcry following the raid and Martin's openness to an inquiry, and had planned a press conference the very day the surprise announcement of the inquiry came.[326]

The political party in power, as well as individual leaders, can make a difference to civil society human rights campaigns, depending on attitudes towards

[321] Pither, *Dark Days*, 321.
[322] Mazigh, *Hope and Despair*, 238.
[323] ibid, 240, 243.
[324] ibid, 244.
[325] Martin, *Hell or High Water*, 228; Mazigh, *Hope and Despair*, 244.
[326] Pither, *Dark Days*, 325.

the sector.[327] Party ideology in Canada noticeably affected the way the executive viewed civil society and the ability of NGOs to influence government policy after 9/11. A Liberal Government was in power in 2001. Prime Minister Chrétien had signed an accord with Canada's voluntary sector promising a collaborative approach to civil society.[328] It was inspired by a similar compact negotiated by the UK Blair Government.[329] The accord came out of work undertaken in the late 1990s by a concerned voluntary sector and a cooperative Government, both keen to relieve tensions and improve relations with the other.[330] This followed a 'rocky' previous two decades particularly under the influence of the neo-liberal policies of the Conservative Mulroney Government (1984–93).[331] This inclusive attitude changed abruptly with the election of the Conservative Harper Government.[332] Prime Minister Harper adopted a populist discourse evocative of Australian Prime Minister John Howard. That is, he promised to govern for the 'mainstream', and promoted the idea that social movements were elitist and motivated by self-interest.[333] Prime Minister Harper was also committed to a 'tough on crime' policy agenda, which commentators say influenced his attitude to Khadr, and tried to discredit members of civil society who questioned his approach.[334] Similar to the UK, where the legitimacy of Muslim human rights organisations' critiquing the Government's war on terror policies was challenged, in Canada the Harper Government accused the National Council of Muslims (formerly CAIR-CAN) of having 'ties to a terrorist organisation such as Hamas'.[335]

A number of civil society actors directly attribute the Arar campaign's success in moving government policy on his case to the political party in power. One argued, 'I think in some respects if Maher's case had come along just a little bit later, once the Conservatives were a little bit more into governing, he may not have had quite the same warm final chapter that he did.'[336] Similarly, another activist believes

[327] Jeffrey M Ayres, 'Political economy, civil society, and the deep integration debate in Canada', *American Review of Canadian Studies* 34(4) (2004), 622; Susan D Phillips, 'Canada: Civic society under neglect', *The Philanthropist* 23(1) (2010), 65, 69.

[328] Voluntary Sector Initiative, *Government-Sector Relationship: An Accord between the Government of Canada and the Voluntary Sector*, December 2001.

[329] Susan D Phillips, 'In accordance: Canada's voluntary sector accord from idea to implementation' in *Delicate Dances: Public Policy and the Non-Profit Sector*, ed Kathy L Brock (Montreal: McGill-Queen's University Press, 2003) 18–19.

[330] Kathy L Brock, 'Sustaining a relationship: Insights from Canada on linking the Government and Third Sector,' *Working Paper No 1*, School of Policy Studies, 1 June 2000, 2.

[331] Phillips, 'In accordance', 18, 22.

[332] Phillips, 'Canada: Civic society under neglect', 65.

[333] Marian Sawer and David Laycock, 'Down with elites and up with inequality: Market populism in Australia and Canada', *Commonwealth and Comparative Politics* 47(2) (2009), 137–38.

[334] Dave Snow and Bejamin Moffitt, 'Straddling the divide: Mainstream populism and conservatism in Howard's Australia and Harper's Canada', *Commonwealth and Comparative Politics* 50(3) (2012), 281–82.

[335] National Council of Canadian Muslims, 'NCCM Commences Defamation Lawsuit Against PMO', press release, 26 May 2014.

[336] Human rights NGO official, tel interview, 21 February 2013.

Prime Minister Chrétien would have eventually ordered a public inquiry into Arar's case under pressure from his party, had he remained in power, but Prime Minister Harper never would have: 'If it had been the Conservative majority government we have now, I'm not sure that we would have won this.'[337] We thus see in this feature of post-9/11 Canadian politics an example of the closing of political opportunity structure. Civil society's strong perception was that it became more difficult to influence public policy on human rights matters because of the new Government's unaccommodating attitude towards the third sector.

Civil society, in its tardiness in taking up Khadr's case, missed opportunities it may have had to influence Liberal governments, which were less dismissive of the views of human rights NGOs on public policy than the Conservatives. Khadr was detained, tortured and tried by a deeply flawed US military commission under two Liberal governments. But during their administrations, civil society was virtually absent in demanding they protect Khadr's rights.

Conclusion

Canada's response to the torture of its citizens detained in the war on terror was the most engaged of the three liberal democracies examined. Canada was, however, inconsistent in its responses to the cases of Arar and Khadr. On Arar, Canada engaged in robust accountability of its own actions in his extraordinary rendition to Syria where he was tortured. On Khadr, Canada refused for a decade to defend his human rights under domestic and international law. His lawyer, Edney, summed up Canada's response after Khadr was finally freed on bail, saying:

> [W]e were the only Western country that didn't request one of their detainees to return home. We left a child, a Canadian child, in Guantánamo Bay to suffer torture. Not only did we leave a child to suffer torture, we, Canada, participated in this torture.[338]

This statement does not sit easily with Canada's traditional domestic and global identity, where its respect for rights distinguishes it from the US and unifies a nation otherwise divided for reasons to do with history and language.

Electoral politics partly explain the failure of successive governments to defend Khadr's rights, given his family's deep unpopularity with the Canadian public. However, I argue that Canada's inconsistent responses to the torture of citizens also demonstrates the powerful role that civil society can have in shaping state responses to international human rights violations. The Canadian Government faced strong pressure early on from civil society over the treatment of Arar. Arar's articulate and persistent wife led his campaign, and was careful to frame claims

[337] Human rights activist, tel interview, 28 January 2013.
[338] 'What Omar Khadr's lawyer said: "Mr Harper is a bigot"', *Toronto Star*, 7 May 2015.

about his situation in ways that appealed directly to Canada's dominant rights-based identity. She attracted many other civil society supporters to Arar's cause. By contrast, for at least five years Khadr had no support from Canadian civil society beyond his two lawyers. Khadr was an unappealing victim whose case repelled civil society actors due to his family's ongoing public support for terrorism. Because of this, the Canadian Government did not, for many years, come under any sustained pressure to defend Khadr's rights.

An examination of Canada's domestic legal and political context for human rights activism reveals many features that were enabling of mobilisation on international human rights. While Canada's political rights culture is more complex than often assumed, imbued with tensions tied to its dual linguistic and cultural heritage, it has strong legal structures in the form of the Charter. The judicial system offered Khadr his only forum for accountability on torture. Khadr successfully invoked the Charter in Canadian courts, and this encouraged domestic civil society to overcome some of its fear about advocating for him. In the first years after 9/11, Canadian politics was characterised by more open political opportunity structures, with a Government that was receptive to the advocacy role of NGOs. This worked powerfully in Arar's case, where his supporters were able to attract individual champions in the Canadian Parliament, who lobbied the Government over his situation. However, by the time civil society realised the enormity of Khadr's human rights abuses, political opportunity structures in Canada had closed, with a Government less receptive to civil society's views on its human rights policies in power. The cases of Arar and Khadr illustrate the importance of civil society seizing political opportunities when they present.

There developed a significant degree of self-awareness on the part of Canadian civil society in relation to its early lack of activism on Khadr.[339] From 2007 onwards, a powerful movement grew around his case. But his case is revealing of the vulnerabilities of self-interested human rights activists and NGOs around the imperative to attract and keep public support, and demonstrates how such pressures can drive individuals and groups to choose popular causes. The Canada case suggests that civil society possesses significant power to shape government behaviour on international human rights issues when it organises early and collectively, and where domestic political conditions are favourable. Canada's many enabling features for human rights activism were, ultimately, not strong enough to overcome competing interests of civil society groups concerned with their own survival.

[339] *Omar Khadr, Oh Canada*, ed Janice Williamson (Montreal: McGill-Queen's University Press, 2012).

8

Conclusion

Introduction

In this book, I have examined the conditions under which three liberal democracies responded to the torture of their citizens detained in the war on terror. Against the background of the challenge to the international prohibition on torture by the United States (US) after 11 September 2001, it has asked why Australia, Canada and the United Kingdom (UK), three liberal democracies sharing a common Anglo political and legal heritage that values the protection of individual rights, responded so differently when their detained citizens were tortured? The evidence suggests that there were many contributing factors, including alliance politics, national security pressures and the differing number of detainees involved. The UK had more citizens (plus residents) involved than did Australia or Canada, meaning that torture was a quantitatively bigger issue there.

Beyond these disparate and, of themselves, incomplete accounts of state behaviour, less obvious forces were at play. These concerned the domestic pressures executive governments faced from a range of local actors—parliaments, courts and members of civil society—to uphold the rights of citizens not to be tortured. Human rights activism on the issue of the torture of citizens detained in the war on terror differed across the three countries, and this profoundly influenced the responses of governments to the issue.

A comparison of successes and failures in holding governments to account across the three cases indicates that civil society activism sometimes played an important role in achieving positive outcomes for citizens whose rights were violated. Here, I discuss how civil society's effectiveness in this role often depended on its working with and through Parliament and the courts, and that while civil society's willingness to defend rights is never assured, the existence of certain legal and political conditions made it easier or harder for actors to engage. Though the analysis here is framed in terms of accountability, the evidence shows that international human rights commitments, and the public standards they embody, empower materially weak civil society actors to influence national politics.

Political Accountability on Torture

Political accountability is the obligation of democratically elected governments to answer to citizens for their decisions and conduct. In the cases examined in this book, those activities related to how executive governments responded to the torture of citizens and residents overseas, and the role of intelligence and security agencies in that treatment. As discussed in Chapter 3, a traditional mechanism for achieving accountability is by way of the tripartite separation of powers: the legislature, the executive and the courts. A broader way to think about limiting executive power is in terms of pluralised 'separations of power'.[1] Freedom from arbitrary state power is guaranteed by networks of checks and balances, and civil society plays a vital role in this.

The arbitrary exercise of power refers to behaviour that goes beyond simply being unlawful, and includes inappropriateness, injustice and a lack of predictability and due process.[2] Chapters 5–7 offer examples of unconstrained and unreasonable exercises of state power. The Australian Government's behaviour might be considered inappropriate in failing to object robustly to US proposals to transfer a citizen to detention in Egypt, where it knew prisoners were tortured. The UK Government failed to observe due process when it prevented its embassy officials from offering consular assistance to a dual citizen in Zambia in breach of established policies. The Canadian Government's actions were arguably unjust in failing to act on a Supreme Court finding that a citizen's rights under the Canadian Charter of Rights and Freedoms had been breached. These examples highlight how liberal democracies are vulnerable to exercises of arbitrary executive power that can encroach on individual rights. Whether arbitrary executive power is checked is a test of the effectiveness of a liberal democracy's arrangements, formal and informal, for political accountability.

This section studies the relationship between traditional mechanisms of institutional accountability and civil society members acting as agents of accountability.

Civil Society's Interactions with Government

Multiple sources of accountability are important in holding governments to account, because the different branches sometimes lack the resources and will to check executive power when individual rights are violated. This is particularly so in times of high national security threat, when governments are expected to act to keep citizens safe. Australia, the UK and Canada share political systems based on

[1] John Braithwaite, Hilary Charlesworth and Aderito Soares, *Networked Governance of Freedom and Tyranny: Peace in Timor-Leste* (Canberra: ANU E Press, 2012) xii.

[2] Human Rights Committee, *Views: Communication No 458/1991*, UN Doc CCPR/C/51/D/458/1991, 21 July 1994 (*Mukong v Cameron*) [9.8].

the Westminster system, where, theoretically, the executive government is responsible to Parliament and an independent judiciary upholds the rule of law. The reality today is that Parliament tends to be subordinate to the executive.[3] This is the result of the high level of control party politics exert over parliamentary processes. In addition, the checking roles that Parliament and the judiciary play vary across the three countries according to historical, institutional and temporal factors. These include the method by which members of the upper house are selected, the existence of a bill of rights that can enhance the judiciary's role, whether the government holds power by a clear lower house majority and so forth. In some of the countries examined, the Parliament and/or the judiciary played substantial roles in constraining the executive on the torture issue; in others they did not. These formal institutions were most effective when they collaborated with, or buttressed the role of, civil society acting as agents of external accountability.

In Australia, the parliamentary committee system was a source of modest accountability on the torture of Mamdouh Habib, especially the Senate Estimates process, because of its unique ability to question civil servants. For example, a Greens Senator, working with Habib's wife, used committee hearings to expose information about the knowledge of government officials regarding his extraordinary rendition to Egypt. In the UK, the role of parliamentary committees was mixed. The Joint Committee on Human Rights (JCHR), established after the passage of the Human Rights Act (HRA) 1998 and which provides openings for civil society to engage with parliamentary processes, eventually became a vocal proponent of a public inquiry into complicity in torture. Members of the All Party Parliamentary Group on Extraordinary Rendition also collaborated with media and human rights non-governmental organisations (NGOs) to pressure the UK Government over torture complicity. In Canada, where Parliament's role in scrutinising the executive is weak, committees played a minor role on the issue of detainee torture. A handful of individual parliamentarians, however, provided crucial practical assistance to Maher Arar's campaign, including organising meetings between his wife and government ministers during his detention in Syria.

We see a similar variation in the role courts played in checking the executive government on the issue of detainee torture. Where courts were involved, in the UK and Canada, their rulings proved critical to campaigning, providing legitimacy to detainees' claims and bolstering the confidence of civil society. In the UK, where detainees launched litigation relying on rights under the HRA 1998 and common law, the courts criticised the executive's conduct and Guantánamo Bay itself. The UK courts also ordered the disclosure of documents showing the complicity of UK intelligence agencies in the detention and mistreatment of residents, providing powerful arguments subsequently used by parliamentarians and civil society actors to argue that the Government had a moral responsibility to assist the men.

[3] Janet L Hiebert, 'Governing under the Human Rights Act: The limitations of wishful thinking', *Public Law* 27 (January 2012) 43.

The Canadian courts had an important impact on Khadr's case, with the Supreme Court of Canada ruling that his Charter rights had been violated. The Supreme Court offered limited redress in refusing to order Khadr's repatriation, but its rulings proved critical by enlivening the civil society campaign around Khadr, which until then was weak, with activists unwilling to take up his cause because of his terrorist-sympathising family. The Supreme Court's disclosure in 2008 of video showing Canadian intelligence agents interrogating a sobbing 16-year-old Khadr at Guantánamo Bay galvanised Canadian civil society. In Australia, where there is no bill of rights, the courts played a minor role on detainees' cases, particularly when the men's advocates only launched legal proceedings many years after their detention began.

Civil Society as Agents of Accountability

We can see from the previous discussion that civil society often worked alongside the traditional branches of the legislature and judiciary to check executive governments. Certain individuals and groups from civil society acted as 'accountability agents', seeking to impose accountability on governments from the outside.[4] Accountability agents pay attention to the conduct of governments, make judgements about whether they are sufficiently respectful of the rights of individuals or appropriately accountable for the effects of their actions, voice their claims and try to inspire others to support them. Ultimately, these agents are self-appointed and self-authorised, their claims are grounded sometimes in law but often in morality, and they derive their legitimacy from the fact that they are part of the national polity, though located outside the formal structures of the political system. On the issue of the torture of citizens, civil society accountability agents were also empowered by their states' normative and legal commitments regarding the absolute prohibition on torture.

The accountability agents active in the cases included a diverse range of non-government actors. I focused on five distinct categories: lawyers and the legal profession, human rights NGOs and activists, Muslim community groups, the media, and family members of the citizens and residents alleging torture. The roles of these different actors varied in terms of the methods used and how engaged they were with the issue of the torture of detained citizens. Their methods included launching legal proceedings, intervening in detainee litigation, compiling reports, giving evidence to parliamentary committees and international forums, issuing press releases and holding press conferences, lobbying parliamentarians and government ministers, writing letters, holding public demonstrations, placing advertisements, giving public talks, lobbying other NGOs not yet involved, writing

[4] Mark H Moore, 'Accountability, legitimacy, and the court of public opinion' in *The Oxford Handbook of Public Accountability*, ed Mark Bovens, Robert E Goodin and Thomas Schillemans (Oxford: Oxford University Press, 2014) 633.

opinion articles in the media and exposing governmental wrongdoing through investigative journalism. In doing this, civil society groups used a combination of informal accountability mechanisms, such as demonstrations, advertising and engaging the media, which were particularly effective in the lead-up to national elections. They also triggered formal accountability mechanisms that otherwise might not have acted, by pushing for parliamentary or judicial or other government-related inquiries. The proper working of accountable government requires the operation and collaboration of all mechanisms of accountability, formal and informal.

The examples of accountability successes and failures highlighted below demonstrate civil society's sometimes pivotal role in determining whether arbitrary power is checked. They focus mostly on one traditional locus of power, the executive, though there were other sources of political influence. Events such as terrorist attacks and wars tend to strengthen the power of executive governments, based on the assumption that crises require urgent action that they are better equipped than legislatures to take, with individual liberties an almost inevitable casualty.[5]

Accountability Successes

When were governments' policies relating to the mistreatment and torture of citizens and residents detained in the war on terror changed as a result of domestic pressures? Here are three types.

A Willingness to Stand Up to the US

Executive power was successfully constrained in the UK when the Blair Government reversed its position supporting the detention of citizens at Guantánamo Bay within a couple of years of their transfer to the US naval base. This reversal occurred under sustained domestic pressure that was driven by members of the country's legal profession. The UK initially supported the Bush Administration's decision to withhold the protection of the Geneva Conventions from detainees. However, unlike governments in Australia and Canada, the UK refused to allow its citizens to be tried under the US military commission system, which permitted evidence obtained by coercion, determining that it did not offer 'sufficient guarantees of a fair trial in accordance with international standards'.[6] The UK Government had, by then, already brought home five citizens, and shortly after demanded

[5] John E Owens and Riccardo Pelizzo, 'Introduction: The "war on terror" and the growth of executive power? A comparative analysis' in *The 'War on Terror' and the Growth of Executive Power*, ed John E Owens and Riccardo Pelizzo (New York: Routledge, 2010) 1–2; Fiona De Londras and Fergal F Davis, 'Controlling the executive in times of terrorism: Competing perspectives on effective oversight mechanisms', *Oxford Journal of Legal Studies* 30(1) (2010), 23.

[6] Lord Goldsmith, 'Lord Goldsmith's speech in full', 25 June 2004, http://news.bbc.co.uk/2/hi/uk_news/politics/3839153.stm.

the return of the remaining four. Australia and Canada both permitted citizens to be tried under the military commission system. Two citizens, Hicks and Khadr, were repatriated only after making guilty pleas. Of course, the UK had more citizens at Guantánamo: nine, compared to Australia's two and Canada's one.

One of the key factors in the UK's willingness to stand up to the US for its citizens' rights when other liberal democracies did not was because of the civil society campaign on Guantánamo Bay detainees, which began almost immediately in 2002. In Australia and Canada, civil society activism was delayed by many years. Chapter 6 documented the various sources of early domestic pressure on the UK Government to defend the rights of detained citizens. Significant pressure came early from legal activists who worked with detainees' families and supportive legal professional organisations. A small cohort of British human rights lawyers used press conferences, sympathetic sections of the media and the UK courts in their campaign demanding that the Blair Government protect the rights of citizens, including the right not to be tortured. The lawyers were in some cases approached by detainees' families to take on cases.[7] But they also had backgrounds in campaigning for civil liberties (some of them in Northern Ireland), made personal judgements that the US war on terror detainee policies were illegal or immoral, and were primed to act. One lawyer, Clive Stafford Smith, for example, recalled hearing in January 2002 of the US plans to hold prisoners at Guantánamo Bay. He 'emailed round some friends in the death penalty world to find out who else wanted to sue Bush and put a stop to this ill-conceived plan'.[8]

The lawyers gave powerful voice to their claims that the UK Government was obliged to intervene in detainees' cases with the US. Lawyer Louise Christian wrote in the *Guardian* about her 'tortured clients', and noted that 'if the British government were not so craven, it could be demanding a proper inquiry' into citizens' claims of mistreatment.[9] By framing the detainee issue this way, Christian tapped into strong anti-Iraq war sentiment in the UK (not prevalent in Australian or Canadian politics), and into the general belief that the Blair Government was too deferential to the US. The lawyers also deployed more traditional mechanisms for government accountability, seeking recourse for clients in the UK courts. They had early, though mixed, success with the 2002 Court of Appeal judgment in *Abbasi v The Secretary of State*, which relied on rights under the European Convention on Human Rights (ECHR), including the right not to be tortured.[10] The detainees' lawyers were able to make arguments about the citizens' ECHR rights in UK courts

[7] Gareth Peirce, *Dispatches from the Dark Side: On Torture and the Death of Justice* (London: Verso, 2010) 18.

[8] Clive Stafford-Smith, *Bad Men: Guantánamo Bay and the Secret Prisons* (London: Phoenix, 2007) 22.

[9] Louise Christian, 'Comment and analysis: Letters: My tortured clients', *Guardian*, 15 September 2004, 25.

[10] *The Queen on the Application of Abbasi v The Secretary of State for Foreign and Commonwealth Affairs* [2002] EWCA Civ 1598.

because of the HRA 1998, which gave effect to them as domestic statutory rights. The Court in *Abbasi* ruled in favour of the Government, but nevertheless offered a scathing critique of the US detention regime. This lent significant moral weight to the detainees' claims, and was a turning point in shifting public opinion and attracting further civil society support.

Holding Public Commissions of Inquiry

Canada provides an example of the successful checking of arbitrary executive power through the establishment of a public commission of inquiry into allegations of government complicity in a citizen's torture overseas. This followed a sustained campaign led by the victim's wife. The Arar Commission was the first instance where any of the three US allies was subjected to public scrutiny on the issue of the torture of citizens in the war on terror, and remains the most thorough exercise of its kind. It was 'an extraordinary exercise in accountability for secret national security activities'.[11] The inquiry held 127 days of hearings, many of them public, and released thousands of previously unseen government documents.[12] The final report ran to multiple volumes and was highly critical of the actions of Canadian officials. Political rivalries and personal politics played a role in the Martin Government's decision to hold an inquiry. In addition, judicial inquiries in Canadian politics, where Parliament's oversight powers are limited, tend to be the preferred response to government-related scandal. However, the build-up of domestic political pressure, driven by intense civil society campaigning for official accountability over Arar's transfer to torture in Syria, was a critical factor.

Arar's sympathetic, articulate and persistent wife, Monia Mazigh, gained the backing of experienced human rights activists from the NGO sector, Muslim community and academia, as well as some parliamentarians. She wrote letters to ministers, organised vigils, gave media interviews, wrote her own newspaper opinion articles and gave public talks. One of Mazigh's most important allies was an activist who worked full-time on the case and had a sophisticated understanding of how to harness the media's power in human rights campaigning. Kerry Pither's media strategy illustrates an important feature of how accountability agents can work to bring about changes in governments' human rights policies. Pither was receptive to media demands, organising interviews with Amnesty International when a 'human rights perspective' was sought and the Council on American-Islamic Relations Canada (CAIR-CAN, as it was then known) when a 'Muslim perspective' was required.[13] Journalists were presented with factual chronologies of what was known about Arar's treatment and the involvement of Canada's security agencies,

[11] Kent Roach, *The 9/11 Effect: Comparative Counter-Terrorism* (New York, NY: Cambridge University Press, 2011) 413.

[12] Commission of Inquiry into the Actions of Canadian Officials in Relation to Maher Arar (Arar Commission), 'The Arar Commission has completed 127 days of testimony and made public thousands of formerly secret documents relating to the Arar affair', press release, 14 September 2005.

[13] Muslim Human Rights Activist, tel interview, 13 January 2013.

and what was not. 'I believe that we were able to bring the majority of Canadians on side because we asked for something very few could disagree with: the right to due process', an activist said;[14] 'We did not tell Canadians they should believe Maher Arar was innocent … We were also very careful not to "accuse" Canadian authorities of misconduct.' The Arar campaign was deliberately measured in its approach, and Mazigh framed her claims carefully in terms of Canadian values of justice and citizenship.

Using National Elections

A third example of successfully holding the executive government accountable rests on national elections. In Australia, civil society activists used the 2007 federal election to pressure the Government into intervening in Hicks's military commission and bringing him home from Guantánamo Bay. The Hicks case illustrates how elections can offer critical points of pressure for activists to influence governments in the course of ongoing human rights campaigns. Elections can make politicians pay attention to what the public wants.

As Chapter 5 documented, the campaign to repatriate Hicks built steadily throughout 2006. The Howard Government had been indifferent to Hicks's situation since he was first detained in 2002, but this changed with the looming election in 2007, amid strong indications that the issue was finally exercising voters. Prime Minister John Howard was sensitive to this shift in public opinion, and in late 2006 and early 2007 he spoke to US President George W Bush about the urgency of bringing Hicks to trial, 'stressing the domestic political problems for my Government'.[15] There were two reasons why the 2007 federal election proved pivotal for influencing the executive over Hicks, when the previous poll in 2004 had not. One was the changing mood in the Australian electorate over the Government and its treatment of Hicks. The other was the formation in 2005 of new human rights-focused NGOs, whose founders identified gaps in the sector that were evident in the limited campaigning around the Government's war on terror policies.

The activism of one organisation in particular, GetUp!, had a profound effect on shifting government policy on Hicks, because it directly targeted the Government's re-election prospects. GetUp! transformed the campaign to bring Hicks home. It framed the issues animating the Hicks campaign in terms of reclaiming Australia's independence and autonomy, and standing up to the US for its beliefs in the rule of law, a view that in the pre-2007 election climate was gaining increasing resonance in the Australian community. GetUp!'s campaign on Hicks was specifically built around the exploitation of opportunities connected to the federal election. Its tactics included conducting public opinion polling, using paid advertising and holding rallies to reinforce to the Government how public sentiment on

[14] Human Rights Activist, tel interview, 28 January 2013.

[15] John Howard, *Lazarus Rising: A Personal and Political Autobiography* (Sydney: Harper Collins Publishers, 2010) 634.

Hicks was moving in a way that could affect its performance at the election. The GetUp! campaign helped turn what began as a human rights issue into 'a political hot potato that needed to be solved by the government quickly'.[16] While GetUp!'s campaign on Hicks increased government accountability on human rights, with Australia intervening in his case and bringing him home, the claims underpinning it were based on the right to due process, not the prohibition on torture. Activism on Hicks stopped when he returned home.

Accountability Failures

Accountability failures refers to cases where the executive government remained indifferent towards the alleged breach of a citizen's human right not to be tortured, and the state's involvement in that treatment went unchecked.

Failing to Stand Up for the Rights of Citizens

The refusal by the state over a sustained period to defend citizens' rights, where multiple breaches under domestic and international law were unquestionably occurring, represents a clear example of the failure to constrain arbitrary executive power. This occurred in the Australian case with respect to citizens, but was most pronounced and prolonged in the Khadr case. Canada only permitted the teenager (aged 15 when captured by US forces) to return after a decade, under pressure from the Obama Administration, which wanted to close the Guantánamo Bay detention facility. Canada was able to neglect Khadr's rights because, for many years following his detention, he had few supporters in Canadian civil society. The breaches of Khadr's rights included his abuse and possible torture in Afghanistan and Guantánamo Bay in contravention of the CAT. The Canadian Supreme Court found that aspects of Khadr's treatment, including sleep deprivation and lengthy periods of isolation ahead of his interrogations by Canadian officials, violated his rights under the Geneva Conventions and the Charter.[17] Khadr's rights as a child soldier under the OPCRC were arguably violated as well.[18]

When Khadr was first detained in 2002, the Liberal Chrétien Government was in power. Stephen Harper's Conservative Government, which was less committed to promoting human rights in foreign policy and took a particularly hard-line approach towards Khadr, came to power in 2006.[19] If political ideology explains the Harper Government's position on Khadr, it is less clear why two Liberal

[16] GetUp! official, tel interview, 21 February 2013.

[17] *Canada (Prime Minister) v Khadr* [2010] 1 SCR 44.

[18] Christopher Dore, 'What to do with Omar Khadr? Putting a child soldier on trial: Questions of international law, juvenile justice, and moral culpability', *Marshall Law Review* 41(4) (2007–2008), 1281–320.

[19] Roland Paris, 'Are Canadians still liberal internationalists? Foreign policy and public opinion in the Harper era', *International Journal* 69(3) (September 2014), 274–307.

Governments ignored transgressions of his rights for four years. The Chrétien Government had been embarrassed before, in the mid-1990s, for supporting the Khadr family, and the Liberals were not inclined to have this happen again.[20] An additional reason why Liberal Governments were able to ignore Khadr's case for so long was because there was no strong civil society campaign demanding accountability for his mistreatment.

Lawyers, journalists, parliamentarians and activists familiar with Khadr's case attest to the reluctance for many years of civil society groups to advocate for his rights or pressure the Government over his situation. Khadr's was a 'very difficult case to actually present and package and convince policy makers and the public of'.[21] This was due to his unsympathetic family, who were known Al-Qaeda associates, and the nature of the charges against Khadr (killing an American soldier). Khadr's case presented too big a risk for politicians concerned about their standing with the electorate, for human rights NGOs and legal professional associations worried about funding and members, and for Muslim community organisations nervous about public attitudes towards Muslims in the post-9/11 environment. Journalist Michelle Shephard observed in 2008, '[T]he fact that the Canadian federal government and the public have never been able to separate Omar from his family has left Canada standing virtually alone in its support of Guantánamo Bay.'[22]

Civil society actors lacked neither a moral nor a legal basis for taking on the Canadian Government over Khadr's treatment, as Supreme Court of Canada decisions made clear. Rather, much of Canadian civil society judged Khadr's case as one for which it would be difficult to find wider popular support, and worried that lobbying for him could damage their reputations. This only changed from 2007 when, aided by the passage of time, the outcome in Hicks's case, and Supreme Court of Canada decisions on Khadr, civil society attitudes began to shift.

Failing to Investigate Torture Allegations

Another example of the failure to check executive power occurred in Australia, where governments did not publicly and independently investigate substantive allegations that citizens were tortured in the war on terror. This failure was a consequence, at least in part, of the lack of any civil society campaign demanding that an inquiry be established. There has been no Australian investigation into Hicks's torture allegations. Under the Labor Gillard Government, the Inspector-General of Intelligence and Security conducted a closed inquiry into Habib's extraordinary rendition to Egypt, but no public investigation into his claims of torture has ever been held.[23] The Howard Government consistently suggested that the men's

[20] Audrey Macklin, 'From cooperation, to complicity, to compensation: The war on terror, extraordinary rendition, and the cost of torture', *European Journal of Migration and Law* 10(1) (2008), 20.

[21] Muslim Human Rights Activist, tel interview, 2013.

[22] Michelle Shephard, *Guantánamo's Child* (Mississauga: John Wiley & Sons, 2008) xiv.

[23] Vivienne Thom, *Inquiry into the actions of Australian Government agencies in relation to the arrest and detention overseas of Mr Mamdouh Habib from 2001 to 2005*, December 2011, https://www.igis.gov.au/sites/default/files/files/Inquiries/docs/habib-inquiry.pdf.

torture allegations should not be believed, and questioned the motives of anyone who suggested the claims should be tested.[24] Amid pressure prompted by the 2004 Abu Ghraib abuse scandal, the Howard Government sought the Bush Administration's assurances that Hicks and Habib had not been mistreated, and relied on the results of US internal reviews to deflect calls for further investigations, as did the Labor Rudd Government.[25]

Australia failed to properly investigate the torture allegations of Hicks and Habib because there was no concerted domestic campaign around the need for an inquiry. Civil society's calls for accountability on the torture of citizens overseas were sporadic and generally made in international forums—namely the Committee Against Torture—rather than at home. Most of the advocacy that occurred around the cases of Australian citizens at Guantánamo Bay was limited to issues of procedural fairness tied to Hicks's military commission, not torture. Civil society actors believed that arguing for a fair trial and repatriation were more achievable objectives than campaigning for a torture inquiry. Human rights activists from a variety of backgrounds—legal, judicial, civil liberties, NGOs—shared a belief that campaigning for a torture inquiry was futile.

Australia had fewer detainees who alleged they had been tortured in the war on terror than did the UK, where civil society campaigned hard for an inquiry. However, as the Arar case in Canada demonstrated, the number of torture victims does not necessarily have a bearing on whether an inquiry is called, nor on its scale or thoroughness. Habib's allegations of rendition to torture in Egypt were of similar gravity to the experiences of Arar. Civil society in Australia formed the view that campaigning for a torture inquiry was pointless, partly because of the lack of legal levers to enforce the prohibition on torture. Australia has no bill of rights and no constitutional prohibition against torture. The inadequate institutional framework around the ban on torture meant that when activists framed their claims about the need to defend the rights of detained citizens, it was more often around fair trial and due process guarantees. As one legal activist noted, it was about 'the legal hooks we had available to us'.[26]

Civil Society Engagement on Torture

The preceding discussion has shown that domestic pressure was an important factor for shaping the responses of liberal democracies to the torture of citizens in the war on terror. In the face of competing concerns to support a close and powerful ally, and to protect their populations from future Al-Qaeda-inspired terrorist attacks, executive governments in Australia, the UK and Canada confronted

[24] 'Interview—2UE IV with John Laws—Habib', 2UE, 14 February 2005 (Alexander Downer), radio.

[25] Deborah Snow and David Marr, 'Sitting alone on our hands', *Sydney Morning Herald*, 16 May 2009, 6.

[26] HRLC official, tel interview, 19 June 2013.

domestic demands to protect the rights of citizens detained by the US. These demands for accountability varied across the countries, according to differences in government structures that affected the roles the Parliament and judiciary played in checking the executive and that also influenced civil society engagement on the issues. In general, executive governments were held accountable when the detainees' cases threatened a government's political future, or when embarrassing details of official complicity were exposed, undermining the executive's legitimacy with its citizenry. Materially weak civil society actors, empowered by their states' human rights commitments and values, and often working with and through the Parliament and courts, played a significant role in making this happen and bringing these details to light.

Civil society is not a monolithic entity, nor does it possess an inherently normative purpose. While civil society's willingness to defend human rights is never assured, the existence of certain legal and political conditions makes it easier or harder for actors with a particular interest in upholding rights (human rights activists, lawyers and journalists acting as watchdogs of public interest, for example) to engage on a given issue.

Environments for Activism

The environments for activism in the three countries differed in ways that enabled or constrained civil society actors. From their behaviours in checking the executive government on torture, we can deduce that it is easier for civil society to mobilise under certain conditions.

In the UK, we saw the existence of a number of enabling conditions for activism. This included a group of lawyers who had seen their Government detain, abuse and torture terrorist suspects before, in Northern Ireland, and so were familiar with the issues. Under the HRA 1998, these lawyers were able to sue the Government in the UK courts for the breach of citizens' rights under a regional human rights convention, including the right not to be tortured, and consequently engaged the courts early and often. Because of the deep unpopularity of the Iraq War, activists could readily frame their media campaigning in ways that resonated with a public already angry about their Government's role in the war on terror.

In Australia, there was a different set of conditions for activism, with many constraining factors, some of which became more enabling over time. Amid a national rights culture where rights are not well understood or institutionalised, civil society was overwhelmed by the high volume of issues after 9/11 and activism was delayed. Freedom from torture is not a well-established right under Australian law, and the activism that did occur (with greater intensity over time as political opportunities opened up) was focused on legal process issues to do with unfair military commissions.

The Canada case is more difficult to explain, as enabling conditions existed for activism but additional factors to do with self-interest and insecurities on the part of non-state actors came forcefully into play. On the one hand, we saw the effects of enabling conditions for activism in the way campaigners on the Arar case appealed to Canada's identity as a rights-respecting country and were assisted by favourable political opportunities, including a change of prime minister to one who was more open to holding an inquiry. In Khadr's case, Charter rights were critical to his lawyers' ability to belatedly build civil society support after successfully suing the Government. However, closed political opportunities in the form of a Conservative Government with a tough-on-terrorists agenda prevented an invigorated campaign from shifting official policy.

Elements of Activism

In Chapter 3 I developed a framework of enabling and constraining factors through which to analyse the way in which different political and legal conditions affect civil society activism in liberal democracies. I highlighted three interconnected factors—political culture, political and legal institutions and political opportunities—that make it easier or harder for activists to mobilise on a given human rights issue. Underpinning the framework is the understanding that a higher level of rights consciousness and sense of legitimacy in claiming rights, the existence of relevant institutional tools through which to access the political and legal system, and openings in the political system for influencing government, can facilitate rights activism.

Political Culture

Political culture is an historically transmitted pattern of meanings, according to which members of a polity interpret their experiences, frame problems and decide upon their actions.[27] Political culture can be imprecise and incomplete. It refers to ideas that are often contested within a polity, that are shared by a broad cross-section of the community, yet can exclude certain members such as indigenous groups, whose experience of history differs from that of the majority. Political culture can enable or constrain human rights activism according to how it affects the way members of a polity understand the relationship between the individual and the state. Historical legacies, including the way a country achieved independence, ongoing internal struggles, former racial policies and past encounters with political violence, precondition how members of a modern polity think about themselves as rights-bearing individuals, and can influence the willingness of citizens to act on new cases of rights infractions. Political culture can shape the make-up of a country's political and legal institutions, by suggesting whether rights should be institutionalised in order to protect individuals from the state, or whether the state should be considered the appropriate protector of rights. Rights cultures are

[27] Clifford Geertz, *The Interpretation of Cultures* (New York, NY: Basic Books, 1973) 89.

not necessarily static and can also be influenced by the establishment of new institutional arrangements for protecting rights.

Political culture does not explain activism, but it can provide a more nuanced appreciation of a polity's dominant ideas about rights, and can thus shed light on some features of the activism that occurred in a particular country on a given issue. This might include why activists framed a problem in a certain way, or why they focused their efforts on particular kinds of rights. A strong rights culture requires a consciousness at different levels of the polity, from the institutions of government in terms of the way rights inform decision making, to citizens who must be prepared to demand their rights. It reflects 'a way of seeing the world through the lens of human rights and consequently with the principles of human dignity and equality'.[28] I selected two features through which to examine a country's political culture in order to ascertain prevailing understandings about rights: historical legacies of rights and political violence, and public discourse on rights. Applied to the three countries, these ideas about political culture assist with understanding the different cultural norms with which activists operated after 9/11 in relation to advocating on human rights. I have described Australia's rights culture as weak, the UK's as stronger and Canada's as aspirational.

The foundation for Australia's weak political culture is the predominance of a utilitarian view of rights.[29] Partly because of the peaceful way the Australian colony gained its independence, the polity takes an instrumental view of the state that readily sanctions interventionist governments and is less concerned with protecting individual freedoms. Reflecting this history, Australia's Constitution is largely silent on rights, and international human rights standards are marginal to political debate and policy development.[30] Repeated attempts to introduce a bill of rights, in part out of a concern to create a stronger rights culture, have failed. Australia was less familiar with terrorism on 11 September 2001, and civil society was ill-equipped to deal with the large volume of human rights issues that arose in the aftermath, including the Government's hyper-legislative response to the attacks, and lost focus and became demoralised.

I described UK rights culture as stronger than that of Australia because of two features. The first is its previous experience of torture and terrorism connected to the conflict in Northern Ireland. Familiarity with terrorism can threaten a country's democratic character and lead to greater public support for draconian security measures, which occurred to an extent in the UK.[31] But it can also make

[28] Julie A Mertus, 'Human rights and civil society in a new age of American exceptionalism' in *Human Rights in the 'War on Terror'*, ed Richard Ashby Wilson (New York, NY: Cambridge University Press, 2005) 325.

[29] Hilary Charlesworth, *Writing in Rights: Australia and the Protection of Human Rights* (Sydney: UNSW Press 2002).

[30] Simon Rice and Scott Calnan, *Sustainable Advocacy: Capabilities and Attitudes of Australian Human Rights NGOs* (Sydney: Australian Human Rights Centre, 2007) 10.

[31] Bruce W Warner, 'Great Britain and the response to international terrorism' in *The Deadly Sin of Terrorism: Its Effect on Democracy and Civil Liberty in Six Countries*, ed David Charters (Westport, CT: Greenwood Press, 1994).

sections of civil society more aware of the potential for human rights transgressions of target suspect groups. In a more practical sense, it can mean that there are lawyers and activists with personal experience of working and campaigning on similar issues. My research indicated that the experiences of internment and detainee abuse in Northern Ireland formed a prism through which some lawyers and human rights NGOs viewed the treatment of citizens and residents at Guantánamo, and influenced their readiness to act after 9/11. A second feature that pointed to a stronger rights culture in the UK was the HRA 1998. The Act was introduced specifically to promote a stronger rights culture across the institutions of government, and across the political community more widely.[32]

I characterised Canada's rights culture as aspirational because its celebrated commitments to the idea of rights mask complexities and tensions that are the result of historical legacies. Rights feature prominently in discussions about Canadian global and national identity. In the international sphere, Canada has sought to distinguish itself from the US by its commitment to multilateralism and activism on human rights treaties.[33] Domestically, appeals to a common commitment to respect individual rights have underpinned a continuing political project to unify a nation divided by its dominant distinct dual Anglo and French heritage and uncertain of its future.[34] The 1982 constitutional Charter represented a robust attempt at unifying the polity through a new common rights-based identity. The Charter has influenced Canada's political culture, arguably making courts less deferential to executive and legislative action that infringes individual rights.[35] However, the failure by the executive and, for a long time, Parliament and civil society to defend Khadr's rights reveals significant gaps in Canada's rights project.

Political and Legal Institutions

Institutions are relatively stable organisational arrangements—rules and practices—that define the setting within which governance and policy making take place. Institutions order democratic political life by allocating resources, empowering and constraining actors, and helping them define their interests. In a human rights context, institutions enable citizens to enjoy their rights as a matter of course through the existence of effective national legal systems of human rights enforcement.[36] National frameworks for protecting human rights differ substantially across liberal democracies, shaped by historical and cultural forces. This has

[32] Lord Irvine, 'The development of Human Rights in Britain under an incorporated convention on human rights', Tom Sargant Memorial Lecture, Law Society Hall, London, December 1997.

[33] Alison Brysk, *Global Good Samaritans: Human Rights as Foreign Policy* (New York, NY: Oxford University Press, 2009) 66.

[34] Michael Ignatieff, *The Rights Revolution* (Toronto: House of Anansi Press, 2007) 77.

[35] Kent Roach, 'Uneasy neighbors: Comparative American and Canadian counter-terrorism', *William Mitchell Law Review* 38(5) (2012), 1709.

[36] Jack Donnelly, 'The virtues of legalization' in *The Legalization of Human Rights: Multidisciplinary Perspectives on Human Rights and Human Rights Law*, ed Saladin Meckled-Garcia and Basak Cali (New York, NY: Routledge, 2006) 76.

consequences for how civil society responds to human rights issues, making it easier or harder to engage in activism according to whether institutional levers are adequate, can be readily activated and are judged as likely to result in successful claims making.

I focused on three kinds of legal and political institutions: bills of rights, other domestic legal and constitutional protections around the right not to be tortured, and parliamentary processes for accountability on human rights. A bill of rights, in particular, can have a profound effect in terms of empowering civil society actors to make rights claims by providing judicially enforceable mechanisms to individuals whose rights have been violated. It can also deepen respect for rights across a polity's institutions and the public more generally. In addition, robust parliamentary committee processes can provide civil society with openings into the political system and occasions for demanding accountability on rights. Australia's political and legal institutions were limited in their capacity to protect human rights mainly because of the absence of a bill of rights, compared to the UK, which has the HRA 1998, and Canada with its constitutional Charter.

Australia's human rights framework after 9/11 had a number of inadequacies, including the absence of a bill of rights and piecemeal domestic laws prohibiting torture. A bill of rights can remind governments and communities of a society's basic values and of the principles that might otherwise be compromised at a time of grief and fear.[37] Australia lacks these institutional reminders. While the lack of a Commonwealth offence prohibiting torture did not directly affect Hicks and Habib, it did suggest a less than complete commitment by Australia to its international legal obligations regarding torture. These shortcomings shaped civil society activism around the issue of detainees, affecting actors' views of their capabilities and what was achievable, and directing them to focus their efforts on due process and fair trial rights rather than human dignity and torture. Legal activists suggested that the reason civil society did not campaign on the need for torture accountability was not simply because there were fewer cases of citizens detained in the war on terror alleging mistreatment (compared to the UK), but also because of the absence of legal hooks around which to frame claims about torture.

Civil society actors in the UK had access to more effective institutions for protecting human rights, because of the UK's membership of the Council of Europe and the passage of the HRA 1998, which allowed individuals to litigate breaches of their ECHR rights in domestic courts, including the right not to be tortured. I do not suggest that the UK was a model case for protecting the rights of individuals not to be tortured. The UK's record on using state sanctioned torture is blemished, and its laws and jurisprudence indicate an ambiguity with respect to the absolute ban on torture. However, civil society actors involved in the detainee torture issue in the UK emphasised the importance of the 1998 Act, which made it easier to bring cases and meant that domestic courts were more open to challenging

[37] George Williams, 'Balancing national security and human rights: Lessons from Australia', *borderlands: new spaces in the humanities e-journal* 4(1) (2005), paras 27, 29.

the Government on human rights issues. The HRA 1998 was invoked in many cases brought by the detainees and their lawyers and families against the UK Government.[38]

Canada was the only country of the three to have a constitutional rights charter, which included a prohibition on the use of 'cruel and unusual treatment or punishment' (section 12). However, the Canadian case also demonstrates that political and legal levers are no guarantee that civil society will adopt a particular human rights cause, or that it will be effective in campaigning when it does. The Charter operated in Khadr's case in two ways, providing a judicial mechanism for his lawyers to challenge the executive's treatment of him and, through successful court rulings, providing a timid civil society with confidence to support his cause. Civil society actors acknowledged the Charter's role in Khadr's case. A human rights NGO official, for example, said, '[A]s there started to be a growing number of court decisions saying this is wrong … all of that gave greater confidence to organisations.'[39] Crucial Supreme Court of Canada rulings upholding his Charter rights came late, however, and their mobilising effect on civil society had limited effects for Khadr's campaign.

Political Opportunities

More dynamic and transient changes in the political environment in the form of emerging or disappearing opportunities can also make activism easier or more difficult. Political opportunity structures are consistent, but not necessarily formal or permanent, dimensions of political environment that provide incentives for collective action by affecting people's expectations for success or failure.[40] The cases I have presented illustrate how political opportunities affect activism: widening or shrinking the space within which citizens perceive that they can legitimately make claims, revealing new allies and exposing the weaknesses of governments, and suggesting ways to frame messages dynamically, though framing is also informed by cultural factors. The cases also highlight how political opportunities are often fleeting and sometimes accidental. Actors, to be effective, had to be alert to this dimension, watching out for opportunities, biding their time (but still doing the ground work) until the right political opportunity presented, recognising it when it arrived and anticipating its possible transience.

I investigated different types of political opportunities that emerged across the cases. They included the attitude or ideological position of the political party in

[38] *The Queen on the Application of Abbasi v The Secretary of State for Foreign and Commonwealth Affairs* [2002] EWCA Civ 1598; *The Queen on the Application of Al Rawi v The Secretary of State for Foreign and Commonwealth Affairs* [2006] EWCA Civ 1279; *The Queen on the Application of Binyam Mohamed v Secretary of State for Foreign and Commonwealth Affairs* [2008] EWHC 2048 (Admin); *The Queen on the Application of Binyam Mohamed v Secretary of State for Foreign and Commonwealth Affairs* [2010] EWCA Civ 65.

[39] Human Rights NGO official, tel interview, 21 February 2013.

[40] Sidney Tarrow, *Power in Movement: Social Movements and Contentious Politics* (New York, NY: Cambridge University Press, 1998) 76–77.

power towards civil society and human rights; the electoral cycle and the effects of national elections; the unity of government where the formation of minority governments or conflicts among political elites can provide potential allies for civil society actors; and the impact of related issues running concurrently in domestic politics. I suggested that a more open polity, offering more points of vulnerability to pressure the government, made activism easier. In Australia, political opportunities were scarce after 9/11, but this shifted after five years. The UK and Canada had more open political systems than Australia after 9/11.

In Australia, the Conservative Howard Government harboured negative views about the legitimacy of the non-government sector, and for many years the Prime Minister ran a tightly controlled ministry and backbench, with few public dissenters. This changed as Prime Minister Howard's popularity weakened and as the 2007 federal election drew near, and opportunities for mobilisation in the political system were identified and successfully exploited by some NGOs.

In the UK, Prime Minister Tony Blair's Labour Government had a more inclusive attitude towards NGOs. More significantly, there were various points of political vulnerability for the Government relating to the war on terror. This included widespread discontent over the UK's involvement in the Iraq War, allegations that UK military forces had abused Iraqi detainees, and controversy over the Government's domestic internment policies for non-nationals who could not be deported because they faced possible torture. Debates around these concurrent issues created openings in the UK's political system that meant it was easier for supporters of detainees at Guantánamo to find public support for their cases.

In Canada, political opportunities closed with the arrival of the Conservative Harper Government, with consequences for the Khadr campaign. Political party ideology in Canada noticeably affected the way the executive viewed civil society, and hence the ability of NGOs to influence government policy. Civil society, whose activism on Khadr was delayed for many years, failed to take advantage of the more open political system that existed after 9/11, when Liberal governments who were more receptive to the third sector's role in public policy held power, a factor that had aided the Arar campaign. Khadr's ill-treatment began and continued for four years under Liberal governments. But during this time, civil society was virtually absent in demanding Khadr's rights be protected. By the time civil society awoke to the gravity of Khadr's situation, political opportunity structures in Canada had shifted against it.

The Limits of Civil Society

Civil society encompasses a range of individuals and groups with diverse interests and values, not all of them supportive of human rights or of human rights for everybody. Civil society is not a panacea for the problem of executive governments exercising arbitrary power. Conditions conducive for human rights activism make it easier for domestic actors to engage with a particular human rights cause, but—as demonstrated by the Canadian case—they do not guarantee that they will. Sometimes other factors will override an actor's inclination to back a particular human rights cause. Security imperatives may cause sections of civil society to back a government's downgrading of human rights protections—for example, against torture. This occurred in the case of some media and academics after 9/11, including in Australia. Internal concerns to do with an organisation's public image or ability to attract public support may cause it to engage in opportunistic behaviour and avoid involvement in an unpopular cause. We saw this in relation to activists in Australia and Canada, who were reluctant to back more unpopular victims.

More fundamentally, civil society is itself a site of power and an instrument for the consolidation and imposition of historical inequities and entrenched interests.[41] These histories and interests can influence which human rights causes, and which victims, mainstream or dominant NGOs (including powerful transnational organisations) are prepared to support. For example, Muslim human rights activists in the UK questioned the initial reluctance by transnational NGOs to take up the cause of Guantánamo detainees because of what they suspected was an unspoken consensus that the religious beliefs of these individuals made them undesirable subjects for advocacy. This was before the full extent of the mistreatment of detainees was known. Human rights NGOs derive legitimacy from being law-abiding and from moral claims based on the importance of their work in defending individual rights.[42] Civil society is critiqued for its claims to representativeness, however, when organisations are unelected and self-appointed, and where NGOs exist to reflect their own principles, not to represent a constituency to whose interests and desires they must respond.[43] Those who constitute 'civil societies' tend to be white and male, from the middle or upper class and caste, practising the dominant religion and speaking the dominant language.[44] Jai Sen argues that civil society is a site of exclusion, ruled by norms of 'civility', where those considered not to conform (the 'incivil' or, worse, 'uncivil' because of their purported criminal intent) are subjugated and either ignored or destroyed.[45]

Post-9/11 controversies in the UK and Canada over certain Muslim groups and their alleged sympathies for extremist ideologies illustrate Sen's categorisation of civil society organisations based on perceived levels of domestication and civility. Cage, a UK Muslim activist organisation set up because existing Muslim community groups were unwilling to get involved in defending the rights of detainees

[41] Jai Sen, 'The power of civility: Some critical reflections on global civil society', paper presented at *Global Civil Society: More or Less Democracy?* World Social Forum, Nairobi, Kenya, 22 January 2007.

[42] Peter J Spiro, 'Accounting for NGOs', *Chicago Journal of International Law* 3(1) (2002), 161–69.

[43] Kenneth Anderson and David Rieff, '"Global civil society": A sceptical view', Research Paper No 2008-69, Washington College of Law, American University, 2008, 1.5.

[44] Sen, 'The power of civility', 58.

[45] ibid, 54.

at Guantánamo Bay, has been accused of supporting extremist ideologies.[46] Similarly, the UK's Islamic Human Rights Commission and the Council on American Islamic Relations (whose Canadian arm CAIR-CAN is now the National Council of Canadian Muslims) have been labelled apologists for Muslim fundamentalist political movements.[47] Elsewhere in Canada the office of Prime Minister Harper claimed that CAIR-CAN had ties to terrorist organisations.[48] These accusations cast such Muslim organisations not only as 'incivil' but as potentially 'uncivil'. These disputes indicate how, in the area of international human rights, the notion of civil society—who constitutes its members and what comprises a legitimate political position—is contested. Given the considerable power civil society actors can exert at domestic and international levels of politics, it is reasonable to question their own lack of accountability, including to the global system of which they are a part.

Conclusion

This study was motivated by an apparent inconsistency concerning liberal democracy after 11 September 2001: a failure by some US allies, but not others, to protest the use of torture in a war that was premised on defending freedom.[49] The central argument of this book is that domestic legal and political conditions influenced activism on the issue of detainees tortured in the war on terror, and that the level of activism influenced government accountability on the way citizens were treated. I acknowledge that there were also other factors at work that shaped government responses, such as alliance pressures and the number of detainees involved. We have also seen that the existence of favourable conditions for activism does not alone guarantee that civil society will mobilise on a particular human rights issues. But appreciating how domestic conditions affect activism can help us to understand how international human rights operate at the domestic level. Since 11 September 2001, some of these conditions, including aspects of the legal and political structures around the prohibition against torture, have altered across the liberal democracies studied here, or there are plans to alter them.

Some of the conditions I have highlighted, such as political opportunities, can be transient or accidental, and therefore are unpredictable. Other conditions, such as political culture, are influenced by history and thus more deeply embedded.

[46] Karima Bennoune, *Your Fatwa Does Not Apply Here* (New York, NY: WW Norton & Company, 2013) 16; Douglas Murray and Robin Simcox, 'The evidence shows that Cage is a pro-terrorist group', *Telegraph*, 21 July 2014.

[47] Bennoune, *Your Fatwa Does Not Apply Here*, 16.

[48] National Council of Canadian Muslims, 'NCCM commences defamation lawsuit against PMO', press release, 26 May 2014.

[49] George W Bush, 'Remarks by the President in photo opportunity with the National Security Team', White House, Washington, DC, 12 September 2001.

Political and legal institutions are also more permanent structures, but can be established or dismantled, sometimes with the express desired effect of modifying cultural norms around the awareness of rights across a polity. Australia, after 2007, briefly considered introducing a bill of rights, but once again shelved the idea. Instead, it passed legislation to close gaps in its federal laws around torture, and established a new Parliamentary Joint Committee on Human Rights to better scrutinise legislation for compliance with international human rights treaties.[50] The UK passed the Justice and Security Act in 2013, which established 'closed material procedures' in civil cases involving national security issues. This was adopted amid embarrassing litigation brought after 9/11 that exposed UK complicity in rendition and torture.[51] Under the new law, courts can now consider evidence from the Government without having to disclose it to other parties, if disclosure would be 'damaging to the interests of national security' (section 6). The Cameron Government had also intended to repeal the HRA 1998 and replace it with a 'British Bill of Rights', in order to dilute the influence of the European Court of Human Rights on domestic courts, though whether the new Prime Minister Theresa May will proceed with her predecessor's plans is unclear.[52] The Justin Trudeau Government in Canada is considering establishing a new parliamentary committee with powers to monitor security and intelligence agencies.[53] There has also been much self-criticism by Canadian civil society about its failings in the Khadr case.[54] It is possible that shared norms around torture have been shaped by the contrasting experiences of the Arar and Khadr cases in ways that might affect future activism in Canada on this issue. As these developments show, liberal democracies learnt from the experiences around detained citizens tortured in the war on terror. Some of these lessons have been positive for the protection of human rights, leading to the strengthening of relevant institutions and others, as evidenced by the UK case, have not.

In this book, I have exposed some of the vulnerabilities of liberal democracies to arbitrary exercises of executive power. I have shown that the role of resisting and checking arbitrary power is dispersed in different ways across liberal democracies. Civil society is one potential realm of power used to protect basic legal freedoms. It relies on a state's undertaking commitments to protect human rights, and involves

[50] Crimes Legislation Amendment (Torture Prohibition and Death Penalty Abolition) Act 2010 (Cth); Human Rights (Parliamentary Scrutiny) Act 2011 (Cth); Human Rights (Parliamentary Scrutiny) (Consequential Provisions) Act 2011.

[51] Tom Hickman, 'Turning out the lights? The Justice and Security Act 2013', 11 June 2013, UK Constitutional Law Association, blog.

[52] Ashley Cowburn, 'Plans to replace Human Rights Act with new "British Bill" could be scrapped, *Independent*, 11 August 2015.

[53] Craig Forcese and Kent Roach, 'Bridging the national security accountability gap: A three-part system to modernize Canada's inadequate review of national security', Forcese/Roach/01/16 working draft, 11 January 2016.

[54] Janice Williamson (ed), *Omar Khadr, Oh Canada* (Montreal: McGill-Queen's University Press, 2012).

holding the state accountable to those commitments. The need for civil society to engage in political accountability on human rights arises because the traditional accountability mechanisms of government are often not enough to guarantee freedom from domination by the executive. However, the willingness of civil society members to act as agents of accountability and organise against the executive government over human rights concerns, and their effectiveness when they do so, is not guaranteed. Activism is easier under certain domestic political and legal conditions that enhance civil society's beliefs in its own legitimacy and capacities.

The norm against torture underwent serious challenges after 11 September 2001, and revealed how tenuous are shared understandings about the absolute prohibition of torture. Some scholars have argued that there are reasons to be optimistic, that such was the revulsion after details of US torture of detainees were revealed, common beliefs that torture should never be used have been reinforced.[55] Continuing debates in the US about torture's utility, including among presidential candidates in the 2016 general election and from former officials from the Bush Administration era, suggest that understandings about the ban on its use are far from settled.[56] As states adjust their laws and practices to deal with evolving national security threats, the capacity for civil society to act as a site for the checking of arbitrary power is critical.

[55] Jutta Brunnée and Stephen J Toope, *Legitimacy and Legality in International Law: An Interactional Account* (New York, NY: Cambridge University Press, 2010) 268.

[56] Ben Jacobs, 'Donald Trump on waterboarding: "Even if it doesn't work they deserve it"', *Guardian*, 24 November 2015; George Tenet et al, 'Ex-CIA directors: Interrogations saved lives', *Wall Street Journal*, 10 December 2014, 19.

BIBLIOGRAPHY

Abel, Richard L, 'Contesting legality in the United States after September 11' in *Fighting for Political Freedom: Comparative Studies of the Legal Complex and Political Liberalism*, ed Terence C Halliday, Lucien Karpik and Malcolm M Feely (Oxford: Hart Publishing, 2007) 361–99.

Ackleson, Jason, 'From "thin" to "thick" (and back again?): The politics and policies of the contemporary US-Canada border', *American Review of Canadian Studies* 39(4) (2009), 336–51.

Alston, Philip and Ryan Goodman, *International Human Rights: The Successor to International Human Rights in Context* (Oxford: Oxford University Press, 2013).

Andreopoulos, George, Zehra F Kabasakal Arat and Peter Juviler (eds), *Non-State Actors in the Human Rights Universe* (Bloomfield, CT: Kumarian Press, 2006).

Arat, Zehra F Kabasakal, 'Looking beyond the state but not ignoring it' in *Non-State Actors in the Human Rights Universe*, ed George Andreopoulos, Zehra F Kabasakal Arat and Peter Juviler (Bloomfield, CT: Kumarian Press, 2006) 3–21.

Arblaster, Anthony, *The Rise and Decline of Western Liberalism* (Oxford: Basil Blackwell, 1984).

Aroney, Nicholas, Scott Prasser and JR Nethercote (eds), *Restraining Elective Dictatorship: The Upper House Solution?* (Crawley, WA: University of Western Australia Press, 2008).

Ayres, Jeffrey M, 'Political economy, civil society, and the deep integration debate in Canada', *American Review of Canadian Studies* 34(4) (2004), 621–47.

Azmy, Baher, 'An insufficiently accountable presidency: some reflections on Jack Goldsmith's power and constraint', *Case Western Reserve Journal of International Law* 45(1&2) (2012), 23–63.

Bagaric, Mirko and Julie Clarke, 'Not enough official torture in the world? The circumstances in which torture is morally justifiable', *University of San Francisco Law Review* 39(3) (2005), 581–616.

Bakir, Vian, 'News, agenda building, and intelligence agencies: A systematic review of the field from the discipline of journalism, media, and communications', *The International Journal of Press/Politics* 20(2) (2015), 131–44.

Barnett, Michael, 'Building a Republican peace: Stabilizing states after war', *International Security* 30(4) (2006), 87–112.

Barry, Donald and Duane Bratt, 'Defense against help: Explaining Canada-US Relations', *American Review of Canadian Studies* 38(1) (2008), 63–89.

Begg, Moazzam, *Enemy Combatant: The Terrifying True Story of a Briton in Guantánamo* (London: Pocket Books, 2006).

Beitz, Charles R, *The Idea of Human Rights* (Oxford: Oxford University Press, 2009).

Benhabib, Seyla, *The Rights of Others: Aliens, Residents and Citizens* (New York, NY: Cambridge University Press, 2004).

Bennoune, Karima, *Your Fatwa Does Not Apply Here* (New York, NY: WW Norton & Company, 2013).

Berlin, Isaiah, 'Two concepts of liberty' in *Liberty: Isaiah Berlin*, ed Henry Hardy (Oxford: Oxford University Press 2002 [1958]) 166–217.

Bernstein, Benjamin, 'Over before it even began: Mohamed v Jeppesen Dataplan and the use of the state secrets privilege in extraordinary rendition cases', *Fordham International Law Journal* 34(5) (2011), 1400–429.

Blair, Tony, *A Journey* (London: Hutchinson, 2010).

Bob, Clifford, *The Marketing of Rebellion: Insurgents, Media, and International Activism* (New York, NY: Cambridge University Press, 2005).

Bovens, Mark, Robert E Goodin and Thomas Schillemans (eds), *The Oxford Handbook of Public Accountability* (Oxford: Oxford University Press, 2014).

Bovens, Mark, Thomas Schillemans and Robert E Goodin, 'Public accountability' in *The Oxford Handbook of Public Accountability*, ed Mark Bovens, Robert E Goodin and Thomas Schillemans (Oxford: Oxford University Press, 2014) 1–22.

Braithwaite, John, Hilary Charlesworth and Aderito Soares, *Networked Governance of Freedom and Tyranny: Peace in Timor-Leste* (Canberra: ANU E Press, 2012).

Brittain, Victoria, 'Besieged in Britain', *Race & Class* 50(3) (2009), 1–29.

Brock, Kathy L (ed), *Delicate Dances: Public Policy and the Non-Profit Sector* (Montreal: McGill-Queen's University Press, 2003).

Brunnée, Jutta and Stephen J Toope, *Legitimacy and Legality in International Law: An Interactional Account* (New York, NY: Cambridge University Press, 2010).

Brysk, Alison, *Global Good Samaritans: Human Rights as Foreign Policy* (New York, NY: Oxford University Press, 2009).

Bukovansky, Mlada, 'Liberal states, international order, and legitimacy: An appeal for persuasion over prescription', *International Politics* 44(2–3) (2007), 175–93.

Burke, Anthony, *In Fear of Security: Australia's Invasion Anxiety* (Sydney: Pluto Press, 2001).

Campbell, Tom, 'Human rights-based judicial review: It seems a good idea at the time', *Dissent* (Spring 2008), 3–15.

Campbell, Tom, Jeffrey Goldsworthy and Adrienne Stone, *Protecting Human Rights: Instruments and Institutions* (Oxford: Oxford University Press, 2003).

Carne, Greg, 'Is near enough good enough?—Implementing Australia's international human rights torture criminalisation and prohibition obligations in the criminal code (Cth)', *Adelaide Law Review* 33(1) (2012), 229–70.

Carpenter, R Charli, 'Setting the advocacy agenda: Theorizing issue emergence and nonemergence in transnational advocacy networks', *International Studies Quarterly* 51(1) (2007), 99–120.

Cellucci, Paul, *Unquiet Diplomacy* (Toronto: Key Porter Books, 2007).

Charlesworth, Hilary, *Writing in Rights: Australia and the Protection of Human Rights* (Sydney: UNSW Press, 2002).

Charters, David A, 'The (Un) Peaceable Kingdom? Terrorism and Canada Before 9/11,' *IRPP Policy Matters* 9 (4) (2008), 1–43.

Charters, David A (ed), *The Deadly Sin of Terrorism: Its Effect on Democracy and Civil Liberty in Six Countries* (Westport, CT: Greenwood Press, 1994).

Chrétien, Jean, *My Years as Prime Minister* (Toronto: Vintage Canada, 2008 [2007]).

Clark, Kathleen, 'Ethical issues raised by the OLC torture memorandum', *Journal of National Security Law & Policy* 1(1) (2005), 455–72.

Coates, David and Joel Krieger with Rhiannon Vickers, *Blair's War* (Cambridge: Polity, 2004).

Cobain, Ian, *A Secret History of Torture* (Berkeley, CA: Counterpoint, 2012).

Cody, Howard, 'Stephen Harper, Michael Ignatieff, and Canada's politics of identity', *Southern Journal of Canadian Studies* 3(1) (2010), 17–27.

Cohen, Jean, *Globalization and Sovereignty: Rethinking Legality, Legitimacy, and Constitutionalism* (New York, NY: Cambridge University Press, 2012).

Cohen, Jean and Andrew Arato, *Civil Society and Political Theory* (Cambridge, MA: MIT Press, 1992).

Cohn, Marjorie (ed), *The United States and Torture: Interrogations, Incarceration, and Abuse* (New York, NY: New York University Press, 2011).

Cole, David, *Engines of Liberty: The Power of Citizen Activists to make Constitutional Law* (New York, NY: Basic Books, 2016).

——, *The Torture Memos: Rationalizing the Unthinkable* (New York, NY: The New Press, 2009).

——, 'The taint of torture: The roles of law and policy in our descent to the dark side', *Houston Law Review* 49(1) (2012), 53–69.

——, 'Where liberty lies: Civil society and individual rights after 9/11', *Wayne Law Review* 57(4) (2011), 1203–267.

Cole, David and Jules Lobel, *Less Safe, Less Free: Why America is Losing the War on Terror* (New York, NY: The New Press, 2007).

Cook, Robin, *The Point of Departure: Why One of Britain's Leading Politicians Resigned over Tony Blair's Decision to go to War in Iraq* (London: Simon & Schuster, 2003).

Cooley, Alexander and Ron James, 'The NGO scramble: Organizational insecurity and the political economy of transnational action', *International Security* 27(1) (2002), 5–39.

Cordelli, Chiara, 'How privatization threatens the private', *Critical Review of International Social and Political Philosophy* 16(1) (2013), 65–87.

Crawford, Neta C, *Argument and Change in World Politics: Ethics, Decolonization, and Humanitarian Intervention* (Cambridge: Cambridge University Press, 2002).

Cruft, Rowan, S Matthew Liao and Massimo Renzo (eds), *Philosophical Foundations of Human Rights* (Oxford: Oxford University Press, 2015).

Dai, Xinyuan, 'The conditional effects of international human rights', *Human Rights Quarterly* 36(3) (2014), 569–89.

——, 'The conditional nature of democratic compliance', *Journal of Conflict Resolution* 50(5) (2006), 690–713.

Danchev, Alex, 'Accomplicity: Britain, torture and terror', *The British Journal of Politics and International Relations* 8(4) (2006), 587–601.

Danner, Mark, *Torture and Truth: America, Abu Ghraib, and the War on Terror* (New York, NY: New York Review of Books, 2004).

De Londras, Fiona and Fergal F Davis, 'Controlling the executive in times of terrorism: Competing perspectives on effective oversight mechanisms', *Oxford Journal of Legal Studies* 30(1) (2010), 19–47.

Denbeaux, Mark and Jonathan Hafetz, *The Guantánamo Lawyers: Inside a Prison Outside the Law* (New York. NY: New York University Press, 2009).

Dershowitz, Alan M, *Why Terrorism Works: Understanding the Threat, Responding to the Challenge* (New Haven. CT: Yale University Press, 2002).

Dershowitz, Alan, 'Tortured reasoning' in *Torture: A Collection*, ed Sanford Levinson (New Haven, CT: Oxford University Press, 2004) 257–80.

Doern, G Bruce (ed), *How Ottawa Spends 2003–2004: Regime Change and Policy Shift* (Don Mills, Ontario: Oxford University Press, 2003).

Donnelly, Jack, 'The virtues of legalization' in *The Legalization of Human Rights: Multidisciplinary Perspectives on Human Rights and Human Rights Law*, ed Saladin Meckled-Garcia and Basak Cali (New York, NY: Routledge, 2006) 67–80.

Dore, Christopher, 'What to do with Omar Khadr? Putting a child soldier on trial: Questions of international law, juvenile justice, and moral culpability', *Marshall Law Review* 41(4) (2007–2008), 1281–320.

Dryzek, John, David Downes, Christian Hunold and David Schlosberg, with Hans-Kristian Hernes, *Green States and Social Movements: Environmentalism in the United States, United Kingdom, Germany and Norway* (Oxford: Oxford University Press, 2003).

Duffy, Helen and Stephen A Kostas, '"Extraordinary rendition": A challenge for the rule of law' in *Counter-Terrorism: International Law and Practice*, ed Ana Maria Salinas de Frias, Katja LH Samuel and Nigel D White (New York, NY: Oxford University Press, 2012) 539–78.

Duffy, Helen, *The 'War on Terror' and the Framework of International Law* (New York, NY: Cambridge University Press, 2005).

——, 'Human rights litigation and the "war on terror"', *International Review of the Red Cross* 90(871) (2008), 573–97.

Dumbrell, John, 'Working with allies: The United States, the United Kingdom, and the war on terror', *Politics & Policy* 34(2) (2006), 452–72.

Dunne, Tim, '"The rules of the game are changing": Fundamental human rights in crisis after 9/11', *International Politics* 44(2–3) (2007), 269–86.

——, '"When the shooting starts": Atlanticism in British security strategy', *International Affairs* 80(5) (2004), 893–909.

Dworkin, Ronald, 'Why it was a great victory', *New York Review of Books*, 14 August 2008.

Elkins, David and Richard Simeon, 'A cause in search of its effect, or what does political culture explain?', *Comparative Politics* 11(2) (1979), 127–45.

Elshtain, Jean Bethke, 'Reflection on the problem of "dirty hands"' in *Torture: A Collection*, ed Sanford Levinson (New York, NY: Oxford University Press, 2004) 77–89.

Emy, Hugh V and Owen E Hughes, *Australia Politics: Realities in Conflict* (Melbourne: The Macmillan Company of Australia, 1988).

Epp, Charles R, *The Rights Revolution: Lawyers, Activists, and Supreme Courts in Comparative Perspective* (Chicago, IL: University of Chicago Press, 1998).

——, 'Do bills of rights matter? The Canadian Charter of Rights and Freedoms', *American Political Science Review* 90(4) (1996), 765–79.

Evans, Harry, 'The case for bicameralism' in *Restraining Elective Dictatorship: The Upper House Solution?* ed Nicholas Aroney, Scott Prasser and JR Nethercote (Crawley: University of Western Australia Press, 2008) 67–80.

Fallon, Richard H, 'The Supreme Court, Habeas Corpus, and the war on terror: An essay on law and political science', *Columbia Law Review* 110(2) (2010), 352–98.

Feldman, David, 'Democracy, law, and human rights: Politics as challenge and opportunity' in *Parliament and Human Rights*, ed Murray Hunt, Hayley J Hopper and Paul Yowell (Oxford: Hart Publishing, 2015) 95–113.

Finnemore, Martha, 'Legitimacy, hypocrisy, and the social structure of unipolarity: Why being a unipole isn't all it's cracked up to be', *World Politics* 61(1) (2009), 58–85.

Franklin, Mark N, Stuart Soroka and Christopher Wlezien, 'Elections' in *The Oxford Handbook of Public Accountability*, ed Mark Bovens, Robert E Goodin and Thomas Schillemans (Oxford: Oxford University Press, 2014) 389–404.

Gal-Or, Noemi, 'Countering terrorism in Israel' in *The Deadly Sin of Terrorism: Its effect on Democracy and Civil Liberty in Six Countries*, ed David Charters (Westport, CT: Greenwood Press, 1994) 137–72.

Gamson, William A and David S Meyer, 'Framing political opportunity' in *Comparative Perspectives on Social Movements: Political Opportunities, Mobilizing Structures, and Cultural Framings*, ed Doug McAdam, John D McCarthy and Mayer N Zald (New York, NY: Cambridge University Press, 1996) 275–90.

Garran, Robert, *True Believer: John Howard, George Bush and the American Alliance* (Sydney: Allen & Unwin, 2004).

Gearty, Conor, '11 September 2001, Counter-terrorism, and the Human Rights Act', *Journal of Law and Society* 32(1) (2005), 18–33.

Geertz, Clifford, *The Interpretation of Cultures* (New York, NY: Basic Books, 1973).

Gellner, Ernest, *Conditions of Liberty: Civil Society and its Rivals* (London: Penguin Books, 1996 [1994]).

Goldsmith, Jack, *Power and Constraint: The Accountable Presidency after 9/11* (New York, NY: WW Norton & Company, 2012).

——, *The Terror Presidency: Law and Judgment Inside the Bush Administration* (New York, NY: WW Norton & Company, 2009 [2007]).

Goodman, Ryan and Thomas Pegram (eds), *Human Rights, State Compliance, and Social Change: Assessing National Human Rights Institutions* (New York, NY: Cambridge University Press, 2012).

Gordon, Philip and Jeremy Shapiro, *Allies at War America, Europe, and the Crisis over Iraq* (New York. NY: McGraw-Hill, 2004).

Gray, John, *Liberalism* (Milton Keynes: Open University Press, 1986).

——, *Two Faces of Liberalism* (New York, NY: The New Press, 2000).

Greenberg, Karen J (ed), *The Torture Debate in America* (New York, NY: Cambridge University Press, 2006).

Greenberg, Karen J and Joshua L Dratel (eds), *The Torture Papers: The Road to Abu Ghraib* (New York, NY: Cambridge University Press, 2005).

Habermas, Jurgen, 'The Public Sphere' in *Jurgen Habermas on Society and Politics: A Reader*, ed Steven Seidman (Boston, MA: Beacon Press, 2005) 231–36.

Habib, Mamdouh with Julia Collingwood, *My Story: The Tale of a Terrorist Who Wasn't* (Melbourne: Scribe, 2008).

Hafetz, Jonathan, *Habeas Corpus After 9/11: Confronting America's New Global Detention System* (New York, NY: New York University Press, 2011).

——, 'Resisting accountability: Transitional justice in the post-9/11 United States', *The International Journal of Human Rights* 19(4) (2014), 429–46.

Hall, Peter A, *Governing the Economy: The Politics of State Intervention in Britain and France* (Cambridge: Polity Press, 1986).

——, 'The movement from Keynesianism to monetarism: Institutional analysis and British economic policy in the 1970s' in *Structuring Politics: Historical Institutionalism in Comparative Analysis*, ed Sven Steinmo, Kathleen Thelen and Frank Longstreth (Cambridge: Cambridge University Press, 1992) 90–113.

Halliday, Simon and Patrick Schmidt (eds), *Human Rights Brought Home: Socio-Legal Studies of Human Rights in the National Context* (Portland, OR: Hart Publishing, 2004).

Halliday, Terence C, Lucien Karpik and Malcolm M Feely (eds), *Fighting for Political Freedom: Comparative Studies of the Legal Complex and Political Liberalism* (Oxford: Hart Publishing, 2007).

Hardy, Henry (ed), *Liberty: Isaiah Berlin* (Oxford: Oxford University Press, 2002 [1958]).

Hartog, Hendrik, 'The constitution of aspiration and "the rights that belong to us all"', *The Journal of American History* 74(3) (1987), 1013–1034.

Hartz, Louis, *The Founding of New Societies: Studies in the History of the United States, Latin America, South Africa, Canada and Australia* (New York, NY: Harcourt Brace Jovanovich, 1964).

——, 'The fragmentation of European culture and ideology' in *The Founding of New Societies: Studies in the History of the United States, Latin America, South Africa, Canada and Australia* (New York, NY: Harcourt Brace Jovanovich, 1964) 3–23.

Harvey, Frank P, 'Canada's addiction to American security: The illusion of choice in the war on terrorism', *The American Review of Canadian Studies* 35(2) (2005), 265–94.

Hathaway, Oona A, 'Do human rights treaties make a difference?', *The Yale Law Journal* 111(8) (2002), 1935–2042.

Hawes, Michael K, 'Introduction: Managing Canada-US relations in difficult times', *The American Review of Canadian Studies* 34(4) (2004), 593–602.

Hewitt, Steve, *The British War on Terror: Terrorism and Counter-Terrorism on the Home Front Since 9/11* (London: Continuum, 2008).

Hicks, David, *Guantánamo: My Journey* (Sydney: William Heinemann, 2010).

Hiebert, Janet L, 'Governing under the Human Rights Act: The limitations of wishful thinking', *Public Law* 27 (January 2012), 27–44.

——, 'Parliamentary review of terrorism measures', *The Modern Law Review* 68(4) (2005), 676–80.

Hirst, John, *Sense and Nonsense in Australian History* (Melbourne: Black Inc Agenda, 2005).

Hocking, Jenny, 'Academic freedom in Australia in an age of terror' in *Free Speech in Fearful Times: After 9/11 in Canada, the US, Australia and Europe*, ed James L Turk and Allan Manson (Toronto: James Lorimer and Company Ltd, 2007) 216–33.

Holmes, Stephen, *Passions and Constraint: On the Theory of Liberal Democracy* (Chicago, IL: University of Chicago Press, 1995).

Hopgood, Stephen, *Keepers of the Flame: Understanding Amnesty International* (Ithaca, NY: Cornell University Press, 2006).

Howard, John, *Lazarus Rising: A Personal and Political Autobiography* (Sydney: Harper Collins Publishers, 2010).

Hunt, Murray, 'Introduction' in *Parliament and Human Rights*, ed Murray Hunt, Hayley J Hopper and Paul Yowell (Oxford: Hart Publishing 2015) 1–25.

——, Hayley J Hopper and Paul Yowell (eds), *Parliament and Human Rights* (Oxford: Hart Publishing, 2015).

Ignatieff, Michael, *The Rights Revolution* (Toronto: House of Anansi Press, 2007 [2000]).

——, *The Lesser Evil: Political Ethics in an Age of Terror* (Edinburgh: Edinburgh University Press, 2005).

Ikenberry, G John, 'Conclusion: An institutional approach to American foreign policy', *International Organization* 42(1) (1988), 219–43.

Ip, John, 'The Supreme Court and House of Lords in the war on terror: Inter Arma Silent Leges?', *Michigan State Journal of International Law* 19(1) (2010), 1–61.

Jackson, Richard, 'Language, policy and the construction of a torture culture in the war on terrorism', *Review of International Studies* 33(3) (2007), 353–71.

Jetschke, Anja and Andrea Liese, 'The power of human rights a decade after: From euphoria to contestation?' in *The Persistent Power of Human Rights: From Commitment to Compliance*, ed Thomas Risse, Stephen C Ropp and Kathryn Sikkink (New York, NY: Cambridge University Press, 2013) 26–42.

Jiwani, Yasmin, 'Omar Khadr, The carceral net, and the Muslim body' in *Omar Khadr, Oh Canada*, ed Janice Williamson (Montreal: McGill-Queen's University Press, 2012) 376–89.

Kahn, Paul W, *Sacred Violence: Torture, Terror, and Sovereignty* (Ann Arbor, MI: University of Michigan Press, 2008).

Kaldor, Mary, *Global Civil Society: An Answer to War* (Cambridge: Polity, 2003).

Kampfner, John, *Blair's Wars* (London: Free Press, 2004).

Katzenstein, Peter, 'Introduction: Alternative Perspectives on National Security' in *The Culture of National Security: Norms and Identity in World Politics*, ed Peter Katzenstein (New York, NY: Columbia University Press, 1996) 1–32.

——, 'The West as Anglo-America' in *Anglo-America and its Discontents: Civilizational Identities Beyond West and East*, ed Peter Katzenstein (New York, NY: Routledge, 2012) 1–30.

—— (ed), *Anglo-America and its Discontents: Civilizational Identities beyond West and East* (New York, NY: Routledge, 2012).

—— (ed), *The Culture of National Security: Norms and Identity in World Politics* (New York, NY: Columbia University Press, 1996).

Kavanagh, Aileen, 'The Joint Committee on Human Rights: A hybrid breed of constitutional watchdog' in *Parliament and Human Rights*, ed Murray Hunt, Hayley J Hopper and Paul Yowell (Oxford: Hart Publishing, 2015) 115–39.

Keck, Margaret E and Kathryn Sikkink, *Activists beyond Borders* (Ithaca, NY: Cornell University Press, 1998).

——, 'Transnational advocacy networks in the movement society' in *The Social Movement Society: Contentious Politics for a New Century*, ed David S Meyer and Sidney Tarrow (Lanham, MD: Rowman and Littlefield Publishers, 1998) 217–38.

Keeble, Richard (ed), *Communication Ethics Now* (Leicester: Troubadour Publishing Ltd, 2008).

Keith, Linda Camp, 'The United Nations International Covenant on Civil and Political Rights: Does it make a difference in human rights behaviour?', *Journal of Peace Research* 36(1) (1999), 95–118.

Keith, Linda Camp, Banks P Miller and Jennifer Holmes, 'How draconian are the changes to US asylum law? A monthly time series analysis', *Human Rights Quarterly* 37(1) (2015), 153–87.

Kelly, Paul, *The March of the Patriots: The Struggle for Modern Australia* (Melbourne: Melbourne University Press, 2009).

Kelly, Tobias, *This Side of Silence: Human Rights, Torture, and the Recognition of Cruelty* (Philadelphia, PA: University of Pennsylvania Press, 2012).

Kendall, Jeremy, 'The mainstreaming of the third sector into public policy in England in the late 1990s: Whys and wherefores', *Policy & Politics* 28(4) (2000), 541–62.

Kende, Mark, 'The US Supreme Court, the war on terror, and the need for thick constitutional review', *Mississippi Law Journal* 80(4) (2011), 1–23.

Kennedy-Pipe, Caroline and Andrew Mumford, 'Torture, rights, rules and wars: Ireland to Iraq', *International Relations* 21(1) (2007), 119–26.

Kettell, Steven, *New Labour and the New World Order: Britain's Role in the War on Terror* (Manchester: Manchester University Press, 2011).

Kinley, David, 'Finding and filling the democratic deficit in human rights' in *Parliament and Human Rights*, ed Murray Hunt, Hayley J Hopper and Paul Yowell (Oxford: Hart Publishing, 2015) 29–37.

Kinley, David and Christine Ernst, 'Exile on Main Street: Australia's legislative agenda for human rights', *European Human Rights Law Review* 1 (2012), 158–70.

Klein, Woody, *The Inside Story of Modern Political Scandals* (Santa Barbara, CA: Praeger, 2010).

Koh, Harold Hongju, 'Friedmann Award Essay: A world without torture', *Columbia Journal of Transnational Law* 43(3) (2004), 641–61.

Kornberg, Allan and Harold D Clarke, *Citizens and Community: Political Support in a Representative Democracy* (Cambridge: Cambridge University Press, 1992).

Krook, Mona Lena and Jacqui True, 'Rethinking the life cycles of international norms: The United Nations and the global promotion of gender equality', *European Journal of International Relations* 18(1) (2010), 103–27.

Langbein, John H, *Torture and the Law of Proof: Europe and England in the Ancien Regime* (Chicago, IL: University of Chicago Press, 2006 [1976]).

Langmore, John, *Dealing with America: The UN, the US and Australia* (Sydney: UNSW Press, 2005).

Larkin, Phil and John Uhr, 'Bipartisanship, partnership and bicameralism in Australia's "war on terror": Forcing limits on the extension of executive power' in *The 'War on Terror' and the Growth of Executive Power*, ed John E Owens and Riccardo Pelizzo (New York, NY: Routledge, 2010) 136–56.

Lasner, Thomas R, 'No empty vessel—media roles in human rights' in *Non-State Actors in the Human Rights Universe*, ed George Andreopoulos, Zehra F Kabasakal Arat and Peter Juviler (Bloomfield, CT: Kumarian Press, 2006) 249–71.

Levinson, Sanford (ed), *Torture: A Collection* (New York: Oxford University Press, 2004).

Lewis, Jane, 'Reviewing the relationship between the voluntary sector and the state in Britain in the 1990s', *International Journal of Voluntary and Non-Profit Organizations* 10(3) (1999), 255–69.

Liese, Andrea, 'Exceptional necessity: How liberal democracies contest the prohibition of torture and ill-treatment when countering terrorism', *Journal of International Law and International Relations* 5(1) (2009), 17–47.

Lipset, Seymour Martin, *Continental Divide: The Values and Institutions of the United States and Canada* (New York: Routledge, 1990).

Locke, John, *Two Treatises of Government*, ed Peter Laslett (Cambridge: Cambridge University Press, 1988 [1689]).

——, 'Second treatise,' *Two Treatises of Government*, ed Peter Laslett (Cambridge: Cambridge University Press, 1988 [1689]) 265–428.

Louis, WM Roger and Hedley Bull, *The Special Relationship: Anglo-American Relations Since 1945* (Oxford: Clarendon Press, 1986).

Luban, David, 'Human rights pragmatism and human dignity' in *Philosophical Foundations of Human Rights*, ed Rowan Cruft, S Matthew Liao and Massimo Renzo (Oxford: Oxford University Press, 2015) 263–78.

——, 'Liberalism, torture, and the ticking bomb' in *The Torture Debate in America*, ed Karen J Greenberg (New York, NY: Cambridge University Press, 2006) 35–83.

——, 'Liberalism, torture, and the ticking bomb', *Virginia Law Review* 91(6) (2005), 1425–61.

MacDonald, David and Brendan O'Connor, 'Special relationships: Australia and New Zealand in the Anglo-American world' in *Anglo-America and its Discontents: Civilizational Identities Beyond West and East*, ed Peter Katzenstein (New York, NY: Routledge, 2012) 176–203.

Macklin, Audrey, 'The rule of law, the force of law, and the rule of force' in *Omar Khadr, Oh Canada*, ed Janice Williamson (Montreal: McGill-Queen's University Press, 2012) 222–46.

——, 'Comment on *Canada (Prime Minister) v Khadr* (2010)', *Supreme Court Law Review* 51 (2010), 295–331.

——, 'From cooperation, to complicity, to compensation: The war on terror, extraordinary rendition, and the cost of torture', *European Journal of Migration and Law* 10(1) (2008), 11–30.

Maddison, Sarah and Greg Martin, 'Introduction to "Surviving neoliberalism: The persistence of Australian social movements"', *Social Movement Studies: Journal of Social, Cultural and Political Protest* 9(2) (2010), 101–20.

Maiman, Richard J, '"We've had to raise our game": Liberty's litigation strategy under the Human Rights Act 1998' in *Human Rights Brought Home: Socio-Legal Studies of Human Rights in the National Context*, ed Simon Halliday and Patrick Schmidt (Portland, OR: Hart Publishing, 2004) 87–109.

Malloy, Jonathan, 'Canada's "war on terror", parliamentary assertiveness and minority government' in *The 'War on Terror' and the Growth of Executive Power*, ed John E Owens and Riccardo Pelizzo (New York, NY: Routledge, 2010) 157–80.

March, James G and Johan P Olsen, 'The logic of appropriateness' in *The Oxford Handbook of Public Policy*, ed Michael Moran, Martin Rein and Robert Goodin (Oxford: Oxford University Press, 2008 [2006]) 689–708.

Margulies, Joseph, *Guantánamo and the Abuse of Presidential Power* (New York NY: Simon & Schuster Paperbacks, 2006).

Marr, David and Marian Wilkinson, *Dark Victory* (Sydney: Allen & Unwin, 2003).

Martin, Paul, *Hell or High Water: My Life In and Out of Politics* (Toronto: Emblem/McClelland and Stewart, 2009 [2008]).

Mayer, Jane, *The Dark Side: The Inside Story of How the War on Terror Turned into a War on American Ideals* (New York, NY: Doubleday, 2008).

Mayerfeld, Jamie, 'Playing by our own rules: How US marginalization of international human rights law led to torture', *Harvard Human Rights Journal* 20 (2007), 89–140.

Mazigh, Monia, *Hope and Despair: My Struggle to Free My Husband, Maher Arar* (Toronto: McClelland and Stewart, 2008).

McAdam, Doug, John D McCarthy and Mayer N Zald (eds), *Comparative Perspectives on Social Movements: Political Opportunities, Mobilizing Structures, and Cultural Framings* (New York, NY: Cambridge University Press, 1996).

McAdam, Douglas, Sidney Tarrow and Charles Tilly, *Dynamics of Contention* (New York, NY: Cambridge University Press, 2001).

McCormack, Timothy, 'David Hicks and the charade of Guantánamo Bay', *Melbourne Journal of International Law* 8(2) (2007), 273–91.

McCoy, Alfred, *A Question of Torture: CIA Interrogation, from the Cold War to the War on Terror* (New York, NY: Holt Paperbacks, 2006).

——, 'Mind maze: The CIA's pursuit of psychological torture' in *The United States and Torture: Interrogations, Incarceration, and Abuse*, ed Marjorie Cohn (New York, NY: New York University Press, 2011) 25–52.

McRae, Kenneth D, 'The structure of Canadian history' in *The Founding of New Societies: Studies in the History of the United States, Latin America, South Africa, Canada and Australia*, ed Louis Hartz (New York, NY: Harcourt Brace Jovanovich, 1964) 219–74.

Meckled-Garcia, Saladin and Basak Cali (eds), *The Legalization of Human Rights: Multidisciplinary Perspectives on Human Rights and Human Rights Law* (New York, NY: Routledge, 2006).

Merry, Sally Engle, *Human Rights and Gender Violence: Translating International Law into Local Justice* (Chicago, IL: University of Chicago Press, 2006).

——, 'Transnational human rights and local activism: Mapping the middle', *American Anthropologist* 108(1) (2006), 38–51.

Mertus, Julie A, *Bait and Switch: Human Rights and US Foreign Policy*, 2nd edn (New York, NY: Routledge, 2008).

——, 'Human rights and civil society in a new age of American exceptionalism' in *Human Rights in the 'War on Terror'*, ed Richard Ashby Wilson (New York, NY: Cambridge University Press, 2005) 317–33.

Meyer, David S, 'National human rights institutions, opportunities, and activism' in *Human Rights, State Compliance, and Social Change: Assessing National Human Rights Institutions*, ed Ryan Goodman and Thomas Pegram (New York, NY: Cambridge University Press, 2012) 324–34.

Meyer, David S and Sidney Tarrow, *The Social Movement Society: Contentious Politics for a New Century* (Lanham, MD: Rowman and Littlefield Publishers, 1998).

Moore, Mark H, 'Accountability, legitimacy, and the court of public opinion' in *The Oxford Handbook of Public Accountability*, ed Mark Bovens, Robert E Goodin and Thomas Schillemans (Oxford: Oxford University Press, 2014) 632–46.

Moran, Michael, Martin Rein and Robert Goodin (eds), *The Oxford Handbook of Public Policy* (Oxford: Oxford University Press, 2008).

Moravcsik, Andrew, 'The new liberalism' in *The Oxford Handbook of International Relations*, ed Christian Reus-Smit and Duncan Snidal (Oxford: Oxford University Press, 2008) 234–54.

——, 'The origins of human rights regimes: Democratic delegation in postwar Europe', *International Organization* 54(2) (2000), 217–52.

——, 'Taking preferences seriously: A liberal theory of international politics', *International Organization* 51(4) (1997), 513–53.

Morton, FL and Rainer Knopff, *The Charter Revolution and the Court Party* (Toronto: Broadview Press, 2000).

Mouffe, Chantal, *The Democratic Paradox* (London: Verso, 2000).

Mumford, Andrew, 'Minimum force meets brutality: Detention, interrogation and torture in British counter-insurgency campaigns', *Journal of Military Ethics* 11(1) (2012), 10–25.

Münch, Richard and Neil J Smelser (eds), *Theory of Culture* (Berkeley, CA: University of California Press, 1992).

Mutua, Makau, 'Human rights international NGOs: A critical evaluation' in *NGOs and Human Rights: Promise and Performance*, ed Claude E Welch, (Philadelphia, PA: University of Pennsylvania Press, 2001) 151–63.

Nash, Kate, *The Cultural Politics of Human Rights: Comparing the US and UK* (New York, NY: Cambridge University Press, 2009).

Neumayer, Eric, 'Do international human rights treaties improve respect for human rights?', *Journal of Conflict Resolution* 49(6) (2005), 925–53.

Ní Aoláin, Fionnuala, 'The European Convention on Human Rights and its torture prohibitions' in *Torture: A Collection*, ed Sanford Levinson (New York, NY: Oxford University Press, 2004) 213–27.

Nicol, Danny, 'The Human Rights Act and the politicians', *Legal Studies* 24(3) (2004), 451–79.

Norris, Pippa, 'Watchdog journalism' in *The Oxford Handbook of Public Accountability*, ed Mark Bovens, Robert E Goodin and Thomas Schillemans (Oxford: Oxford University Press, 2014) 525–41.

Norton, Philip, *Parliament in British Politics* (London: Palgrave MacMillan, 2005).

Nossal, Kim Richard, 'Defense policy and the atmospherics of Canada–US relations: The case of Harper Conservatives', *American Review of Canadian Studies* 37(1) (2007), 23–34.

O'Connor, Michael P and Celia M Rumann, 'Into the fire: How to avoid getting burned by the same mistakes made fighting terrorism in Northern Ireland', *Cardozo Law Review* 24(4) (2003), 1657–751.

Oikarinen, Jarmo, 'Parliamentary oversight of counter-terrorism policies' in *Counter-Terrorism: International Law and Practice*, ed Ana Maria Salinas De Frias, Katja Samuel and Nigel D White (New York, NY: Oxford University Press, 2012) 936–64.

Owens, John E, 'Congressional acquiescence to presidentialism in the US "war on terror"' in *The 'War on Terror' and the Growth of Executive Power*, ed John E Owens and Riccardo Pelizzo (New York, NY: Routledge, 2010) 34–86.

Owens, John E and Riccardo Pelizzo, 'Introduction: The "war on terror" and the growth of executive power? A comparative analysis' in *The 'War on Terror' and the Growth of Executive Power*, ed John E Owens and Riccardo Pelizzo (New York, NY: Routledge, 2010) 1–32.

—— (eds), *The 'War on Terror' and the Growth of Executive Power: A Comparative Analysis* (New York, NY: Routledge, 2010).

Paris, Roland, 'Are Canadians still liberal internationalists? Foreign policy and public opinion in the Harper era', *International Journal* 69(3) (September 2014), 274–307.

Parmar, Inderjeet, '"I'm proud of the British Empire": Why Tony Blair backs George W Bush', *The Political Quarterly* 76(2) (2005), 218–31.

Parry, John T, *Understanding Torture: Law, Violence, and Political Identity* (Ann Arbor, MI: The University of Michigan Press, 2010).

——, 'The shape of modern torture: Extraordinary rendition and ghost detainees', *Melbourne Journal of International Law* 6(2) (2005), 516–33.

——, 'Escalation and necessity: Defining torture at home and abroad' in *Torture: A Collection*, ed Sanford Levinson (New York, NY: Oxford University Press, 2004) 145–64.

Pauly, Louis and Christian Reus-Smit, 'Negotiating Anglo-America: Australia, Canada and the United States' in *Anglo-America and its Discontents: Civilizational Identities beyond West and East*, ed Peter Katzenstein (New York, NY: Routledge, 2012) 127–51.

Peirce, Gareth, *Dispatches from the Dark Side: On Torture and the Death of Justice* (London: Verso, 2010).

Peruzzotti, Enrique, 'The societalization of horizontal accountability: Rights advocacy and the Defensor del Pueblo de la Nación in Argentina' in *Human Rights, State Compliance, and Social Change: Assessing National Human Rights Institutions*, ed Ryan Goodman and Thomas Pegram (New York, NY: Cambridge University Press, 2012) 243–69.

Peters, Edward, *Torture: Expanded Edition* (Philadelphia, PA: University of Pennsylvania Press, 1999 [1985]).

Phillips, Susan D, 'Canada: Civic society under neglect', *The Philanthropist* 23(1) (2010), 65–73.

——, 'In accordance: Canada's voluntary sector accord from idea to implementation' in *Delicate Dances: Public Policy and the Non-Profit Sector*, ed Kathy L Brock (Montreal: McGill-Queen's University Press, 2003) 17–61.

Pither, Kerry, *Dark Days: The Story of Four Canadians Tortured in the Name of Fighting Terror* (Toronto: Viking Canada, 2008).

Pitts, Jennifer, *A Turn to Empire: The Rise of Imperial Liberalism in Britain and France* (Princeton, NJ: Princeton University Press, 2005).

Pratt, Sheila, 'Khadr's Canadian defence: Two Edmonton lawyers, a professor, and the rule of law' in *Omar Khadr, Oh Canada*, ed Janice Williamson (Montreal: McGill-Queen's University Press, 2012) 210–21.

Price, Richard, 'Reversing the gun sights: Transnational civil society targets land mines', *International Organization* 52(3) (1998), 613–44.

Pye, Lucian W, 'Introduction: The elusive concept of culture and the vivid reality of personality', *Political Psychology* 18(2) (1997), 241–54.

——, 'Introduction: Political culture and political development' in *Political Culture and Political Development*, ed Lucian Pye and Sidney Verba (Princeton, NJ: Princeton University Press, 1965) 3–26.

Pye, Lucian W and Sidney Verba (eds), *Political Culture and Political Development* (Princeton, NJ: Princeton University Press, 1965).

Radin, Margaret, *Reinterpreting Property* (Chicago, IL: University of Chicago Press, 1993).

Ratner, Michael, 'From Guantánamo to Berlin: Protecting human rights after 9/11' in *The United States and Torture: Interrogations, Incarceration, and Abuse*, ed Marjorie Cohn (New York, NY: New York University Press, 2011) 203–14.

Rejali, Darius, *Torture and Democracy* (Princeton, NJ: Princeton University Press, 2007).

Reus-Smit, Christian, 'Human rights in a global ecumene', *International Affairs* 87(5) (2011), 1205–18.

Reus-Smit, Christian and Duncan Snidal (eds), *The Oxford Handbook of International Relations* (Oxford: Oxford University Press, 2008).

Rice, Condoleezza, *No Higher Honor: A Memoir of My Years in Washington* (New York, NY: Crown Publishers, 2011).

Rice, Simon and Scott Calnan, *Sustainable Advocacy: Capabilities and Attitudes of Australian Human Rights NGOs* (Sydney: Australian Human Rights Centre, 2007).

Riddell, Peter, *Hug Them Close: Blair, Clinton, Bush and the 'Special Relationship'* (London: Politico's, 2003).

Risse, Thomas and Kathryn Sikkink, 'Conclusions' in *The Persistent Power of Human Rights: From Commitment to Compliance*, ed Thomas Risse, Stephen C Ropp and Kathryn Sikkink (New York, NY: Cambridge University Press, 2013) 275–95.

Risse, Thomas, Stephen C Ropp and Kathryn Sikkink (eds), *The Persistent Power of Human Rights: From Commitment to Compliance* (New York, NY: Cambridge University Press, 2013).

Risse-Kappen, Thomas, 'Public opinion, domestic structure, and foreign policy in liberal democracies', *World Politics* 43(4) (1991), 479–512.

Roach, Kent, *The 9/11 Effect: Comparative Counter-Terrorism* (New York, NY: Cambridge University Press, 2011).

——, *September 11: Consequences for Canada* (Montreal: McGill-Queen's University Press, 2003).

——, 'The varied roles of courts and legislatures in rights protection' in *Parliament and Human Rights*, ed Murray Hunt, Hayley J Hopper and Paul Yowell (Oxford: Hart Publishing Ltd, 2015) 405–21.

——, 'Substitute justice? Challenges to American counterterrorism activities in Non-American courts', *Mississippi Law Journal* 82(5) (2013), 907–74.

——, 'Uneasy neighbors: Comparative American and Canadian counter-terrorism', *William Mitchell Law Review* 38(5) (2012), 1701–803.

——, 'The role and capacities of courts and legislatures in reviewing Canada's anti-terrorism law', *Windsor Review of Legal and Social Issues* 24 (2008), 5–56.

Ron, James and David Crow, 'Who trusts local human rights organizations?: Evidence from three world regions', *Human Rights Quarterly* 37 (2015), 188–239.

Rose, David, *Guantánamo: The War on Human Rights* (New York, NY: The New Press, 2004).

Rosecrance, Richard N, 'The radical culture of Australia' in *The Founding of New Societies: Studies in the History of the United States, Latin America, South Africa, Canada and Australia*, ed Louis Hartz (New York, NY: Harcourt Brace Jovanovich, 1964) 275–318.

Rumsfeld, Donald, *Known and Unknown: A Memoir* (New York, NY: Sentinel, 2011).

Said, Edward, *Orientalism* (London: Penguin Books, 2003 [1978]).

Sales, Leigh, *Detainee 002: The Case of David Hicks* (Melbourne: Melbourne University Press, 2007).

Salinas de Frias, Ana Maria, Katja LH Samuel and Nigel D White, *Counter-Terrorism: International Law and Practice* (New York, NY: Oxford University Press, 2012).

Samuel, Katja, 'The rule of law framework and its lacunae: Normative, interpretive, and/or policy created?' in *Counter-Terrorism: International Law and Practice*, ed Ana Maria Salinas de Frias, Katja LH Samuel and Nigel D White (New York, NY: Oxford University Press, 2012) 14–53.

Sands, Philippe, *Torture Team: Rumsfeld's Memo and the Betrayal of American Values* (New York, NY: Palgrave Macmillan, 2008).

——, *Lawless World* (New York, NY: Penguin Books, 2005).

——, 'Terrorists and torturers' in *The United States and Torture: Interrogations, Incarceration, and Abuse*, ed Marjorie Cohn (New York, NY: New York University Press, 2011) 261–80.

Sarup, Raj, 'Torture under the European Convention on Human Rights', *American Journal of International Law* 73(2) (1979), 267–76.

Sassen, Saskia, *Territory Authority Rights: From Medieval to Global Assemblages* (Princeton, NJ: Princeton University Press, 2008 [2006]).

Satterthwaite, Margaret L, 'Rendered meaningless: Extraordinary rendition and the rule of law', *The George Washington Law Review* 75 (2007), 1333–420.

Sawer, Marian, 'Populism and public choice in Australia and Canada: Turning equality-seekers into "special interests"' in *Us and Them: Anti-Elitism in Australia*, ed Marian Sawer and Barry Hindess (Perth: Curtin University of Technology, 2004) 33–55.

—— and Barry Hindess (eds), *Us and Them: Anti-Elitism in Australia* (Perth: Curtin University of Technology, 2004).

—— and David Laycock, 'Down with elites and up with inequality: Market populism in Australia and Canada', *Commonwealth and Comparative Politics* 47(2) (2009), 133–50.

Scheinin, Martin, 'Resisting panic: Lessons about the role of human rights during the long decade after 9/11' in *The Cambridge Companion to Human Rights Law*, ed Conor Gearty and Costa Douzinas (New York, NY: Cambridge University Press, 2012) 293–307.

Schmitt, Carl, *Political Theology*, trans George Schwab (Chicago, IL: University of Chicago Press, 2005 [1922]).

——, *The Concept of the Political*, trans George Schwab et al (Chicago, IL: University of Chicago Press, 1996 [1932]).

Schneiderman, David, 'Property rights and regulatory innovation comparing constitutional cultures', *International Journal of Constitutional Law* 4(2) (2006), 371–91.

Seidman, Steven (ed), *Jurgen Habermas on Society and Politics: A Reader* (Boston, MA: Beacon Press, 2005 [1989]).

Shephard, Mark, 'Parliamentary scrutiny and oversight of the British "war on terror": Surrendering power to parliament or *plus ça change*?' in *The 'War on Terror' and the Growth of Executive Power*, ed John E Owens and Riccardo Pelizzo (New York, NY: Routledge, 2010) 87–116.

Shephard, Michelle, *Guantánamo's Child* (Mississauga: John Wiley & Sons, 2008).

Shue, Henry, *Basic Rights: Subsistence, Affluence, and US Foreign Policy* (Princeton, NJ: Princeton University Press, 1996 [1980]).

——, 'Torture in dreamland: Disposing of the ticking bomb', *Case Western Reserve Journal of International Law* 37 (2&3) (2006), 231–39.

——, 'Torture' in *Torture: A Collection*, ed Sanford Levinson (New York, NY: Oxford University Press, 2004) 47–60.

——, 'Torture', *Philosophy and Public Affairs* 7(2) (1978), 124–43.

Sikkink, Kathryn, 'The United States and torture: Does the spiral model work?' in *The Persistent Power of Human Rights: From Commitment to Compliance*, ed Thomas Risse, Stephen C Ropp and Kathryn Sikkink (New York, NY: Cambridge University Press, 2013) 145–63.

Simmons, Beth A, *Mobilizing for Human Rights: International Law in Domestic Politics* (New York, NY: Cambridge University Press, 2009).

Singh, Uday Mehta, *Liberalism and Empire: A Study in Nineteenth-Century British Liberal Thought* (Chicago. IL: University of Chicago Press, 1999).

Slaughter, Anne-Marie, 'A liberal theory of international law', *American Society of International Law Proceedings* 94 (2000), 240–48.

Slaughter, Joseph, 'A question of narration: The voice in international human rights law', *Human Rights Quarterly* 19(2) (1997), 406–30.

Smelser, Neil J, 'Culture: Coherent or incoherent' in *Theory of Culture*, ed Richard Münch and Neil J Smelser (Berkeley, CA: University of California Press, 1992) 3–28.

Smith, David E, *The Canadian Senate in Bicameral Perspective* (Toronto: University of Toronto Press, 2003).

Snow, Dave and Bejamin Moffitt, 'Straddling the divide: Mainstream populism and conservatism in Howard's Australia and Harper's Canada', *Commonwealth and Comparative Politics* 50(3) (2012), 271–92.

Sokolsky, Joel J, 'Northern exposure? American homeland security and Canada', *International Journal* 60(1) (2004/2005), 35–52.

Soysal, Yasemin Nuhoglu, *Limits of Citizenship: Migrants and Postnational Membership in Europe* (Chicago, IL: University of Chicago Press, 1994).

Spiro, Peter J, 'Accounting for NGOs', *Chicago Journal of International Law* 3(1) (2002), 161–69.

Stein, Janice Gross and Eugene Lang, *The Unexpected War: Canada in Kandahar* (Toronto: Penguin Canada, 2007).

Steinmo, Sven, Kathleen Thelen and Frank Longstreth (eds), *Structuring Politics: Historical Institutionalism in Comparative Analysis* (Cambridge: Cambridge University Press, 1992).

Stephens, Philip, *Tony Blair: The Price of Leadership* (London: Politico's, 2004).

Steyn, Johan, 'Guantánamo Bay: The legal black hole', *International and Comparative Law Quarterly* 53(1) (2004), 1–15.

Strong, Tracy B, 'Foreword' in Carl Schmitt, *The Concept of the Political* (Chicago, IL: University of Chicago Press, 1996) ix–xxxi.

Sunstein, Cass R, 'Rights after Communism', *East European Constitutional Review* 4(1) (1995), 61–62.

Tarrow, Sidney, *Power in Movement: Social Movements and Contentious Politics*, 2nd edn (New York, NY: Cambridge University Press, 1998).

——, '"Aiming at a moving target": Social science and the recent rebellions in Eastern Europe', *Political Science and Politics* 24(1) (1991), 12–20.

——, 'National politics and collective action: Recent theory and research in Western Europe and the United States', *Annual Review of Sociology* 14 (1988), 421–40.

Tasioulas, John, 'Towards a philosophy of human rights', *Current Legal Problems* 65(1) (2012), 1–30.

Taylor, Charles, *Reconciling the Solitudes: Essays on Canadian Federalism and Nationalism* (Montreal: McGill-Queen's University Press, 1993).

Thwaites, Rayner, *The Liberty of Non-Citizens* (Oxford: Hart Publishing, 2014).

Tolley, Michael C, 'Parliamentary scrutiny of rights in the United Kingdom: Assessing the work of the Joint Committee on Human Rights', *Australian Journal of Political Science* 44(1) (2009), 41–55.

Tomkins, Adam, 'National security and the due process of law', *Current Legal Problems* 64(1) (2011), 215–53.

Tulloch, John, 'Normalising the unthinkable: The British Press, torture, and the human rights of terrorists suspects' in *Communication Ethics Now*, ed Richard Keeble (Leicester: Troubadour Publishing, 2008) 3–18.

Turk, James L and Allan Manson (eds), *Free Speech in Fearful Times: After 9/11 in Canada, the US, Australia and Europe* (Toronto: James Lorimer, 2007).

Tushnet, Mark, 'Defending Korematsu? Reflections on civil liberties in wartime', *Wisconsin Law Review* 2 (2003), 273–307.

Tyrie, Andrew, Roger Gough and Stuart McCracken, *Account Rendered: Extraordinary Rendition and Britain's Role* (London: Biteback Publishing, 2011).

Vidal-Naquet, Pierre, *Torture: Cancer of Democracy—France and Algeria 1954–62* (Harmondsworth: Penguin Books, 1963).

Vincent, RJ, *Human Rights and International Relations* (New York, NY: Cambridge University Press 1986).

Volpp, Leti, 'The citizen and the terrorist', *UCLA Law Review* 49(5) (2002), 1575–600.

Vucetic, Srdjan, 'Why did Canada sit out of the Iraq war? One constructivist analysis', *Canadian Foreign Policy* 13(1) (2006), 133–53.

Waldron, Jeremy, *Torture Terror and Trade-offs: Philosophy for the White House* (Oxford: Oxford University Press, 2010).

——, 'Torture and positive law: Jurisprudence for the White House', *Columbia Law Review* 105(6) (2005), 1681–750.

——, 'Vagueness in law and language: Some philosophical issues', *California Law Review* 82(3) (1994), 509–40.

Walt, Stephen M, 'Alliances in a unipolar world', *World Politics* 61(1) (2009), 86–120.

Wark, Wesley, 'Learning lessons (and how) in the war on terror: The Canadian experience', *International Journal* 60(1) (2004/2005), 71–90.

Warner, Bruce W, 'Great Britain and the response to international terrorism' in *The Deadly Sin of Terrorism: Its Effect on Democracy and Civil Liberty in Six Countries*, ed David Charters (Westport, CT: Greenwood Press, 1994) 13–42.

Warren, Mark E, 'Accountability and democracy' in *The Oxford Handbook of Public Accountability*, ed Mark Bovens, Robert E Goodin and Thomas Schillemans, (Oxford: Oxford University Press, 2014) 39–54.

Welsh, Jennifer M, 'The 2005 international policy statement', *International Journal* 61(4) (Autumn 2006), 909–28.

Whitaker, Reg, 'Arar: The affair, the inquiry, the aftermath', *IRPP Policy Matters* 9(1) (2008), 1–43.

——, 'More or less than meets the eye? The new national security agenda' in *How Ottawa Spends 2003–2004: Regime Change and Policy Shift*, ed G Bruce Doern (Don Mills: Oxford University Press, 2003) 44–58.

White, Robert W and Terry Falkenberg White, 'Repression and the liberal state: The case of Northern Ireland, 1969–1972', *Journal of Conflict Resolution* 39(2) (1995), 330–52.

Williams, AT, *A Very British Killing: The Death of Baha Mousa* (London: Vintage Books, 2013 [2012]).

Williams, George, *A Charter of Rights for Australia* (Sydney: UNSW Press, 2007).

——, 'A decade of Australian anti-terror laws', *Melbourne University Law Review* 35(3) (2011), 1161–76.

——, 'Balancing national security and human rights: Lessons from Australia', *borderlands: new spaces in the humanities e-journal* 4(1) (2005).

——, 'Constructing a community-based bill of rights' in *Protecting Human Rights: Instruments and Institutions*, ed Tom Campbell, Jeffrey Goldsworthy and Adrienne Stone (Oxford: Oxford University Press, 2003) 247–62.

Williamson, Janice (ed), *Omar Khadr, Oh Canada* (Montreal: McGill-Queen's University Press, 2012).

Wilson, Richard, Ashby (ed), *Human Rights in the 'War on Terror'* (New York, NY: Cambridge University Press, 2005).

Wintemute, Robert, 'The Human Rights Act's first five years: Too strong, too weak, or just right?', *Kings College Law Journal* 17(2) (2006), 209–27.

Zald, Mayer N, 'Culture, ideology, and strategic framing' in *Comparative Perspectives on Social Movements: Political Opportunities, Mobilizing Structures, and Cultural Framings*, ed Doug McAdam, John D McCarthy and Mayer N Zald (New York, NY: Cambridge University Press, 1996) 261–74.

Zelikow, Philip, 'Codes of conduct for a twilight war', *Houston Law Review* 49(1) (2012), 1–52.

Zine, Jasmin, 'Stolen youth: Lost boys and imperial wars' in *Omar Khadr, Oh Canada*, ed Janice Williamson (Montreal: McGill-Queen's University Press, 2012) 390–411.

INDEX